Butterworths Guides to Information Sources

Information Sources in
Architecture

Butterworths Guides to Information Sources

A series under the General Editorship of
D. J. Foskett, MA, FLA
and
M. W. Hill, MA, BSc, MRIC

This series was known previously as 'Information Sources for Research and Development'. Other titles available are:

Information Sources in Agriculture
    edited by G. P. Lilley

Information Sources in the History of Science and Medicine
    edited by P. Corsi and P. Weindling

Information Sources in Education and Work
    edited by E. H. K. Dibden and J. C. Tomlinson

Use of Chemical Literature (Third edition)
    edited by R. T. Bottle

Use of Engineering Literature
    edited by K. W. Mildren

Use of Mathematical Literature
    edited by A. R. Dorling

Use of Medical Literature (Second edition)
    edited by L. T. Morton

Use of Physics Literature
    edited by H. Coblans

Use of Reports Literature
    edited by C. P. Auger

Use of Social Sciences Literature
    edited by N. Roberts

Butterworths Guides to Information Sources

Information Sources in
Architecture

Editor
Valerie J. Bradfield, BA, DipLib, ALA
Academic Librarian, Leicester Polytechnic

Butterworths
London Boston Durban Singapore Sydney Toronto Wellington

All rights reserved. No part of this publication may be reproduced or transmitted in any form or by any means, including photocopying and recording, without the written permission of the copyright holder, application for which should be addressed to the Publishers. Such written permission must also be obtained before any part of this publication is stored in a retrieval system of any nature.

This book is sold subject to the Standard Conditions of Sale of Net Books and may not be re-sold in the UK below the net price given by the Publishers in their current price list.

First published 1983

© **Butterworth & Co (Publishers) Ltd 1983**

British Library Cataloguing in Publication Data

Information sources in architecture. – (Butterworths guides to information sources)
 1. Architecture – Information services
 2. Architecture – Bibliography
 I. Bradfield, Valerie J.
 720'.7   NA2540

ISBN 0-408-10763-4

Photoset by Butterworths Litho Preparation Department
Printed and bound in Great Britain by Mackays of Chatham

Series Editors' Foreword

Daniel Bell has made it clear in his book *The Post-Industrial Society* that we now live in an age in which information has succeeded raw materials and energy as the primary commodity. We have also seen in recent years the growth of a new discipline, information science. This is in spite of the fact that skill in acquiring and using information has always been one of the distinguishing features of the educated man. As Dr Johnson observed, 'Knowledge is of two kinds. We know a subject ourselves, or we know where we can find information upon it.'

But a new problem faces the modern educated man. We now have an excess of information, and even an excess of sources of information. This is often called the 'information explosion', though it might be more accurately called the 'publication explosion'. Yet it is of a deeper nature than either. The totality of knowledge itself, let alone of theories and opinions about knowledge, seems to have increased to an unbelievable extent, so that the pieces one seeks in order to solve any problem appear to be but a relatively few small straws in a very large haystack. That analogy, however, implies that we are indeed seeking but a few straws. In fact, when our information arrives on our desks, we often find those few straws are actually far too big and far too many for one person to grasp and use easily. In the jargon used in the information world, efficient retrieval of relevant information often results in information overkill.

Ever since writing was invented, it has been a common practice for men to record and store information; not only facts and figures, but also theories and opinions. The rate of recording accelerated after the invention of printing from moveable type, not because that in itself could increase the amount of recording but because, by making it easy to publish multiple copies of a document and sell them at a profit, recording and distributing information became very lucrative and hence attractive to more people. On the other hand, men in whose lives the discovery or the handling of information plays a large part usually devise ways of getting what they want from other people rather than from books in their efforts to avoid information overkill. Conferences, briefings, committee meetings are one means of this; personal contacts through the 'invisible college' and members of one's club are another. While such people do read, some of them voraciously, the reading of published literature, including in this category newspapers as well as books and journals and even watching television, may provide little more than 10% of the total information that they use.

Computers have increased the opportunities, not merely by acting as more efficient stores and providers of certain kinds of information than libraries, but also by manipulating the data they contain in order to synthesize new information. To give a simple illustration, a computer which holds data on commodity prices in the various trading capitals of the world, and also data on currency exchange rates, can be programmed to indicate comparative costs in different places in one single currency. Computerized data bases, i.e. stores of bibliographic information, are now well established and quite widely available for anyone to use. Also increasing are the number of data banks, i.e. stores of factual information, which are now generally accessible. Anyone who buys a suitable terminal may be able to arrange to draw information directly from these computer systems for his own purposes; the systems are normally linked to the subscriber by means of the telephone network. Equally, an alternative is now being provided by information supply services such as libraries, more and more of which are introducing terminals as part of their regular services.

The number of sources of information on any topic can therefore be very extensive indeed; publications (in the widest sense), people (experts), specialist organizations from research associations to chambers of commerce, and computer stores. The number of channels by which one can have access to these vast collections of information are also very numerous, ranging from professional literature searchers, via computer intermediaries, to Citizens'

Advice Bureaux, information marketing services and information brokers.

The aim of the Butterworths Guides to Information Sources is to bring all these sources and channels together in a single convenient form and to present a picture of the international scene as it exists in each of the disciplines we plan to cover. Consideration is also being given to volumes that will cover major interdisciplinary areas of what are now sometimes called 'mission-oriented' fields of knowledge. The first stage of the whole project will give greater emphasis to publications and their exploitation, partly because they are so numerous, and partly because more detail is needed to guide them adequately. But it may be that in due course the balance will change, and certainly the balance in each volume will be that which is appropriate to its subject at the time.

The editor of each volume is a person of high standing, with substantial experience of the discipline and of the sources of information in it. With a team of authors of whom each one is a specialist in one aspect of the field, the total volume provides an integrated and highly expert account of the current sources, of all types, in its subject.

D. J. Foskett
Michael Hill

Preface

Several years ago I was asked to condense some of my teaching handouts and leaflets into a format suitable for use with a group of experienced architects in a concentrated session on sources of information. The result was a rather large booklet from which this book has developed. More information has been included and some has been omitted to make this a national guide. The aim is still similar – to assist in educating architects, builders, building surveyors and all others involved in the construction process in the sources and nature of information available. There was no single complete guide in existence at the time. Although there are now some useful guides, none are very comprehensive. Many tackle the historical discussions better than the present-day construction process.
    This volume therefore attempts to review the coverage of information over the whole of the construction processes, showing all appropriate sources of information and access to them. Researchers will find it useful, especially those in the final stages of their training, and those already in practice should find guidance on all aspects of construction. To this end it has been written with the professional in mind, and the language of the librarian has been avoided as far as possible – but not entirely, since many librarians entering the construction industry information services will find it invaluable as a starting point, to be reinforced by membership of the Construction Industry Information Group, whose members and meetings have been useful to me over the last twelve years.

This is, however, a guide. It aims to indicate where to look for information, not to list comprehensively all the sources. A reasonable knowledge of the industry will sometimes be found useful and is assumed in places. Most sources of information are referred to, with some indication of availability and content as well as critical comment where necessary.

Initially, the structure of the volume was shown by the use of three parts; the introductory chapters discussing sources or location of information and assistance, the techniques of searching for and presenting information. Then follow several chapters examining certain types of material, the information from the government, the trade and technical literature which is almost unique to this profession, the periodicals and visual information, before the major chapters discussing the actual information necessary at each stage in the building process, from design through to finishing and including a section on conservation (or rehabilitation, as it is increasingly becoming) and a brief section on identification of buildings, their locations and their architects. Historical guidance will be provided in another book in this series, although Ruth Kamen's excellent *British and Irish Architectural History: A Guide to Sources* (Architectural Press, 1981) has recently filled this need. The plan is still the same but there are no sub-sections. Having discussed the general needs for information and sources in the sense of libraries and advice services, the methods of information retrieval and presentation are discussed, with particular emphasis on the development of computerized methods. The many reference handbooks, from dictionaries and encyclopedias through to databooks and manuals, are explained and examined, with a section on indexing and structure of information to assist with their efficient usage. Then the chapters on types of material discuss periodicals, trade and technical literature and standards, government publications and statutes, slides, maps and other visual resources. The remaining chapters follow the construction process, from the initial needs for design and site data through to the erection of the various parts of a building, the finishing, the management and the contractual side of the process.

Limitations are naturally imposed by the space available to cover a very broad subject. Bibliographic citation is essentially Harvard style but with further information sometimes inserted to assist with the identification and retrieval of sources. References are to representative items rather than providing a comprehensive bibliography. They have been selected from experience for their content and ease of use when answering the problems, or questions, which crop up daily. One or two items from a series may be quoted to give an idea of content overall. Full lists, although useful, are too long for inclusion and would be out-of-date almost immediately, as publishing is currently still increasing – usually in the realm of the pamphlet literature, which is not easily located and indexed.

Currency is difficult to achieve, let alone to maintain. Many references indicate where series are continuing, or were at the time of publication. Changes have been made up to the end of June 1982. In some cases references have been left open to prevent dating. Having praised the GLC's *Development and Materials Bulletin* not only in Chapter 8 but throughout, I learned at the end of July that this, too, is to cease publication. The process of change and development is continuous, and everyone in the industry knows that there is no way of ensuring absolute currency.

Abbreviations common in the industry have been used throughout, but for newcomers and the 'occasional' user they have been listed at the back with the list of addresses and names of associations. Again, this was correct at the time of writing, but it would be advisable to check with a current listing when using the addresses.

Finally, I would like to acknowledge the assistance of many friends and colleagues, in particular those at work, Carolyn Hall and Charles Doidge, for help with reading through the text, and all the others for putting up with me. Jacqui Ollerton helped with some of the information in Chapters 1 and 4 as well as her own and thanks are due to George Atkinson, whose work was not included in the final version. Thanks are due to all the contributors for their work and the ease with which they have agreed to amendments being made or given me freedom to make them. Discussions with many others in the field have been very useful. My friends and family all deserve thanks for their support through the last two years.

Contributors

John Barrick
Librarian, Royal Town Planning Institute

Anthony J. Coulson
Liaison Librarian (Arts), Open University Library

Bob Frommes
Standing committee Urban and Building Climatology, Luxembourg

Margaret Hallett
Overseas Affairs Secretary, Royal Institution of British Architects

Shirley Herbert
Deputy Librarian, Tropical Products Institute
Formerly at the Property Services Agency Library, Department of the Environment

Ruth H. Kamen
Head of Library Information Services, British Architectural Library, Royal Institution of British Architects

Andrew McDonald
Planning Librarian, Library, University of Newcastle-upon-Tyne

Jacqui Ollerton
Senior Information Officer, Research Library, Greater London Council

xiv Contributors

Chris Parker
Information Officer (Physical Sciences and Engineering), University of Southampton Library

Charles Rogers
Chief Librarian, Property Services Agency, Department of the Environment

John F. Smith
Curator, Stamford Museum
Formerly of the Institute for Advanced Architectural Studies, University of York

Ken Turner
Faculty Librarian, Faculty of the Built Environment, Polytechnic of the South Bank

Contents

Series Editors' Foreword		v
Preface		ix
Contributors		xiii
1	Introduction: information for architects *Valerie J. Bradfield*	1
2	Libraries *Ruth H. Kamen* and *Valerie J. Bradfield*	18
3	Information retrieval techniques *Valerie J. Bradfield*	37
4	Computerized information retrieval *Valerie J. Bradfield*	58
5	Using and presenting information *Chris Parker*	76
6	Sources and organization of information *Valerie J. Bradfield*	96
7	Periodicals *Ken Turner*	124
8	Trade literature, technical information and standards *Valerie J. Bradfield*	136
9	Government publications, legislation and statistics *Charles Rogers*	167

xvi Contents

10	Maps, drawings and slides	
	Valerie J. Bradfield	187
11	Developing a design	
	Design data	
	Valerie J. Bradfield	210
	Site survey	
	Andrew McDonald	219
	Land use	
	John Barrick	227
	Climatic data	
	Bob Frommes	238
12	Executing a design	
	Valerie J. Bradfield	246
13	Finishing a design	
	Landscape	
	Shirley Herbert	291
	Interior design	
	Anthony J. Coulson	299
14	Managing the design and the office	
	Contracts	
	Ken Turner	311
	Working abroad	
	Margaret Hallett	318
	Running the practice	
	Ken Turner	324
	Information in the office	
	Jacqui Ollerton	329
	Setting up an office information unit	
	Ken Turner	336
15	Conservation	
	John Smith	343
16	Buildings, people, places: background information	
	Valerie J. Bradfield	361
Appendix 1	Outline classifications	379
Appendix 2	Associations and abbreviations used	398
Index		404

1
Introduction
Information for architects
Valerie J. Bradfield

The need for information

This guide is a discussion of the sources of information and of the appropriate retrieval techniques available to the professional architect and to others in the construction industry. This introduction will look at the reasons for needing information, the ways in which it is supplied and the sorts of information which are essential, not just to the design process but to the successful completion of a construction project. In doing this it is also necessary to outline the development of information services to the construction industry as a whole to show the role of specialist establishments in the process of providing information. Information itself is useless without communication, organization and presentation. The plan and rationale for this guide may be seen by examining these concepts and their relevance to the construction process.

One definition of the design process expressed recently in *Building Design for Energy Economy* (Ove Arup Associates, Construction Press, 1980) was that the 'designer's immediate objective is to utilise all his knowledge of the past and present, combine it with the new technology in a balanced and compatible manner and thus produce a result that can be defined as architecture'.

In the design process information is needed before synthesis or analysis can take place to produce a design. Reviewing some of the many different views of the design process in *Design in Archtecture* (Wiley, 1973) Broadbent showed how important information is in design. Recent checklists of information needs, published in the Department of the Environment studies, also show this role for information. The information ranges widely, from site and briefing data to legislation, standards and product information, with increased emphasis on technical data as techniques change or develop. As the scope increases so, too, does the rate of change and yet the approach to new knowledge is often conservative.

Practical guidance on integrating information into designs exists in many texts, ranging from Alexander's *Pattern Language* (Oxford University Press, 1978) to Christopher Jones' *Design Methods* (2nd edn, Wiley, 1981). The latter prepares the ground for the present guide in his chapter on 'Literature Searching', which points out that a 'literature search' involves perceiving the problem and its structure, then exploring the situation. Relevant published literature should be found without unacceptable cost or delay, and to do so one must have some idea of what it is and how to find it. In stressing this his chapter introduces the need for guidance in information retrieval and sources.

In 1968 Bullivant identified seven categories of 'producers of information' in discussing the information 'explosion'. In so doing he equated information production with publishers, that is, the producers of useful publications. He discussed the output of these publishers. But this represents a false assumption. In architecture not all information is produced in literary form, on paper, nor is it to be found in a library. Discussions of information and communication of information using drawings are both important. The method of communication of information should be appropriate both to the information being conveyed and to the needs of the architect at that time, that is, appropriate to content and context. Rapidly changing technology is affecting both retrieval and presentation.

Information and information problems are encountered in training and in practice. The student is involved in reading, writing and learning how to handle information. He searches for books and articles containing facts and explanations of techniques and learns to solve design problems. Information handling is an integral part of educational development. Information requirements become increasingly complex and generate further requirements. Whether it is the information on user needs at the beginning of the design process or the detailed information on products or techniques when working out a solution, the information is always a means to an end. The architect cannot usually effectively design buildings without consulting a wide range of design guides, regulations, standards and catalogues in conjunction with the offices' data files and sets of drawings. Information is the backbone in this sense. Information is essential to the production of first, the drawings and then finally, the building.

Information may range widely both in content and format. Some might prefer information to be available 'pre-packaged' for specific needs. Such pre-packaging destroys some of the opportunity to exercise judgement and the faculties of selection. Pre-selection, unless extremely skilfully done, limits the breadth of understanding conveyed to the user:

> Regardless of what form it takes, people use information, called knowledge and experience – *knowledge* may be defined as information acquired by learning and *experience* as information acquired by applying knowledge in practice. (CIB, 1978)

Knowledge is constantly being updated and augmented, and its possession enables the professional to recognize formally the need for more knowledge and for precise information.

> The essence of professionalism is judgement. What distinguishes the judgement of a professional from that of a lay person is the professional access to relevant information, his accumulated knowledge and his ability to apply this information and knowledge appropriately. Traditionally these capacities have been the results of the interests, education and experiences of the individual architect. (Burnette, 1979)

The architect places a heavy reliance on his own information systems and experience (digested and remembered information), spending as little time as possible in gathering externalized data. A Building Design Partnership survey quoted in Broadbent, *Design in Architecture* (1973, p. 205) showed that the young job architect may spend 7.6% of his time in information-seeking, half of which is spent in locating the type of information described in this book. But is this enough? The percentage may have increased in the last ten years, with the increase in the volume of information available. Time needs to be saved. Time is money, and both are usually scarce. Even free information takes time to sift, organize and file. Information is needed quickly and in sufficient detail. It is needed in the appropriate format, breadth, depth and degree of accuracy.

Much has been written in each generation about this volume of information with which the professional must come to terms. A measure of its importance to the architectural profession might be the space that the major weekly *Architects' Journal* has devoted to the 'Annual Review' each January since 1977. Is this used? By whom? Such listings are essential to keep abreast of changes but not all professionals can, or wish to, find time to read them. Changes can find the student hunting for the *IHVE Guide* because he has been told by his mentor that it contains the required information. Unfortunately, the senior architect still using his own copy in his office is unaware that the revised edition of his familiar three-volume handbook has been issued in about twenty pamphlets, and that the IHVE is now called the CIBS, with the appropriate change of title. Such changes take time to penetrate. Much new information is published. The qualified architect acquires a knowledge of and should develop an instinct for the best resources to answer many of the technical problems and questions which he encounters. The student is learning. But both encounter similar problems when their own reserves fail to provide answers. The the search for information must be widened. Both must be kept up-to-date.

In putting forward this view of the need for information and weighing the need against the time available and the inclination to discover new or related information other points must be remembered:

> It may of course be that the 'need-to-know' is not as great as imagined by members of the information profession and given the time at his disposal, the engineer may indeed be using this time to his best advantage. (Mildren, p. 174)

Although it is often tempting to do without information which is not readily to hand, recent moves towards increasing the architect's liabilities for the design and performance of buildings emphasize the need for a conscientious search for accurate and comprehensive information. The results of research are available. But related research needs to be identified and efficiently applied to new problems.

Research generates information. Research is not necessarily academic but practical, including feedback and deductions from current work. The *Oxford English Dictionary* defines research as 'careful search or inquiry *after* or *for* or *into*; endeavour to discover new or collate old facts, etc. by scientific study of a subject; course of critical investigation'. But the dissemination of research is not as effective or as widespread as many researchers and investigators feel that it should be if mistakes are not to occur or recur. 'Practitioners cannot easily be persuaded to even consider new methods,' commented S. Hendy at the seventh CIB conference, and he continued, 'I wonder if anyone has tried to discover the extent of this resistance, why it exists and how it can be overcome' (*Construction Research International*, Vol. 2, Construction Press, 1978, p. 434). Hendy is perhaps more aware than other architects of the need to apply research to the construction industry (see also p. 9).

Failures have occurred, both large and small. Feedback from the subsequent investigations is available. Such information is not necessarily widely disseminated. The late 1970s have seen an increase both in related publications (see p. 8) and in cases where liability has been proved, varying from planning applications to design defects and defective workmanship. Such cases are diverse. Examples include that of the *London Borough of Merton* v. *George Lowe and Partners* (see *Building Design*, 24 April 1981, p. 5) regarding the specification of materials for a ceiling which subsequently failed. *B. L. Holdings Ltd* v. *Robert J. Wood and Partners* (1978) concerned the architect's responsibility for obtaining the correct planning permission for a Brighton office development where the architects claimed that they could not be held responsible for planning applications. The case went to appeal and was allowed in 1979. Such cases have resulted in some questioning of the architect's liability for decisions in the press. (See *Building Trades Journal*, 9 May 1980, pp. 43–44 for discussion of this case.)

Information relevant to some failures publicized in recent years was available in the literature if one bothered, or knew how and where to look for it. This was demonstrated after the high alumina cement 'panic'. The crucial nature of the mix had been pointed out as a result of failures in the USA ten years previously and reports were available. All in the construction industry might benefit from reading and pondering Andrew Rabeneck's contribution to the *AJ* 'Aids to Practice' series, in which he reviews the aspects of the construction process which need attention and information. He ends by suggesting a need for a service on similar lines to the French *ARIANE* (see p. 66) as well as much-improved communications within the industry in Britain (*AJ*, 15 April 1981, pp. 715–718).

Designers must now conform with voluminous legislation varying from place to place, country to country. Legislation is not normally presented in a readily comprehensible form. Guides are essential. Ignorance is no excuse. Recent developments occur here as in every other sphere, often with immediate effect. Currency of information is necessary in every aspect of the design process also. Feedback information may be valuable but design ideas change and products change. With product changes, so understanding of new techniques becomes necessary. Clients 'hear' about new design ideas and include them in the brief to their architect. The architect must determine how to comply with a request to install a solar heating system in a new small factory unit when most of the technical information relates to houses. Should he investigate such details as the running costs and inform the client? Is his responsibility to apply the brief or to advise on its suitability? Here also is an example where both breadth and depth of information are needed to use existing knowledge with inspiration to produce a functional design.

New work comes to the architectural practice from recommendation and example – completed projects are advertisements in themselves. The application of information and the depth of knowledge usually affects the successful completion of the project and its reputation in use.

The architect is dependent in many senses on others and their skills – the larger the project the more so, and yet he must coordinate and successfully combine the skills of others into a finished whole. To do this not only must he be abreast of developments of immediate concern to him in design, materials and construction techniques but also in the surrounding professions, as the planning case cited above demonstrates. Where does this information all come from?

The information 'explosion'

Skills were once learned by example from craftsmen. Masons were the first architects. literacy has changed our ways of coping with information. Instructions and information can be drawn, written and interpreted more readily. Written information developed in the seventeenth and eighteenth centuries and has increased immeasurably in the twentieth. Initially there were just books. Printing made feasible the multiple duplication of books. Then lists of books (bibliographies) became necessary, followed by lists of bibliographies. Then the government began to publish technical leaflets and manufacturers' published catalogues containing technical details. Then also associations of manufacturers, promoting the use of their products, began contributing to the flow of paper. This volume of publications made guides necessary.

The construction industry has a well-documented history of information and communication problems. The large, complex, fragmented and diverse nature of the industry and the separation of design from construction are contributing factors, augmented by new technologies, new materials and techniques. There has been a continuous expansion of information produced with subsequent rising costs and an increase in the number of information sources:

> Few people associated in whatever way with the construction industry can be unaware of, or unaffected by the frightening increase in the amount of information being produced, circulated and stored. (DoE, 1979)

This information emanates from many different sources resulting in overlap and duplication. The government, since the Woodbine Parish Report of 1964, has attempted to coordinate and improve the information systems and services available to the whole construction industry. However, the increase in the 1970s in government publications and British Standards 'which appear to be doubling every 5 years' (DoE, *Computing and Communication in the Construction Industry,* DoE, 1978) is not to be outdone by the costs which are also increasing – by 18.5 per cent in 1978 (ibid.). But by the 1980s 'The era of cheap paper-based government-sponsored information, which started after the last war, had clearly ceased. . . .' (Bullivant, 1980). The decrease in the size of the DoE *Annual List of Publications* also shows this. Some sections of the industry feel that they do not have the time, means or inclination to keep abreast of developments.

The explosion is a feature of industry in general. The volume of bibliographical references available has increased phenomenally, as shown in *Figure 1.1*. The result is user 'dependence', or information dependence, on services such as the online computer services described in Chapter 4, and the dependence of information seekers on those with appropriate skills and knowledge of information resources, since it is no longer possible to keep in touch with everything. In an attempt to help with this, however, many of the chapters following include hints on keeping up-to-date.

Eighty years ago Lord Rayleigh pointed out that

> By a fiction as remarkable as any to be found in law what has once been published, even though it be in the Russian language, is spoken of as *known*, and it is too often forgotten that the rediscovery in the library may be a more difficult and uncertain process than the first discovery in the laboratory. (Vickery, p. 18)

8 Introduction: information for architects

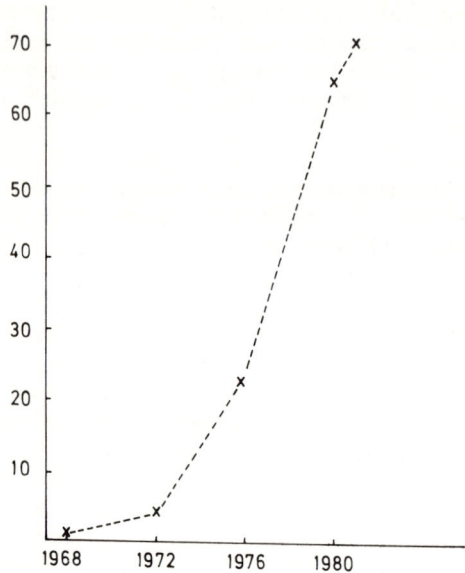

Figure 1.1 The volume of bibliographical references (From, J. Hall *Online bibliographic databases*. 2nd edn. Aslib, 1981)

The growth not only of information but also of its recorded forms and channels of communication has made rediscovery sometimes easier but also a more complex skill. There has been a growth in alternative representations of data for differing purposes as well as in the reporting of new facts. Thus abstracts of the Building Research Establishment research papers (*Current Papers*) are published in its *Information Directory* each year and longer digests of the same appear as *Information Papers* in an effort to increase awareness of developments and enable architects to apply new knowledge. Such overlap is an essential feature of the 'explosion'. Not all published is 'new' and much is of dubious quality, but a degree of skill, awareness and basic knowledge is necessary to sort the good from the bad.

In other countries the development and coordination of information handling and its communication has been ahead of work in Britain. Sweden has developed an information network, as has Denmark. France has a computerized databank for construction information (see p. 66).

Introduction: information for architects 9

In 1949 following a UN initiative the International Council for Building Documentation was established and extended in 1953 into the International Council for Building Research Studies and Documentation (usually abbreviated to CIB using the French initials, Conseil International du Batiment pour la Recherche l'Etude et la Documentation). In his opening address to the 7th Triennial Congress in Edinburgh G. MacKenzie, Minister for State at the Scottish Office, stated that 'the work of the CIB is continuous and that the benefits of research can be reaped only if communications are good and if the knwledge gained from research can be effectively applied' (*Construction Research International*, Construction Press, 1978, p. 351). The organization aims to encourage cooperation at non-government level in all aspects of the construction industry both in research and in practice. This work is little known in Britain. Mr Hendy, an architect from Newcastle-upon-Tyne, stated that 'Until I was invited to join the Organising Committee for the Congress I knew very little about CIB or its work. I think this is typical of most architects in Britain and I think it is a great pity' (ibid., p. 434).

The work is organized from the Secretariat in Rotterdam. There are a number of Working Commissions and Study groups through which work is carried out, W 52 deals with information research and its dissemination. Such work will increase with the use of computerized networks for international information dissemination. The value of such work is apparent when one begins to appreciate the number of information producers in the construction industry in any one country.

The producers

The centre of information in construction in Britain, since its foundation in 1921, has been the Building Research Establishment (BRE, formerly the Building Research Station). It was the first such organization in the world. There, research and practical advisory services have been united. In 1972 it was merged with the Fire Research Laboratory (formerly the Joint Fire Research Organization) and the Princes Risborough Laboratory (formerly the Forest Products Research Laboratory). An information unit developed, now called the Communications and Services Department, to serve its research and industrial staff working both on government and consultancy-funded projects. The large and specialist library has suffered recently from cuts in funding but was acknowledged as the leading source of information in the country.

10 Introduction: information for architects

A useful abstracting service, *Building Science Abstracts*, was established before many others existed but ceased in 1976. It covered developments in the world building industries, taking particular interest in Commonwealth countries, which was also reflected in the work of the overseas divisions. The publishing side of the BRE is essentially separate and an exercise in dissemination of information. Much is published from the BRE itself rather than through HMSO, but fewer publications are now free of charge than formerly. Literature searches may be requested through the advisory services and are charged according to the length and difficulty of the search and the work previously in existence.

Other large construction libraries within the government produce information and give services firstly to their members (see Chapter 2). All have to be aware that, because they are part of the government, information from them may be taken as authoritative where it is in reality no more so than that obtained from local libraries unless it has gone through departmental professional architects.

Research and practice need to be brought together, and this was also recognized in 1964 with the creation of the Civil Engineering Research Association, which in 1967 became the Construction Industry Research and Information Association (CIRIA). Information is an essential feature of its work, but its duty is primarily to its membership, though this now extends to a wide range of bodies concerned with construction. Results of such work may be published, however, in an effort to disseminate the information gathered. In the same way the National Building Agency, set up in 1964, is described as a 'gulf-bridging concern, (*House's Guide to the Construction Industry*, 8th edn, p. 159) to coordinate experience and ideas in construction. Again the results of work have been published for dissemination. The consultancy basis of the NBA failed to secure its survival through the 1981 –1982 crisis and it was wound up in February 1982. It published information but did not provide any kind of active information service, having a minimal library. Some of the consultants hope to continue similar work privately.

The research and information associations set up by members of the various industries such as the Building Services Research and Information Association, the Timber Research and Development Association and the Cement and Concrete Association, for example, aim to promote their product. They and their publications are discussed in Chapters 2, 8, 11, 12 and 13. Many more are listed in *House's Guide*. Advice and information is available from all and voluminous from some. The largest have information officers and libraries of a high calibre which produce bibliographies for members and architects seeking information as well as on a commercial basis. Subscribers may benefit from experience in the very specialist fields of an association like BSRIA, which can provide bibliographies of substantial length on topics such as the installation of services in specific types of buildings ranging from hotels to old churches.

Communication and presentation

Coordination of needs, of resources and of communication is essential if information is to be successfully presented to the architect in the design office *and* from the architect to others in the construction industry to enable a building to be successfully completed. As long ago as 1965 Higgin and Jessop described the communication problems in the industry following their research with the Tavistock Institute, and concluded (in *Communication in the Building Industry*, Tavistock, 1965) that 'there is a lack of match between the *technical interdependence* of the resources and organisational *independence* of those who control them' (p. 77) and that relationships must control and coordinate both to effectively improve communications. In 1979 the Department of the Environment's General Information Group came to similar conclusions *but* more closely related to the provision, presentation and communication of information in that

> 7.4. a) It is *recommended* that a survey be conducted of the provision and use of information resources within a particular region. . . .
> b) It is *recommended* that a comprehensive guide to sources of information (defined in the broadest sense) be prepared and updated as frequently as may be necessary. It is *recommended* that CIRIA and the Building Centre Trust should take the initiative in this by setting up a consultative group, drawn from the industry, in order to build on their previous work in producing guides to sources. (DoE, 1979)

In addition a basic library of resources should be listed, there should be improved coordination of bibliographic resources and of presentation of information in publications and some central mechanism should be set up to achieve these ends. With the government cutbacks and withdrawal of funds from research and industry, the Property Services Agency and the Building Research Establishment as well as the National Building Agency and other groups this appears remote at present.

Presentation of information is also important. Written information is not necessarily the best way to communicate with the designer, although it may be preferred by other professionals in the industry. As formulae and symbols are to the scientist so the drawing is to the architect. But much information is not available in this way. The work of Alex Gordon showed that feedback information was unused while it remained in written format or was referred to from other sources, but was included in future designs when it was itself entered upon, or stored with, office standard details. The studies by Mackinder and by Goodey and Matthew (see p. 19) have proved this need, but there is little sign of its implementation unless it be in the increasing number of detailing manuals and standard design drawings published in the late 1970s.

There are varying types of formats for information used at different stages of a project. The component parts of the industry do not necessarily use the guides and information prepared by each other, as pointed out by Higgin and Jessop.

Information is not necessarily reaching those who need it. Communication fails because it faces barriers of understanding, acceptance and retrieval. Work is being done on the communication of information and this guide, among others, attempts to improve one aspect of communication by developing awareness not only of the availability of information but also of the techniques for locating and using it. The foreword to the first issue of *Construction Papers* by the CIOB stated that the institute has 'no established tradition for publishing the results of its work and it would be of considerable benefit if the expertise which exists in all areas of technology, management and economics was more widely disseminated'. Whether all branches of the construction industry will get to read these papers has yet to be seen. There are few 'academic' journals in architecture – *AJ* provides references and bibliographies but many others rely on pictures, not necessarily plans and drawings. The books are similar.

A guide to information

It should be clear that this guide is attempting to fill a gap. No-one else is known to be actively attempting to do this, although the publication of the volume *Information Practice in the Construction*

Industry by the defunct National Building Agency might have gone some way towards it. This has now been withdrawn from publication by HMSO and there are no plans to find another publisher. Since it was ready for publication in 1979 it would need heavy revision before it could now be published. The *AJ*'s pages are beginning to provide a somewhat scattered guide. *House's Guide to the Construction Industry* is also moving further that way both in its lists of sources, associations, etc. and its chapters describing information providers, resources and communications. The pattern adopted in this guide differs in approach perhaps because the editor is a librarian rather than an architect, and because the aim is to make this useful not only to the architect but to *all* those involved in the construction industry – builders, surveyors, managers, etc. – including those who provide information to the professionals, some of whom may have a limited awareness of the sources, insufficient time to search and therefore rely on external services. It should have a value for researchers also by providing an initial guide to sources, although it will be necessary to look beyond its pages for more detailed discussions according to the depth and nature of the work in hand. Such individuals might turn to works such as Mildren's or Parker and Turley, *Information Sources in Science and Technology* (Butterworths, 1975), where greater emphasis is placed on the use of the more obscure report, conference, translation or patent literature which the average user of this guide will never need.

In showing what is available to the profession this guide will not venture in depth into the thorny problem of the suitability of that information to the purposes for which it is required.

Many parts of the guide will relate to the traditional forms in which information is presented. These are essentially:

Books, handbooks and monographs on specific topics, design guides
Reference handbooks, directories, lists, dictionaries
Journals or periodicals and the services indexing and abstracting them
Maps and plans
Official publications from the government and other bodies, often only pamphlets but representing advice and data
Legislation, Acts of Parliament, statutory instruments (regulations) and by-laws
Codes and Standards, mainly from the BSI, but also from other organizations
Approvals and test certificates such as Agrément certificates

Product literature, manufacturer's catalogues, handbooks, price lists, data sheets, directories, samples, trade association publications
Project information, drawings specifications, bills of quanties
Project standards, details, feedback information and job records
Cost indices
Publicity material

Many of these are 'products' of the age of multiple copies, cheaper printing and extensive documentation – the information 'explosion'. Most will be covered but not topics like publicity and job records.

A resource is 'a stock or reserve upon which one can draw when necessary' (*Oxford English Dictionary*). In this context therefore it is used to mean information itself or something which is used to find information, whether that is a colleague, a repository of literature (that is, a library, a databook or catalogue) or even a textbook. This introductory chapter has discussed information in general, the concepts, the needs, the difficulties and preconceptions, in an effort to 'set the scene' for what follows and to draw together the threads of the chapters following.

The chapters are arranged in groups covering retrieval and presentation of information, general sources of information according to their format or mode of presentation, then specific information required for the development of a brief from the initial stages to completion, including its management, and the management of the office. The two final chapters cover information which relates to many of the foregoing but which required separate discussion and without which the guide would be incomplete.

Thus Chapter 2 discusses the use of contacts in particular libraries, but goes beyond that in suggesting advice centres. Chapters 3 to 5 discuss techniques for finding and using resources. Then Chapters 6 and 10 provide essential background information on types of literature preliminary to the discussion of topics in Chapters 11 to 15. These suggest specific information resources and places to find information on certain problems and in the very specific topic areas related to the construction process. They start with the 'brief' and move through to the final landscaping of the finished building before looking at aspects of managing the work. Conservation and rehabilitation, restoration or preservation of buildings are currently of great importance and form a large volume of work currently in hand. They are therefore worthy of consideration. The final chapter also applies to the whole process and presents information which may be needed at any stage in the work, whether new or old. Hence its separation from the other sections and its inclusion to round out this guide in preference to referring all users to another guide to amplify this section, as none exists.

This briefly explains the plan of the guide. I make no apology for adopting what may seem to some a 'librarian's approach' to the discussion of various types of written resource before giving subject-oriented information. This is not intended as a guide for librarians, although they will use it. It was essential, however, to explain the organization, function and retrieval problems associated with certain types of materials such as government publications, statistics and periodicals. This would disrupt the thread of the discussion related to topics in Chapters 11 to 15 and was therefore brought to the front to enable easy reference to be made to these essential forms of publication in preference to voluminous page references in the index. Similarly these chapters are placed before the specific subject-information because the latter may be more easily understood if the preliminaries have been scanned first.

Following from this it is perhaps also sensible to note that sufficient information on the publishers and dates of books, articles and reports is usually given in the text to enable the user to locate the items concerned. These may not always be the full standard bibliographical details recommended by BS 1629:1976 *Bibliographical References*. This is because too much detail would make it difficult to see the wood for the trees. In my experience, even if it is given, most users (except librarians) will ignore it (and the librarians should know how to locate it). Adequate data are always given for location purposes; hence the extra details given where items may be a little more obscure or publishers not well known. So, too, with *AJ* and *Building*, in particular, references are frequently given to the date of the issue without the volume number, since this is usually the most accurate way of locating the information, especially with the latter's complex numbering system and the practice in many of the offices and personal collections to stack copies in date order. Volume numbers do not appear as readily on the covers as dates.

Mention should be made of the manner in which the guide has been compiled. It is neither a fully contributed work nor one written entirely myself. Therefore different styles will be obvious throughout the chapters as the authors vary. The exercise of editorial discretion should leave the individual style to come across to the user, keep the information clear and coordinate the chapters to show inter-relationships and minimize unecessary duplication. The styles reflect differing approaches from a variety of minds, not all in regular contact with architects, some professionals in related fields, some librarians. Length varies with style and content – it is not always easy to be brief or uniform in this type of work. Some sections are more bibliographical than others because with a more stable literary content they can be so. By contributing to the information 'explosion' one is also anxious not to do so to such a great length that the weight and the resultant price placed on the volume (or guide) by the publishers is prohibitive, preventing the guide from reaching its audience.

The aim is guidance. Data will not be provided except when discussing organization of information – the sources will be indicated. Some of these will be readily to hand, or should be, but others will not be available locally. The discussion of places where they may be found, and where enquiries may be made, is therefore given priority. The loan of urgently required material can usually be secured. Few practices or institutions can nowadays afford a comprehensive collection of resources on site. Computerized centralized databanks may be the information providers of the future. It may be that information needs will change also when the more basic data is also computerized. This has yet to be seen. Predictions and some analysis of possible future developments will be made. However, the needs and sources of information outlined here are unlikely to change radically in the immediate future.

References

* indicates useful further reading.
* Atkinson, G. (1981). 'Sorting out information', *Building*, 9 January, pp. 39–40
Bullivant, D. (1968). 'Can we survive the information explosion?' *RIBA Journal*, 553–559
Bullivant, D. (1980). '1980 Review of the Year', *Architects' Journal*, 9 January, 92–93
Burnette, Charles, and Associates (1979). *The Architect's Access to Information: Constraints on the Architect's Capacity to Seek, Obtain, Translate and Apply Information.* Prepared for National Engineering Laboratory (NBS), Washington DC, US Department of Commerce National Technical Information Service (PB – 294 855)
* Cabinet Office. Advisory Council for Applied Research and Development (1980). *Information Technology*, HMSO
CIB, Conseil International du Bâtiment pour Recherche l'Étude et la Documentation/International Council for Building Research Studies and Documentation (1978). *Evaluation of Information Systems for the Construction Industry: Report from a Subgroup of CIB Working Commission W52* (Publication 47)

DoE (1979). *General Information: Towards the Better Use of Existing Construction Industry Information Resources. Final Report of the General Information Group of the National Consultative Council of the Building and Civil Engineering Industries.* Department of the Environment

Goodey, J. and Matthew, K. (1971). *Architects and Information.* University of York, Institute of Advanced Architectural Studies (Research Paper 1)

Gordon, A. (1968). Design and Information Flow. Report 13B in CIB *Information Flow in the Building Process*, CIB

Mackinder, M. (1980). *The Selection and Specification of Building Materials and Components: Study in Current Practice and Educational Provision*, 2nd edn, University of York, Institute of Advanced Architectural Studies (Research Paper 17)

Mildren, K. (1976). *Use of Engineering Literature*, Butterworths

Woodbine Parish, D. E. (1964). *Building Research and Information Services: Report of a Working Party* (Ministry of Public Building and Works), HMSO

2
Libraries
Ruth H. Kamen and Valerie J. Bradfield

Since the first printed and illustrated edition of Vitruvius, architecture has been practised against an ever expanding accumulation of information in books, magazines, reports, pamphlets and now computer displays and print-out.

Architects need information for a variety of reasons. The practice may be commissioned to design a type of building with which it is unfamiliar or the location where a building is to be constructed presents problems not previously encountered. For example, when a building is to be sited near an airport, ways of combatting aircraft noise will have to be taken into account. Since information needs cannot all be anticipated and not all information needed will be at hand, the architect should be able to turn to advisory and information services, including libraries.

Architects are often, by nature, disinclined to turn to outside resources to solve their information problems; 'in common with many other information users, [architects] prefer more informal information communication, perhaps because this is also the easiest – the personal library, use of colleagues and manufacturer's representatives' (Snow, 1974). Lack of training in problem-solving and information-seeking may also limit the use and awareness of information and enquiry services (MoPBW, 1968). But the developments in building technology, new products and methods were recognized as increasing the dependence of architects on information and advisory services by the Woodbine Parish Report in 1964.

Personal collections of information and the knowledge of colleagues are not necessarily the most reliable sources of information. They have their pitfalls and biases. Some professionals may not, however, be familiar with the more sophisticated libraries and information services despite the efforts of the technical press to publicize them. Skill is necessary for effective use. Where students receive education in information skills a recent study found that 'at the time of receiving it they had little appreciation of its value as they were ignorant of its relevance to the practice of architecture' (Mackinder, 1980). There are guides, lists and assistance offered, but not all architects are aware of their existence. In many instances libraries may be the best source of information on technical problems, such as the background information on a new technique or a type of building not previously, or recently, tackled by the enquiring practitioners. Certain building types have evolved since the professional architect's student days. The motel has entered Britain, new sports such as skateboarding have required new facilities and an increasing concern for the disabled has affected the design of all types of building. An information service may be the best source of advice about materials or on the solution of a tricky design question. The choice is wide as there are many services serving the construction industry.

Library or information service?

It is sometimes difficult to see the difference, especially when many libraries are changing their titles. We have the RICS Technical Information Service and the Leicestershire Library and Information Service. Colleges have Learning Resources Centres. Once all were simply called libraries. The concept has changed less than the image. Many libraries were always active providers of information but others were, and may still be, passive storehouses of documents.

The library principally provides the architect with published information and with guidance in locating it. Although some may also have advisory services they will normally be restricted to providing a précis of the literature unless there are technical staff within the same institution who can be called upon to evaluate the literature or to discuss the particular problem, e.g. at the BRE, where the library will refer complex questions and matters requiring advice to the Advisory Service.

The literature provided may range from basic reference books, texts and reports, to specialist periodicals, large collections of manufacturers' literature and technical information services such as the *Barbour Design Library* and the RIBA'S *Product Data* service. Complete sets of British Standards and some foreign standards may be available, together with Agrément Certificates and some relevant government publications. In-house guides and indexes to these are sometimes available. The information is there but the architect must often go and use it himself.

An information service is one which answers an enquiry with facts, information and advice, not necessarily literary. When required, most enquiry services will go beyond their own resources to other information services. Alternatively an enquirer might be referred to another source which is better able to deal with a particular problem. An information service often provides evaluations and précis of the literature, e.g. technical digests, and some are closely linked with advisory centres. 'The aim of the information function . . . [is] the translation into practice of existing knowledge and the fruits of new thinking and research' (Woodbine Parish, 1964). This function is often executed through publications, and the Construction Industry Research and Information Association (CIRIA) was set up in the 1960s to try to coordinate the effort and bring information services to the notice of those requiring them, from the architect to the site-foreman.

However, for the sake of simplicity, throughout this chapter the term library will be used in the widest sense. Advisory and evaluation services will be specifically mentioned.

What can a library provide?

Patricia Calderhead (1972) pointed out than an architectural practice 'must rely on directories and outside sources of information to augment its own stock of reference material'. The majority of library and information services offer a wide range not only of resources but of assistance to the enquirer. Skilled staff available to answer specific enquiries are often subject specialists and aware of the likely context and scope of most questions. This enables them to exploit the resources of their library and, if necessary, either to refer the enquirer elsewhere or to contact other libraries for an answer. In such cases locating the answer may take time. The degree of urgency involved should be indicated since while most answers are required immediately, some are more urgent and the questions should have been asked the day before yesterday.

Reference collections of documents are the key to most enquiry services offered to architects and it is not always possible to borrow materials. Photocopying is the modern solution to this problem. In many academic and public libraries this is self-service, and users should observe the copyright regulations.

Active responses to questions can involve librarians in lengthy literature searches and the preparation of bibliographies for the architect. In most cases this will be based on already published work, but some services can provide information covering unpublished research and investigative work. Any searching done in response to an enquiry will always depend on the context and the complexity of the problem as well as the time available. The use of on-line search facilities (see Ch. 4) greatly assists the compilation of bibliographies and the search for solutions to technical problems but is still subject to the availability of databases. Publications may already exist on topical or frequently occurring questions. Selective Dissemination of Information (SDI) services may exist to keep the regular enquirer up-to-date with developments in specifically defined fields. Translation services are available when the literature is not in English. ASLIB and the British Library, Science Reference Library, hold indexes of translated articles and further sources of translations are given in Mildren (1976) or *Aslib Proceedings* (1979).

While many items identified by a literature search may not be available locally, the inter-library loans services will usually be able to obtain copies (or photocopies) from other libraries, although a time delay is inevitable. The overwhelming information explosion of the 1970s makes it impossible for any library to acquire all the literature which its users may require, but a wide network exists to enable each library to locate and obtain identified items required by its users as a result of searches or specific enquiries.

When to use a library

The office reference collection or library varies in size. If the answer to an enquiry is not immediately found there it is necessary to go elsewhere, to ring or call around to a library or information service. Some of the guides described below should be available in the office library to indicate who is most likely to assist with a particular type of question. For example, when searching for the address of Brown, Brown and Brown Ltd, which appears not to be in the telephone directory, the *Barbour Compendium* or the RIBA *Product Data*, all of which are in the office, the local public library will probably be able to assist. The nearest Building Centre, the local college, polytechnic or university library may also have suitable directories to answer this. In the same way the address of the manufacturer of a product known only by its trade name, the location of a specific publication, whether a manufacturer's handbook, a BRE *Digest* (missing from the office set) or other government reports should be found in local libraries.

Complex technical information can sometimes be provided locally but the enquiry is often better directed to a more specialist information service. For example, the Department of the Environment has been doing a lot of work with flat roofs and might be looked to for technical advice with such a problem. The British Architectural Library at the RIBA has outstanding architectural collections and is admirably placed to answer enquiries relating to specific types of buildings. Where a specific type of building is involved such as a school or hospital then it is worthwhile considering the Department of Education and Science (DES) Library or that of the Department of Health and Social Security (DHSS). Likewise the Sports Council can be useful when designing sports facilities. Technical problems can occur with materials and the many trade and research associations can provide answers to technical enquiries, often with assistance in evaluating the information rather than just providing the literature.

Other professional problems often relate to the work of specialist research establishments. The requirements of the Fire Officer may present a problem in compliance which the BRE Boreham Wood Laboratory can solve. Timber decay information is the province of the BRE Princes Risborough Laboratory, and the National Physical Laboratory has done much work on noise. But the enquiry calling for information on noise levels around airports, especially Heathrow, is one which only specialist architectural and construction libraries can answer. The list of examples is endless. The guides listed on pp. 28ff. below should indicate where and how to select a source for any enquiry. The use of modern telecommunication facilities, like the Telefacsimile Information Network Data, which can transmit drawn data in the way telex transmits the printed word, when used in conjunction with the telephone should reduce the barrier of distance suffered by many working outside London.

How to use a library

Telephone inquiries

It is often as easy to ring as to visit the local information service if you know that the answer to your enquiry can be easily reported to you over the telephone. You can explain your needs and have them phone back later rather than wait while an answer is found. In the near future, viewing facilities developed by the National Building Agency for the transmission of plans and drawings may be more widely available, but at present for this type of visual information an architect must either be prepared to wait for the post to deliver the response or to visit the library.

The 'Annual Review' of information sources in the *Architects' Journal* (January) gives only telephone numbers of information sources since a majority of enquiries are made this way. But not all enquiries can be answered immediately or accurately by telephone.

Postal inquiries

A complex technical enquiry requiring visual information may be made and answered by post if distance and time prevent visits. In this case it is best to try to give as much information as possible relating to the context of the enquiry in order to assist the information service to provide a suitable response. A telephone number should be given in case they need to ring you to clarify information.

Personal visits

Time often precludes visits. However, if visiting an information service or library, especially if travel is involved, it is advisable to ring or write ahead to make sure that the library is open and can provide what is required instantly. Some places, like the British Architectural Library's Drawings Collection, need notice to produce items from stores located away from the building or in other less accessible parts of the building. An unannounced day-visit may be insufficient. Check also on opening times, as there may be discrepancies with published hours, with vacations or illness forcing unexpected closures, especially in small services. If contact is made first it may not even be necessary to go. They can indicate whether the material required is available.

Some information and research associations actively discourage visits for inquiry purposes unless at their invitation. If the solution to a difficult technical problem is involved then they may be prepared, or even request, to visit your site. Payment may then be involved.

In a small library or research and information unit personal assistance is usually available to familiarize visitors with the organization and layout of the area and to assist with locating the information sought. Such personal attention is less obvious in the larger organizations with open access, e.g. public and academic libraries, although they may be the most freely available locally. In such cases it is advisable to look around for plans and guidance and to ask for assistance, which is usually available to casual users to enable them to use the catalogues and to find special collections, special indexes and categories of publication which might otherwise be difficult to locate. Publications providing guidance and explanations to the resources are now produced in many large institutions.

Making enquiries

Getting the right answer is as much the responsibility of the enquirer as of the librarian. It is frustrating to expend effort locating the information only to find that it is not what was required because the question was not clearly explained in sufficient detail. Be prepared also for the answer not to be quite what was expected; the right response can be rejected because it is unexpected.

Whether enquiries are made in person or by telephone a sensible technique may get the right answer more quickly with less or no frustration. The Department of the Environment publication *How to Find Out*, gives useful hints:

There are seven simple rules:
1. Ask personally. A question can be completely altered if it has been passed through several people – so ask personally.
2. Say who you are.
3. Say why you need the information.
4. State the urgency. A quick and short answer may be more useful than a week's delay and a more comprehensive answer.
5. Be accurate and concise.
6. Give as many relevant facts as possible.
7. Don't anticipate the answer.

Communication involves transmitting, understanding and receiving a message. Understanding must be achieved by both parties. Therefore it is important to be able to express a question clearly to get the right answer. Enquirers may expect to be questioned and should explain in detail the question, its origin, and the amount, level and complexity of the information needed.

Any names or unusual words should be spelled. It is helpful to know how recent or current that particular information needs to be, what steps have already been taken to locate it and whether foreign-language material is acceptable. It is best to explain as though talking to a colleague without simplifying. If the librarian does not understand then questions will clarify points, but simplification can distort and present the wrong terminology. Alternative words may be sought in an effort to clarify an enquiry or find index terms. Most specialist librarians have a wide understanding of the relevant terminology. Since there may be a delay in providing the answer it is also sensible to indicate where and when to telephone.

Which library to consult

Office libraries

Most practices have their own small collections of information. Some are larger than others and may be available to other local practices. Those of the Local Authority Architects and Planning Departments may be able to help other local architects. The scope of the GLC's ACCESS is far larger than most. Some of the major manufacturers maintain information services covering applications and techniques; Pilkington and Kodak, for example. The commercial office services, the *Barbour Index* and *Barbour Design Library*, the RIBA Office Library Service and *Product Data*, are received in many office libraries and may be available for use by the smaller practice.

Building centres

Through these the Building Centre Group aims to provide information on building products, materials and services, not just in London but in the main provincial areas, although the principle that no-one should be above one hundred miles from a Centre is not always met. They have libraries as well as exhibitions and operate the Data Express service to distribute technical literature and an information service (FIND) if research is needed to provide an answer. International information and energy conservation information are also provided by special sections.

Professional institutions

Most professional associations have a library service and most will assist other professionals with enquiries in their field of interest. In addition to the RIBA's British Architectural Library the architect should also note those that are likely to cover particular problems from the Chartered Institution of Building Services, the Royal Town Planning Institute, the Landscape Institute, the Institutions of Civil and Structural Engineers and the Royal Institution of Chartered Surveyors to the British Institute of Management and the Institute of Housing.

Trade and research organizations

These are set up by a particular group of industries to promote, to research into and to develop their products. Some take an outward-going approach to this and provide many services freely, but others make charges for services and publications. Not all have information services and libraries, but the largest ones do, and names like the Brick Development Association (BDA), the Timber Research and Development Association (TRADA), the Building Services Research and Information Association (BSRIA), the Cement and Concrete Association (C&CA) and the Aluminium Federation will recur constantly in these pages. Many are known by the acronyms. 'It should be recognised when seeking advice from trade associations that they exist primarily to promote the products, materials or services of their members. Nevertheless many can provide valuable technical information in their own field, some produce excellent technical literature and many are represented on BSI and other technical committees and also produce their own codes of practice' (*AJ*, 1979).

Government departments

The Department of the Environment (DoE) and the Property Services Agency (PSA) and its branches have their own comprehensive libraries. Many enquiries can be answered here if time permits, but it should be remembered that they exist primarily to serve their own staff and are not generally available to the public. However, every government department has its library and the related building types are usually well covered there. Thus, for example, the DHSS publishes technical notes on hospitals, other health care facilities and their equipment needs. Law courts are covered at the Home Office library.

Government research establishments

Separate from but related to the government departments are the research establishments supported by the government and other funds. The Building Research Establishment (BRE), which also covers timber and fire research, is only one of these. Others with relevance to architects range from the National Physical Laboratory (noise research) to the UK Atomic Energy Authority.

Public libraries

Although few public libraries have large architecture and building collections most have basic texts and they are a useful source of a wide range of background and technical information. Commercial and business information services are usually found in major towns and the City of London Business Library is one of the best in the country. Addresses can always be found through public libraries and many have collections of British Standards. The largest libraries in this category are the divisions of the British Library, in particular the Science Reference Library, which holds a large proportion of the technical literature and of manufacturer's literature covering many industries and countries.

Academic libraries

Often the only local specialist collections which also hold the more expensive reference tools and manufacturer's literature are the academic institutions with schools of architecture or construction. Most are accessible to anyone on introduction to the librarian and may have special arrangements with the local society of architects, as at Leicester. The schools of architecture are listed in the RIBA *Directory of Members* and the CIRIA *Guide*, while the libraries of institutions with building courses are described in Harlow's *Search* from the Chartered Institute of Building (1977). However, the latter should be used with care, as it minimizes the size of some collections and enhances that of others.

Other libraries

Miscellaneous other services include those of the Centre on Environment for the Handicapped, the Farm Buildings Information Centre and many other associations like the National Playing Fields Association, the Sports Council and the Fire Protection Association. Such organizations usually cover information on specialist building requirements as did the Zoological Society for a recent enquiry on the construction of camel stables for a Middle Eastern client or the BBC for information on television studios. The scope is endless, and it is in finding these that the general directories listed below are especially useful.

How to find appropriate libraries

There are many guides in existence to tell you which library or association to consult. Some of those mentioned are produced primarily for the architect, are easily and cheaply available and are frequently up-dated, and are therefore not only of greater use than some of the weighty tomes produced for the librarian but also should be available for desk-side reference and for everyday use in the office.

When using them remember that address and telephone numbers date quickly, and it may be necessary to telephone directory enquiries to correct some information. No guide is comprehensive, although some that claim to be are sometimes the least comprehensive. Therefore more than one guide is a necessity; do not rely on just one list, however good it may be, or may seem to be.

Guides not only cover libraries but they also mention associations and services which provide the various types of information service already discussed. The distinction is sometimes difficult to draw. The first three guides listed are reliable but do not go beyond their authors' definition of an architect's needs. Many of the others include a wider range of organizations and are useful for enquiries relating to specific types of buildings.

The Architect's Guide to Sources of Information and Advice (Bullivant, annual) is published in the form of a wallchart. It covers about two hundred organizations, indicating which have libraries and which provide information services. If organizations charge for their services this is indicated. One must scan the list to determine who to contact for a specific subject enquiry and there is no subject index. Organizations are arranged under the following headings:

> General information and advisory services, including bodies principally concerned with supplying information and/or advice not limited by product or technique, including permanent exhibitions;
> Building Centres, comprising the Association of Building Centres in England and Scotland;

General libraries, including the larger libraries with a broad coverage of their main field;
Professional institutes and learned societies, including bodies promoting a specific subject field and the interests of individual members;
Government departments (including GLC), including any office of central government and the nationalized industries (excepting research establishments);
Government research establishments, including stations and laboratories which are wholly part of central government;
Research associations including stations and laboratories organized by industry and central government;
Standards, testing, inspection and approval organizations (including bodies financed partly or wholly by government, industry, users and consumers) largely concerned with products and services;
Trade associations including bodies financed by industry for promotion, development and information supply regarding products and contracting services;
General bookshops.

How to Find Out (PSA, 1980) is a four-page pamphlet available free from the PSA Library. A few organizations are described in detail and hints are given on making enquiries but the most valuable section is the list of just over a hundred information organizations, ranging from government departments to trade associations, They are listed in alphabetical order, giving just addresses and telephone numbers. It was regularly revised but 1980 was the last edition. Although smaller, it complements the wallchart described above. For example, of the manufacturers' associations given, thirty-five are listed by both, thirty-nine by the wallchart only and thirty by the PSA only.

The *Barbour Design Library* index volume lists over three hundred organizations (including trade associations, government departments, advisory services, societies, etc.) concerned with the construction industry. Since it is revised three times a year, addresses and telephone numbers are more up-to-date than in any other of the directories described in this chapter. The index caters for both subject and alphabetical approaches. To identify an organization which might be able to help with a specific subject enquiry (e.g. lighting) one consults the subject index. This refers you to the section which lists documents in the *Design Library* from the relevant organizations and which also provides the names of organizations not represented by the literature. The addresses and telephone numbers are found in the alphabetical list on the yellow pages at the back. Not all will be able to offer advice, nor do they all have libraries, but the notes sometimes indicate this. Unfortunately, the index is available only to subscribers.

The Building Centre and CIRIA Guide to Sources of Information (3rd edn. 1979, Supplement 1981; 4th edn due 1982) also lists major associations of all types including government departments and research bodies. Information about each is given with its address and telephone number. A subject index is provided to the main alphabetical sequence. The range of coverage is wide and at £4 this represents good value, although new editions tend to be four to five years apart.

House's Guide to the Construction Industry, although more expensive at £25 in 1981, also describes, briefly, the services mentioned, including library availability, publications and contact names. It aims to present this from the 'single viewpoint . . . of the practising architect in a busy office' who is 'accustomed to treading in minefields' where information is concerned. It certainly covers more than the other guides in general information content but tends to skim some areas; for example forty-eight major contractors are listed with only eight specialists named – this is hardly a substitute for a full directory of contractors. The list of trade associations numbers one hundred and forty-two, with thirty-four research associations extending beyond the narrowly defined range of the construction industry as defined by the PSA and Bullivant, to include councils, pressure groups and amenity societies from the Science and Engineering Research Council to the Dartington Amenity Research Trust, for example. Societies are not listed extensively in the other guides. Before going on to provide a digest of information on the industry itself, major reports and some major bodies are described in detail and government bodies are listed, again ranging widely and including all nationalized industries. There is also a very comprehensive list of libraries and information services. Formerly this was known as *Construction UK*, and before that the *Redland Guide to the Construction Industry*.

Technical Services for Industry (1981) is produced by the Department of Industry and describes the various services provided by government and quasi-governmental bodies. Unfortunately, the present economic stringencies are forcing government departments to cut down on services to those outside their own departments. Nevertheless, they are often among the most comprehensive and least-publicized information services in the country. Telephone numbers, addresses, contact names and publications are given in this free publication, which is revised every four to five years and has a good, detailed subject index.

Technical Help to Exporters is another publication relating to government information services, and since it is geared to the export market it is particularly useful for architects requiring information relating to overseas work.

The 'Guide to Information Sources' published by the *Architects' Journal* (1979) may lie unheeded in many offices. The list covers research and advisory bodies and trade associations which were present at Interbuild 1979 and who responded to a questionnaire asking for a brief account of their activities. They are perhaps therefore among the most active. Although there is an overlap with other guides, some organizations not mentioned elsewhere are included. The information was up-dated in the 'Guide to Information Sources' published as part of the *AJ Annual Technical Review* in January 1981, and may, in future, become annual.

A directory of organizations which describes more than two hundred relevant associations, societies, institutions, libraries and other data relevant to architects forms a large part of *British and Irish Architectural History: A Bibliography and Guide to Sources of Information* by Ruth Kamen, Head of Library Information Services at the British Architectural Library (Architectural Press, 1981).

All associations in Britain, not just those relevant to construction, are listed in the *Directory of British Associations* (6th edn, 1980). The architect can often find sources of information relating to different types of building here. Although presented in alphabetical name order, the detailed subject index will soon locate national and local associations. The information supplied by the associations is detailed and notes the services available, but not all of the many voluntary organizations are included, especially small local ones. However, the publishers do hold information on many unlisted bodies and they operate an enquiry service. There is a certain overlap with other publications mentioned and with Millard (see below), but since the scope is different they tend to be complementary. For example, this directory lists thirty-four conservation bodies where Millard lists fifteen, but not all of those are included in the former's thirty-four. Two companion volumes complement this, the *Directory of European Associations* (2nd edn, 1976 and 1979) and *Councils, Committees and Boards* (5th edn, 1982). The 'advisory, consultative, executive and similar bodies' listed in the latter are both local and central, including government advisory committees, commissions of inquiry and consultative bodies. Chairmen and subjects are indexed and the main entries describe the board fully, giving its activities, publications and location. It should be noted that not all can give advice and information.

Patricia Millard's *Trade Associations and Professional Bodies of the UK* is in preparation and new editions usually appear every two to three years. Since it covers all topics it is a useful adjunct to other lists and it is the only guide with a geographical index to assist those working out of London. Chambers of Commerce and Trade are included but not the small bodies found in the *Directory of British Associations*. However, associations like the Architectural Metal Craftsmen's Association and the Association of Builders' Hardware Manufacturers do not appear in the *Directory*, the PSA leaflet or other lists above.

The guides discussed above generally deal with associations and their services rather than specifically with library and information services, which are more particularly the province of the following directories.

The Construction Industry Information Group (CIIG) was formed in the 1960s to bring together librarians and information officers in architectural practices and libraries. Its current membership of approximately seventy-five organizations includes all kinds of libraries, from small architects' offices to government departments and civil engineering firms. Its list of members is issued annually and the *Directory to Members' Libraries* (1981) can help in identifying many libraries and proving a contact name. The standard comprehensive listing of libraries and information services in the UK is the *Aslib Directory* (4th edn, 1977 and 1980). The two volumes cover the whole range of topics likely to tax the architect and all libraries listed have some external services. The fourth edition has ceased to provide a geographical approach to the libraries listed, but there is a good index and some place names are included. The special libraries are sometimes very small but others are large and each entry gives key information such as address, contact name, telephone numbers (although some of these have been found to be wrong), opening hours, subject coverage and publications issued. Of especial value are the many company libraries listed, such as British Gypsum Ltd and ICI.

The *Guide to Government Departments and Other Libraries* (British Library, 1982), now in its 25th edition, lists government department libraries comprehensively without duplicating the information in the *Aslib Directory* or *Technical Services for Industry*. Since all subjects are covered it is possible to locate assistance here easily and most libraries listed will handle enquiries from outside. Ten major libraries are listed specifically under the heading 'construction' but other topic headings are also relevant. For each library the guide gives address, telephone number and contact name, stock and coverage, services and publications and hours where known.

Libraries in the UK and the Republic of Ireland (9th edn, Library Association, 1981) gives only basic address and telephone information for public and academic libraries. There is no subject index. The regional guides compiled by the branches of the Reference Special and Information Section of the Library Association provide a subject-indexed list of local services. These guides provide a good description of each library and list all types of library in the region, from the large public and academic establishments to the one-man company services.

Specialized lists

The number of handbooks and directories for different subject areas is increasing. Lists of information services may also be found in the back of many handbooks. All libraries holding complete sets of British Standards are listed in the *BSI Yearbook*. The Crafts Advisory Committee have produced the *Conservation Sourcebook* (1979, Supplement 1980) to give those involved in all types of conservation a guide to organizations offering assistance and information. It is organized by subject. There are about two hundred and sixty-five fully descriptive entries covering organizations which can help with technical advice, library services, publications, etc. The information assistant at their headquarters can also be contacted for up-dated information.

Knowhow (British Library, 1979) is the unusual title of a small, unpretentious guide by Graine Morby to a wide range of information sources covering health, security and fire, housing and pressure groups. Although aimed at advisory services, it provides a very wide range of informal contacts for information, most of which will not be found in other sources. Community Action's *Investigator's Handbook* (1975) is another similar type of publication developed for pressure groups but with some useful advice on locating information which will not be found elsewhere. The Departments of Environment and Transport publish subject guides to information and organizations in their *Information Series*. Each of these describes organizations, journals and major reference works in a particular subject area. Topics covered so far include housing, town and country planning, environmental pollution, traffic, transport, new towns, quality of urban life, local government and sport and recreation. In the latter are given the main contacts and organizations for all major sports, a boon to the architect providing sports facilities. Many bibliographies list organizations to contact (see below). The architect should already be familiar with those in *Specification*, and the RIBA *Product Data*, which provide such lists after the Bibliography or References.

Printed library catalogues

Many libraries have actually had their catalogues published in printed format. Although those from the major national libraries are to the fore in this sphere, notably the British Museum, the Library of Congress and the Bibliothèque Nationale, one of the first printed catalogues to appear was that of the RIBA Library (*RIBA*, 1937, 1938). The publishing firm of G. K. Hall (Boston, Mass.) specializes in reproducing in book form the card catalogues of major libraries. Of particular relevance to the architect are: *Catalogues of the United Kingdom Department of the Environment Library* (1977), *Catalog of the Warburg Institute Library* (2nd edn, 1967+), *National Art Library Catalogue, Victoria and Albert Museum* (1972), *Catalog of the Avery Memorial Architectural Library of Columbia University* (2nd edn, 1968+), *Catalog of the Harvard University Fine Arts Library (The Fogg Art Museum)* (1971+), *Catalog of the Library of the Graduate School of Design, Harvard University* (1968+), *Catalog of the Library of the Museum of Modern Art (New York)* (1976), *Dictionary Catalog of the Art and Architecture Division, the Research Libraries of the New York Public Library* (1975), which is supplemented by the annual *Bibliographic Guide to Art and Architecture* which also includes Library of Congress additions, *Dictionary Catalog of the United States Department of Housing and Urban Development Library and Information Division* (1972+) and *Library Catalog of the Metropolitan Museum of Art* (New York) (2nd edn, 1979+).

Because they are so expensive, these catalogues are generally found only in the largest architectural libraries and some university libraries. It is, however, useful to know of their existence, as they can help the researcher to identify a wealth of published information which previously could only be obtained by travelling to the individual libraries.

Other published catalogues include the *Catalogue of the Drawings Collection of the Royal Institution of British Architects* (20 vols, 1969–).

The *British National Bibliography* is published weekly with annual cumulations and this provides a current listing of all books published in Britain and deposited with the British Library (formerly the British Museum Library). Although it is not the equivalent of the above catalogues it does provide similar information, by subject, author and title.

Foreign sources of information

When engaged on an overseas project it may be necessary to search further afield than the British sources of information described above. *Construction Industry Europe* (1976–1977, House Information Services, 1979, with Supplement 1980–1981) surveys twenty-two countries in Eastern and Western Europe. For each country it provides an article describing the construction industry, market prospects and client organizations, building regulations and town planning controls, standards, testing, research and information, professional practice and a summary of key facts. This is followed by a directory section which lists government and public authorities, professional bodies, trade, industry and other organizations, employers' organizations, trade unions, information, research, testing, standards and approvals organizations and information sources (i.e. a bibliography with names and addresses of publishers and bookshops). Addresses and telephone numbers are provided for each organization and entries are coded to indicate whether an advisory service or technical consultancy is offered. There is a subject index to products and services.

The BRE Overseas Division produces *Building Research Centres and Similar Organisations throughout the World* (Building Research Establishment, 1978) which covers about one hundred and fifteen countries. It begins with a list of some international organizations and then, for Africa, the Americas, Asia, Australasia and Europe, lists regional organizations and national centres, by country, giving addresses only. Summaries of the structure and activities of slightly more than six hundred institutes in fifty-two countries are given in the *Directory of Building Research Information and Development Organizations* (CIB, 1979). It begins by providing information on nearly fifty international organizations and then, for each country, a summary of the pattern of building research, and for each organization details such as addresses, telephone numbers, telex, brief history, name of director, staff and structure, field of work and publications. It includes an index to the names of organizations.

Research Institutions around the World concerned with Housing and Urban Development (HUD, 1980), produced by the Office of International Affairs of the US Department of Housing and Urban

Development, lists institutions in one hundred and twenty different countries. It includes organizations involved in urban and regional research, especially in the broad field of housing and urban development. Those included are mainly government or government-related institutions. The arrangement is by country. The address (but not the telephone number) is provided for each institution and sometimes a note of the subjects covered, but there is no subject index.

Overseas architectural institutes are listed in the *RIBA Directory of Members* and the *Handbook* of the Commonwealth Association of Architects gives further information. See also Chapter 14 below for further information.

Conclusion

Although this chapter attempts to describe and list some of the many guides to libraries and sources of information it is by no means exhaustive. Books and bibliographies will often add the name of a useful association when discussing particular types of project or technique. Many architects will find that it is useful to maintain their own list of names and addresses which have proved helpful.

References

Aslib Proceedings (November 1979), **31** (11). This issue devoted most of its pages to studying the provision of technical translations but in particular pp. 500–511 provide locations for translations

Calderhead, P. (1972). *Libraries for Professional Practice*, Architectural Press

Mackinder, M. (1980). *The Selection and Specification of Building Materials and Components:* a study in current practice and educational provision, 2nd edn, York, University of York, Institute of Advanced Architectural Studies (Research Paper 17)

Mildren, K. (1976). *Use of Engineering Literature*, Butterworths, pp. 57–61

Ministry of Public Building and Works. Directorate of Research and Information (1968), *The Use of Information in the Construction Industry:* a study of twenty-five firms, MoPBW (R & D Paper)

Snow, C. (1974). 'Some information habits and preferences of architects', *CIIG Bulletin*, p. 6

Woodbine Parish Report. Ministry of Public Building and Works. (1964). *Building Research and Information Services*, HMSO

Note: While this chapter was being proof-read the Construction Industry Research and Information Association published a useful short *Guide to International Organisations of Interest to the Construction Industry* (1982, Special Publication 24). Compiled by J. S. Armitage, this is a handy booklet which gives a considerable amount of information about each organization and also includes a brief guide to further such lists.

3
Information retrieval techniques
Valerie J. Bradfield

The analysis and digestion of new information is the result of either research or everyday work in the professional practice and produces data. Much of the work in architectural offices is not research in the academic sense but, in applying known facts to new situations and in analysing the results, new information is created. That information is used in creating a building, which may then be reviewed in the professional literature. If it is not reviewed then the information will be absorbed and used internally only – but if published information is created, then that information enters the 'information chain'. Once the chain of reporting in the literature is understood then it is possible to enter the literature at the appropriate level for the information required. *Figure 3.1* represents the stages of publication of information, showing the levels of 'digestion' and the names that are given to the retrieval tools appropriate to each level. The tertiary level of lists is not shown. These are the guides to using and finding literature as well as lists of bibliographies, databases, indexing services and so on which are useful to anyone requiring guidance in information retrieval.

This chapter aims to discuss the nature of the information usually required in construction processes, examining suitable approaches to the information retrieval process. A basic search technique exists. The skills involved in information retrieval are discussed in some detail, giving hints on keeping records and presenting bibliographical information.

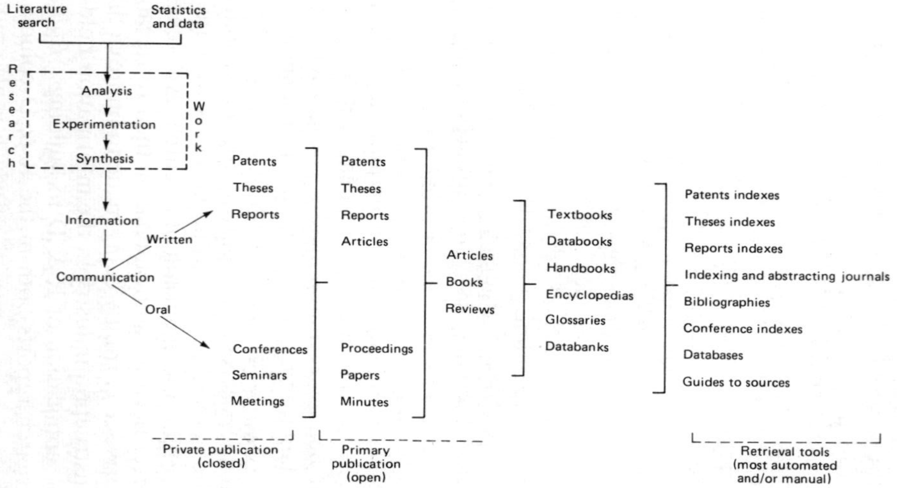

Figure 3.1 Generation of information

The nature of searches

It is always easier to ask someone else to find information, but there are occasions when there is no-one to ask or when it is profitable to do it yourself. No-one can achieve the same understanding of the requirement as the originator, nor have others the same ability to recognize what is useful, to assess and to integrate the findings with the problem instantly while assimilating additional information which might otherwise have been unnoticed.

Everyday information requirements are usually for established facts, design data, manufacturer's addresses, product names and features. Many are swiftly found by consulting desk collections, the office 'library' or colleagues. Sometimes these fail. The address is not there. The tables seem to give every figure except the one sought. Then one must look elsewhere. In performing these searches one goes through a process or series of processes without conscious thought once the usual procedures have been learned. Finding more complex information entails thinking through those processes methodically. Information needs are also highly individual, depending upon the enquirer, the level of expertise in the profession (ranging from student architect, to recently qualified building surveyor, to experienced civil engineer), the usual field of interest, the depth of knowledge required and the subject characteristics of the information required. All aspects of construction require great breadth of knowledge in the professional and frequent searches for detailed information in narrow technical fields. Thus, when seeking information, available sources may be used for their speed of access, although better, more detailed or more reliable data may lie unsuspected in a less accessible report or article. At some point a decision may be made that there is no necessity to search further or time may prohibit the extension of a search. Awareness of the remoter resources plays a significant part in their retrieval and use. Conscious efforts are currently being made to improve the awareness of the construction industry in the information field in order to improve the application of R & D to buildings. *Building* now lists recent research reports both in the R & D column and the monthly 'Techalert' page, a version of which is also published in *Building Services*.

Basic data may be found quickly by turning to a reference handbook, one of the *AJ* ones, or *Kempe's Engineers' Yearbook* perhaps. The need is clear and easily expressed. The answer is, or should be, obvious when it is found; for example, degree day data for this month, average rainfall at the new site (see pp. 270 and

242). Such facts are usually located in handbooks, and discussions of their use can be located quickly in specialist journals or texts once the source is known or identified. Telephone enquiries for such information are easily answered, as they do not involve searching through a chain of information but just entering the right handbook at the appropriate point. In the future the architect may locate such facts through his VDU using the appropriate databank (see Chapter 4). An instinct for the source of the answer develops. It cannot be easily taught. For a town plan most people will think to go to the road atlas or the *Geographia* plan series. In a large library the development plan or structure plan from the County Council will be available and may give the information required about the site environment in a form more suitable for the purpose. In the same way a dictionary will explain the meaning of a word but an architecture or building dictionary will often be preferable to the *Oxford English Dictionary* and may include tables and other related information such as is found in Cowan's *Dictionary of Architectural Science* (Applied Science, 1973). Whatever the requirement, the data are sought, extracted from the source and the search ends. It is not necessarily a lengthy process.

More often the need is not just for facts but for descriptions of techniques, user requirements, materials, etc. A detailed answer is difficult to find. A new material has been advertised but in what situations has it been tested and used? Manufacturer-independent information is required. Finding the answer may require a long search through many different types of literature involving not only time but lateral thinking. Success may be dependent upon the depth and quality of the indexing in the retrieval tools used as much as upon the skill of the searcher. Mechanized databases can speed up such searches but once references are found, the actual documents must also be sought. Delays are sometimes inevitable. However, precision in answering the enquiry is more vital than the volume of information retrieved.

An exhaustive search may be essential sometimes. An architect may make such a request figuratively, for example, when a client's brief calls for a new type of building with which he has little experience, or which he has not designed recently, and he requests 'all' information on that particular building type. This does not usually mean everything ever published but a selection of keynote, relevant readings and examples of current thinking about that building type and the needs of its users.

However, there are occasions, especially when commencing research projects, when an exhaustive search is needed. All possible sources must be investigated using the type of strategy outlined below in order to ascertain that the work has not been done before, is not currently in progress and has a firm background of established fact on which to build. Many references are sought, only some of which will be followed up. It is an exacting process requiring meticulous documentation. Such searches may continue for a considerable time.

Skills

Skills in successful searching can be developed. However, it is important to recognize when to search personally and when to consult a specialist. There are benefits in searching for information such as a broadening of the general awareness of facts and techniques which are relevant or which may be relegated to the information file and recalled later for another project. If there is doubt about the expression or limits of the enquiry it may be easier to look for the answer than to try to explain. During searching, judgements on relevancy can be made and the course can change to follow useful channels which might have gone unheeded by an information specialist answering a specific enquiry. However, time and knowledge of sources may often militate against this approach.

Flexibility and an open mind are essential in order to exploit all approaches to a difficult problem when it may be useful to back-track, side-step or even start the search again. Records are therefore essential to save time, to remember what has been done and what has been found. A methodical and systematic approach to both searching and record-keeping is essential. Even items which were rejected or useless should be recorded with a note of what was wrong with them so that it is clear that they were consulted and to save time back-tracking later. Answers may not always be found in the expected place – flexibility of approach means that they can be accommodated, especially if a possible solution might be unrecognized because it is farther from the expected answer than was thought possible.

Resourcefulness will uncover alternative sources of information and persistence will be necessary where specific information is required and is fugitive, where dead-ends are met and when the whole process is dull. Browsing has rewards. Where index terms change not only a thesaurus is often necessary but also a degree of lateral thinking – for instance articles on nuclear fallout shelters have existed since World War II but, prior to the 1970s, they were usually indexed under civil defence shelters, air-raids, etc.

Methodology

'Unfortunately the publishing world is not systematic' (Maltha, 1976), therefore any methodology has to take account of the need to skip stages and allow for exceptions. Bibliographies formerly only listed books, but many now include periodical articles, the names of institutions and other sources of information. Some indexing journals include relevant reports and books, especially those journals from government libraries such as *Construction References*, and *DoE Library Bulletin*, which refer to many internal papers not readily located elsewhere. The following paragraphs give an outline of how to proceed; the essence is to start the snowball rolling, since once it is gathering momentum, and hopefully size, the order of procedure may vary. Keeping of records at every stage has already been mentioned as essential. *Figure 3.2* shows clear routes through the most rewarding channels which should be chosen initially according to the subject of the enquiry and should continue into the more specific types of resource using the following hints on technique.

Some processes are automatic, that is, the brain proceeds with them when it recognizes the need for information. Other processes, skills, must be developed. Initially it is important to clarify exactly what information is required. This implies an awareness of any technical limitations, the teminology usually used and the level and amount of information needed at the particular time. Some books and articles may be too technical, too mathematical, or even too simple, or be based on American practices. The exact time-scale and any relevant dates should be checked. For example, information on an event such as the Summerland fire has an exact date before which there will be no information. Although reports are usually published within a few years reassessments may occur as, for example, that in 1981 of the causes of the Ronan Point failure in 1969. At times only very recent information will be needed. Sometimes specific forms of literature will be required, such as standards, and the scope of a search should be narrowed accordingly. Foreign-language material may not be acceptable, or otherwise the barrier between British practice and others will prevent its use, For example, the application of solar energy heating systems depends on the availability of sunshine, and examples from the USA or even France may not be appropriate to the British climate. Some American publishers, e.g. Wiley, are now publishing British texts and vice versa, so that it is no longer possible to reject them instantly as being based on US standards.

Searching takes time, but intelligent guesses can save time. If a lot of information is required, use a bibliography as soon as possible. The index volume to the *Barbour Design Library* is really a classified bibliography, and many publications listed have references leading to other more specific information than that which appears on the microfiche file document. Stop when enough information has been found – most searches could go on forever but the rate of return diminishes.

Where current information is needed, be aware of the delays inherent in publishing processes. Books may be written four years before publication date and only partially up-dated after the submission of text. Publication usually takes six months to one year. Some journals which appear quarterly may also be a long time in publication, especially some indexing and abstracting journals which take time to compile. Other journals may have a tatty appearance but may be very current. Current information is the most difficult to find because of the inadequacy of memory and the delays both in publication and compilation of indexes. Memory usually condenses time or is incomplete but as indexes are not compiled until some time after events have taken place individual issues of journals will need to be searched for information. *Keesing's Contemporary Archives* is current and helpful with national events while *Research Index*, an index to the daily and weekly press, appears within two weeks of the articles listed.

It is helpful to list the sources to be used to retrieve information in the order in which they are to be consulted. If any are remote or need to be contacted by letter they should be contacted early enough not to cause difficulties and delays later. Books may not be the best place to start if the topic is more likely to have been written about in journals. Use any indexing services available. At this stage try to appreciate any other subject approaches. For example, library science journals and books frequently discuss library buildings and their construction. Similarly pit-head baths are likely to be described in mining literature. Other examples can be cited; computer-aided architectural design is written about not only in its own journal but is indexed in *Architectural Periodicals Index* and also in *Computing and Control Abstracts*. New programs are discussed in *Which Computer* as much as in *AJ* or *Computer Aided Design*. Historians are interested in vernacular buildings, especially at the local level, and are far better at writing up information than architects. Will information about noise levels at Heathrow airport be found with discussions of planning, with noise research, with aircraft engineering or with the specialist literature on airport construction, or with the growing literature on types of pollution?

44 Information retrieval techniques

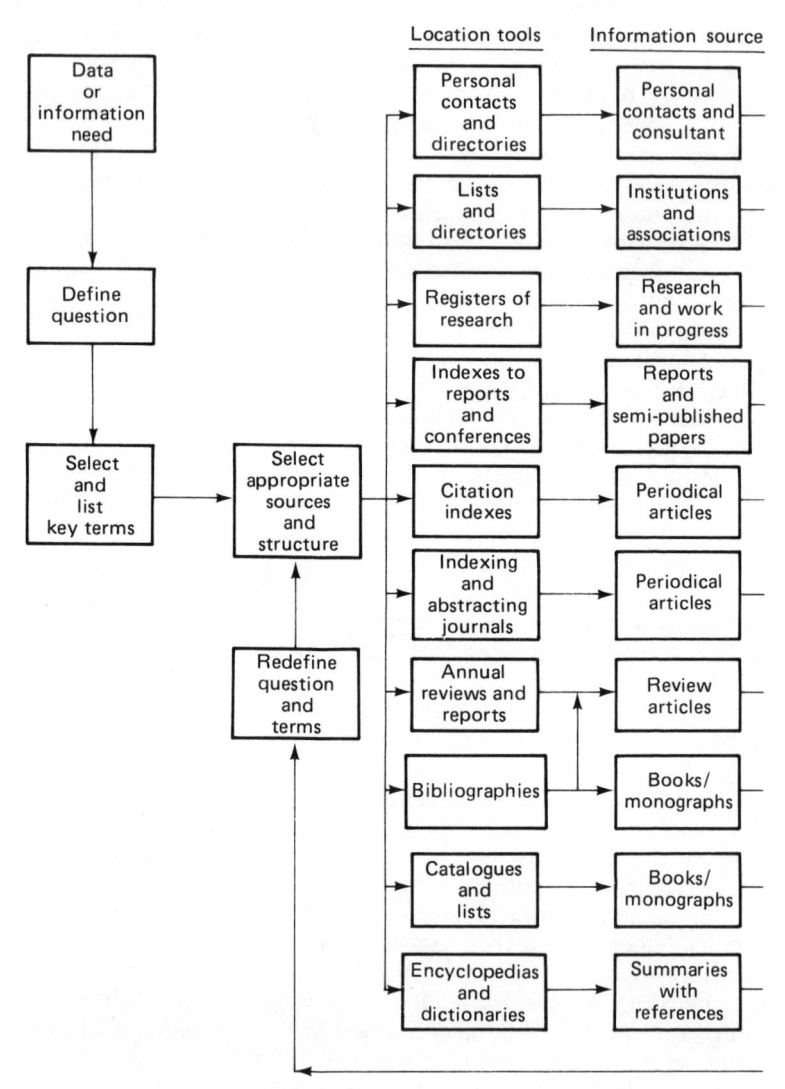

Figure 3.2 Information search chain

Terminology varies between subjects, and between indexers. In searching any type of index to a book, journal or abstracting journal, there may be deviations from architectural language, and terminology may change over the years even within the same indexing journal. Usage also changes with time. Colleagues of the

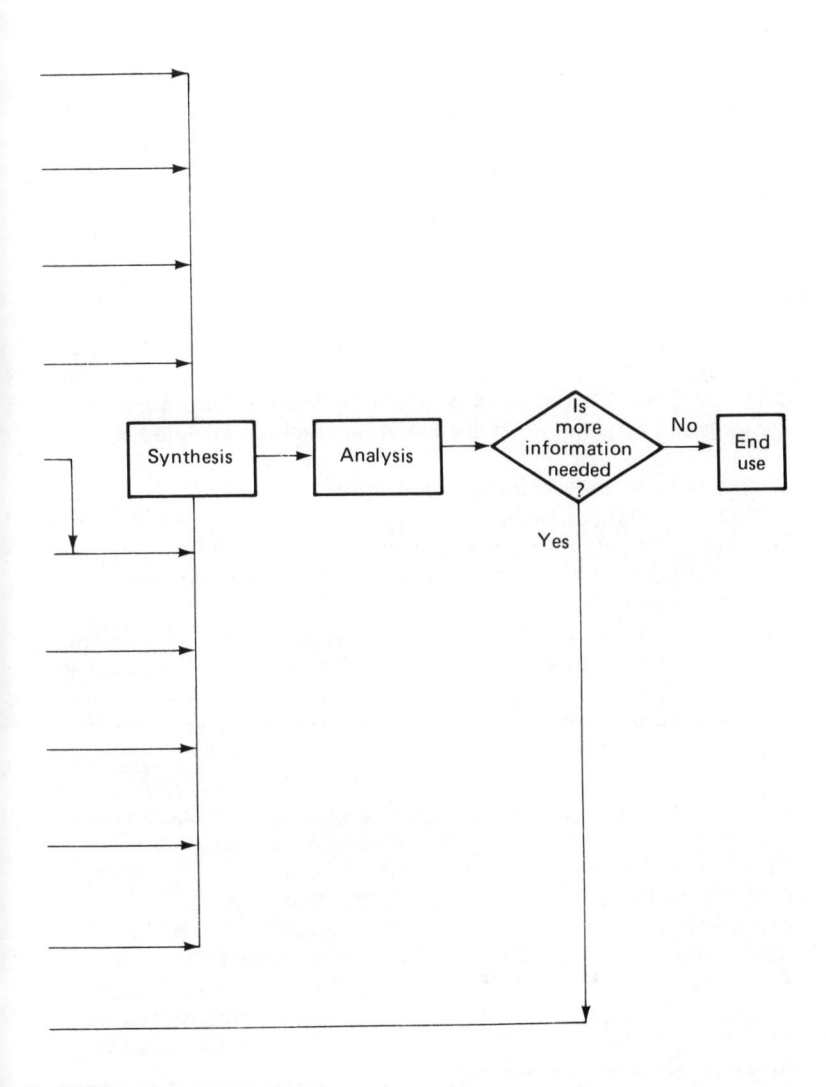

1940s and 1950s might not understand conversations on 'environment', which was once confined in usage to what is now called the habitat of animals. Librarians need to identify the appropriate terminology for the subject according to the source of the information, others may also need to think about word usage.

For example, the search for information on the environment required for zoo animals will produce articles on 'natural habitat' unless 'conditions in captivity' is used.

Similarly, the original definition may appear not to be yielding the sort of information required. Terminology should be redefined, either broadening the field of search because little has been found or narrowing the field because too much was located, some being irrelevant. For example, with the previous instance of noise level around Heathrow airport a number of references may be found on the volume of noise made by aeroplanes, on attempts to control it mechanically, but nothing on the actual recorded levels in and around local buildings and the necessary remedial action. The redefinition will cover the effect of aeroplane noise on buildings near airports, in particular Heathrow, providing information also on the success of attempts to exclude noise from buildings in *any* similar noisy situation, such as elevated motorways.

Any definitions and background information should be sought initially in a handbook but this may not always succeed if depth, breadth or currency of coverage is poor. Some technical information is found most easily in handbooks with less familiar names like *Kempe's Engineers' Yearbook* or the *Electrical Engineers' Reference Book*. For example, the former reprints the 'IEE Wiring Regulations'. Further references may be given in these and in encyclopedias.

'Key' articles sometimes exist which either crystallize information on a topic or which represent the basis from which other work has developed and from which other articles digest or rehash information. Locating one of these quickly may produce sufficient references or provide a good start. A review may perform a similar function in that it will discuss all literature and information on a subject, summarizing the content, discussing it critically and providing a synthesis. Some recent publications from the BRE have done this, e.g. *Wind Environment around Buildings* by Penwarden and Wise (HMSO, 1975) and *Climate and Building in Britain* by Lacy (HMSO, 1976). Subject series entitled 'Advances in. . . .' and 'Progress in. . . .' have been running for many years in some areas of science and technology. In construction such reviews are few. *Progress in Construction* appeared only twice (Construction Press, 1971 and 1972).

Journal articles often discuss topics on which no books exist. Indexes and abstracts to journals are discussed at length in Chapter 7. They will often provide references quickly and have a wide scope. However, their indexing and arrangement are not always helpful to the searcher. Abstracts may provide useful information but critical ones should be used with care. Articles with numerous references can start the information-snowball but in architecture this may be rare – although referencing in journals and books is improving, many do not cite their sources of information as well as those relating to other disciplines.

Key authors may be identified and used in the author indexes of reference tools to locate their other relevant works. Authors may be used in the citation indexes, *Arts and Humanities Citation Index, Science Citation Index* and *Social Sciences Citation Index*. Corporate authors, i.e. companies, practices, used in this way may help to locate a lot more information.

Books may be located via the articles, bibliographies and the catalogues, both printed and library (see pp. 34 and 101). Some abstracting journals include books and government publications. Publishers' lists can be useful. Whenever using books be aware of the effect of changed legislation, standards and advances in technology on the information, as books tend to be older and these aspects change quickly. Throughout a search check references and cross-references. Read. As you read and digest so new lines of approach and reference will arise.

Indexes cover in-house company reports, research reports from academic institutions and reports communicating government-funded research results, among others. The most useful of these indexes are the BLLD's monthly *British Reports, Translations and Theses* which has superseded the *BLLD Announcement Bulletin*, has regular cumulative subject indexes and which now includes *R & D Abstracts* from the Technical Reports Centre of the Department of Industry; the abstracts in the regular 'Techalert' pages in *Building* and *Building Services*; the US Department of Commerce, National Technical Information Service (NTIS) database which is available on-line and its publication, *Government Reports Announcements*. The DoE *Library Bulletin* and *Construction References* cover a few reports, especially government ones. The problems of using and obtaining reports are discussed in greater detail in Auger's *Use of Reports Literature* (Butterworths, 1975) and Chapter 5 of Mildren's *Use of Engineering Literature* (Butterworths, 1976). While books and articles are secondary publications and their content may have been checked for accuracy, reports are the first stage in communicating research and may contain inaccuracies according to their source.

Conference proceedings are another source of information with a separate indexing system. Most detailed and current are the BLLD's *Index to Conference Proceedings*, also available on-line, and the ISI services, *Index to Scientific and Technical Proceedings* and *Index to Social Sciences and Humanities Proceedings*. Not all proceedings published contain full papers: some are summaries, others are fully researched and documented. The discussion is rarely recorded in full, and yet for the participants this is often the major benefit.

Translation services have been covered elsewhere (see p. 21) but those done by the BRE and PSA library services are also subject-indexed in their respective abstracting journals. The development of computers with larger stored capacity has brought with it a new technique for retrieving information: on-line searching of computer-held databases. Some of the manual drudgery is removed but new skills are necessary, since the computer database has to be searched accurately if all the relevant information is to be retrieved. Searching needs increased accuracy and attention to terminology. Databases are discussed in Chapter 4. However, their use is only advantageous when searching for information on very precisely defined topics – where wider topics are sought, the volume of references located on a computer database may be very expensive to print out and more than can be used in the time available.

Evaluation

It is easy to accept information once written as being correct. But is it? Has the printer made an error which proof-reading has failed to correct? If a figure is in error and a calculation is based on it, what could the result be? It is best to be aware of such problems and to 'test' or appraise the information presented. Even *Mitchell's* has errors in printing. There are two levels of evaluation; to decide whether the book or article contains the relevant information and is worth reading, and to assess the validity of its content. Some hints on approach should be helpful in evaluating references found during a search. The evaluation of a reference can be attempted with a minimum of information and can save time and frustration in locating irrelevant items.

The author may be either a well-known authority, an academic with no practical business experience or a journalist who will produce a very chatty account, helpful for background in an unfamiliar area but not always to be relied upon for detailed discussion. The ability to write is often not as good among those whose technical expertise is excellent. Some authors are biased, even in the presentation of facts. Look for biographical information stating where the author is working, what his qualifications are, his nationality. The title page, introduction or preface may help. Dust-jacket 'blurb' is designed to sell. Omission is a favourite ploy. If in doubt, use a biographical dictionary or *Who's Who* (being aware that these entries are written by the persons who may omit or misrepresent information themselves).

Gimmicky titles may indicate poor quality within or may be a sales device. Sub-titles elaborate the content or the tone of the work indicating that a book with a seemingly helpful title is actually irrelevant to the search. The publishers may indicate the tone of a work; some are known for their usual type of publishing. There are scholarly and popular presses or small propagandist private presses. Sweet and Maxwell tend to be law publishers, the university presses are scholarly and, although they usually relate to their country of origin, some in the late 1970s, such as Yale, have published British texts, and vice versa. A number of American publishers have recently published British texts, usually the larger ones like Wiley, McGraw-Hill or Prentice-Hall. Bell tend to produce 'O' and 'A' level texts. Where work is based on standards, law and regulations it is not usually translatable between countries without a great deal of thought and comparison.

Date and edition are vital. Not all information needs to be current. However, where law, standards and advances in technology are concerned currency is essential. There is a difference between a revised reprint and a new edition, but a reprint does not imply revision. Check also the date to which the data in the book relates, especially with reference books or handbooks, as it may well be considerably before the publication date.

The contents list often indicates the scope of the book, its depth and the weighting of various parts. Omissions are noted either in the introduction or the preface, which should indicate also the aims, limitations and level of the material. In an article this should be done in the opening paragraph.

Check the references. Do they appear reliable and are they up-to-date? If you know any authorities you would expect to see quoted, look for them. Is sufficient information given to locate the references? A recent list in Bowyer's *Vernacular Building Conservation* (Architectural Press, 1980) omitted dates and lacked any standardization. This does not instill confidence. Enquiries revealed that it had not been compiled by the author. Many architecture books have in the past lacked references. The results of academic work are usually well referenced. An author may be known by local or specialist libraries to be frequently inaccurate in citing references. For example, Leicestershire Archive Office pointed this out with regard to W. G. Hoskin's *The Midland Peasant* (Macmillan, 1965).

Indexing also varies in quality, as shown on p. 111. Is there an index at all? If you are locating very specific information check that the index is detailed enough to reflect the content adequately. Indexing is not always done by the author and varies in depth.

In reading, try to distinguish facts from interpretation, skimming the less useful sections and scanning others for information. Be sure that hypotheses are substantiated with good evidence, figures, diagrams and references. Style of writing differs and affects comprehension. If an account is difficult to understand a similar version by another author may be presented in a clearer style. Do not accept every word as true. Look for bias and evaluative or critical treatment. After reading a few items on a topic it should be possible to separate facts from opinions and develop a personal viewpoint.

Recording

Records are important, and many architects develop personal record systems at an early stage. Nothing is more frustrating than to be unable to recall what was said yesterday and the source you were told to check in for particular information about a worrying technical problem. . .

When a problem recurs, your records should indicate not only where to find the answer but also the additional hints which were published a month or so ago in one of the journals which are regularly received. Although one cannot remember off-hand such items, the note will provide the reference. The *Barbour Design Library* (see p. 147) is proving of great value in providing current information quickly, but it does not have that personalized touch, and references to odd journal articles or scraps of information mentioned by friends can be extremely useful.

There are two types of record necessary; what was searched and what was found. In recording what was searched, keep a list of sources and check off items making brief notes of problems in using or finding them and of content. In the case of serial publications such as journal indexes, note the years which have been checked. This can be done simply, by noting the date after the title with simple annotations, e.g. *API* $1978^{/}$, $1979°$, $1980^{/}$ or *API* $78^{/}$, $79°$, $80^{/}$, meaning that only those complete years have been checked and, although something was found in 1978 and

Information retrieval techniques 51

1980, nothing was found in 1979 but it was checked. Such shorthand is useful where a lot of checking needs to be done. Fuller notes may not seem necessary but may save time when returning to a source.

Notes of the references found are best kept on slips or cards, since these can be easily filed or shuffled. Larger cards may be used for notes on the subject content, If notes are made on A4 sheets then these should be indexed to the bibliography cards. Size is immaterial. Many people use A5 (5×8), A6 (6×4) or 5×3, according to the volume of detail to be recorded. Basic information noted on bibliography or reference slips should be enough to help to locate the items and to refer to it in written reports etc. according to one of the two systems described on page 88. If the

---

Mildren, K. W. (ed.)
Use of engineering literature.
London, Butterworths, 1976.

Part of a series: v. wide range of contents:
Ch. 1–11 types of literature + Ch. 12 searching;
13 personel indexes; 14–35 various subjects incl.
32 structural engineering (i.e. construction technique mainly)
33 Soil eng.
34 Land survey.

                                Leicester
                                Polytechnic   REF
                                Library   016.62

Figure 3.3 Example of a reference slip, showing the content of the item, the library and the classification mark for ease of reference

item is retrieved it is best to note where it was located, and, if in a library, make a note of the classification number in order to save time should it be needed again. An example of a reference slip is shown in *Figure 3.3*.

Personal reference collections

Experience in teaching architectural and building students has shown that the former tend to begin to develop their own personal reference collection early in their career, frequently with some form of indexing or organization. This often flags later. The latter, in common with many other professionals, collect but do not organize. Scraps of paper, useful addresses and memory tend to get lost or fail. Organizing does take time but repays that time when it is possible to find required information quickly and easily at the deskside. Methods vary and have been described in few texts, the recent ones making the assumption that one has access to a computer, or unlimited funds. Neither may be true at present, although a micro-computer, if available, is certainly a useful option.

Most useful is A. C. Foskett's realistic chapter on *Personal Indexes* in Mildren's *Use of Engineering Literature*, which is a revised and shortened version of his earlier *Guide to Personal Indexes* (2nd edn, Bingley, 1970). Jahoda's more complex *Information Storage and Retrieval Systems for Individual Researchers* (Wiley, 1970) has an American bias and there is also Stibic, *Personal Documentation for Professionals: Means and Methods* (North-Holland, 1980).

There are a few points which may be useful when trying to organize information. Integration of cross-referencing between various shapes and sizes of information-bearing documents ensures that nothing is omitted or overlooked when retrieving data. Thus notes from reading, reference record cards, trade catalogues, technical leaflets and slides, etc. should all be located using the same system. Ideally this should be simple. If notes are filed in ring-binders these can be numbered using codes and the contents indexed. Files of catalogues may be kept in broad subject order, perhaps using the CI/SfB outline. Again the names or codes can be used for reference. This way a subject file may be identified for information on a general topic such as roofing, while the reference index should provide specific indication of where the information on problems with flat roofs will be found within the sub-collections of documents.

Such an index is time-consuming to prepare. If bibliography cards are kept as described above they can be organized alphabetically by subject headings. Again, CI/SfB can provide useful headings, as can any of the other classification schemes. Author-order does not provide instant subject access, and to try to maintain files in both orders entails constant duplication and is not necessarily recommended. All systems, however, may require some duplication where two or more subjects are covered in one document.

The address book or file may be kept on cards or in a book. It should be remembered, however, that books get full, and unless ring-binders allow pages to be added, copying into a larger book is tedious, and maintaining a second when the first is full always means looking in two places. Bibliographic references may be kept separate from a data file but each should contain cross-references (cards indicating where related information may be found). For example, when the file is arranged according to CI/SfB, Table 1, literature on heating, which also discusses solar energy in housing design, should be referred to under housing and solar energy,

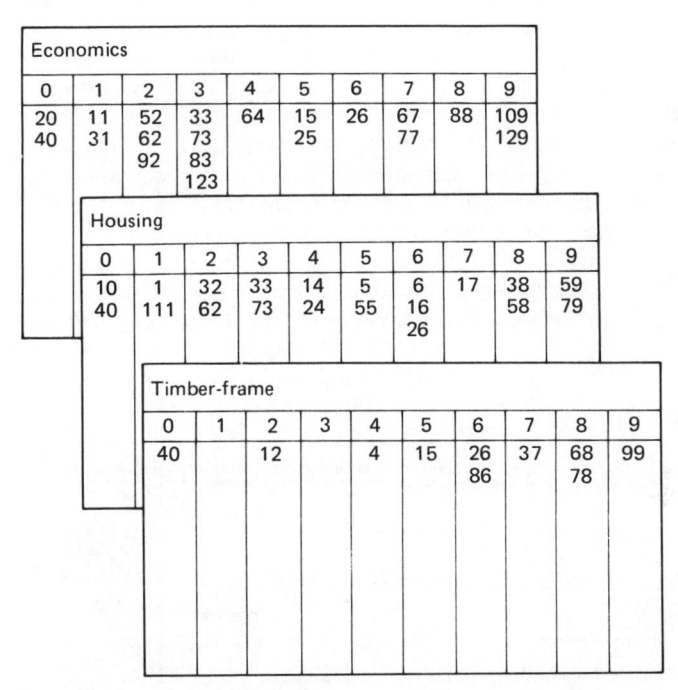

Economics									
0	1	2	3	4	5	6	7	8	9
20 40	11 31	52 62 92	33 73 83 123	64	15 25	26	67 77	88	109 129

Housing									
0	1	2	3	4	5	6	7	8	9
10 40	1 111	32 62	33 73	14 24	5 55	6 16 26	17	38 58	59 79

Timber-frame									
0	1	2	3	4	5	6	7	8	9
40		12		4	15	26 86	37	68 78	99

Figure 3.4 Coordinate index cards

perhaps by a separate sheet of paper at those locations, noting that information will also be found in document x in the heating file.

It is possible to develop increasingly sophisticated methods of indexing collections of literature and references. All are subject to the problems mentioned in Chapter 5. Any classification scheme can be used for subject organization but indexing is essential to access it, and in any personal subject heading system problems of terminology will arise as the system grows – thesauri will be necessary, albeit simple ones. The simplest method of coping with this is not to develop a thesaurus but to keep at hand a copy of a

54 *Information retrieval techniques*

building dictionary, the *Ci/SfB Indexing Manual* or the *Construction Industry Thesaurus* in its abridged form, and every time you use a term to underline it to show that it exists in your system. The indexing and cross-referencing will be already done within the volume used.

Other forms of indexing require expenditure in money and effort. Coordinate indexing is perhaps the least expensive. Documents and references need to be organized in such a way that they can be given numbers which act as location keys. Each is also given sufficient 'keywords' to describe its content. Each keyword itself has an index card on which is entered the number of every item in the office to which that keyword is assigned. To retrieve information, the appropriate keyword cards to describe the problem adequately are located. The numbers are matched as in *Figure 3.4*, where it can be seen that information on the economics of timber-frame housing will be found in documents 26 and 40, which can then be located in the office.

This system is relatively cheap. Similar more sophisticated versions work on the same principles but with alternative methods for matching numbers. The Peek-a-boo cards illustrated in *Figure*

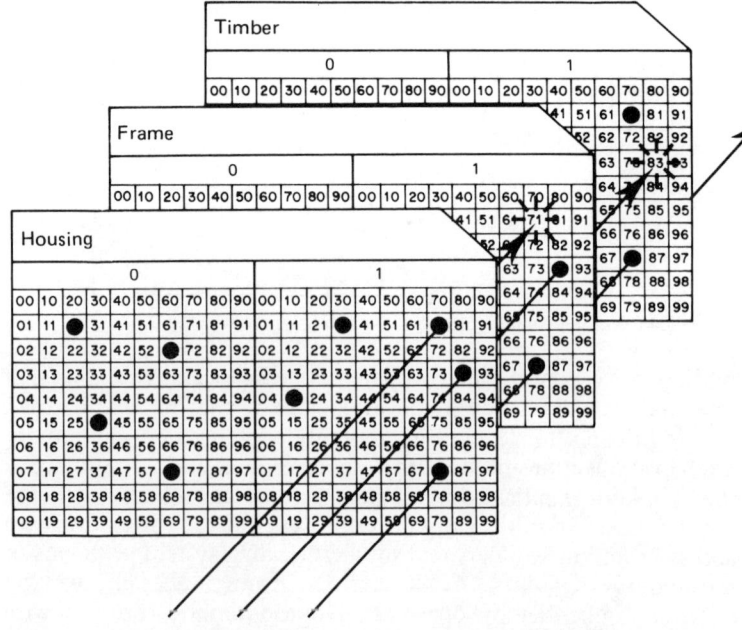

Figure 3.5 Peek-a-boo cards (Courtesy ISS Information Systems and Services Ltd)

Information retrieval techniques 55

3.5 have holes punched to represent the document number. These are matched by holding the chosen cards to a light source. Edge-notch cards are shown in *Figure 3.6*. Here the information is entered on the card itself and encoded around the edge using various predetermined combinations of notches. The pack of cards may be kept in any order. When information is required the appropriate codes are identified and needles are inserted through the pack so that the relevant cards drop down. These may be

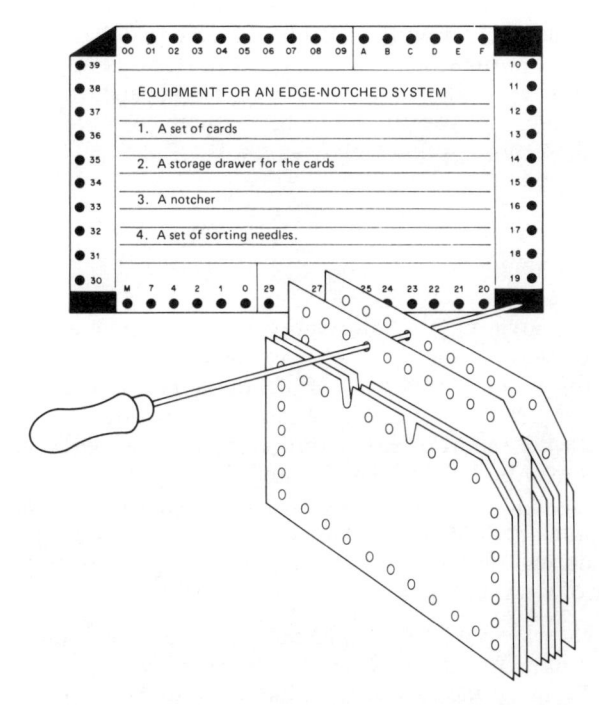

Figure 3.6 Edge-notch cards (Courtesy ISS Information Systems and Services Ltd)

needled again on another code to narrow the field of information and so on, until the required degree of precision is reached. Very complex codings can be achieved according to the types of card purchased, and all cards can be blank or pre-printed according to the information to be entered. Microfiche may be mounted on such cards for instant retrieval of a greater volume of information.

These systems are described in more detail in the sources mentioned above but as micro-computers become available more cheaply so personal document systems may rely on them for indexing. However, organization is still necessary in the document store. Reference and information retrieval is feasible provided that the program is adequate to a basic search and match using keywords. The principles are the same as those described above, with the computer doing the work of card matching and sorting. The most recent discussion of this is in Stibic (*op. cit.*), who cites a number of articles on specialist applications. Some software houses produce suitable programs. Only the computers with larger memories can store and retrieve the information itself and, although this sounds very useful, it must be remembered that there is labour involved in inputting that information from its original paper format. Sometimes keeping the information in paper format and referencing it on the computer may be far more cost-effective and accurate than transcription (see Chapter 4).

Presenting a search

The result of a search may be information which is immediately applied to produce a drawing, to ring a manufacturer or to compile a bill of quantities, etc. If it is a list of bibliographical references this must be organized and presented either as a separate item or as the final part of a report or a dissertation. Some brief notes on how to do this may be helpful. The information to include is set out on p. 89. There must be some clear order. Simple alphabetical order of author may be adequate. (Those items without authors go under title, ignoring 'the', 'a' etc.) However, for longer lists there are a number of alternatives:

> Bring major works to the fore, alphabetically by author, with annotations on their value and content. Follow this with other references in one of the two orders below: By form, books, reports, articles, etc. alphabetically by author or title within each. (If authors are known it is unusual to use titles for such lists); By subject where there are sufficient references to make this the easiest way of representing them. Alphabetical author order will be observed within each subject heading and the breakdown into books and articles can be applied if necessary.

Any limitations to the content should be stated at the beginning, with an explanation not only of the topic but also of the resources used to find the information.

In conclusion it should be remembered that this guide is about finding and using information. The architect has a wider scope for information search than many other professionals, since the diversity of projects and the building process itself lead him into subject fields ranging from education and law, to housing, technology and science according to the type of building and its functions. Architectural books are often glossy, lacking indexes and references. Science books are usually dull but fully referenced. In general, science and technology queries may be easier to solve because there are more retrieval tools, a more precise terminology, more reliance on journals and more basic factual information. In humanities, social sciences and the arts even terminology varies widely, and searching becomes difficult without the same legacy of well-developed information retrieval aids.

Reference

Maltha, D. (1976). *Technical Literature Search and the Written Report*, Pitman

4
Computerized information retrieval
Valerie J. Bradfield

The increasing storage capacity of computers has given the information profession a means of automating some of the more time-consuming processes of information retrieval. A large store with an efficient search mechanism can provide current and retrospective information to the construction industry quickly and accurately. That information may be in the form of bibliographic references, data, figures, diagrams or standards. This chapter will outline the development of services and examine their use to the architect and building profession. It will not discuss the applications of computers to architectural design, structural calculations and project scheduling, etc. This has been done elsewhere, for example, in the new *AJ* series on computing and in many texts; or contact may be made with the Construction Industry Computing Association. Programmes are listed in Hutton and Rostron's *Computer Programs for the Construction Industry* (Architectural Press, 1978), which is regularly revised.

Development and availability

Advances in technology over the past decade have provided larger storage capacity in smaller devices with simpler procedures for the man in the office utilizing the services of the machine. The specialist programmers and electronics staff have made the 'chip' useful not just to program the washing machine, to program the heating services for a building or to assist with the production of drawings but also to store data required for processes which have not yet been mechanized and may never be.

Many of the abstracting and indexing services referred to in Chapter 6 are compiled on computers which can sort and print the references quickly and accurately. The cumulation of monthly or weekly parts into annual issues has also become simple and speedy using a computing or word-processing facility.

Once the information is available on the computer it can be reorganized and used in a variety of ways. The initial growth of these databases was slow in the 1960s. Services such as *Biological Abstracts* have had an author-index on-line since 1957 and a subject-index since 1959, and *Chemical Abstracts* began *Chemical Titles* database in 1962. The databases created can be made available as machine-readable services on a national and international basis. Researchers experimented in the later 1960s and commercially available services began in the USA, with Lockheed and Systems Development Corporation (SDC) being the first firms to offer the facility. Europeans were able to use their services when in 1974 the Tymshare telecommunications network made access available in Europe. Since then the growth has been dramatic, as *Figure 4.1* shows. However databases are still specialist. Many are small and few cover a large time-span as yet (see *Figure 4.2*). The construction industry has few databases, although it will be seen that improvements are in hand and information is available provided one is aware of the capabilities of a wide range of databases.

There are many guides available (see p. 71) and each 'host' offers a booklet or manual containing information on all the databases which they offer. Some of the many guides are given at the end of this chapter, but first the main information-providers are discussed and the contents of some of their databases are outlined.

Host, supplier or vendor are the names given to a commercial organization with large sophisticated computers which makes databases available on-line to any user using a VDU/terminal and 'dialling in' from remote points. Users subscribe to one or more hosts or suppliers, paying a nominal fee. Use of databases is usually charged monthly, according to usage on an hourly basis, and varies with each database.

Costs are composed of a number of charges. The operator-time is not included and variables include the database used, the type of contract as a subscriber to the supplier and the prints made. The main features are the telecommunications charge while connected to the host computer, the charge for connect-time into a database, the charge for off-line prints according to volume and the monthly or annual charge for a password to the system. This latter is often minimal, but if access is to be available for a number of systems to extend the range of databases available these charges could mount

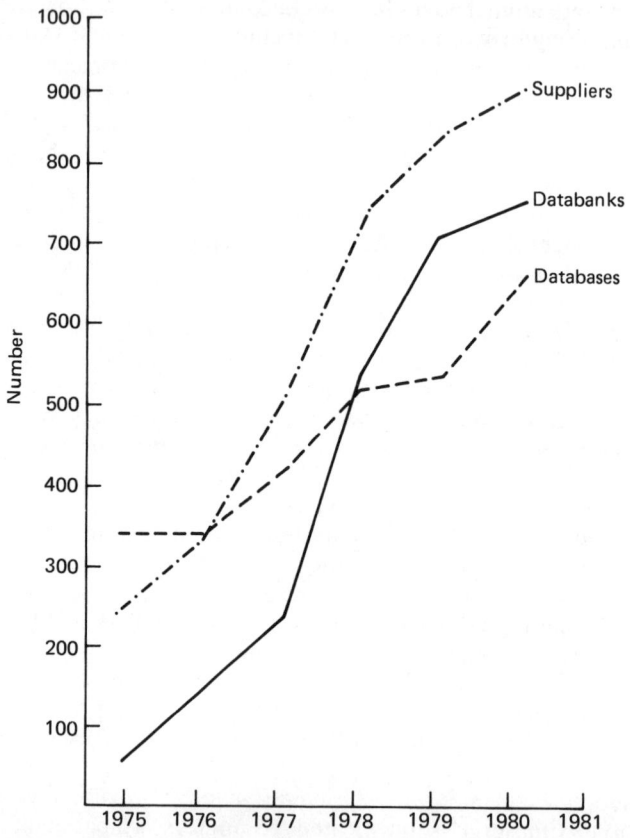

Figure 4.1 Growth of on-line data using figures taken from *Eusidic Database Guide 1981*

up considerably. Each supplier details charges per database in its manual.

Contact is made with the supplier using a password. This means that although many databases are theoretically available it is necessary to contact each host organization separately to register and obtain a password. This is not as complex as it may seem at first, since some of the largest suppliers offer over a hundred databases to subscribers and where some databases are only available via one supplier, others, like *MEDLINE* or *COMPENDEX*, are available from many. Many European suppliers have linked together to form the *Euronet DIANE* group – Direct Information Access Network for Europe. This is sponsored by the Commission of the European Communities and is a communications network. Subscriptions have to be made to individual hosts

Years covered	Percentage databases
1980	100
1976–1980	86
1970–1980	50
1960–1980	6

(a)

No. of references included	Percentage databases	Percentage by size
Up to 50 000	55	46
Up to 100 000	21	small
Up to 200 000	15	
Up to 300 000	6	
Up to 400 000	5	43
Up to 500 000	6	medium
Up to 1 000 000	11	
Up to 2 000 000	7	11
Up to 4 000 000	2	large
Over 4 000 000	2	

(b)

Figure 4.2 (a) Time span of references in databases (figures from Hall, 2nd edn); (b) Size of databases by number of references included (figures from Hall, 2nd edn)

as it is a communications and cooperative network rather than a host organization itself. In Britain access may be made via *DIALTECH*. The *Euronet Diane Directory* explains procedures and lists databases, with a subject-index as well as addresses.

The main British suppliers are *BLAISE*, based at the British Library, *DIALTECH*, based at the Technical Reports Centre, Kent, and *INFOLINE*, run by Pergamon Press. They issue brochures describing their services. All brochures are up-dated regularly. Subscribers also receive a manual explaining the commands used, the specific search procedures and details of each database available. New subscribers are usually given an allocation of free time to get used to the system in the first month. Training sessions are also available. The British Library Automated Retrieval System, *BLAISE*, offer bibliographic databases, databases containing information on literature in catalogue format, databases containing data on research, chemical substances and toxicity and databases containing thesauri to assist with searching the bibliographic databases. Access is made in the usual way on the telephone lines, or from outside Britain on *Euronet*. Back-up services are available and, for users without terminals, searches can be made from postal requests to the BL. 'Factsheets' explain all services.

The *DIALTECH* service operates from the TRC, St Mary Cray, through a minicomputer link-up which automatically connects to the European Space Agency computer at Frascati. The host is actually the ESA–IRS service at Frascati near Rome. A manual and assistance are available from Kent. Pergamon's *INFOLINE* is developing its database range to offer many not yet available elsewhere, but at the time of writing it still has a limited range including *PATSEARCH*, *Geomechanics Abstracts*, *World Textiles*, *Management and Marketing Abstracts* and *PIRA Abstracts*, as well as *Chemical Abstracts* and *COMPENDEX*. Facilities may be used to build up private data files.

Many people in Britain also use *DIALOG*, from Dialog Information Services Inc., which started in 1972 and is owned by the Lockheed Corporation. In early 1982 it was put up for sale but the purchasers are not yet known. Some one hundred and forty-five databases were available in May 1982, a larger number in comparison to the above, but some, such as the *ASI*, Congressional Information Service Inc., are oriented to US business needs. The other main hosts in the USA, also accessible in Europe, are SDC Orbit and BRS.

The main European hosts are listed in the *Euronet Directory* and include Compagnie Internationale de Services en Informatique (CISI), Centre d'Information Temps Riel Europe (CITÈRE), Data Star (Switzerland), Deutsches Institut für Medizinische Dokumentation und Information (DIMDI), Informationsystem Karlsruhe (INKA) and Télèsystèmes Questel.

For those without terminals it is still possible to use these services through the local library service, if it has facilities. The large public and academic libraries usually have services – Birmingham Public Library has a printed leaflet introducing its services.

Aslib offers search facilities to members for a fee representing the on-line time, telecommunications and a handling charge. The BL offer a similar service to the public generally. Techsearch at the Technology Reports Centre offer on-line search services. Many libraries use such services as a means of locating information quickly as part of their usual information retrieval service.

Brokerage services developed in the USA and there are a few in Britain. The consultant Gordon Pratt, formerly of Lockheed Dialog, discussed their work in his talk to CIIG on 18 March 1980 when he outlined the present and future developments in databanks in the British construction industry. *NPM Information Services* offer retrieval services and their work was outlined in *Online*, July 1981. Capital Planning Information undertake consultancy work especially on the planning side. Most such brokers can be located by contacting the Institute of Information Scientists, Aslib, by using the *Information Trades Directory* and by using other directories and professional press. General assistance in locating any retrieval services is offered by the UK Online Information Centre based at Aslib headquarters.

Databases

The reason for the use of a database in preference to a manual abstracting service is that a search can be conducted quickly and easily, at a greater depth and accuracy. However, searches are most effective if they are for a very precise topic. For example, the National Technical Information Service database in the USA covers publications of the building research institutions, including references to research carried out in the 1960s on high-alumina cement concrete problems influencing failure in a tower block. If this information had been located and utilized in Britain it might have helped to avoid the recurrence of the same problems here in the 1970s. However, NTIS covers a large proportion of US government publications and their research and reports database might not have seemed an obvious source of construction information. The broader a topic the more difficult it is to specify terminology precisely enough to use the on-line services efficiently and the more print-out will be required to study the results, making the search expensive.

At present there is only one British database covering construction. This is *ACCOMPLINE*, from the GLC Research library. *ACCOMPLINE* has been developed from *Urban Abstracts*, formerly *Planning and Transportation Abstracts*. It covers over

64 Computerized information retrieval

100 000 references on all aspects of construction, architecture, services, maintenance, housing, planning, transport, local government and social and administrative problems. Thus architectural design and construction information is limited. Subject terminology is restricted and proper names have not been consistently entered. However, until anything else is available this is useful. In 1977 the BRE promised a database replacing *Building Science Abstracts* but this has not yet appeared. *Architectural Periodicals Index* is expected to be available on-line at the end of 1982.

The Swedish Institute of Building Documentation has a reference service called *BYGGDOK*, which covers housing, planning, environment, construction, civil engineering and energy. It corresponds partly (30%) with the abstracting journal *Byggreferat* and has recently become available via *Euronet*. Much information referred to is in Scandinavian languages and search terms are in Swedish. Also in Sweden *BYGGVARUREGISTRET* (Swedish Building Centre) covers information on 45 000 products and their suppliers (*c.* 12 000) and corresponds to their printed building products catalogue. Both date from 1975. In Germany *BAUFO* is available from INKA. This has indexed building research projects since 1970. The French *ARIANE* is discussed below.

Many general databases include items of interest to the architect. For instance, *Conference Proceedings Index* from the BL is available on *BLAISE* and *DIALOG* offer *Conference Papers Index* (US). Both cover all topics and conferences are often very useful sources of further information. The *GPO Monthly Catalog* (the US Government Printing Office), *NTIS* (above), which now includes Concrete Society publications as well as US government research reports, HMSO catalogues which are due to be available by 1983, *Research and Development Abstracts* from the TRC and the *Research in British Universities, Polytechnics and Colleges*, are all available as databases and include many important titles discussing government regulations, standards and recommendations on building. They will be particularly useful for user-studies, structural and materials problems, energy and environmental matters, as research and reports cover a very wide range.

Different types of buildings are indexed in relevant subject databases. *AGRICOLA, AGRIS* and *CAB Abstracts* index work on agricultural buildings. Waterside buildings are referred to in *AQUALINE*, libraries in *LISA*, schools and colleges in *ERIC* and health buildings in *EXCERPTA MEDICA* and *MEDLARS*. These last are widely available. The coverage of *Energy Abstracts* and *Energyline* is obvious. *ENVIROLINE* and *Pollution Abstracts* refer to all types of pollution including noise. Less obvious perhaps

Computerized information retrieval 65

are *ARGODATA* and *Sociological Abstracts* for design information assisted by *ARTBIBLIOGRAPHIESMODERN* for the more abstract side of design.

BEOREF, GEOARCHIVE and *Meteorological and Geophysical Abstracts* all cover survey and geology references. None are based in Britain, however, and, although referring to literature in English, area studies may be in any of the English-speaking countries. Planning is not covered in any other than *ACCOMPLINE* in Britain, although *Euronet* gives access to services such as the French *URBAMET* and the German *RSWB*, these may include references in English but not necessarily to English practices (see below).

Technical information is easier to obtain from a wide range of sources. Patent literature can provide useful specifications and references are available from *INPADOC, PATSEARCH* and *WPI (World Patents Index)*. Standards in France are referenced in *NORIANE* and in Norway on *STANDARD NORSK* but not elsewhere as yet. *Engineering Index* produce *COMPENDEX*, which includes references on structures and materials from a wide database reflecting world literature, mainly in English. It has the largest coverage of building as a general subject, but it is important to remember that the terminology in the headings and keywords is usually American, although sometimes British in the texts. When searching both English and American spellings should be entered to ensure full retrieval. The ASCE also offer a database covering structures. *INSPEC*, the publishing sector of the Institution of Electrical Engineers, offers a British-based service with references up-dated monthly since 1969 covering all subject areas within physics, electrical and electronic engineering, computing and control engineering. This will therefore assist with many information problems in the environmental and services area, especially as services become more influenced by computer technology. In this sphere also, there is the *IBSEDEX* database at BSRIA which can be interrogated internally for enquirers and which is now available freely to members or on subscription to non-members.

Chemical Abstracts, the 'mother' of databases, is wider in scope and uses than its name implies. Among the journals indexed are titles such as *Concrete* and *Construction* (USA). Any reaction or materials problems, e.g. corrosion, are likely to be referenced here. It also has a number of derivative databases and the manuals should be checked carefully to ensure which part of the service is appropriate to the enquiry. Research on metals will be indexed in *Weldasearch, ISMEC* (Information Services in Mechanical Engineering, USA), *METADEX, BNF-metal, ALUMINIUM* and

World Aluminium Abstracts. Other useful sources covering materials include the Rubber and Plastics Research Association's database. *RAPRA*, the Forest Products Service, AIDS, and *Beton-index* from France (concrete). Many include references beyond national boundaries.

For several reasons the construction industry in most countries has only limited interest in foreign information. Application of standards and regulations is still national despite the work of the ISO. Differences in climate and social circumstances affect information needs and relevance, whilst the language barrier is a major problem. As more companies become involved in overseas work the needs will change. The International Council for Building Documentation is investigating the possibilities for an international database. *CIBDOC* has been set up by Working Commission 57 of the Council and will gather construction information from all relevant *existing* databases to create a unified file using common indexing terms. This is being done in cooperation with Unesco's *ARKISYST*, the UIA study of the information problems of architects and builders. It will be extended to databank information if possible and hopes to overcome barriers of language and size. The project is reported in greater detail by A. Stern in *Housing Science*, from the Swedish Institute of Building Documentation in Stockholm (**4**(2), 1980, 75–79) and in the *Unesco Journal of Information Science, Librarianship and Archives Administration* (**3**(4), 1981, 210–216). An earlier issue (**3**(1), 1981, 18–28) contains a full discussion of *BYGGDOK* by Karl Tegner.

Databanks

The French *ARIANE* system has been referred to already and provides a useful illustration of the transition from database to databank, from references to literature, to direct retrieval of facts and the required data. Few descriptions exist. There is one by J. Devoge in *Transfer of Information for Industry*, a symposium (Luxembourg, Commission of the European Communites, 1979, pp. 40–48) and one can be obtained from their offices. With the support of the Fédération Nationale du Bâtiment, the Centre d'Assistance Technique et de Documentation (CATED) in 1970–1972 developed a databank oriented to the needs of small- and medium-sized construction firms using highly qualified personnel and supplying technical data, standards and regulations information as well as references. This is backed by a personal enquiry service for practices, operated by subject experts. The database refers to microfiche copies of documents, by number, when information beyond what is already in the databank is required and these can be transmitted via the system page by page, or subscribers may hold sets. The concept appears very useful to information-workers also and would appear to operate like an amalgam of the *Barbour Design Library* with a database as yet not available in Britain.

Some large offices have developed internal databanks for their own design information, working with purchased programs for such tasks as structural calculations and referring directly to that practice's preferred details. This means that structural data can be retrieved, as for example load data, rather than retrieving a reference which then has to be located and which can prove time-consuming.

The developments in this field commercially are behind the database preparation but in the 1980s are progressing and may well catch up with and overtake database provision. Already much business and company financial information in France, Germany and the USA is available in this format as well as some of the printed directories described in Chapter 8. In Britain the *Prestel* service is being used for this function, and has available company financial and planning information, some product information and data services from prominent names in the business information field. These include Fintel, Extel, Frost & Sullivan, ICC Business Ratios, The Henley Centre for Forecasting, Jordans and the Department of Industry, the BOTB and Central Statistical Office. The Statistical Information Service in the USA has also made figures available on-line. This may eventually lead to the end of expensive printed publications on statistics as a databank direct from the information, as collated, cuts communications costs considerably. It is also more up-to-date.

The legal community has developed a cross between databanks and databases containing references and facts. *LEXIS* from Butterworths maintains 'libraries' of legal texts on-line with English and American options and with cases and statutes. Statutory instruments are listed, with full text, and subject services exist, such as the tax library with case law dating back to 1875. However, subscribers must rent a special terminal and subscription is high, making this only feasible for those in the legal profession rather than those needing access to legal information on a less regular basis. Searching is over the whole text using the natural language of the legal world. Such a databank is the natural development of HMSO's use of computer-typesetting for legal publications like statutes. *Hansard* may follow when the new computerized press gets established and creates a databank as an offshoot from its daily publishing activity. *EUROLEX* is a developing full-text retrieval system from the European law centre run by the Thomson Organization and covering some subjects in law, the law of Western countries, European Community law and patent law, but it does not require special terminal equipment. *INFOLEX* has been on *Prestel* since 1975 and is mainly a case law reference service with *All England Law Reports*, *Times Law Reports*, *Weekly Law Reports* and *Solicitors Journal* on-line. Databanks on building regulation data could also be developed for the industry, depending on the necessity after the revision and simplification at present under discussion.

The House of Commons Information Service has developed a system called *POLIS* to provide immediate information of all types to their membership. Daily indexing of *Hansard* and other government documents is discussed by C. C. Pond of the Public Information Office, House of Commons Library, in *Aslib Proceedings* (**33**(11/12), 1981, 418–426). SCICON, the computer experts involved, are making the service available commercially and this should be advantageous for all types of information, especially when building regulations and other construction industry matters are discussed in Parliament or its committees.

Viewdata and Teletext

The transmission of text to a television screen by the broadcasting networks is known as *TELETEXT*. The constantly changing databank has defined information, regularly up-dated by the networks, and the frames are beamed continuously. The receiver 'catches' the required frame as it comes by. The BBC/ITV services, *CEEFAX* and *ORACLE*, have a limited content for the businessman, although useful. They are now well established.

Still developing is *VIEWDATA*, 'a system for diplaying information – words, figures, diagrams – on the ordinary television screen' (Winsbury, 1980). The *Prestel* receiver dials into the computer and requests the frames required using numbers. Each frame is selected from the hierarchical display system enabling the user to work from a general to a very specific answer to an inquiry. This does not require the formulation of a search in the way described in Chapter 3. It is the technique also used by *ARIANE* to get into their databank. However, this can be a long and tedious process and can be short-circuited by obtaining the number of a 'page' of information sought, or at least the earlier sub-divisions of the subjects, from the user's handbook. The Post Office *Prestel* service began in 1975 experimentally and has been developed to around 4000 users in 1980–1981. These are concentrated around the computers already available. Many articles are available dicussing *Prestel*, its value and uses, including those in their own regular user's journal. The *Prestel Business Directory* is available quarterly (FT Business Publishing) and *Prestel User*, from Printel Ltd, is also quarterly. Discussion of its potentialities, linking it with the French, Canadian and Japanese systems, *TELETEL, TELEDON* and *CAPTAIN* respectively, appeared in *Undercurrents* (No. 40, 1980, 16–19) and in Winsbury. In most other countries the same type of system is known as *VIDEOTEX*.

Information providers pay the costs to 'put up' information frames on the service while the subscribers pay telephone charges and a charge per frame used which is set by the provider and may range from ½p to 30p or even 50p. Guide frames are usually free. Information is selected by pressing out the numbers on a keypad connected to a specially adapted television set. More sophisticated users may purchase sets with full keyboard like a VDU but these are usually limited to office users with private information files on the same system, hosted by *Prestel*. *Prestel* information-providers range from British Rail to *Which*? but of particular interest here are relating to construction.

The Department of the Environment, Property Services Agency, sponsored the National Building Agency to investigate the potential use of viewdata to the construction industry. This pilot project involved the National Building Agency in coordinating some leading construction industry information-providers to provide the service known as *Contel* within the *Prestel* service. These providers included government departments, trade associations, publishers, professional institutes and individual practices. The main types of information considered were statutory and codes, technical, cost, product, news, directories and advertisements. It was launched at the National Exhibition Centre, Birmingham, in 1979, and ceased in early 1982 with the demise of the NBA.

Information available covered that from BSRIA on heating and ventilating, market information and company contacts. The pilot project has been carefully monitored and the user-survey was carried out in 1980. This showed that the most heavily used section was cost information and specifically the NEDO cost indices. It also became apparent in discussion with users that the product data information service would be desirable giving costs, specification changes and availability. A report has been issued on the lessons learnt (NBA, 1981), and the future of the project is now under review. The system is described in *House's Guide to the*

Construction Industry (8th edn, 1981), in *Building* (30 November 1979, 52–53) and in *Architects' Journal* (28 November 1979, 1163–1164).

Prospects for the future of a similar service to *Contel*, using *Prestel*, look brighter in 1982 with the formation of the Association of Construction Information Providers (ACIP) under the Chairmanship of Harold Stoddard (C & CA). Working through the Computel computer bureau, it is hoped to make available current information on products both for architects and builder's merchants with information on tenders, costs, contracts, markets, standards, contractor's and consultant's services and a guide to associations. Earlier than this the Building Services Viewdata Association, an original subgroup of *Contel*, intend to launch building services information. The possible future use of *Gateway*, British Telecom's latest service launched in 1982, permits use of the *Prestel* network to access other computer databases and databanks, Access to these can be by keyword as with other database services, and there can be free text input and ordering. The RIBA is also discussing computerized information services linking with these.

A + B Viewdata, the Architectural Press in conjunction with the Building Bookshop, provide a catalogue and order service on *Prestel* already and information for the architect, quantity surveyor, contractor and buildings services engineer in the form of costs, price-adjustment formulae (NEDO), appointments, BSI monthly news, amendments and withdrawals and trade news. The building cost information is that from the pages of *Building*, covering prices, measured rates, wages, plant hire and domestic heating. This particular use of *Prestel* is as a vehicle for presentation of information already available elsewhere in print. The same is true of the information provided by the Thomson Organization under the main headings of *Building Trades Journal* and *Construction News*. This taps into the A + B information also and has similar coverage.

Developments of this nature are working towards the provision of the first national information service, although this was not the original aim when *Prestel* hoped to penetrate a domestic market. There is a parallel development in France in *TÉLÈSYSTEMES-QUESTEL*, but other countries are still developing the idea.

Video disc

A growth area in future is the use of the video disc for information services. In 1982 Pergamon's *INFOLINE* made available *VIDEO*

PATSEARCH from the *PATSEARCH* database indexing US patents since 1971. The subscriber receives eight video discs with an up-dating service and necessary equipment. When searching, the screen is able to display the full front page of the patent specification with drawings as well as the usual bibliographic details and abstract. Their literature explains the new venture in more detail but video discs are already being discussed as the next development from on-line searching.

Sources of information

The most current general guide which discusses the concepts and provides a list of database and hosts with an outline of search strategy is W. Henry's *Online Searching: An Introduction* (Butterworths, 1980). However, as with the guides below, any list of databases and mention of charges is likely to be out-of-date before publication. For instance, while this was being written a further kind of charge was announced on some databases; a royalty charged on every time an abstract is displayed on the screen, thus acting rather like a fee.

The European Association of Scientific Information Dissemination Centres publishes *Eusidic Database Guide* annually (ed. A. Tomberg, Oxford, Learned Information). This is a straightforward list of databases with a subject index and list of organizations. Descriptions are brief giving only the broad subject field, the date started, the number of abstracts added per annum and availability. More detail is given in J. Hall's *Online Bibliographic Databases* (2nd edn, Aslib, 1981). More detailed breakdowns of subject coverage are given and the number of items included is analysed. However, coverage differs since Eusidic includes databanks and Hall only databases.

The increase in guides is swift at present. Many others exist such as *Databases Online* from the American Society for Information Science (1981) and Williams' *Computer-readable Databases Directory and Data Sourcebook* (Knowledge Industry Inc., 1980). The *Information Trade Directory 1982* from Learned Information Ltd includes database publishers, terminal manufacturers, agencies and a useful service listing on-line user groups and information brokers. These are useful contacts if starting in the field. It covers Europe and America, although it is marketed in America by Bowker as *Information Industry Market Place 1982*.

Also useful for their descriptive listings are the *Encyclopaedia of Information Systems and Services* (4th edn, J. Schmittroth, Jr and

A. T. Kruzas (eds), Gale, 1980) and the *Directory of Online Databases* (2 p.a., Cuadra Associates, California).

Searching

The guides referred to, especially Henry and Hall, give advice on search technique. While any topic may be searched on-line the more precise the request the more accurate the answers that will be provided. Databases are either interrogated by searching all the terms used in the title, the abstracts (if present) and the subject index keywords, or just the keywords. In some cases now natural language may be used. The first stage in making a 'search profile', once it has been decided which databases are to be used, is to check the manuals for coverage, specific search limitations and idiosyncracies of vocabulary.

The topic itself must also be thought out to ensure that all implications are discovered and all terms found. This is where a thesaurus is useful. Some databases like *BIOSIS, ERIC* and *MEDLARS* have their own. In other cases *CIT* and the BS *Glossary of Construction Terms* (1981) are most helpful. Alternative spellings should be checked as the English/American spelling is often not standardized. Words which are capable of many endings can be contracted unless the search required the distinction to be made between building and buildings. Truncations are performed in various ways using *? and +. Thus heat? will retrieve heats, heater, heating, heaters, heated, etc. Building* may indicate just one letter missing, or Alumin+m indicate that one or more may be missing.

Planning the procedure before going on-line will save costly time. Some systems using microprocessors are now available to record and store a search sending it to the host more quickly than can be done manually and storing the result for use later. These devices may be useful if a lot of work is done.

When on-line the computer responds to each word input as a search term by indicating how many times that word appears in the database. It is necessary to decide in what order and in what combinations a search will be structured to achieve the maximum relevant output. Thus a very simplified version of a search for information on the use of heat pumps for domestic hot water installations in Britain might appear as three parts initially;

(heat AND pumps)
(houses AND Britain)
(hot AND water AND installations)

Then the sum of the first two would be added to the third, i.e. $[(a+b) + (c+d)] + (e+f+g)$. In this example it would be necessary to use also alternative terms for Britain, e.g. UK, England, and for houses, e.g. domestic. With the assistance of the training seminars offered by the hosts, sometimes free of charge, this technique is soon learned.

Figure 4.3 shows the output from a search. This is the record of the search strategy sent out to the user with the off-line print-out of search results. The search was made using *DIALTECH* to ESA

```
****************************************************
*                                                  *
*                                                  *
*         ESA  INFORMATION RETRIEVAL SERVICE       *
*                                                  *
*                                                  *
****************************************************
```

USER1287   DATE:05/17/82   TIME:17:36:01

	SEARCH HISTORY			PRINT SUMMARY		
SET	ITEMS	DESCRIPTION	NO.	FILE	ACCN/SET FMT	ITEM-RANGE
1	12260	CONCRETE	1	4	12 4	1–65
2	176	PAVING	2	4	3 4	1–53
3	53	1★2	3	4	16 4	1–3
4	9383	DEFECT?	4	4	21 4	1–246
5	3199	FAULT?	5	4	23 4	1–27
6	6018	FAILURE?	6	4	8 4	1–274
7	18093	4+5+6				
8	274	1★7				
9	9687	REINFORCED				
10	2500	1★9				
11	14956	CORROSION				
12	65	10★11				
13	4	ALKALI(W)ATTACK				
14	3	SULPHATE(W)ATTACK				
15	7	13+14				
16	3	1★15				
17	3	16–3				
18	4822	CONVERSION				
19	706	SHRINKAGE				
20	5528	18+19				
21	246	1★20				
22	270	8–21				
23	27	HIGH(W)ALUMINA(W)CEMENT				
24	389	3+12+16+21+23				
25	383	24–8				
26	268	8–24				

SRCH TIME   14.25   PRINT COUNT   668   DESCS.:   17

Figure 4.3 Output from a search on *COMPENDEX* from *DIALTECH*

and then File No. 4, which is *COMPENDEX*. Each input line is called a set and is numbered consecutively by the computer. 'Items' represents the number of times the terms, or combination of terms, input by the user appears in the database. These are the computer's replies to the user's questions entered under 'description'. Everything under the the latter head was entered into the computer with a prefatory sign meaning 'look for all entries containing. . . .'. The logic shows how to cope with only entering one point at a time and at the end Sets 24, 25, 26 show that an attempt to compare different combinations resulted in little new – the output being scanned on-line and not printed out. The print-out is listed on the right, showing that it is given in Format 4, which includes full bibliographic details and an abstract. This can be interpreted thus:

Set 12 has 65 references to corrosion in reinforced concrete;
Set 3 has 53 references to concrete paving;
Set 16 has 3 references to alkali/sulphate attack on concrete;
Set 21 has 246 references to conversion and/or shrinkage of concrete;
Set 23 has 27 references to high alumina cement;
Set 8 has 274 references to failure, defects and faults in concrete.

Although simplified, this should help to understand the concepts involved in a search – the search had to specify certain types of failure in concrete in order to get all references to defects and failures. The output from Set 8 did not correspond with the others, many of which failed to use the terms associated with their outcome.

Conclusion

This section has been considerably condensed to cover a mass of information. Keeping up-to-date with the new databases requires checking with journals like *Online* and *Online Review* (see Henry) and noting news items displayed when 'logging on' to a search with any host. *AJ* or *Building* are likely to note any new developments for construction. Relatively little has been said here about the search process because this is a guide not a text. Those using databases need thorough understanding of indexing, classification and literature searching.

New developments are occurring regularly. *Prestel* hosts *EURONEWS*, a fifty-frame journal giving European news on R &

D, calls for tenders, conference announcements and technical publications reviews. A cassette tape unit has been developed to allow a search to be pre-recorded before going on-line and transmitted more speedily once on-line. In the same way units are being developed to record and store searches for replay later and for printing later if required. Techniques will become simpler as time elapses and probably there will be increased uniformity of databases.

The DoE General Information group, reporting in May 1979, 'observed that this service would be greatly enhanced for the industry if other databases were added, such as *Geodex, British Technology Index* and the RIBA *Architectural Periodicals Index*'. Their resumé of databases available for the UK construction industry, while being sufficient and clear (*General Information*, DoE, 1979), points the way forward since with the 'enormous proliferation of technology, databases, database suppliers and networks, the developments still seem to be appearing faster than applications. It is vital that there should be a careful appraisal of future possibilities and the formulation of immediate solutions should be as flexible as possible. . . . but any bibliographic database must be backed up with an efficient document delivery system.'

Reference

Winsbury, R. (ed.) (1980). *Viewdata in Action: A Comparative Study of Prestel*, McGraw-Hill, p. 3

5
Using and presenting information
Chris Parker

Introduction

We spend a large part of our lives receiving, processing and transmitting information, and it is a sad fact that relatively little is generally known about this subject and that it is not widely taught in schools or colleges.

The main reason for 'handling' information at work is usually an objective which involves influencing or affecting other people in a desired way. One of the main problems is to integrate all the aspects of information handling with the objective. It is all too easy to isolate the various tasks and aims and forget that they are interdependent. For example, some people might be tempted to acquire a comprehsive set of manufacturers' literature on a given product, when a small selection would have proved perfectly satisfactory. Another example is the piles of 'relevant' xerox copies and pamphlets which grow on some peoples' desks, accumulating dust and waiting for the magic moment when there will be time to read them or to transfer their contents to a report. And lastly there are those talks where the speakers 'read' their paper and show unreadable slides because they have forgotten what it is like to be on the receiving end of this type of presentation.

Objectives

In our real-life situations, objectives are often mixed and complicated. The best approach is probably to look objectively at a given situation from a number of different points of view.

Information

As far as information is concerned it should always be considered as having a subject and an object – information is never required for its own sake, or put another way, it is what you do with the information that counts, or what the information (if you communicate it) can do for you.

You should consider how information can help you in the short term in a number of ways:

Stimulation: e.g. to help you to be creative and motivated or interested;
Current awareness: e.g. to keep you up-to-date with the 'competition' and developments;
Methodology: e.g. to tell you how to do something;
Theory: e.g. to predict different or future phenomena;
Data: e.g. to compare your own results or use in calculations;
Solutions: e.g. to show how other people dealt with similar problems;
Education: e.g. to give background details in a new field or to pass an exam.

Communication

You should consider the method that you will use to communicate the results of your work:

Proposals: e.g. to sell a product or service;
Reports: e.g. to satisfy an employer of progress;
Talks: e.g. to persuade clients to adopt a design solution;
Plans: e.g. to satisfy authorities that regulations have been obeyed;
Articles: e.g. to demonstrate professional expertise;
Drawings: e.g. to express a design to clients and contractors.

You will also need to consider your abilities, timing and production services in relation to whatever form of communication you intend to use.

The receiver

The last, and for some, the most important consideration should be of the recipient of your communication. What are their objectives and how are they able and willing to attain them? Can their objectives be compatible with yours? Again a process of integration is necessary. The specific points to consider are:

How do you wish to influence them?
What level do they understand?
What will they use the information for?
How much time will they spare to read it?
How would they prefer to receive information, a long essay, drawings or brief, clear notes?

Of course, an appreciation of all these considerations should influence literature searching and personal records. Literature searching is dealt with in an earlier chapter, but a few examples of these influences are:

If you are in a hurry for information do not bother to look in indexes to remote documents which cannot be obtained quickly;
Make sure that 'relevance' applies to your objectives and not just the subject of your search.

Personal records of references are also dealt with in the chapter on literature searching, but their relationship to objectives is covered in this chapter, where it will be shown how they should be far more than mere records of what you have found, but working documents which will play a direct role in helping you to achieve your objectives, develop working drawings, write your report, etc.

To summarize, the key concept is the integration of all aspects of your objectives and the method of achieving those objectives. In particular:

Decide exactly who you wish to influence and in what way;
Imagine yourself in their position and decide what would influence you in the desired way.

Do not forget your priorities and your timing, as you may find that the advice that follows is just a counsel of perfection, that time has evaporated and that you must make the inevitable compromises.

Gathering and organizing information

Apart from the concept of integrating the gathering and organizing of information with objectives and presentation of information, the most important thing to remember is that this stage reflects *the way you work* and tends to develop into a *habit* very quickly.

The problems

The problem for some people is that it is easy to drift into sloppy habits and very difficult to break out of them. The message in this section is to develop a sound procedure and then stick to it if at all possible. Some examples of where things go wrong are

It is time to write your report, you are in a desperate rush and you are not sure which items in the pile of literature on your desk are really relevant, without re-reading the lot.
You remember lending a vital article to someone, but to whom?
A conference proceedings arrives two months after you requested it on loan, and you cannot remember why you ever wanted it.
A really useful photocopy of an article contains no details of its source, so now you do not know how to quote it.
The substance of the good idea you had, and which seemed so vivid that you'd never forget, has evaporated by the next day.

First of all, it is usually best to deal with references and documents or copies as they appear. This can save time in reorientation after an interlude of forgetfulness and can prevent a demoralizing back-log of the kind mentioned earlier.

Secondly, at the most basic level it is essential to keep a proper record of what you have done and what you have to do. A simple way to deal with these is to use the following.

Day book or journal

In this you record those aspects of what you have done which you may need to recall; for example, who you rang and what information they gave you; where you searched for a reference to a new material and what you found; a possible solution to design problems. In other words, this book should be the equivalent of a scientist's laboratory notebook. If duplicate copies of entries are required for cross-filing or sending elsewhere, carbon or xerox copies can be made, or if copies are going to be needed frequently, special notebooks with duplicate pages are available.

Diary

Preferably of the large desk variety, this can be a very helpful workhorse if used properly as an extensive *aide-mémoire*. Apart from appointments you can note, for example, the names of those people who you have to contact tomorrow or next week and their telephone numbers; regular chores like checking accounts or pending trays, personal deadlines and even running or continuous tasks which have to be done 'some time' – these can be kept in the weekend sections.

Pocket notebook

For some people this is a vital 'mobile memory'. It can be divided into sections such as books or references to be looked up, things to do and 'ideas'. The last suggestion is essential for the many people who remember or think of things to do while at home and forget them before they get back to work.

Of course, the habit of using these recording devices must include cross-references, transferring appropriate details from one to another and also to other records, e.g. ideas from the pocket notebook to the diary for action, or information from the day book to reference cards or other working documents. The contents of all of them should be regularly reviewed and pages crossed through when 'dead' as far as future use or action is concerned.

Reference extension

The basic principles of recording references or constructing personal reference collections were dealt with in the earlier chapter on literature searching. The purpose of this section is to show how these records may be extended to increase their usefulness.

Figure 5.1 shows a reference card designed to do just this. The three boxes along the top edge are to enable easy filing under Author and/or Subject and/or End Document. For example if you were interested in a particular subject but with no end document (such as a report) in mind, all the reference cards pertaining to that subject could be labelled accordingly and stored in alphabetical author order in the section of your card index system for that subject.

'REF 1' is for recording a reference in a particular house-style, e.g. where the reference is to be cited in a particular journal or company report and where there are strict rules for writing references (see also *List of References*, page 88).

'REF 2' allows for a second, different house-style for the same reference – you may want to cite a reference in two different documents which have different editorial rules.

'FULL REF' contains any missing details from 'REF 1' or 'REF 2' so that there is always sufficient detail to accommodate any

AUTHOR	SUBJECT	DOCUMENT
REF 1		
REF 2		
FULL REF		
LOCATION	REF SOURCE	
REQUESTED	USE	
REASON		

Figure 5.1 Card for reference extension (© C. C. Parker, Southampton University, 1981)

other house-style. If no end document is in view the complete reference is entered in this box. The point of 'REF 1' and 'REF 2' is to save time when compiling a bibliography or list of references for a report, article, etc. The appropriate set of cards can be handed to a typist in the correct order with the instruction to say – type only 'REF 1' items.

'LOCATION' is for locating the document or copy. This can work in various ways: it may indicate a place in your main xerox file, a shelfmark and book number in your local library or a colleague's desk drawer. Alternatively it may show a temporary location in a file specially compiled to write a report, or even a loan to a colleague in another office and the date they borrowed it.

'REF SOURCE' is to record your source of reference so that you or anyone else can check on the accuracy of your reference or so that you can extend your search if appropriate. Accuracy here is very important for identification and for inter-library loan purposes.

'REQUESTED' is for recording attempts to obtain the original document or a copy. This may involve a book order or reservation, a request via an inter-library lending department, a direct request for a reprint to an author or an on-line document order following a computer search – all noting the date requested. All cards referring to awaited items can be stored in a separate part of the file, reviewed regularly for action, the date noted on arrival and the card ultimately refiled in an appropriate section.

'USE' is for a list of the actual or potential applications for the information in the original document. This might include specific end documents or more general 'education'.

'REASON' is for noting what it was about the information in the original document that made it worth a record. Perhaps it was an excellent example of a previous practice which would be suitable for introduction into a new design. Perhaps it was a new technique which should be borne in mind by the contractor when making tenders for a particular kind of construction work.

Lastly the reverse of the card may, if an end document is to be written, be used to write an essential extract of the original, so that when reporting or writing commences there is something to build on, or even use if appropriate, without starting again from scratch.

Originals and copies

When dealing with originals, reprints or copies it pays to treat them as working documents (provided they are yours and not office or library stock). Extend them in just the same way as the reference cards, to enhance their usefulness and to make them work for you rather than against you. For example, do not be afraid to mark up the margins with pencil comments or to highlight lines using fluorescent marker pens. You may agree or disagree, you may think something is a good new idea or you may be stimulated to think of something quite different – in all cases note it down. If you do have the misfortune to have to go back through a number of documents at reporting time, at least you will not have to read every line to see what it was that originally caught your eye.

Evaluating information

All stages in the process of finding information involve some degree of evaluation but you should always try to adopt a critical approach to recorded information – it may be wrong! If your work depends, for example, on certain basic data, the origin of the data should be checked, i.e. original journal article, measurement method, etc. Data from handbooks may be vaguely defined and misleading; for example, properties of materials may vary with environmental conditions. Ideally the data should also be cross-checked with other sources of information (e.g. independent calculations, measurements, theories, etc.) through your own findings or via the advice of a colleague or an expert in the subject.

When evaluating documents or their component parts (e.g. articles in journals, chapters in books), publishers, authors and their place of work, dates and journals may be critically considered where appropriate. People frequently rely on the date more than anything else, assuming that the most recent information is the best. Although this is frequently found to be a correct assumption in the case of scientific research, the critical approach should never be neglected. In the case of printed material you should always check in the appropriate guides, or with the publisher, that you have the latest edition. You can sometimes find helpful reviews in appropriate journals. It is always a sound practice to obtain any review articles in your field, and these will frequently contain a comparative or critical evaluation of journal articles.

Some types of publication contain sections which assist evaluation. These include contents pages, abstracts, indexes, introductions, conclusions, lists of references, illustrations, tables, graphs, etc.

Presenting information

Communication is essential to our way of life. We shall only briefly discuss here that part of communication which deals with informing others of the results of our work. Performing successful work offers no personal advantage until the results are properly communicated.

Written versus verbal

Normally the choice is made for us, but the important thing to remember is that you may cause a greater impact with verbal communication – for example, the great political speeches – but with written communications you have much greater control. If you make a mistake when talking to an audience, it is difficult to correct it, even if you spot it. When talking, you may suffer from nerves and perhaps lack of experience, and also from the effects of your surroundings, including your audience. With writing and drawing you can normally correct the finished product before it reaches the client.

Written communication

This usually takes the form of a letter, memorandum, report, design, contract or periodical article. The presentation of drawn information should need no discussion and is ably covered in the following works among others: R. F. Reekie, *Draughtsmanship* (3rd edn, Arnold, 1976), L. Dudley's *Architectural Illustration* (Prentice-Hall, 1977) and *The Thames and Hudson Manual of Rendering in Pen and Ink* (Thames and Hudson, 1973). We shall briefly consider reports as an example.

Report writing

There is no rigid procedure, but the notes below coupled with a flexible approach should offer some help. You should check whether your organization issues any instructions on layout, house-style, etc.

Prepare a statement of intent (refer back to Objectives), This can prove an invaluable yardstick when deciding whether or not to include items of information.

TIMING

Work out a time schedule. This means fixing or acknowledging a deadline for completion of the report. Then check the availability and speed of production facilities, typing, reproduction, photography, binding, etc. This will then enable you to work out how long you have to actually write the report. Sometimes the production of the report causes more problems than the writing.

INFORMATION

Assemble the results from your work and any other relevant material, bearing in mind your statement of intent. Some people find that it helps to have a card or folder, for example, for each section of the report or for each subject-division of the work they are reporting. As you acquire information or ideas, you can add them to the appropriate collection. Ideas can be very fleeting; you should note them down as they occur. As a part of your work, you should have examined all the ideas and information with a critical eye, particularly checking for accuracy and comparing your results and ideas with previous work. Time spent in simply thinking around the material you have and how you might present it is never wasted. At this stage it can help to write out a provisional list of section headings covering the work you have done or the information you wish to present. These headings can then be arranged into a logical order, and shown to colleagues for comment. Even at this early stage criticism can be helpful. If you have problems in deciding on the structure of the report as far as the work done is concerned, or how to organize your work into sensible chapters, then consider the alternatives and take the one that fits best with your objectives.

Each heading can be expanded by adding brief notes about your own work, ideas and information from other sources which relate to that heading. Use your objectives to guide you as far as selecting which topics require special emphasis, and try to predict questions that may arise in the minds of the people you expect to read your report.

WRITING

Writing the report can best be described by considering its various parts. A typical layout is given next and you should try to arrange the material and the ideas that you have to fit this type of pattern. Reports are usually best written over a short period of time to preserve continuity. Do not wait for perfect sentences to form in your mind, but write whatever comes to mind. This way you will find it easier to start, and you will find it is always easier to criticize and correct something on paper, rather than something in your mind.

LAYOUT

The accepted page size is now A4 (210 mm × 297 mm), and it is usually to put page numbers centrally at the bottom of each sheet. The various parts of the report are considered below.

Front cover. This should contain the following:
Report number: may be used for physically storing and retrieving report, if it is part of a series.
Title: must be descriptive, as it may be used to retrieve the report by subject, or it may be used to decide if the report is worth reading.
Author's name.
Name of organization producing the report.
Date when writing was completed.
Security classification if necessary.

Title page. This usually contains the information already given on the front cover, perhaps with a little more detail, such as sub-titles, names of sponsoring bodies, contract numbers and acknowledgements. The signature of the writer and his supervisor or senior executive, if required, should always appear here.

Summary page. The summary or abstract of the report is best kept to one page. It should be written as though it might be the only part of the report that a busy executive will have time to read. It must contain the 'message' that the report is trying to communicate. At the very least, the summary is the bridge between the title and the body of the report.

Table of contents. This should list all the principal headings in the report in the order in which they appear, giving appropriate page numbers. The table should allow a reader to see at a glance how the report is laid out and to quickly locate any section which he wishes to read. Contents pages are usually written last because they have to cover the entire contents. It helps sometimes to write a draft contents page to see how well the report is 'balanced' in terms of structure and headings. It is usual to number (or letter) sections as well as pages. Sections may be systematically broken down by numbers and letters or by decimals. For example:

Principal Section	1		1
Main Section	(a)	or	1.1
Sub-Section	(i)		1.11

Introduction. This should give the reason behind the report, the objectives, terms of reference, background, state-of-the-art, previous work and any appropriate discussion which should justfy the work which follows.

The work done. The work done is usually split into two main parts: (1) experimental or investigatory, method and results, (2) discussion and theoretical interpretation. This is the vital section when it comes to details and accuracy. Make sure you have covered all the influencing variables. If you have trouble in breaking the work down into logical sections see the earlier paragraph on 'Information'. Diagrams, pictures, graphs, tables, etc. should only be used when they represent the best way of communicating information. If you do decide that diagrams, drawings, graphs, etc. ('figures') are the best way to convey what you want to say then, bear in mind that scaled drawings are the most popular way of illustrating architectural reports. If one of your 'figures' is referred to in detail from just one part of the text, or it is essential to the understanding of the text, that 'figure' should be positioned adjacent to the corresponding text (preferably opposite, not over the page). If neither of these apply, or the 'figure' is referred to from numerous parts of the text, or the size and number of illustrations would unbalance the text making it difficult to follow, the 'figures' should be placed in the 'appendices' section.

The text should refer to the figures via figure numbers or codes and/or page numbers. Codes can be a simple running number right through the report or a compound number made up of chapter number/section number/type of figure, etc. E.g. 'Table 4.12.2' in the text could mean a table in Chapter 4 section 12 paragraph 2, and 'Fig. 45' could simply refer to *the* 45th 'figure'. From the text point of view you should make sure that your reference to a 'figure' will make sense to your reader, so explain why you are referring to that 'figure'. From the 'figure' point of view you should make sure that it emphasizes the point you have made in the text, that its title, labelling, symbols and units are all crystal clear, well defined, make sense and are in a form that your reader can easily use if he has to. Use footnotes or annotations if necessary to avoid overcrowding a drawing. Lastly do not forget that 'figures' cause the most problems in their making and reproducing – so check on what can or cannot be done first.

Conclusions and recommendations. These form the end-product of your work and will hopefully justify your efforts. Like the summary, these may be some of the only parts of your report that are actually read by 'busy' managers or customers, so again special care is required.

Appendices. These may include the following:
Tables, graphs, photographs, diagrams, drawings, etc. (only when it is not appropriate to include these in the body of the report – see 'The Work Done').

List of references. This is often a neglected area and as a result causes all sorts of problems. There are two points to remember: first of all the whole reason for having these references is for other people to obtain the original documents, and therefore it is vital to be accurate and to give as much information as possible. For example the title will help them to decide if the original is worth having; the issue date should be included, even if it duplicates volume and issue numbers, as a double-check in case you make a mistake and to give an idea of currency; the complete pagination will give an idea of the length of the item and hence one measure of its usefulness; the complete title of a journal will prevent misinterpretation of abbreviated journal titles. The second point is to check whether there is an imposed house-style for references, as mentioned earlier in 'Reference Extension'. Whether or not there is a house-style, you should be consistent in the way you record your references (for example you can indicate 'volume' by volume, Volume, vol., Vol., vol, Vol, v., V., v, V, or by underlining or by using bold print!).

There are two main ways of linking the text of your report with individual references in the list; these are the Harvard System as used in this book, and the numeric system as frequently found in journal articles. Quite a lot of detail may be found in the appropriate British Standards, but briefly the two systems work as follows:

Harvard system. This uses authors' surnames and year as the link, e.g. the text may contain inserts such as 'the method used by Jones (1980) was also . . .' or 'the established method (Brown

1960) was also . . .'. In this system the list of references would be in alphabetical/date order and of the form

> BROWN, J. 1960. Title of the Article. *Journal Name*, Vol. 6, No. 3, March, pp. 542–584.
> JONES D. 1980. Title of the Article. *Journal Name*, 28, No. 6, June. pp. 33–34.

Numeric system. This uses numbers as the link, e.g. the text may contain inserts such as 'the method used by Jones[4]. . .' or 'the method (5) used by us . . .'. In this system the references are listed in number order in the same order as they first appear in the text, e.g.

> 4. JONES, D. Title of the Article. *Journal Name*, Vol. 28, No. 6, June 1980. pp. 33–34.
> 5. BROWN, J. Title of the Article. *Journal Name*, Vol. 6, No. 3, March 1960. pp. 542–584.

Both systems have their advantages and disadvantages and, depending on what you are writing, you may find one better than the other, or alternatively you may find a hybrid or extended system the best for your purposes.

If you think that new references may have to be added as you go along, the pure numeric system may prove awkward if you have to re-number all the text/reference numbers. If you want to be able to refer from your references to the text, the numeric system is the best, although any list of references may be annotated by adding those page or paragraph numbers* where the text refers to the references,

e.g. BROWN, J. 1960. Title of the Article. *Journal Name*, Vol. 6, No. 3, March. pp. 542–584 [42, 43, 80]*

Where such annotations are used, an appropriate explanatory note should be given at the beginning of the list. If you think it is important that the reader should know who wrote a particular reference and when, as it is referred to in the text, then the Harvard system is the best. The Harvard system can be bulky, and upset reading flow if a number of references are cited close together. Various other addenda may include any acknowledgements, a glossary, list of abbreviations and symbols with explanations and distribution list. It is most important to clearly define any units which are used in the report. If the report is long enough to justify an index, it should always be given one.

REVISION

This is an essential part of report writing. It is a good idea to give the proofs to a colleague for comment, and also to put the report aside for a few days before revising it yourself.

Further reading

The details here are merely an introduction to written communication. The serious writer should take the time to study a few of the many books, pamphlets or journal articles on this subject. For example:

Barrass, R. (1978). *Scientists must Write: A Guide to Better Writing for Scientists, Engineers and Students,* Chapman and Hall
Cooper, B. M. (1964). *Writing Technical Reports,* Penguin
Day, R. A. (1979). *How to Write and Publish a Scientific Paper,* Philadelphia, ISI
Gray, D. E. (1970). *So You Have to Write a Technical Report: Elements of Technical Report Writing,* Washington, DC, Information Resources Press
Kirkman, J. (1980). *Good Style for Scientific and Engineering Writing,* Pitman
Mitchell, J. (1974). *How to Write Reports,* Fontana

There are numerous British Standards which are helpful; the following is just a selection:

BS 4811: 1972. The presentation of research and development reports
BS 4821: 1972. The presentation of theses
BS 1629: 1976. Bibliographical references
BS 1191: 1969. Building drawing practice
BS 5605: 1978. Citing publications by bibliographic references
BS 3589: 1963. Glossary of general building terms
BS 1991: parts 1–6. Letter symbols, signs and abbreviations
BS 3700: 1976. Recommendations for the preparation of indexes for books, periodicals, and other publications.
See also British Standards Yearbook.

One should always have a good English dictionary close at hand when writing a report.

Two additional reference books which help with language difficulties are

Roget's Thesaurus of English Words and Phrases, R. A. Dutch, (ed.) (1977). Longman
Fowler's Modern English Usage. 2nd edn, rev. by E. Gowers (1965). OUP

Verbal communication
(With acknowledgement to Dr R. V. Turley, Southampton University.)

Just as with written communication the main thing is to consider your readers so with verbal communication the main thing is to consider your audience: what are the listeners going to get out of your talk? Will they be bored? Are they going to understand what you say? Will they be able to interpret any slides you may show? Is there enough 'new' information to make the talk seem worthwhile? Giving a talk (or lecture) ought to be an *enjoyable* experience both for the audience and for you. Your enthusiasm for the subject (or lack of it) will be communicated to your listeners. Unlike written communication, a speaker and his audience are in a 'live' situation where it is essential to take into account the interest (and comfort) of the listeners at every stage. If one or two members of the audience become restless, this will be communicated to the others: watch for the warning signs (excessive yawning, undue movement of chairs, expressions of boredom or non-comprehension, muttering, people walking out!), but remember, you should be able to control this situation to some extent by varying your presentation (perhaps even departing from your original intention in extreme cases).

There are various kinds of verbal communication, ranging from a simple telephone conversation, through committee meetings and interviews, to the formal lecture (including delivery of conference papers, talks on radio and television, etc.). We shall briefly consider the preparation and delivery of a lecture as an example.

Giving a talk

Objective

Decide exactly what your talk is to achieve, remembering that you will be able to impart only a comparatively limited amount of 'new' information during the length of an average talk (i.e. do not cram too much in – you can always distribute a handout covering the details which have to be omitted). Give careful consideration to the nature of your audience and the reason for the lecture, which will determine your approach: e.g. are you trying to sell something, describe your own work, review the work of others, instruct your audience on a particular subject, or what? Estimate, as accurately as you can, the amount of knowledge possessed by your listeners: you must not waste time unnecessarily by telling them what they know already, or pitch the talk at so high a level that you will not be understood. If you have to address a 'mixed' group of people, in the sense that they have different subject backgrounds or levels of ability to understand, try to make sure each section of the audience is catered for, i.e. that everybody will ger *something* out of your talk. Remember, particularly, that if you had to prepare talks based on given material to (say) your company's sales staff, and its research staff, the approaches adopted should be rather different: in the former case, for example, lengthy attention to technical minutiae would be inappropriate, while in the latter it might even be welcomed! It may help to write a short statement of your objective to keep before you throughout the time spent on preparation.

Timing

Work out a time schedule. You will generally know the date of the talk, and think that there is plenty of time in hand. Remember, it takes *very much* longer to prepare a talk than to deliver it (a rough estimate is at least ten hours to prepare a one-hour talk but for a prestigious event it could take a *great* deal longer). Also, be aware that visual aids take time to produce (especially if made professionally), so allow for this in your schedule.

Information

Gather your information as described in the previous section on report writing. You will generally acquire rather more than you intend to use, making selection of material possible.

Preparation

Your talk should consist of a logical progression of ideas leading, if the material permits, to a climax. In other words, it must have a well-defined structure designed to ensure that each point is grasped by the audience before you proceed to the next.

Some people prefer to work out what they are going to say and then write brief notes for use in the talk; others prepare a complete text which they intend to read (this method should be avoided if at all possible, as it generally creates a very bad effect): in either case think in terms of composing a speech from a play rather than a written report. Do not be afraid of adopting a slightly dramatic approach to your audience (but, of course, do not overdo it!)

Your listeners will assume you are an expert (since you presume to address them): let them retain this impression. You must have confidence in your own knowledge of the subject, backed by thorough preparation of your material. Remember to give the audience something to look at from time to time. The importance of *good* visual aids simply cannot be overestimated. But there are pitfalls for the unwary. For example: does the slide contain too much, or not enough information? Will the people at the back of the room be able to read any writing without difficulty? Are there too many slides, or too few? The answers to these questions are best obtained by consulting visual aids experts: your organization may have staff trained to advise on or prepare slides, transparencies for overhead projection, working models, large-scale diagrams, etc., or the items mentioned in the 'Further Reading' section (see later) may help.

Organization

If you are responsible for the organization of your talk, make a list of everything that needs to be done and see to it in good time (e.g. booking a room; making sure a projector is available, if needed; arranging publicity material; signposting the room on the day, if it is hard to find). Be prepared for last-minute hitches, especially where other people are involved. Even if you are not organizing the talk yourself, you must make sure that the organizer is aware of your need for special equipment (projectors, etc.) and has arranged for it to be provided. You should also familiarize yourself with the place where the talk will be given, covering such points as layout of the room, location of switches for lights and projector, position of blackboard and chalk. At least plan to arrive well before you are due to start; you may waste time looking for the room if you have not used it previously.

Delivery

You will, of course, have rehearsed the talk (perhaps with the aid of a tape-recorder) before delivering it (!). This helps to give you confidence, find the best way of making certain points and ensure the talk is of the right length.

What is the secret of good technique? It is the ability to exercise self-control coupled with a relaxed approach. Try to speak clearly, naturally and not too quickly, guarding against verbal mannerisms: '*Well*, Ladies and Gentlemen – *um,er* – *Well*, Mr Chairman, I must first thank you for your – *um* – opening remarks and – *er* – the kind – *er* things you have said about my – *um* – work. *Well*, Ladies and Gentlemen, this evening I want to . . .'. This sort of thing is maddeningly hard for the inexperienced speaker to avoid, especially at the start of a talk (when he is particularly vulnerable), but a determined effort should be made to begin clearly and decisively: 'Mr Chairman, thank you for you kind remarks! Ladies and Gentlemen, this evening I am going to . . .'.

Stand still, or relatively still: do not juggle with the chalk, your notes, or anything else – you are not a circus act.

Look the audience in its face, if you can: after all, there is no need to be ashamed (unless you have skimped the preparation of your material). Your listeners wil hear you better if you face them (remember those in the back row also have a right to hear what is said) and will feel more involved if you look at them, individually, from time to time.

Try to judge audience reaction as you go along, and respond when the need arises. If you make a mistake, correct it without a lot of fuss – and carry on: do not be thrown.

Humour in a 'serious' talk can be overdone. Your audience will no doubt appreciate a brief, relevant, anecdote (or humorous turn of phrase) occasionally, but forced humour and irrelevant jokes are out of place. Leave this sort of thing alone unless it comes naturally to you. Allow time to answer questions; perhaps at the end of the talk or, better still, during its course (which increases the sense of audience-involvement). Remember that even an expert cannot be expected to know everything about a subject, so it is better to give no answer than one which is incorrect ('I need notice of that question!'). Sometimes you can stall for time ('I am afraid I do not understand your question. Would you mind rephrasing it?') or even stimulate another member of the audience to reply – the possibilities are endless.

Finally, your audience deserves to be thanked for listening.

The other forms of verbal communication present different problems, the main factor being that you cannot predict exactly what you are going to say (e.g. during a telephone conversation, at an interview or committee meeting). You can, however, form a clear idea of the points you wish to make, if necessary writing them out on paper, trying to express them simply and concisely when the time comes.

You may have the 'gift' of verbal communication; otherwise you will need to work hard to master its techniques. There is no substitute for experience, expecially in acquiring the difficult art of self-control.

Further reading

The British Association for Commercial and Industrial Education has published a useful booklet entitled: *Tips on Talking* (2nd edn, 1960). A more substantial volume is H. H. Manko's *Effective Technical Speeches and Sessions: A Guide for Speakers and Program Chairmen*, McGraw-Hill, 1969.

Of particular interest to those concerned with the preparation and use of visual aids are the following titles:

Brown, J. W. (1976). *Audiovisual Instruction: Media and Methods*, 5th edn, McGraw-Hill.

Atkinson, N. J. and J. N. (1975). *Modern Teaching Aids: A Practical Guide to Audio-visual Techniques in Education*, 2nd edn, MacDonald and Evans.

Jay, A. (1974) *Effective Presentation: The Communication of Ideas by Words and Visual Aids*, British Institute of Management.

The British Institute of Management Foundation in London (BIM) also produce a number of useful publications, e.g. Checklist 61, *Using Visual Aids Effectively*, Checklist 50, *Giving a Talk*, and Checklist 2, *Report Writing*.

6
Sources and organization of information
Valerie J. Bradfield

The previous chapters have discussed resources generally, the libraries, search techniques and skills required to find information. This chapter is moving forward to begin the discussion of the 'tools' available to assist in the search for information. Many such tools will be discussed with the appropriate topic but some terms and types of tool do need understanding and discussion separately. Many practising architects and builders may be tempted to skip this section, leaving it for the librarians in practices or larger libraries, but an understanding of the nature of the reference tools and their organization, that is, the indexing and classification systems described, is essential to effective use of information sources. Thus this chapter consists of five sections:

(1) General introduction.
(2) Guides and bibliographies.
(3) Reference tools.
(4) Catalogues and indexes.
(5) Classifications.

Introduction

Many architects have a small basic 'library' of information sources, including books, pamphlets, catalogues and articles. 'It has been recognized for a long time . . . that only a small percentage of the total range of documents are of real importance and/or are referred to regularly,' and that a 'high proportion of queries [are] answered from a very few documents basic to each collection' (National Consultative Council, 1979). Such essential items are subject to individualistic selection, although they have been listed in works such as Calderhead's *Libraries for Professional Practice* (Architectural Press, 1972). There are frequent occasions when these resources are insufficient and need supplementing. Specialist sources are available as guides to assist in locating relevant information, as well as providing sample lists of the contents of the basic technical library (*AJ* 'Annual Review', Bibliography, January each year).

Since these sources are important and not always easy to locate it is useful to know what types of publication to look for and the titles of the most useful. First, it will be advantageous to define the terminology usually used to describe these works.

This section then discusses the types of publication before giving guidance on the location and use of some types.

Definitions

GUIDES TO SOURCES

This whole book is a guide. There are others like it on various topics (see p. 99). While some guides tell you which publications to consult they are more than simple lists – they discuss methods and point the user down the right path to the source of the information required.

BIBLIOGRAPHIES

A list of books and articles is usually called a bibliography. Each item is often called a 'reference'. Many bibliographies on technical topics also include institutional sources of information and research known to be in progress. Some are pure lists, while others are 'annotated', that is, they briefly describe the scope and sometimes comment on the merits of each item.

The length of a bibliography may vary from six to seven references at the end of an article to the *AJ*'s 'Annual Review' or the full-length hardback book like John Smith's *Bibliography on Conservation* (see Chapter 15). The larger collections of these and of guides are usually to be found in professional and academic rather than public libraries.

REFERENCES

As mentioned above, a reference is 'the thing referred to', whether it is another book, an institution or other source of information. There should always be adequate information given to locate any reference; for a book that is; the author, title, publisher and date, and for a journal article; the author, title, journal, volume, issue, date and pages.

REFERENCE WORKS

'Every special library should have the main reference works and handbooks of its field on the shelves' (Batten, 1975). These are specially designed handbooks, data books, etc. to enable users to find specific information quickly. They are not meant to be read thoroughly. The major categories are:

Dictionaries give, in alphabetical order, the spelling, pronunciation and definition of words in one or more languages, or of terms in one or more special fields.

Encyclopedias provide an extended summary of all knowledge either generally or over a specific subject, usually in an organized (frequently alphabetical) format with an index, cross-references and some references to further reading;

Directories usually list, either in subject or alphabetical order, people, organizations, products, research, etc., sometimes including brief notes of useful information and always including addresses of contacts:

Handbooks and manuals provide the facts and figures which are established and regarded as standard information in the relevant field and are most frequently needed. While the good ones include references some others assume a high level of understanding in the field;

Yearbooks combine directory and handbook information in areas where this changes frequently and is always needed in its current form, but the term is often used in the titles of reference works which would otherwise be called handbooks or directories, for example, the *RIBA Directory and List of Members* or the *Institute of Building Yearbook*. They include the same type of information.

Guides and bibliographies

Guides to information

In some instances it is very difficult to distinguish between a guide which discusses sources of information and indicates to the architect where specific types of query may be answered and a bibliography, especially an annotated bibliography.

The first guide in the architecture field was written fifteen years ago before the Department of the Environment amalgamated three former ministries under its umbrella. Denison Smith's *How to Find Out in Architecture and Building: A Guide to Sources of Information* (Pergamon, 1967) discussed the profession and the library classification of architecture and building disproportionately to the guidance it gave on sources. General chapters on dictionaries and encyclopedias, periodicals, directories and libraries were followed by bibliographies on building, planning, architectural history, building types and details. Much of the material is now dated, if readily available at all. The period since its publication has also seen a vast increase in the volume of published information, particularly from the government.

Two series, *How to Find Out* From Pergamon and *Sources of Information* from Butterworths are useful because the architectural profession so often needs to locate information in subject areas beyond the immediate scope of buildings. Thus Parker and Turley's general volume, *Information Sources in Science and Technology* (Butterworths, 1975), provides a useful background and is supplemented by D. J. Maltha's *Technical Literature Search and the Written Report* (Pitman, 1976) which, although taking most of its examples from agriculture, provides a most lively and readable guide to the actual process of finding information. Other volumes in the series will quickly give an indication of where to locate the answers to specific enquiries in other fields, ranging perhaps from current trends in primary school teaching methods (needed to establish criteria for an infant's school), in Foskett's *How to Find Out: Education Research* (Pergamon, 1965), to the law on partnership in Dane and Thomas, *How to Use a Law Library* (Sweet and Maxwell, 1979), or some figures on the use and availability of office space in the statistics chapter of Fletcher's *The Use of Economics Literature* (Butterworths, 1971), and recent information on work study in small organizations, K. D. C. Vernon's *Use of Management and Business Literature* (Butterworths, 1975). Other useful volumes include Bakewell on management (Pergamon, 1970), Burrington on the social sciences (Pergamon, 1975), Palmer on the EEC (Mansell, 1979) and White on iron and steel (Pergamon, 1970).

Although several guides exist in the art field which purport to cover architecture this is, almost invariably, a historical treatment. *Sources of Modern Architecture* by Sharp (2nd edn, Architectural Press, 1980) is a cross between a bibliography and a guide but is essentially historical, since it discusses the works of modern architects and modern architectural design, giving lists and bibliographies, but does not develop the theme into construction techniques or building types.

The Scarecrow Press is currently publishing several volumes by J. B. Godel called *Sources of Construction Information* (Vol. 1, 1977). Although described as a guide and working tool for professionals, only the first volume on books has so far appeared, and it is not only more in the form of an annotated bibliography but it is also heavily biased towards American texts and practices. Also biased towards American practice but with some European references are the guides to sources of information from Gale Research Company of Detroit. Topics range widely from broad to precise topics; for example, *Theatre Planning*.

Planning has been fortunate in its bibliographical coverage, as can be seen below and in Chapter 11. However, Brenda White's *Sourcebook of Planning Information* (Bingley, 1971) was one of the early guides which set a tone of excellence in its learned discussion of the value of the sources indicated and, although dating from 1971, it still retains its relevance and has quite a wide scope.

Almost unique also is *Registers and Records*, by Trevor Aldridge (3rd edn, Oyez, 1976) which provides a reliable, regularly up-dated indication of, or guide to, the sources of the very specific types of information, usually giving names and addresses or lists rather than references to books and articles. Topics range from births, wills and service records to finance, property and professional advice, including land registration, site layouts, maps, rights of way, etc. The monthly 'Techalert' series in *Building* should not be overlooked. It aims to guide readers to the most important recent research reports, often from the USA, by providing a summary of their content. All have international applications and are readily available in Britain from the Technology Reports Centre of the Department of Industry, often quite cheaply.

Lastly, but by no means least, the *Architects' Journal* has, each January since 1977, provided its own guide to information sources in the 'Annual Review'. Intitially this was a guide to sources of information giving essential and additional reading lists which are now supplemented by annual summaries of the past year's work in, and additions to, the bibliography of each of the topics covered. These range from the major building types to construction, energy, law, fire, practice and planning. The value of this guide is cumulative. But each year the second part also contains a brief guide to the services available to the architect to assist in finding information. It should therefore remain at hand all year as the most current guide available.

Bibliographies

Many bibliographies useful to the architect do, in fact, contain a certain amount of guidance and lists of sources to consult other than the written page.

AJ 'Annual Review' has been mentioned and the *AJ* handbooks should by now be familiar resources to most architects. In many handbooks the bibliographies are developed in each relevant section. However, the one with the widest scope, the *New Metric Handbook* (Architectural Press, 1980), has only scanty bibliographies following each section. These are updated regularly by the 'Annual Review'. New handbooks are frequently being published in the *AJ* and revised for hardback issue by the Architectural Press. The main published handbooks are *AJ Handbook of Building Enclosure*, *AJ Handbook of Building Structure*, *AJ Handbook of Environmental Powers*, *AJ Handbook of Urban Landscape*, *AJ Legal Handbook*, *Housing Rehabilitation Handbook* and *Use of Redundant Buildings*. Most recently the *Handbook of Sport and Recreational Building Design* (4 vols, Architectural Press, 1981) is an expansion of the *AJ Handbook*, while Duffy and Worthington's *Planning Office Space* (Architectural Press, 1976) was the *AJ Handbook of Office Planning* originally. Others such as those on architectural ironmongery, building environment, factory design, fixings and fastenings and industrial storage remain as series of articles.

Specification has been at the right hand of many architects for a long time and the lengthy bibliographies to most sections should not be forgotten. They include Regulations and Standards as well as references and names and addresses of relevant associations. They are complemented by the similar sectional bibliographies in other 'trade' information services, in particular, the bibliographies of the RIBA *Product Data* and the *Architects' Standard Catalogue* (see Chapter 8). (Revision is now at about eighteen-month intervals by the Architectural Press.). The strength of these bibliographies perhaps indicates how essential they are to the profession.

CATALOGUES AND LISTS

As many centres and institutes offer book-purchasing facilities to their members so many of them also publish lists and catalogues of their stock which often read like a bibliography of the essential items in each field. Thus the annual RIBA *Booklist* is 'a general guide'. The catalogues of the Building Bookshop at the Building Centre, the Cement and Concrete Association, TRADA, and the Institute of Housing, among others, also form useful lists, with indexes. Some libraries publish catalogues and these have been mentioned earlier (see Chapter 2). For those wishing to purchase books, *British Books in Print* can be located using the annual listing (bibliography) of that name. It can be found in most bookshops and libraries. It lists by author and title all items in print when it went to print, giving their publisher and price. But it does not always include the books and pamphlets from very small presses, associations, educational institutions and government departments, which are useful if not essential in practice. These are often difficult to locate (see Chapter 9 for government publications). *Books in Print* is the American equivalent and has a separate subject listing. However, bookshops may still have stocks of books which are registered in these lists as 'out of print' so do not be deterred from asking for what you require, especially if published fairly recently.

British National Bibliography can be useful when trying to locate the author of a book known only by a vague title since it lists, in subject order, a majority of everything published in Britain and placed with the British Library on copyright deposit. The use of this for providing subject bibliographies can be a bit daunting since the lists are voluminous and material may not be easy to obtain locally although known to be available at the British Library Reference Division. To use this effectively some idea of the publication date of any book or pamphlet is necessary.

The publishing company of G. K. Hall has, for a number of years, issued an annual *Art and Architecture Book Guide* which is very comprehensive in its coverage of British and American titles. *Information* from the Building Research Establishment is a concise, free, annual list of relevant publications and a useful bibliography to have on hand. The new series of *Information Sheets* from the BRE are mentioned regularly in this and provide a useful condensed version of current research and developments.

Many of the libraries of the construction industry keep users aware of new publications by listing additions to the library either as a separate publication, such as the RIBA's list and that of the Centre on Environment for the Handicapped, or as a section in the regular journal, like the Cement and Concrete Association's quarterly list in the *Magazine of Concrete Research* or the Institution of Structural Engineers' monthly list in *Structural Engineer*, Part A.

Bibliographical series

Both associations and departments of the government have issued bibliographies which have been compiled in their libraries as a result of requests. Lists of titles in the various series are a useful reference. Restrictions on finance in the early 1980s are slowing the output of those from some public bodies such as the Building Research Establishment ('Library Bibliographies'), the Department of the Environment ('Bibliography Series' and 'Information Series') and the Greater London Council ('Research Bibliographies' renamed 'Research Documents Guides' in 1980). All bibliographies are of general interest and not specific to the department or council. Those from the RIBA and C & CA are no longer frequent, but the Building Services Research and Information Association and the Institute of Building still issue many. TRADA issue fairly regular bibliographies and other similar associations issue them less frequently such as Fox's *A Review of the Literature on the Racking Strength of Brickwork* from the British Ceramic Research Association (1979).

The *Vance Bibliographies* from Monticello, Illinois, formerly known as the Council of Planning Librarians' 'Exchange Bibliographies', and now issued in either the Public Administration series or the Architecture series, are not always biased towards the USA where they are produced. A prolific series, they are sometimes published on British topics, and they are always wide-ranging and lengthy in the items listed.

The Property Services Agency issues a number of bibliographies compiled in the Library on topics such as *Solar Energy II: An Annotated Bibliography* (1979) and *Landscape Design: Guide to Sources of Information* (1978). These are usually revised regularly. In particular there are two series of six titles under the headings of *Current Information on Maintenance* (including Cleaning, Design and Maintenance, Management and Economics, Building Services Engineering, Deterioration and Weathering of Materials, Preservation and Restoration of Buildings) and *Current Information on Energy Conservation* (including District Heating, Total Energy, Energy Conservation in Building Design, Thermal Insulation, Systems and Systems Control, Boiler Plants for Domestic, Commercial and Industrial Use), which are particularly useful. Many parts are now in their third editions in 1981.

Longer bibliographies

A full bibliography may be a very lengthy book, like Singh's *Bibliography of Structural Failure 1850–1970* (BRE, 1976), or it may be a pamphlet such as those from the Centre for Environmental Studies. Examples are numerous. The *Bibliography of Vernacular Architecture* by de la Zouche Hall and the PSA's series above were the only bibliographies touching conservation until John Smith's exhaustive volume in 1978. The list of topics is endless, and serves to illustrate the importance of checking for the existence of a bibliography before re-doing the same work oneself. Some other examples are T. M. Russell, *Building Environment Technology: A Bibliography* (University of Edinburgh, Dept of Architecture, 1980); *Building Services for Hotels* (BSRIA, 1977); D. H. Manning, *Disaster Technology: An Annotated Bibliography* (Pergamon, 1973); *Solar Energy for Domestic Heating and Cooling* by Eggers-Lora (Pergamon, 1979); D. F. Cheshire's *Bibliography of Theatre and Stage Design: A Select List of Books and Articles Published 1960–1970* (British Theatre Institute, 1974).

Bibliographic Index (H. W. Wilson, 3 p.a.) is one means of finding relevant bibliographies since it lists any containing over fifty references under subject headings whether they appear independently or as part of a book or article. The terminology has to be used with care since it originates in America, but its European coverage is good and it is unique.

Notes on using bibliographies

It is essential to appraise the value of any bibliography for each particular use and need. Subject indexing may or may not enable users to find the relevant sections quickly. Currency may not always matter, but many topics date quickly. Indexes to journals will help up-date a bibliography quickly (see Chapter 7). Look at the coverage of a bibliography in terms of books, articles and the more difficult to locate report and ephemeral literature, as well as the depth of the treatment of the topic and the annotations, which can give a better clue than the title as to whether a reference is worth following up. In some cases regional or national bias is clear, as in the series from the Gale Research Company of Detroit (p. 1). But some American publishers and bibliographies do frequently treat British information very well. Depth may not always be necessary and the few references in the *New Metric Handbook* or Mills' *Planning* (6 vols, Newnes, 1976–1977) may be sufficient. There may even be sufficient 'leads' in a reference book or ordinary text. A bibliography becomes essential when there is a need for a lot of information or when it is difficult to find anything at all on a topic.

Reference sources

Many good handbooks are designed to make working life easier. A dictionary is essential. The *Oxford English Dictionary*, concise or full edition, takes its definitions from precedent. The definitions given in the American *Webster's New International Dictionary* are based on current usage and sometimes easier to understand. One-volume encylopedias are little more than enlarged dictionaries. Some contain 'further reading'. Background information on a wide range of topics is best found in the *McGraw-Hill Encyclopedia of Science and Technology* or the *Encyclopedia Britannica*, now more frequently revised than formerly. *Chambers' Encyclopedia* is the equivalent British publication but it is less up-to-date.

Single-volume encyclopedias vary in quality. Many are repetitive, despite slight variations in title. The *Macmillan Encyclopedia of Architecture and Design* (P. Guedes (ed.), 1979) is one of the few recent British ones. Whittick's *Encyclopedia of Urban Planning* (McGraw-Hill, 1974) tends towards the biographical and theoretical coverage, with a few bibliographies and many entries for architects. Less well referenced but with good definitions and many diagrams as well as illustrations is Harris' *Dictionary of Architecture and Construction* (McGraw-Hill, 1975).

Dictionaries in architecture tend to be only very finely distinguished from brief encyclopedias. The Penguin series are designed to complement each other in architecture, building and civil engineering. The latest architecture edition is illustrated clearly and even includes bibliographies. Among others the *Dictionary of Architectural Science* (Applied Science, 1973), with clear, concise entries and a brief literature survey, is very useful.

Similar dictionaries exist in all subject fields and should be checked for vocabulary when working with specialist buildings. There are also dictionaries of more general application such as the *McGraw-Hill Dictionary of Scientific and Technical Terms* (2nd edn, 1978).

Language dictionaries often bear very similar titles to the above and may be needed with overseas work or for translating the wording on plans and sections in foreign journal articles where no British information exists. *Dictionary of Architecture, Building Construction and Materials* (H. Buksch, Macdonald and Evans, 1974 and 1975) is in fact a *German–English, English–German* volume, where the *International Dictionary of Building Construction* (A. C. Schwickers (ed.), Technoprint International with McGraw-Hill, 1972) covers English, French, German and Italian, and an earlier *Dictionary of Architecture and Building Trades in Four Languages* (Pergamon, 1963) added Polish and Russian to this list.

Lists of schools of architecture world-wide will be found in the *UIA Handbook* and overseas architectural institutes are listed in the *RIBA Member's Directory*. The handbook of the Commonwealth Association of Architects also lists members and schools in the countries covered.

Lists of practices will always be found in the yearbook of the appropriate professional institution, usually accompanied by a list of members. Few are in two volumes like the RIBA *Directory of Members* and *Directory of Practices*, both annual. *The Register of Architects* (ARCUK) is also published annually and lists all practising architects. Also useful are volumes like the *National Register of House Builders and Developers* (7th edn, National Housebuilders Council, 1977), which also explains the scheme of registration. Selective lists of practices have been published in the 1970s like the *Selective List of Practising Architects* from British Data Services (Essex) (n.d.) or the Data Research Group's *UK Architectural Partnerships* (Amersham, 1977) but they cannot be taken as authoritative and need to be up-dated regularly if they are to be of any use. Architects and their departments in public service and industry are listed in *Directory of Official Architecture and Planning* (Godwin, annual).

Local authorities, their functions and officers are listed in the annual *Municipal Yearbook* (Municipal Journal) which also gives addresses, some local information and names of councillors for all county and district councils in the United Kingdom.

Grants available for research, visits and study are listed in a number of publications from the main donors like the Social Science Research Council and the Science Research Council, but are most comprehensively described and indexed in *The Grants Register* (Macmillan, annual).

Events of the past year are listed and summarized in the *Annual Register of World Events . . .* (Longman, annual) which also covers recent developments in the arts, sciences, technology and society. A weekly digest of recent events will be found on most public library shelves in *Keesing's Contemporary Archives* (Edinburgh, Keesing, 1931–), a weekly news digest presenting an impartial review of events and developments in all walks of life.

Governments, their working and chief personnel throughout the world, are described in the *Statesman's Yearbook* (Macmillan, annual), along with brief statistics and bibliographies. Similar information is also found in the annual *Europa Yearbook* (for all countries, not just Europe), and the *Yearbook of the United Nations* (United Nations, Department of Public Information, annual) which relates also to international organizations.

A brief description of the workings of Britain and the British way of life is presented succinctly in the annual handbook *Britain* (HMSO). The judical and the prison systems are described alongside the setting up and maintenance of the National Parks, British Gas and many others.

If they have no other handbook, all practices should own a copy of *Whitakers Almanac* published within the previous four years. This is a fund of all types of basic information, facts and data, ranging from addresses of government departments and names of personnel (available in greater detail in the annual *Civil Service Yearbook* (HMSO)) to actual statistics on education, insurance, sports, etc., all of which can be located elsewhere in greater detail but are found here in a 'handypack'.

Addresses, figures and facts about most everyday features are available in a wide range of annual handbooks. Some examples will indicate the range:

Schools are listed in the *Education Authorities Directory* (Redhill, School Government Publishing Company, annual).

Universities and colleges, their subject coverage and staff are listed in *The World of Learning* (Europa, annual) or the *Commonwealth Universities Yearbook* (Association of Commonwealth Universities, annual).

Social services are described in the *Guide to the Social Services* (Family Welfare Association, annual) or the *Social Services Yearbook* (Longman, annual). Sources of charitable help are described by subject in *Charities Digest* (Family Welfare Association, annual).

Hospitals are described in *Hospital and Health Services Yearbook and Directory of Hospital Suppliers* (Institute of Health Service Administrators, annual).

Qualifications are explained and indexed in *British Qualifications* (9th edn, Kogan Page, 1978).

Abbreviations may be identified in a list or dictionary, but some have more than one meaning according to the context and country of use: *Pugh's Third Dictionary of Acronyms and Abbreviations* (Bingley, 1977) is just one example.

Parliamentary procedures are described in Wilding and Laundy's *An Encyclopedia of Parliament* (4th edn, Cassell, 1971) while *Dod's Parliamentary Companion* (Dod's, annual) will always give the current names of MPs, their constituency and majorities.

108 Sources and organization of information

Places can always be located in the Ordnance Survey or *Times Gazetteer*, if not found in one of the popular motoring atlases. Town plans in Britain have been published in an AA volume of *Town Plans* and many are sketchily shown in motoring atlases. Museums and places of interest are listed in the annual *Museums and Art Galleries Great Britain and Ireland* (ABC, annual) as well as in *Historic Castles and Gardens* (ABC, annual).

Among the guides with special concern for the environment are the Civic Trust's *List of Conservation Areas* (1974) and their *Environmental Directory* (5th edn, 1981).

Management information and office practice information needs vary widely, from the resources of the loose-leaf *Management Information Manual* (Cromer, 1978–) covering law, finance, tax, travel, property, manpower and government to the British Overseas Trade Board's *Export Services Handbook* (HMSO, 1978). The *Creative Handbook* (Creative Handbook, annual) lists agencies for all types of design work, advertising and exhibitions. *Personnel Training and Management Yearbook* (Kogan Page, annual) provides the employer with a guide to all aspects of employment.

Technical information is a field too wide to detail adequately but a few reference tools should be useful, ranging from the new edition of Black's *Builder's Reference Book* (Northwood, 1980) to the standard, annual, *Kempe's Engineers' Yearbook* (Morgan-Grampian) providing basic information, regulations and tables relating to all materials, structures, surveying, services, safety and fire. Every aspect of housebuilding from management and design to finishing is referenced in Powell's *House-builder's Reference Book* (Newnes–Butterworth, 1979). Although the *CIBS Guide* well known (formerly the is *IHVE Guide*) McGuiness' *Mechanical and Electrical Equipment for Buildings* (Wiley, 1980), now in its sixth edition, or the *Insulation Handbook* (Comprint, annual) are less well known.

The list is endless. The large public and academic libraries can supply a reference handbook on most topics. The major ones which are more widely available have been mentioned here.

There are guides to such books. Walford's *Guide to Reference Material* (3rd edn, Library Association, 1973–1977) is regularly up-dated and presents a comprehensive list of reference books in classified order (Dewey). The detailed annotations provide guidance on the content of the many titles and most are readily available in Britain. A concise, one-volume edition published in 1981 by the Library Association provides a handy guide. There is a difference between a reference book and a directory, however, and *Current British Directories* (9th edn, CBD, 1979) provides a list of the latter with a clear subject index and brief information on the content of each one. More recently Gavin Higgens has edited a useful volume covering all *Printed Reference Material* (Library Association, 1980).

Basic libraries of recommended sourcebooks have been listed from time to time in a number of publications and the latest report from the Department of the Environment has recommended that a 'basic library' is developed. This would mean 'a small collection of documents described to be as useful as possible at minimum cost . . . based on a good analysis of search patterns so that they do effectively meet certain requirements of different user groups' (National Consultative Council, 1979). Such a library would contain some of the above, and an index or guide to the others.

In 1972 Patricia Calderhead listed the basic needs for the architect's practice library and provided a brief guide to sources of information. Professional institutes list basic texts. The Royal Institution of Chartered Surveyors revises the list published with RICS *Abstracts and Reviews* about every five years. The RIBA issues its *Booklist* annually. Although this latter is a reading list, it also provides a current guide to texts. These serve as a guide to the most useful reference tools.

Conclusion

Evaluating and comparing resources is an everyday activity when using information and might be compared to the way alternative design solutions are evaluated before a final solution is achieved. Coverage and usefulness vary extensively between ostensibly similar titles.

Comprehensiveness is rare unless works reach the size of *Encyclopedia Britannica*. Not all information sought will be found even there. The introduction to a reference work will usually state which topics are excluded and how the work is organized. It helps to check before trying to locate information.

Currency is important sometimes, but not always. Look not only for the date of publication but for the date when entries and amendments ceased to be made and consider how this affects the data required. Publication procedures can take from three to twelve months. A description is often the same from year to year but addresses, local government boundaries, names of officials, etc. vary frequently.

The right book for the task may seem elusive. If you ask for assistance sometimes a handbook may be found which will provide information in the exact way you require it, but often, information available will need sifting to locate the essential facts.

Presentation in some volumes is of the ultimate complexity and may render them almost useless without a clear section headed 'How to use'. The 'Introduction' or 'Preface' may do this. Clear instructions, such as were given to Alice saying 'Eat me', may well be necessary, but they are not always as prominently displayed, especially where publications rely on advertising for finance and place pages of advertisements to the front of the information. A little care may be well rewarded and with it should come the realization that some of the basic facts which once appeared elusive need not be so. A quick telephone call, if the volumes required are not at hand, will hopefully produce many of the answers required as most basic facts, addresses and other information have been gathered together into handbooks, or reference books, provided one can locate the appropriate one.

Catalogues and indexes

In any book or directory the contents are listed and indexed to provide a means of retrieval. Information in a book is usually located by using either its list of contents or its index(es). The catalogue a collection of books and other materials is an index. The mystique often built up around these is largely imaginary and most are not difficult to use unless they themselves are particularly complex in construction. Ease of use does involve a little understanding of techniques.

    Libraries usually have catalogues.
    Many information or resource centres have catalogues.
    Manufacturers produce catalogues.

All that any of these catalogues does is to present a list of, and an index to, the contents and products of that store or firm. This list should be arranged in such a way that it can quickly lead to the answers to the usual questions asked about that range of literature or products. Hence books are usually required by author, title or subject but rarely by publisher; information is usually required by subject; products are usually required by certain characteristics of the product, or by trade name, or by manufacturers' name. Catalogues and indexes usually therefore list them in this way.

Sources and organization of information   111

But there is a bit more to this. Many institutions and publications have a variety of different styles and formats for these indexes and lists. Mastery in understanding these assists exploiting indexes for one's own purposes. For example, frequently when using an index one finds that the term one first thought of is not there. But the information required is thought to be there and probably is there, but under alternative terms. One must then think of these and look for them. Frequently the words themselves have become a stumbling block and barrier to finding information. A dictionary or thesaurus is needed to find alternative words or terms.

```
heat resistant paints, painting 3–200
heat sources:
 – electric, heating 4–192
 – gas, heating 4–191
 – local, heating 4–190
 – oil, heating 4–192
 – solid fuel, heating 4–190
heat store design, hot water supply 4–217
heat stores:
 – indoor poosl as, hot water supply 4–218
 – outdoor pools as, hot water supply 4–217
heat-treatable alloys, metalwork 2–282
heat-treatable wrought alloys, structural
    engineering 4–50
heat-welding PVC pipes, plumbing 4–153
heated ceilings:
 – electrically, heating 4–193
 – heating 4–189
heated floors:
 – domestic, heating 4–189
 – electrically, heating 4–193
heater, types of water, hot water supply 4–908
heaters:
 – central instantaneous gas, hot water supply
    4–208
 – coil, plumbing 4–174
 – commercial:
 – – electric, heating, proprietary 4–197
 – – heating 4–193
 – – heating, proprietary 4–197
 – controls for electric instantaneous, hot water
    supply 4–208
```

Figure 6.1 Index to *Specification 1980*

Heat balance, 70–71, 126–131
Heat gains, 70
Heat loss, 24
Heating, 2, 19, 23–24, 20–33
    43–49, 70–72, 98
    116–131, 155–156
Heating costs (*see* Heating)
Heating installation, (*see* Heating)

Figure 6.2 Index to P. A. Stone, *Building Design Evaluation* (3rd edn, Spon, 1980)

The format of a printed index may also vary a great deal as shown by the detailed index using key terms arranged alphabetically from *Specification* (*Figure 6.1*) in comparison with *Figure 6.2*, showing entries taken from a current textbook and using natural language forms.

Sometimes descriptive entries are compiled by inverting terms, as in *Figure 6.3*. Locating information from these requires an understanding of the way terms are entered and the depth of indexing. It is helpful that currently many of the professional books are adopting the style of indexing used in *Specification* and developed especially for the construction industry by Hutton and Rostron. This relies on the page layout to show the subordination of terms to the main heading but provides very specific and detailed indexing using familiar terminology.

With the development of computer technology such indexes are manipulated automatically and the alphabetization may vary since the listing may use one of two systems. Either words are treated as entities and the order of printing takes account of the gaps in words, or these gaps are ignored, words mean nothing and every entry is organized letter by letter. The example from *Specification* (*Figure 6.1*) is word by word, but when reorganized letter by letter (and temporarily ignoring subheadings) it would vary as shown in *Figure 6.4*.

Health centres
   areas, measurement 193
   basic elements 174, 175
   'cost rent', review of 184
   doctors' requirements 188
   finishes, external and internal 180, 183
   form and scope of 8
   Functionalism, expression of 190, 191
   generally 8
   health services plan, objective 180
   history of 8
   'multi-use' concept 173
   services provided 174, 176 183
   single building, motives for 183, 184
   structure 176, 183
   Thamesmead 172–181
   town planning requirements 174
   treatment areas, plans of 178
   Wellington 182–191
Heat services
   distribution 31
   provision of, generally 30, 31, 45, 116 183
   restaurant and stores 244
   water 32, 45, 208
High Wycombe, Wycombe General Hospital 33–45

Figure 6.3 Index to P. A. Stone (ed.), *British Hospital and Health Care Buildings* (Architectural Press, 1980)

heated ceilings
heated floors
heaters:
heater, types of water, hot water supply
heat resistant paints, painting
heat sources
heat store design, hot water supply
heat stores
heat-treatable alloys, metalwork
heat-treatable wrought alloys, structural engineering
heat-welding PVC pipes, plumbing

Figure 6.4 Index entries from *Specification* (*Figure 6.1*) reorganized letter by letter

When reading a page it is usually easy to see the variation and alternative positions of the words sought. However, the order in *Figure 6.4*, when integrated with the other three or four columns of words beginning 'heat', would be magnified and appear to be more drastically different to word-by-word order. When using card indexes the eye cannot as easily discern such differences because only two or three index terms can be seen at once. The understanding of order is valuable and the Post Office, for example, decided to explain the change on separate pages when it altered the order used in the telephone directories from word-by-word to letter-by-letter.

The library catalogue is only an index. The key to its use is the understanding of the alphabetical order and the ordered sequence of entries, as in a book index. However, just as some books have author, subject and place indexes so there are several parts to most catalogues: the author/title section, the classified subject section and the subject index.

The author/title catalogue lists every item held in any library and indicates the code number or letter at which it may be located. Not all items have obvious authors or editors, so that in some cases the listing may need to be by title either as the best-known 'name' or in the absence of a recognizable author; for example, the *Oxford English Dictionary*. Sometimes an institution or a department of an institution or of the government is responsible for the appearance of the item and is used as the author; for example, the Building Research Station for *Principles of Modern Building*. At other times items are known as part of a series, and although this may not be the proper name for them, extra entries are provided there for users in order to make location easier; for example, Howard King's *Finishes* appearing also under 'Mitchell's Building Construction', the title of the series.

The classified section of a catalogue is like a stock list representing everything which would be on the shelf in subject order if everything were ever there at one time, in one long sequence with nothing on loan and nothing in use. The subject order varies according to the system of classification in use and each subject is usually represented by a code (see below). But, as in the author/title section, extra entries for any items may be inserted to represent that item wherever relevant. This allows access to the item at any subject despite the fact that it can only physically be located in one position and, in any case, may be on loan to another reader when required. It can then be located and recovered. Therefore use of the subject list will often refer the user to relevant information on a topic which is not represented on the shelf at the time of searching because it is either stored elsewhere, is in use, or perhaps covers two topics and is shelved at the alternative one. To save the space required for constant repetition the *see also* instruction is used to help provide related information, and sometimes it is used in the subject index, where a synonym or near-synonym has been used. To control words, especially with the development of computerization which requires great accuracy of usage, we use a thesaurus (see below, p. 121).

114 Sources and organization of information

The subject index is an integral part of the classified or subject catalogue since without it one cannot locate subjects in the numerical, or alpha-numerical, sequence. This alphabetical list of subject headings gives the user an index to the code(s) for the subject sought, thus providing access to the classified catalogue. Some abstract and indexing services (see Chapter 7) are subject-organized and also depend upon their subject index for successful use. Hence the quality of the index directly affects the value of the subject catalogue. Subject indexes need to be compiled with the end-user's vocabulary in mind to enable the user to retrieve the topics required easily using familiar terminology. The more specific such an index is, i.e. the more headings that are used to index any subject, the easier it will be to find very specific information.

There are currently three clearly definable formats in use for library catalogues:

(1) The card catalogue still survives: one card is created for every entry required for each item held. But filing is time-consuming and extra cards need space, therefore only a minimum number of essential entries are usually generated.
(2) The computer-produced catalogue either on paper print-out or on microfiche has gained in popularity. Microfiche production has reduced the cost and is quicker and cheaper than paper print-out. These are also easier to read quickly since both appear in page format rather than the single sequential entries of the card catalogue. The computer can also sort quickly requiring little extra space for increased entries. Therefore not only more subject index entries but title, series and author entries can be made in the catalogue.
(3) Xeroxed or printed catalogues were referred to in Chapter 2 (see p. 34). These have been produced by some major libraries in the world in order to provide an indication of their stock to the potential users who cannot always visit. They read like bibliographies and most have either been type-set for printing in page format, e.g. the British Museum, the Library of Congress, the RIBA; or the catalogue cards have been xeroxed, e.g. the G. K. Hall series covering the architecture collection of the Avery Library of Columbia University, New York, the art and architecture collection of the New York Public Library, the architecture and desgn collection of Harvard Graduate School of Design and most recently the Department of the Environment Library. These do not all reproduce the parts of the catalogue mentioned above, mainly because in America a system of alphabetical subject headings is often

preferred to the classified subject catalogue and is sometimes integrated with the author/title listing into one long sequence.

Lists similar to those described will be produced in simpler form for small collections of literature as well as large libraries. Some may just be entries in exercise books in roughly alphabetical order, perhaps listing manufacturers for whom catalogues are held. Others may be more elaborate and use various forms of indexing stationery available from the larger office equipment suppliers. Lists of all types are essential for retrieval purposes. Their success as retrieval tools varies with the accuracy and amount of detail included in their compilation. In situations where there is a large amount of information to be stored these need to be organized. Subject organization is called classification, and is essential to the production of systematic lists and indexes. Some of the more common standardized schemes are described below but for a small collection of information the simplest of outline groupings of subjects may be not only adequate but better.

Classification

In the construction industry 'Classification of information . . . is widely acknowledged to be the most complex, controversial and fundamentally important component in the development of data coordination, since it is basic both to general information systems and to the structuring of project information' (M. Phillips, 'Putting data on tap', 1976). The DoE Working Party on Data Coordination reporting in 1971 on *An Information System for the Construction Industry* pointed to the need for uniformity, but many different schemes still abound. CI/SfB is the major one, designed especially for the construction industry and used independently and as a basis for systems such as National Building Specification. Universal Decimal Classification (UDC) is used in many libraries. The CIT Agency developed a special scheme for the *Construction Industry Thesaurus* (see p. 121). These are just some of the best-known schemes. Others of local invention, modification and use were described by Alan Gilchrist in the BRE's survey of classifications (CP 11/69, 1969).

Geoffrey Broadbent and Christopher Jones, among other architects, have written about the flow of information in the design process, but articles on the problems of information organization in practice by architects are more rare. Alex Gordon, at the CIB conference on *Information Flow in the Building Industry* (1968), pointed out that when the computer is to be used to organize data in practices the organization and coding of the data is crucial to success.

Every writer concludes that certain features are essential if successful coordination of office work is to be achieved with the minimum of duplication between projects and if feedback information on successes and failures is to be integrated into future designs. The computer has been involved in information retrieval in a few practices to coordinate such information. Its use may increase rather than decrease the need for organization of the information. Every piece of information has to have its place in any computerized system store and this must be logically allocated if it is to be retrieved quickly and efficiently. Understanding the principles of organization ensures that every sub-topic has its place: nothing is omitted and everything is listed when needed. Only computers with very large store capacity can get around this by storing the full text of the information and permitting natural language to be used to retrieve data. However, natural language can present retrieval problems, and a thesaurus becomes necessary to determine the appropriate retrieval terms.

A subject listing of information is usually presented to users in two ways.

(1) An alphabetical arrangement of words and phrases representing the topics, which we call an *index*. This is essential if one is to locate any particular term in the other part.
(2) A logical arrangement of the subjects, grouping them together to keep like with like, part with whole and so on. This latter is *classification*.

Exploiting subject-organized information effectively is enhanced by a background understanding of how the subject system works. Reliance on indexing is only a partial solution and is only as good as the indexing itself.

The basic principles of organization are similar, no matter which final scheme is used. The essentials are given here since many architects require to understand the elements of the organization of information for application during the design process and in the use of local collections of information. Several major schemes are briefly described. There are outlines in the Appendices (p. 379) which show the appropriate breakdown of the schemes for architects.

Classification simply means putting together things which are alike, and separating them from those that are different. Names are given to items to describe or define them. Codes are assigned to these for swift processing and for arrangement. Alphabetical lists of names are created after the basic classification process has decided which are to be included and the codes have been assigned. There are basically two means of organizing the words describing things or their attributes:

(1) By relating each to each other through a family tree – thus creating a hierarchy; e.g. *Figure 6.5*;
(2) By listing each in categories according to the characteristics they share in such a way that there can be no overlap or uncertainty as to the appropriate position of anything; e.g.

Buildings	*Structure*	*Materials*
Factories	Ceilings	Brass
Hospitals	Roofs	Copper
Houses		Lead
Hotels		Perspex

Great intellectual effort and skill is involved in the creation of an appropriate hierarchy for a specific purpose or in the isolation of categories. The standard systems of classification provide the

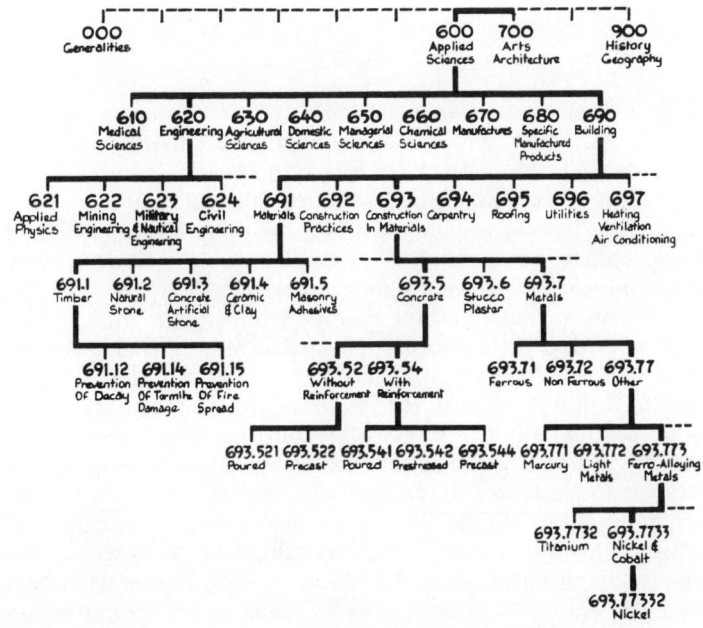

Figure 6.5 Sample of hierachy using Dewey Decimal Classification

option not to 're-invent' every time order is required, but it should be recognized that those systems described here and in other texts have greater suitability to some situations than to others. For example, many architects dislike CI/SfB although it has gained international acceptance and has been adapted for quite specific purposes ranging from the NBS to the Danish computerized information system. UDC was designed to handle information as well as literature but the notation required for precision can be too complex to be fully practical. Dewey was devised to suit literature rather than data. Both the latter are general rather than specific to construction. Nor can everyone agree on the basic categories into which construction information can be divided: some examples are

CIT	CI/SfB	CLASP	CBC	DoE
Construction works	Building type Elements	Building Space use	Element Form	What (site, works) On which
Parts of construction works	Construction form Materials	Project division Element	Labour material Unique job	(documents) Where (location) When (operation)
Materials	Requirements and activities	Design data Feature	codes	How (construction)
Operations and processes		Method		Who involved
Agent of construction		Feature category		
Properties and measures		Unique reference		
Time		Organization		
Place				

Most such analyses of categories reflect the particular purpose for which they are devised. For example, the CLASP and CBC systems were developed for specific projects with computerized organization of the information involved and the need to be able to relate to any very specific part in a building. CIT and CI/SfB were developed for general use and do not have all the above features but do permit the adding of extra facets. Some of the other systems are intended for literature rather than drawings or quantities work and therefore do not perform well when attempts are made to use them for other tasks. In some ways this is where CI/SfB falls down, because it tries to be applicable to literature, drawings and all other aspects of the construction process.

The SfB system (Samarbetskommiten för Byggnadsfragor) was developed in Sweden for the building industry and was recommended for international use by the International Council for Building Documentation (CIB). Agencies were licensed to develop its use in various countries and in 1961 the international edition was published in Britain as SfB. Since then the categories have been changed and developed with the publication of the second and third editions in 1968 and 1976. The first and last tables have been added to cover British needs and the British version is called CI/SfB. Indexing in the *Manual* has been improved and sub-categories developed to take account of developments in production methods and materials. An outline of the system is given in the Appendices.

Hierarchies are constructed with greater difficulty since the family tree has to be developed by starting with the whole concept and breaking it down into component parts. However, at every level of division the same criteria should be applied. This condition sometimes makes it difficult to create divisions, as they do not all seem to flow easily. For example, should you divide walls first by load-bearing and non-load bearing, or by internal and external, and, whichever you use, where do you move to next? Discussion can be heated, and the hierarchy below from the Dewey Decimal Classification reflects all these problems in that it does not obey the principles of strict hierarchial division.

Although both the Dewey Decimal Classification (DC) and its more complex development, the Universal Decimal Classification (UDC), are basically hierarchical classifications stemming from the sub-divisions of the whole of knowledge, problems are evident when an attempt is made to apply such principles to architecture and building (as shown). Many library-users dislike the scatter of documents on what appear to be similar topics across a number of shelves, but it can be seen that this arises because their interests are diverse, and if the books themselves are situated in the classification according to the subject-matter of their content they will inevitably be scattered. Thus books on management in architectural practices will be with those on management in any other type of practice, materials will all be together and structures will be with civil engineering rather than building. At the same time when trying to locate very precise information on the wind-loading of tall buildings, especially offices, there may be several places to look; under structural loading, wind and offices, to name a few only. If a topic is very specific and there is no material available the hierarchy will automatically lead you to less specific topics, including the one sought, or to immediately related topics. Literature on more than one subject or in combination will inevitably be scattered as it can be physically located in only one place. However, catalogue entries can be made as often as necessary to represent other subjects covered.

Outlines of both these schemes are given in the Appendices to aid those needing to fathom their use in libraries and more recently in information systems. Periodical indexes may be organized by a recognized classification scheme. For example, *Construction References* uses UDC.

The only other major scheme which users of some large libraries are likely to encounter is the Library of Congress, which follows neither of the principles above since it was developed to fit the collections of this vast library in the USA rather than on any philosophical principles. Hence every subject has developed separately according to its own rules and is revised as necessary. Appendix 1 lists the main divisions, with a breakdown of the construction numbers. Numerous other subject schemes have been developed over the years for various areas, ranging from medicine to business. As long as the subject indexing is good any system should be easy to follow.

In information retrieval classification assists in selecting terms for a search. When searching manually this initial selection was less important than it now is when using the computer. This is because a person can take in, recognize and change terms or course according to new information received during the search. The computer does not think and is slave to what it is told. The thinking must be done by people before the search commences. As it is not always possible to see and include extra terms during a search these must be selected prior to the start. Since no-one can remember everything quickly and easily the classified sequence of terms indicates the possible terms which one might use in the search, i.e. those which include or are broader than the topic (BT), those which are parts of the topic, sub-divisions of the whole (NT) and those which are related or similar, although not the same (RT). Synonyms will also be found and those which have not been entered in the system will be noted. Thus there will appear to be nothing on wood if the system uses only timber! Effective use of the terminology revealed by the classification and its indexes will enhance the chances of finding the information required. Hence the development of thesauri, which has increased with the advent of the computerized information file.

A thesaurus is basically a word list providing the user with a list of terms both in alphabetical order and in a subject classified order. This latter makes it possible to see, easily, what alternative terms may be used with similar, broader or more precise meanings to the original terms used. Access from the alphabetical to the subject section is usually provided by a numbering sequence which reflects the position of the term in the categories used. From 1969 to 1972 the Department of the Environment, in conjunction with the Polytechnic of the South Bank, developed the *Construction Industry Thesaurus* (*CIT*). Since then it has been refined and is

Sources and organization of information

continually up-dated by the CIT Agency. Terms are categorized into the broad groupings of Construction Works, Parts of Construction Works, Materials, Operations and Processes, Agents of Construction, Properties and Measures, Time and Place. Thus a section from the alphabetical section would look like *Figure 6.6*. This indicates that Heaters is used instead of Heating Plant, and at the latter is an instruction to Use Heaters. Heat pumps appear at

Heat pipes	J50740	Hedges	H43050

Heat pumps	J55112	Height
		  UF Altitude
		    Elevation
			E00910

Heat recovery systems UF Waste heat recovery	J69570		
Heat resistant USE Refractory	E55490	Height measuring equipment	F18820
		Helical	E06510
Heat treated glass UF Tempered glass	H23350	Helical gears	J32538
		Helical reinforcement	J25542
Heat treatment	B06890	Helically threaded nails USE Drive screws	J13890
Heated ceilings	J90986		
Heater batteries USE Preheaters	J55294	Helicopters	B37430
		Heliports	K29150
Heater tees	J51152	Helium	H08490
Heaters UF Heating plant	J55032	Helmets	F20290
Heating (Functional systems)	J99505	Helobise UF Fluvials	B17040
Heating (Operations)	G10030	Helping USE Assisting	G06060
Heating and domestic engineers	F04650		
Heating and drying spaces	K13960	Hemihydrate	H18530
Heating and refrigeration industry	B32183	Hemihydrated	E46350
		Hemispherical	E08550

Heating and ventilating
  engineers
	F07590	Hemlocks
		  UF Tsuga
			B12950

Heating and ventilating industry	B32184	Hemp (Materials)	H39170

Heating and ventilation
  services
  USE Climatic services
	J69500	Hemp (Parts)	J03713

		Hepaticese USE Liverworts	B12470
Heating coils	J55058	Heraldry	B28110

Heating elements
  UF Elements
	J55118	Herbaceous plants
		  USE Herbs
			H43070

Heating equipment	F21930	Herberia	K18770
Heating installations	J12572	Herbs UF Herbaceous plants	H43070
Heating panels	J55038		

Heating plant
  USE Heaters
	J55032	Hermetic
		  USE Hermetically sealed
			E17670

Heating properties	E18010	Hermetic compressors UF Sealed compressors	J51498

Figure 6.6 Construction Industry Thesaurus, alphabetical subject heading list

122 *Sources and organization of information*

J55112, and when this is turned up in section J, the display in *Figure 6.7* is found.

Figure 6.7 shows the many sub-divisions of electric heaters and the fact that they are generally thought of as heaters. However, they are the only ones arranged by principle of operation, and one might need to look at the other categories of sub-division under heaters to see whether other terms might also be applicable to the current work on heat pumps.

As more use is made of computerized databases an understanding of the importance of terminology becomes more important to

	Services: common parts	
	Heat exchangers	
J55026	Coils	Parts of heat exchangers
J55028	Steam jackets	
J55030	Calorifiers *J 55286	
J55032	Heaters (i.e. heat producers and emitters) =	
	Heating plant	
J55034	Superheaters	
J55036	Panelled heaters = Plate heaters	
J55038	Heating panels	
J55040	Embedded panels	
J55042	Oil filled panel heaters	
J55044	Radiators	Heaters by form
J55046	Strip heaters	ditto
J55048	Radiant strips	
J55050	Finned strip heaters	
J55062	Ring shaped heaters	ditto
J55054	Tube heaters	ditto
J55056	Pipe heaters	
J55058	Heating coils	
J55060	Ceiling coils	
J55062	Cartridge heaters	
J55064	Block heaters	ditto
J55066	Conduction heaters = Contact heaters	Heaters by method of distributing heat
J55068	Radiant heaters	ditto
J55070	Overhead radiant heaters	
J55072	Convection heaters = Convectors	ditto
J55074	Natural convection heaters	
J55076	Forced convection heaters	
J55078	Fan heaters	
J55080	Combined radiant and convection heaters	ditto
J55082	Flueless heaters	
J55084	Freestanding heaters	
J55086	Portable freestanding heaters	
J55088	Unit heaters	
J55090	Fires = Hearth fires = Open fires	Heaters by openness
J55092	Built in fires = Inset fires	
J55094	Stoves = Closed fires	ditto
J55096	Charging doors	
J55098	Furnaces	
J55100	Gas furnaces	
J55102	Fire doors	Parts of furnaces
J55104	Grit arrestors	ditto
J55106	Soot arrestors	
J55108	Storage heaters = Heat accumulators	Heaters by output method
J55110	Instantaneous heaters	ditto
J55112	Heat pumps	Heaters by principle of operation
J55114	Electric heaters	Heaters by energy used
J55116	Resistance heaters	Electric heaters by principle
J55118	Heating elements = Elements	Components of resistance heaters
J55120	Exposed resistance heaters = Unenclosed heaters	Resistance heaters by exposed/embedded
J55122	Embedded resistance heaters	
J55124	Sheathed resistance heaters	
J55126	Sheathed wire resistance heaters	
J55126	Underfloor heating cables	
J55130	Incandescent heaters	Resistance heaters by incandescence
J55132	Non luminous heaters	

Figure 6.7 Construction Industry Thesaurus, structured or classified list of subjects

the user. There will not necessarily always be a librarian/information officer interface between the architect and the terminal. But the understanding of basic indexes should assist in the office and in everyday use of directories and guides, since many aspects of paperwork other than books are filed or organized in alphabetical or subject orders, sometimes with some strange and useful/useless results for the staff.

R. M. Rostron, of Hutton and Rostron, found that it became necessary to develop a 'keyword list', i.e. a thesaurus, in order to develop their indexing system for information in the office. Because of the inadequacy of any systems in existence in the 1960s for architecture they developed their own along the principles described above to enable them to set up an information system to index products according to characteristics, availability and the construction techniques used. This is the way in which they are usually used or needed in practice. Their system was described in *Aslib Proceedings* (**20**, No. 3, March 1968, 171–187). P. Miller and M. Roberts recently discussed the use of thesauri in *Building* (28 September 1979, pp. 59–60). A number of other references are listed below for those who wish to follow up this topic. The *CI/SfB Indexing Manual* describes the system, and some others, giving the principles of classification and the applications of CI/SfB to drawings and literature in practices.

References

Batten, W. (ed.) (1975). *Handbook of Special Librarianship and Information Work*, 4th edn, Aslib, p. 308
Broadbent, G. (1973). *Design in Architecture*, Wiley. Department of the Environment, Directorate of development (Housing and construction) (1972). *Structuring Project Information*. HMSO
Foskett, A. C. (1981). *The Subject Approach to Information*, 4th edn, Bingley
Grant, D. P. and Chapman, A. J. (1974). 'A data bank for a small architectural office' in *Information Systems for Designers*, University of Southampton
Jones, C. (1970). *Design Methods*, Wiley
National Consultative Council of the Building and Civil Engineering Industries. Standing Committee on Computing and Data Co-ordination. General Information Group (1979). *General Information; Towards the Better Use of Existing Construction Industry Information Resources*, Department of the Environment, Paragraphs 4.17 and 4.11 respectively
Phillips, M. (1976). 'Putting data on tap', *Construction News Magazine*, **2**(9), 39
Ray-Jones, A. and Clegg, D. (1976). *CISfB Construction Indexing Manual*, 3rd edn, RIBA Publications
Vickery, B. C. (1968), 'Theory of classification' (Paper 3.03), in CIB *Information Flow in the Building Process*, Report 136. See also papers by H. Morris (6.14) and I. Karlen (2.02)

7
Periodicals
Ken Turner

There are many reasons why current issues of periodicals are important to the professional. The information which they contain is likely to be more up-to-date than that found in any other publication, giving information about current projects, practice and techniques. Weekly or monthly periodicals can rapidly become vehicles for debate within the architectural profession. A great deal of the material may never be republished in any other form. Information which is important to researchers and designers but is considered too slight to warrant publication in report or book form will frequently see the light of day in a periodical. In general they contain material from a variety of sources or contributors, ranging from reported news to lengthy technical articles. Information of a purely ephemeral nature, news of topical events, details of conferences, courses and new publications are all ideally suited to this form of publication. Serials, journals and magazines are only alternative names for a publication usually produced at regular intervals, with consecutive issue-numbering and no planned end.

There are two main functions of a periodical: to record knowledge and to disseminate information. Depending on their source and frequency, periodicals will tend to be biased toward one of these functions. For example, those produced by professional associations and learned societies will usually contain a 'newsy' section and a few substantial articles, contributed by members and other specialists in the field. Periodicals produced by commercial organizations may be glossy in appearance and contain considerable advertising but most have a useful technical content. Commercially produced periodicals often attempt to fill the gaps left by the professional society publications providing for new subjects as they become topical. Some are highly academic in approach. The results are not always entirely satisfactory for the architect and can result in repetition of the same information in a slightly different form. The proliferation of periodicals around topics which are in vogue such as 'Conservation', 'Energy' and 'Computing' tend to be reflected in both new titles and changes to existing ones; for example; *Energy and Buildings, Energy Management, Energy Manager* and *Building and Environment* (which was formerly *Building Science*). Many of these are interdisciplinary and, while broadening the architect's outlook, may in fact be rejected as too broad in content or even irrelevant. Keeping up-to-date in one's own field of practice and being able to find out what has been written in the past are problems which every architect faces. Frequently both will be served as well, if not better, by periodicals than by books.

Current information

Being up-to-date or currently informed about news, technical developments, the profession, etc. involves regularly scanning and then perhaps reading part of a number of periodicals. Where groups of people who work closely together are involved, this task may be shared to give greater coverage or to reduce the amount of reading for one individual. However, some reading cannot be delegated.

Current information applies to technical information useful to the job or activity in-hand and to the professional's own self-development and awareness. A periodical, regularly received, may be filed for future use even though it may not always be read before filing.

Each week and month many hundreds of periodicals are published, some of which, and not necessarily the same titles each time, carry articles or information which may be important to the practising architect. Few people have sufficient time or resources to cope with more than a fraction of what is produced. The selection of the important periodicals which an architect should see as they are published is crucial, and probably falls into two categories, the general and the specialist.

General information on news, events and technical innovation is well provided for by the *Architects' Journal* and *Building*; both are published weekly. The *Architect's Journal* is probably the principal news and technical medium for architects. It encompasses most aspects of the profession, spreading its coverage over current events and future activities while also providing longer feature articles and studies, including descriptions of new buildings, technical construction matters and professional practice articles. *Building* is aimed at the construction and design team, and covers all aspects of the construction industry. In addition to giving details of current events it provides a weekly analysis of developments within the industry, including tenders and contracts as well as technical articles and cost information. There is a frequent 'dossier' giving a detailed breakdown of the development, production and costs of individual buildings. These two titles are widely read and are probably the best sources of up-to-date information about current trends and practices. Significant current news and information is also found in *Building Design*, a weekly 'newspaper' with a wide readership. This presents current news in a lively style with comment on new buildings and brief technical information notes.

Less 'newsy' but providing general information for architects in Britain are three monthly periodicals. *Architectural Review* and *Architectural Design* are produced by commercial publishers and design is prominent. *Architectural Review* illustrates current design, mainly in Britain, with some news and editorial comment. On the other hand, *Architectural Design* has changed from being a light-hearted, 'mod' review of architecture in general to a more substantial but theme-based publication. Recent themes have ranged from the Beaux Arts to Stirling and Post-modernism. The *RIBA Journal*, however, ranges widely over Institute and professional news as well as technical matters and product information which the others do not cover.

Specialist periodicals will be selected according to the interests of the user. A few examples might include international design periodicals such as *Domus* (Italy), *l'Architecture d'Aujourd'hui* or *Techniques et Architecture* (France) and *Japan Architect*. Technical journals include *Building and Environment, Concrete Quarterly, Light and Lighting and Environmental Design* and *Brick Bulletin*. Practice and management requires frequent examination of such titles as *Contract Journal, Construction News* and *Management Today*. The list could be endless, since there are numerous periodicals of fringe interest to the architect. The lists found in the front of the indexing and abstracting journals discussed below are usually fairly comprehensive and up-to-date. *House's Guide to the Construction Industry* also lists relevant periodicals under broad subject groupings. For a wider range, *Ulrich* can be used or Woodworth (p. 135). Relevant titles are cited in each sub-section throughout this guide.

Non-current information

For a want of a better word, this refers to material which was published at least a month ago or which could be many years old. The information may still be relevant. It may, in fact, be the only information which was ever published on the topic or indeed is worth reading about the subject.

Which periodical title was the article in? How long ago was it? Which precise issue was it? These questions are asked frequently but can seldom be answered accurately from memory. There are several methods of locating periodical articles each of which has merit; to remove, or copy, and keep required articles; to index required articles; to use the index to each periodical; to use indexing and abstracting services. *Architects' Journal* and some others pre-classify articles for removal and filing. Required articles can be cut out, discarding advertisements, news items and ephemera. These can then be arranged in a useful order such as subject. When this is done on a continuing basis each article, whatever its origin, will be placed next to or with others on a similar subject. This is a little crude and has disadvantages in that a basic filing system must be set up and a subject system developed which in time will become dated and overflow.

It is possible to acquire the indexes that are published by the periodical concerned. These are usually produced covering six-monthly periods for weekly periodicals and yearly periods for those published monthly or less frequently. The indexes, which are generally arranged alphabetically, include subjects (but not always) titles or articles and authors or contributors. This allows one to store periodicals intact and in title, then date, order. The disadvantages are that not all publishers produce indexes. While some are included as part of the last issue of a particular period (e.g. at the end of six months or one year) or with the first issue of the next period, others are published separately and have to be applied for in writing or by telephone. Indeed some take a year or more to be produced following the last issue of a particular volume. Whilst many are good, an equal number are not, suffering from either inaccurate or inadequate indexing, or both. When looking for articles one must scan the index for each periodical title and this can be time-consuming. Thus, while indexes to individual periodicals provide a useful means of locating past articles, there many drawbacks.

Indexing and abstracting services

Indexing publications give purely bibliographical information:

(1) In the case of a periodical article; author and title of the article *plus* the title of the periodical, its issue number, date of issue and the relevant page number.
(2) In the case of a book or a report; author, title, publisher and date of publication.

Abstracting publications, in addition to the above information, may also provide a statement of what the item is about either in the form of a short annotation or as a full abstract sometimes running into several hundred words. The distinction between indexes and abstracts is that the fomer are concerned only with the basic essentials of locating and identifying a particular article while the latter provide a summary of the article in addition. In some cases the summary is so informative as to substitute for the article itself, but in others the summary allows the user to make a judgement about the value of the article without having to locate and read it.

All indexing and abstracting services have their own specific arrangement. This is not standardized. It might be

(1) In classified subject order, either in some detail, using broad subject groups, or using a recognized classification scheme such as CI/SfB or UDC;
(2) In alphabetical order using subject headings;
(3) In simple number order as references are produced, relying on detailed indexes for retrieval;
(4) Any combination of the above.

Depending upon the arrangement used, most services provide supporting indexes. For example, a subject arrangement will have a name index and an alphabetical index of subject headings as an aid; a numerical sequence will have both a name index and a subject index, sometimes combined, but more usually separate.

Much time can be saved by making use of these. Most cover many hundreds of periodical titles and enable users to keep abreast of current developments over a wide field. In addition, they provide a facility for checking back over a period to locate articles by a given person or on a particular subject. They are guides mainly to articles published in periodicals, although some include details of published books and reports. Most are published in monthly or quarterly parts which are then often brought together in annual cumulations. Each publication may be concerned with a single subject (e.g. *Avery Index to Architectural Periodicals*) or aimed at a particular group of people or a profession (e.g. *Architectural Periodicals Index*) – on occasions it may be a combination of both.

Published indexes and abstracts

The *Architectural Periodicals Index*, produced quarterly by the Royal Institute of British Architects, is the major publication for architects. The final quarter of the year is incorporated into an annual cumulative volume. It was established in 1971, replacing the *RIBA Annual Review of Periodicals Articles*. It is aimed at the practising architect and covers in the main articles that have been published on new buildings, conversions and conservation. Design, technology and practice are also covered. The periodical articles are selected from some 450 of the world's architectural periodicals received at the RIBA, including ones which are not in English. The references are grouped under alphabetically arranged subject headings. Under each heading general articles are listed first. These are followed by those which deal with geographical locations alphabetically arranged according to country name, then town or region and sometimes more precise location names. Some care, however, is required in selecting the appropriate subject heading, e.g.

DOMES: GEODESIC (*not* GEODESIC DOMES)
ENTERTAINMENT BUILDINGS (*not* LEISURE BUILDINGS)

First-time users of the index should therefore be prepared to learn the methods employed and note the key phrases using the list of headings which has been published annually since 1978. The annual name index is particularly useful, as it contains the names of architectural firms as well as those of individual architects. In March 1982 the full list of subject headings was published as a separate volume entitled *API Keyword Headings*. This includes cross-references and synonyms of the main headings used in *API* and will prove invaluable to efficient use of the main indexes.

Complementary to the *Architectural Periodicals Index* is the *Avery Index to Architectural Periodicals* (Boston, G. K. Hall). It is produced by the Avery Architectural Library, Columbia University, USA, and covers world periodicals in architecture from the

1930s. Crucial American periodicals, *American Architect, Architectural Forum, Architectural Record* and *Progressive Architecture*, have been indexed in their entirety back to the first issues. Since 1963 *Architectural Review* has been back indexed also. The complete coverage of major American periodicals is its strong point. The index consists of Volumes 1–15 and Supplements 1 (1975), 2 (1977) and 3 (1979). The original index, and all supplements since 1963, were included in the second edition of 1973. The pages of the index are photographed from the cards in the Avery Architectural Library's dictionary catalogue, subject headings and names being in one alphabetical sequence. The size of each volume – they are extremely large – together with the layout of entries on each page, make the index irritating to use at first. However, it is a very comprehensive work covering a wide range of periodicals. The American terminology means that some thought must be given to the selection of subject headings. All place-names used as main headings are followed by the country to which they apply – many are duplicated in Britain and the USA.

Another extremely important index is the fortnightly *Current Information in the Construction Industry (CICI)*. This is compiled by the staff of the Library of the Property Services Agency and is aimed at the architects, surveyors and engineers who work for the PSA. A wide range of material is covered including not only periodical articles but also books, reports and standards (both British and foreign) related to the construction industry. Entries covering each book or periodical article are arranged in a classified subject sequence bringing together material on similar or related subjects. The fortnightly lists are cumulated every six months into a single volume under the title *Construction References*. A subject guide to the classification used is given in this volume as well as an author or name index which serves to provide an additional approach to locating articles. These two indexes are on coloured sheets to provide distinction and easy location. There are no indexes in the fortnightly issues and some abstracts of lesser value are omitted from the cumulated volumes.

A number of other publications of lesser importance to the architect should be mentioned, however. They are *RICS Abstracts and Reviews, Urban Abstracts, Departments of Environment and Transport Library Bulletin, British Humanities Index* and *Current Technology Index*.

The *RICS Abstracts and Reviews* is produced monthly by the Royal Institution of Chartered Surveyors. Its aim is to cover the information needs of surveyors but it appeals to a much wider field. Abstracts of periodical articles, books and pamphlets are arranged in about twenty broad subject areas, e.g. Arbitration, Building and Construction, Compulsory Purchase and Compensation, Housing and Property Management, Insurance, and Property. It has been in existence since 1966. There are no cumulations and the monthly issues can be kept in sequence in specially provided binders. The production of indexes, quarterly and annually, with five-year cumulations which greatly ease searching, has not been kept up-to-date since 1977. However, subject coverage is good. The abstracts are most informative and it is an excellent monthly current-awareness service for many of the more elusive topics of concern to the architect. Its chief value at present is for current scanning, and this can be done quite readily. The *Reviews* part of this service are notes on questions in Parliament and literature reviews on topical subjects published at the end of each monthly issue.

Associated with the *RICS Abstracts and Reviews* is *RICS Weekly Briefing*. The brief abstracts of items of importance from the national and provincial press provide a guide to current developments in housing, construction, land, planning, property, law and economics. On receipt of the publication the abstracts are usually between one and two weeks old.

Urban Abstracts is compiled from periodical articles, reports, books and pamphlets received by the Greater London Council Research Library. From the beginning of 1981 the monthly issues have been published separately as two series of abstracts.

Series 1: Government, management, planning, land use and transport.
Series 2: Building, construction, housing, science, technology, environment and pollution.

A cumulative subject index and corporate author index is produced for each yearly volume of abstracts and is issued about six months after the December issue. From the middle of 1981 the database has been available on-line as *ACCOMPLINE* (see p. 63). A guide to the use of the database was published as *Research Documents Guide No. 19* (GLC Research Library, 1981).

The *Departments of Environment and Transport Library Bulletin* provides informative abstracts from a wide range of periodical articles, books, pamphlets and reports of interest to the staff of these government departments. They are arranged under broad headings including the following: architecture, housing, construction, urban and planning, land use, environmental protection, water, sewerage, transport and local government. Annual indexes are delayed for up to two years and the index in each fortnightly issue is very brief. However, many government papers which may not be listed elsewhere are included.

Unfortunately the very useful *Building Science Abstracts* from the BRE ceased in 1976 and has yet to be resumed as an on-line database. However, in design and technology it can still provide valuable references to work in many countries through its lengthy abstracts of articles and reports. Its computer-produced title index relies upon the use of accurate subject descriptions in the article titles and should therefore be used with care as a supplement to the broad subject categories used to present the abstracts.

The only other major service in the field is *International Building Services Abstracts*, formerly *Thermal Abstracts*, compiled at the BSRIA. The monthly issues cover all aspects of services with lengthy abstracts of periodical articles and a photocopy supply service for members.

Some architects may use *Building Management Abstracts* for references on site and project organization, estimating and costs, education and practice management generally. Produced by the Chartered Institute of Building this bi-monthly service also includes books and reports and organizes abstracts using its own broad subject categories.

Finally, *British Humanities Index (BHI)* covers all aspects of the social sciences, except education (*British Education Index*). Architecture and Town Planning are represented and there is a particularly useful coverage of major newspapers and weekly periodicals. Articles from over two hundred and fifty periodicals published in Britain are selected for inclusion under alphabetically arranged subject headings. It is published quarterly with an annual cumulation and regular author indexes. Its complementary monthly service, *British Technology Index* became *Current Technology Index (CTI)* in 1981 and indexes a similarly wide range of British periodicals in the fields of science, engineering and construction.

No discussion of abstracting and indexing services would be complete without mention of the major American series, since these do include British periodicals and articles of interest to British practice. In particular, construction technology is well abstracted in *Engineering Index*, which often includes lengthy abstracts as well as many foreign-language articles. This is also available on-line as *COMPENDEX*. The equivalent publications to *BHI* and *CTI* are *Humanities Index, Art Index, Social Sciences Index* and *Applied Science and Technology Index*, all published by H. W. Wilson Ltd at varying frequencies. Many of the American series, and all those above, are arranged using alphabetical subject headings rather than classified orders since this obviates the need for further indexes. All cumulate annually.

General assessment of published abstracts and indexes

Subscriptions to these publications are generally quite expensive. Prices range from about £20 per year for the cheapest to many times that amount for the dearest. A great deal of work goes into their preparation and printing and this is reflected in the high cost. But it may be seen that the cost is not as high when it is considered that their services offer:

(1) An accurate record of what has been written;
(2) A relatively easy facility for checking over a wide range of periodicals, most of which will not be purchased on subscription and many of which may be unknown, although useful and relevant.

Currency and frequency of the indexes must also be considered. It has been mentioned that the most frequent can serve as current-awareness devices. In monthly abstract services articles are, or will be, at least two months old on receipt. When technical information is required this will most likely be current enough. Those that are published less frequently will have articles which can be six months old or more.

There are drawbacks in using abstracts and indexes which should not go unmentioned:

(1) It takes time to search for the articles.
(2) If an article, once located, is not in a journal filed away personally or in the firm's library then the particular article or periodical issue must be borrowed from another library or a photocopy obtained.
(3) No two indexes are organized or presented in the same way making it necessary to become acquainted with the objectives and method of arrangement of each one used.
(4) There is often considerable overlap both in subject matter and periodical coverage between indexes produced for different groups of people or on different but related disciplines. Content is complementary.

Nevertheless architects should not be without the *Architectural Periodicals Index*. Other subscriptions should be judged in the light of personal or group requirements:

(1) How well does this cover one's needs?
(2) What areas does it not deal with and which of the other systems will give it the necessary support?

On-line bibliographic databases

Technical developments are taking place in the production process whereby the printed version of an abstracting or indexing periodical is also available on-line via a rapid access computer store (see p. 59). The advantages are clear.

No paper copies of the abstracting or indexing periodicals need to be kept.
An enquiry on a subject usually means that the whole file is searched in one operation.
The response is extremely quick.
The information about the articles is presented in exactly the same way as in the printed form.

At present very little is of direct interest to the architect, as most databases cover the fields of science, engineering and law. Some European building and town planning databases are available for consultation but no comparable British ones as yet except *ACCOMPLINE*.

Locating periodicals

There are so many periodicals in existence that locating the relevant titles when embarking on work in a new field of construction is itself daunting. Some information guides publish lists. Mildren's *Use of Engineering Literature* cites a number of technical construction periodicals. Sections below cite relevant journals, hence the concentration in this chapter on general architectural periodicals. The list of British titles given in *House's Guide to the Construction Industry* is useful but selective, and based mainly on the titles published by institutions and their branches. However, it gives addresses and is up-dated more regularly than other subject lists.

Lists do exist. Price and purchasing information for all periodicals will be found in *Ulrich's International Periodicals Directory* (Bowker, alternate years), which also includes abstracting and indexing services with full subject indexing. Most libraries hold this. Periodicals are sometimes rather irregular, and these are listed in *Irregular Serials and Annuals: An International Directory* (Bowker, alternates with *Ulrich*). British titles are listed in the annual *Willing's Press Guide* or Woodworth's *Guide to Current British Periodicals* (2nd edn, Library Association, 1973), currently being up-dated by CBD Research (Beckenham, Kent) and covering discontinued series as well as abstracts and indexes. The list of many large academic institutions provide a good guide to available titles, as do the lists of titles covered which are included in the front of many indexing and abstracting services. The British Library Lending Division publishes regular lists, for example, *Current Serials Received 1981* (BL, 1981) but there is only one alphabetic order without subject listing or indexing. However, this does indicate the availability of many titles.

Copies of articles identified using indexing and abstracting services or databases may be borrowed from other libraries. The inter-library loan network in Britain is one of the best cooperative systems in the world, and requests sent to the British Library Lending Division at Boston Spa, Yorkshire, will be redirected to appropriate libraries if they are not available among their own holdings. The delay for architectural items varies from one week to one month, within which, experience suggests, most articles can be found in Britain. Only those which have to be sought abroad will then take longer. The process has been hastened since the introduction of computer databases by the use of on-line ordering facilities for items located during such a search. At present the delivery factor, the Post Office or a locally arranged van service in some cases determines the remaining delivery time elapsing.

8
Trade literature, technical information and standards
Valerie J. Bradfield

This chapter aims to draw together information about products and their uses, including standardization and testing procedures information. This important section of information used in the construction industry ranges widely. Although difficult to discuss adequately in a short space, it is possible to summarize the approaches to information retrieval and the types of resources available.

Trade and technical literature

There are few discussions of trade literature in print, and most are out-of-date except for those by Thomson (BL, SRL, 1977) and by the present author, in *Art Library Manual* (Bowker, 1977). However, the Department of the Environment survey of *Commodity Information in the Construction Industry* (HMSO, 1971) investigated the available sources of information on products and the ways in which they filled the users' requirements. At 1971 values the annual cost to architectural firms of locating and using manufacturers' literature was 31 minutes per employee per month, or £2 230 000 per annum, to quantity surveyors the time was the same but the cost was £830 000 and to builders 141–427 minutes per month was spent, at a cost of £3 960 000 per annum. Such figures indicate the large amount of time (and money) which is spent using this type of material.

Manufacturers issue many leaflets about their products either as catalogues, data sheets or other similar leaflets. Martin Thomson in *Trade Literature: A Review and Survey* (BL, SRL, 1977) defined this genre as 'discrete publications issued by or on behalf of a company in order to promote the image and/or products of that company'. They range in size from leaflets to lengthy booklets or binders and in value from essential technical reading to valueless, glossy, picture books. Some manufacturers employ professional technical authors and the services of firms such as Technical Literature Services Ltd to design and produce effective and informative literature. The Property Services Agency publication, *Better Trade Literature* (1979) outlines the recommended content and layout of effective literature in order to bring to the notice of manufacturers the contents of BS 4940: 1973, *The Presentation of Technical Information about Products and Services for the Construction Industry*.

Good catalogues should contain written and drawn descriptions of the product, a data sheet, samples, colours, range and price lists, supply information, with technical and design data, application details, specifications, site-work and user instructions and a list of references. The amount and detail of the content is the best criterion for assessing the quality of such literature. Most categories given in the CIB *Master List of Properties* (2nd edn, CIB, 1972) should be covered. Presentation of drawings should be clear and location drawings should be provided for elements. While some data sheets on specific products fulfil these criteria admirably others are limited in their coverage, and a decreasing number give little specification information. Although BS 4940 requires all information to be dated by the producer and to be regularly revised, much is not, and it is advisable to date-stamp literature on receipt in the office to give some indication of its currency when in use.

In their survey of *Architects and Information* (University of York, 1970) Goodey and Matthew used several differing formats to present similar information to a sample of architects. As a result they were able to recommend to manufacturers methods and styles of presentation for trade and technical information in order to make the information more useful to the architects and specifiers. At the same time it was shown that 90.3% of their sample relied on this source for most of their information.

Walton Markham Associates' telephone survey of architect's use of product information (reported in *AJ*, 26 August 1981) showed that, although architects rely heavily on this type of information, they prefer to send for it rather than be 'bombarded' by mail shots and salesmen. However, despite the earlier research, much of the literature received still gives inadequate information on sizes, weights, fixings and costs. It was also pointed out that 60% of the sample of a hundred architects contacted (there are 27 000 registered architects) maintained personal collections of product data as distinct from the office collection.

Some other types of literature are often kept with, equated to and used with manufacturer's data. These are included in this section. They range from the data books, which are almost technical textbooks, produced by some companies, to company journals or bulletins which may appear sporadically as a glossy advertising publication or which may be a well-developed technical presentation of data on new products and advice on old, designed to be circulated externally or internally as the firm's own communication bulletin. Technical data sheets from government research establishments, from trade associations and other sources are also included in this category of material.

Much of the literature is located through the new products lists in a number of professional journals which also review manufacturers' literature and carry many advertisements. Those reviews in the *Architects' Journal, Building, Building Services* and *Building Specification* are particularly useful. The first two are printed so that they can be cut up and filed in CI/SfB order if time permits. Part of the *AJ* 'Annual Review' each January is devoted to a review of the best new technical literature. *What's New in Building* also produces regular lists and brief reviews, as does *Builder and Merchant*, launched on 1 December 1980.

Trade literature

Several types of information are usually sought from this literature:

(1) Products are required which conform to particular needs in a particular situation;
(2) Manufacturers of named products or of product groupings must be located in order to make contacts;
(3) Data on products is needed to assess their suitability for the situation in hand;
(4) Comparative data is required in order to select products.

The first is sometimes the most difficult to supply because of the variable quality of the indexing in some collections and the individualized presentation of some literature. A number of years ago Hutton and Rostron discussed their method of providing an indexing system to enable an architect to locate products according

Trade literature, technical information and standards 139

to their characteristics (see p. 123). The advent of the microcomputer may assist this function. The second category of information is usually answered by the various directories available. Problems (3) and (4) are solved either by the use of specific manufacturers' catalogues from the nearest collection, or by using a service such as RIBA *Product Data* or by obtaining catalogues from the manufacturer on each occasion. This chapter will indicate the most effective ways of answering the above questions and will provide guidance to the various services available to the construction industry.

FINDING MANUFACTURERS

The annual *Barbour Compendium*, since its introduction in 1977, has become the largest specialist listing of building products. No listing can ever be fully comprehensive since there are over 30 000 companies in the construction industry. However, this has a wide coverage and architects find that the brief, illustrated data sheets, which are provided for some of the products in the volume, are helpful. All names and addresses are listed separately at the back. A trade-name index is incorporated into this alphabetical listing. On the final pages the British Standards are listed under broad subject groups.

In practice the 'big red book' does, however, need to be supplemented by other listings to achieve a more comprehensive survey of products available. There are a number of such listings. The RIBA *Product Data* volumes list many manufacturers under each CI/SfB heading. In 1980 the RIBA also brought these sections together and published a separate *Directory of Manufacturers* (see p. 146). Further lists of manufacturers will be found in the Proprietary section of *Specification*, and subject lists in *Architect's Standard Catalogue* as well as the 'grey pages' in *Building* each week. *Sell's Building Index* also provides a full listing.

The *AJ* 'Products in Practice' series reviews the developments in different product groups, giving a up-to-date general information on each type of product and lists of manufacturers in tabular format. The *RIBA Journal*, the *Architect* and *Architectural Association Quarterly* have changed their formats to provide reviews of different groups of products regularly. (The latter two ceased publication in 1981 but may reappear under new titles.) The relevant parts of these journals can be kept with other trade literature and lists. If this is not done then references should be made to their existence. The monthly *Building Specification* concentrates on a different product each month and not only consolidates advertising but reviews some of the recent uses of the product in specific buildings. Offprints from these articles are sometimes circulated by manufacturers with their literature.

Some associations and publishers issue highly specific product guides containing lists of manufacturers and some additional information. They are usually inexpensive since they rely on advertising finance. They range from *Insulation Handbook, Concrete Yearbook, Building Board Directory* and *Adhesive Handbook* to the *Business Equipment Guide* (which uses a grid system to define attributes of products) and the Design Council's *Street Furniture Design Index*.

The telephone directory *Yellow Pages* provides a local listing covering some companies, although the subject headings are sometimes difficult to understand. The ARTRAD series of trades directories use subject headings to list manufacturers in certain county groupings, mainly over the Midlands and the South. Local Chambers of Commerce sometimes provide officers with company directories. Thomson's series of local directories is being extended to provide Midland and Northern towns with local trades lists but their coverage is erratic and far from comprehensive. Nevertheless, where local suppliers are required these are the main source, since the *Kelly's* local series has now ceased except for the London area and the *Kompass* local volumes have also ceased. However, these local listings, like the telephone directory, usually give only name and address.

There are a wide range of product directories available to cover products beyond the immediate confines of the construction industry. These can be located using the subject index of *Current British Directories*. This lists names, addresses, coverage and frequency of production and is up-dated every couple of years. The most comprehensive general directories will be found in even the smaller libraries. These are *Kompass*, which uses a grid system to relate the product features to a manufacturer's range (*Figure 8.1*); *Kelly's Directory*, which lists names and addresses using subject headings which are more specific than the telephone directory but are based on the entries in the latter. *Kelly's* covers the whole country and also has an international volume; *Sell's Index* is similar and covers all products but gives only name and address; Stubb's *Buyers' National Guide* and *Buyers' International Guide* are similar. These are the most comprehensive directories. All are complementary, and by using several under any product heading the list of manufacturers of any one product can usually be increased.

Trade literature, technical information and standards 141

35-42

Architectural and Builders' Metal Work

Part 3

E Export
I Import
2 Wall Ties, Stainless Steel
3 Wall Cladding, Shaped/Contoured
4 Wall Cladding, Steel
5 - -, Aluminium
6 - -, Metals, N.E.S.

7 - -, Stainless Steel

8 - -, Metal, Insulated or Composite

9 Wall Cladding, Lead.
10 Laminated Sheets, Steel-Asbestos-Steel, etc., with Fire Resisting Qualities to BSS 476
11 Building Panels, Insulated
12 Partitions, Panels etc. Steel Framed
13 - etc., Aluminium Framed
16 - etc., Steel
17 - -, -, Asbestos Bonded; Fire Resistant

18 - -, Aluminium
19 Column Corner Guards, Metal
20 Metal Flue Linings
21 Framed Partitions etc., Steel Panelled
22 - - -, Glass Panelled
23 - - -, Board Panelled
26 Partitions, Panels etc. for Toilet Use

27 Metal Tracks and Fittings for Sliding Glass Doors, Windows, etc.

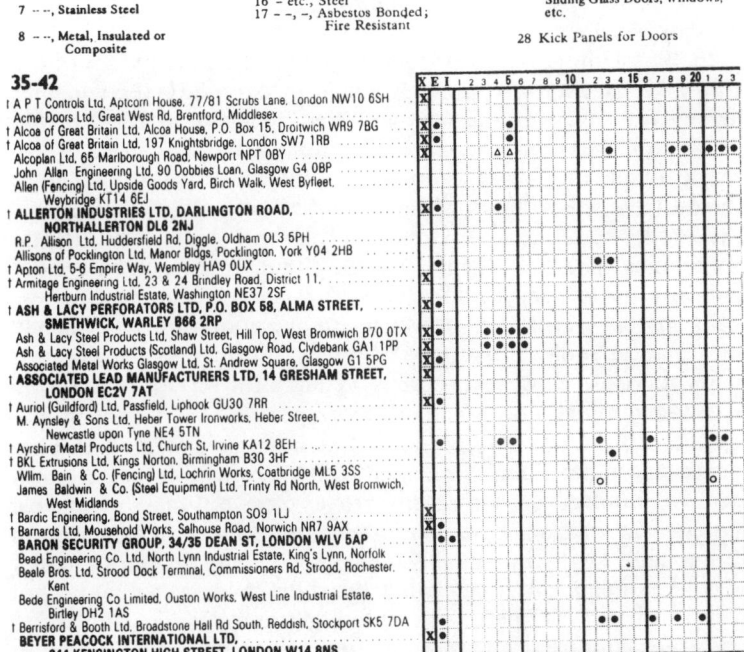

28 Kick Panels for Doors

35-42

† A P T Controls Ltd, Aptcorn House, 77/81 Scrubs Lane, London NW10 6SH
Acme Doors Ltd, Great West Rd, Brentford, Middlesex
† Alcoa of Great Britain Ltd, Alcoa House, P.O. Box 15, Droitwich WR9 7BG
† Alcoa of Great Britain Ltd, 197 Knightsbridge, London SW7 1RB
Alcoplan Ltd, 65 Marlborough Road, Newport NPT 0BY
John Allan Engineering Ltd, 90 Dobbies Loan, Glasgow G4 0BP
Allen (Fencing) Ltd, Upside Goods Yard, Birch Walk, West Byfleet, Weybridge KT14 6EJ
† **ALLERTON INDUSTRIES LTD, DARLINGTON ROAD, NORTHALLERTON DL6 2NJ**
R.P. Allison Ltd, Huddersfield Rd, Diggle, Oldham OL3 5PH
Allisons of Pocklington Ltd, Manor Bldgs, Pocklington, York YO4 2HB
† Apton Ltd, 5-6 Empire Way, Wembley HA9 0UX
† Armitage Engineering Ltd, 23 & 24 Brindley Road, District 11, Hertburn Industrial Estate, Washington NE37 2SF
† **ASH & LACY PERFORATORS LTD, P.O. BOX 58, ALMA STREET, SMETHWICK, WARLEY B66 2RP**
Ash & Lacy Steel Products Ltd, Shaw Street, Hill Top, West Bromwich B70 0TX
Ash & Lacy Steel Products (Scotland) Ltd, Glasgow Road, Clydebank GA1 1PP
Associated Metal Works Glasgow Ltd, St. Andrew Square, Glasgow G1 5PG
† **ASSOCIATED LEAD MANUFACTURERS LTD, 14 GRESHAM STREET, LONDON EC2V 7AT**
† Auriol (Guildford) Ltd, Passfield, Liphook GU30 7RR
M. Aynsley & Sons Ltd, Heber Street Ironworks, Heber Street, Newcastle upon Tyne NE4 5TN
† Ayrshire Metal Products Ltd, Church St, Irvine KA12 8EH
† BKL Extrusions Ltd, Kings Norton, Birmingham B30 3HF
Wilm. Bain & Co. (Fencing) Ltd, Lochrin Works, Coatbridge ML5 3SS
James Baldwin & Co. (Steel Equipment) Ltd, Trinty Rd North, West Bromwich, West Midlands
† Bardic Engineering, Bond Street, Southampton SO9 1LJ
† Barnards Ltd, Mousehold Works, Salhouse Road, Norwich NR7 9AX
BARON SECURITY GROUP, 34/35 DEAN ST, LONDON WLV 5AP
Bead Engineering Co. Ltd, North Lynn Industrial Estate, King's Lynn, Norfolk
Beale Bros. Ltd, Strood Dock Terminal, Commissioners Rd, Strood, Rochester, Kent
Bede Engineering Co Limited, Ouston Works, West Line Industrial Estate, Birtley DH2 1AS
† Berrisford & Booth Ltd, Broadstone Hall Rd South, Reddish, Stockport SK5 7DA
BEYER PEACOCK INTERNATIONAL LTD, 344 KENSINGTON HIGH STREET, LONDON W14 8NS

1100   x indicates expanded entry in volume 2   † denotes member of Confederation of British Industry

Figure 8.1 Kompass grids showing product features and manufacturers

Many of the above include indexes to products. *Specification* and the Barbour *Compendium* are most helpful for identifying the manufacturer of a product known only by its trade name. Should these fail, the product may be identified in the broader-based *UK Trade Names* (7th edn, Kompass, 1982).

There are occasions when it is desirable to 'check out' a supplier financially or to find information about a company and its personnel. This can usually be done without contacting the company by consulting one of the directories or services which give more detailed information than those mentioned above. The *Stock Exchange Official Yearbook* provides a reseumé of the company personnel, background and finance for all public companies. There is less information about each company in Volume 2 of *Kompass*, but it includes many private companies not quoted on the Stock Exchange. Dunn and Bradstreet's *Guide to Key British Enterprises* covers the largest 2000 companies, whether public or private, and has more detail than *Kompass* but less than the *Stock Exchange Official Yearbook*.

In 1981 Dunn and Bradstreet published the first edition of the *Construction Industry Register*, giving facts on 28 000 companies arranged by types of business and then by location. *Construction News* publishes data on some companies regularly and also makes this available on *Prestel*, as do some of the construction companies themselves. Many major libraries subscribe to either the McCarthy or the *Extel* card services covering both public and private companies. These cards condense the annual report, balance sheet and any 'news' items into a very brief space. The *FT Business Information Service* can answer telephone enquiries for company information and offers various company information and business news services. However, there is a charge for services.

Where annual reports and other company-issued documents are required these are held on deposit at Companies House and are available on payment of a search fee. Microfiche copies are now sent to enquirers. If a company proves elusive it may be sensible not just to check the company registration index available from Companies House but also *Who Owns Whom* to ascertain whether it is a holding or subsidiary company. If the holding company is not British then it may be necessary to enquire for similar directories for other countries, and these are usually held only at the largest public libraries. More detail on this type of information will be found in Vernon's *Literature of Business and Management* (Butterworths, 1975) or Campbell's *Business Information Services* (2nd edn, Bingley, 1981).

TRADE LITERATURE IN THE OFFICE

Drawers and shelves stacked with catalogues and pamphlets are to be found in every office. However, if available trade information is to be usable it needs to be organized and gathered systematically.

There have been numerous recent suggestions on how this should be achieved. After studying the many different methods of providing the architect with trade literature Anne Volbeda (1977) suggested that all product literature should be provided on a comprehensive basis, not from manufacturers but from a central system funded by the user or the government. However, at present this has not happened in Britain. There are a number of ways of gathering and organizing product information in the office.

The small office may rely on an in-house system. Literature is gathered by contacting manufacturers when it is needed or by using the reply-paid cards supplied as a reader service in many journals. Requests to be put on mailing lists are not always successful. Only the largest manufacturers seem to maintain such lists effectively. On receipt everything needs to be dated. Some form of organization is essential, the simpler the better, and, if possible, self-indexing to reduce paperwork. Using the CI/SfB system reduces indexing, as the *Manual* can be used (with annotations to suit the particular practice) and most literature is pre-classified, although not all manufacturers are very good at classifying. Some interesting misplacings may arise if a quick check on codes is omitted. A subject grouping on a simpler basis may be developed within the private office to suit specific needs. Such systems are sometimes incapable of sufficient expansion unless the principles of compilation are well understood. The Department of the Environment shelves literature by manufacturer's name and uses a subject index for access. Personal preferences vary, but the alternative is to leave the organization to one of the office library services, of which three have survived from the many offered in the 1960s. A recent brief description was given by the Building Centre Group in its news journal, *Inform* (**2,** No. 5, 1979). The services are *Barbour Index Ltd*, *Building Product Index* and *RIBA Office Services Ltd*.

Barbour Index Ltd Catalogues and technical literature are supplied to *Barbour Index Ltd* by subscribing manufacturers. These are then organized and taken to subscribers' 'libraries' where they are filed in SfB order and the collection thus created is regularly weeded to maintain the currency of all literature. An index binder provides a subject index, a list of manufacturers indicating what literature is included with its classification code, and a note of recent government publications. The Barbour *Compendium* provides the trade-name index and manufacturers' address list. Manufacturers pay to be included in the service and the practice subscribes but the practice is free to add any extra information which will be filed for them. Extra literature covering non-subscribing manufacturers may be requested or provided but, although Barbour run a service to obtain this for subscribers, a recent survey by L. S. Watson of Ealing Technical College, School of Librarianship (1977) showed that only one library of the thirty surveyed used the service. Others preferred to contact manufacturers themselves. The basic service covers a broad subject span and any practice needs to develop its specialist areas. However, the service is cheaper than providing staff-time to maintain a similar collection.

RIBA Office Library Service This is a similar service to the *Barbour Index*. Visiting library staff maintain files which combine technical literature with manufacturers' catalogues. All are arranged by CI/SfB and tailored to suit the requirements of individual offices. The RIBA *Product Data* is automatically supplied (see below) and any extra literature may be added. However, the user pays for the service and the manufacturer does not pay to include literature.

Building Product Index This service provides a library unit, 7 ft × 4 ft × 1 ft, accomodating binders with both manufacturers' literature and technical information sheets. About 1350 manufacturers are covered and up-dating is done monthly in person. An index is provided. This service is, however, more limited than the other two in its size.

Technical Indexes Ltd The Ti system provides subscribers with full trade catalogues on a number of engineering topics which may be useful to some architects, structural engineers, etc. All catalogues are provided on microfilm and revised regularly when the new printed indexes are produced. These use a grid system which makes possible precise location of any product according to specified features. A full set of British Standards is also available as part of the service (as well as US, Canadian, Japanese, German, European and International Standards). Subject files cover Electronic Engineering, Mechanical Engineering, Chemical Engineering, Engineering Components and Materials and Materials Handling. All are available with either a core coverage of major manufacturers or extended range at a higher subscription charge. A US 'Building Products' file is available but not a British one. The services are expensive by comparison with *Barbour Index Ltd*.

Trade literature, technical information and standards 145

PRODUCT INFORMATION SERVICES

Technical and product services are also provided by the Building Centre, the RIBA Services and the Architect Standard Catalogue Service. They offer cheaper alternatives or services complementary to those already discussed.

Data Express was developed by the Building Centre as a service to deliver to architects and specifiers the catalogues which they requested from the central store. Manufacturers' literature was delivered by messenger in London and first-class post in the provinces. This service depended on the cooperation of manufacturers and was operated as part of the Building Centre Information Service and as a back-up to the *Building Documentation UK Commodity File* (Builder Ltd), which ceased early in 1981. At the time of writing the new Building Centre Barbour group have not announced further plans for the replacement of the file.

RIBA *Product Data* is the most comprehensive trade and technical service. Run by RIBA Services and arranged by Ci/SfB, it provides users with a number of readily identifiable orange binders containing both digested data sheets from subscribing manufacturers' product information and a few technical information sheets, mainly from trade associations. Each data sheet is arranged in CIB *Master List* order which makes identification, comparison and selection of products simpler than when the architect is presented with an unsystematic arrangement of facts, as in many trade catalogues. Only explicit and fairly brief technical data sheets are included, and the whole includes a very wide range of information. At the beginning of each section there is a full list of manufacturers for each product (not all of whom are represented by a data sheet) and a list of references to literature, to associations, to regulations, to British Standards and to other applicable legislation. Indexing is provided in a pamphlet 'Desk Index', of which multiple copies are freely available for separate desk use. Entries in the index refer not just to the Ci/SfB sections but also the relevant news sheets which are provided in a separate binder. These news sheets give abstracts of recent articles or publications on Agrément Certificates, Construction Techniques, Practice Procedures and Legislation. They are intended to keep the architect fully up-to-date with practices, problems and even failures. Design will be added to these in 1983. The whole service is up-dated every few months by the insertion or removal of sheets. *The Directory of Manufacturers* is being superseded by the *Product Selector*, in three volumes, giving an alphabetical list of manufacturers with addresses, product lists and a trade-name index. Bibliographical references are given but this is a comprehensive listing similar to the Barbour *Compendium* and data sheets will not necessarily be found in the binders for every company mentioned in the *Directory*. Because of their different subscription lists, coverage complements the *Compendium*. The *Directory* is available as a separate publication and in 1982 the RIBA Services launched an A5, three-volume *RIBA Product Selector*, claiming to cover 6000 suppliers in 450 CI/SfB product groups with an A–Z index.

Architects' Standard Catalogue and *Interior Design Catalogue* will be found in many offices, usually because they are cheap. However, since only four and two volumes respectively are issued annually, into which are bound manufacturers' leaflets, their coverage cannot be as wide as the above. Often the leaflets are not very informative. But each CI/SfB section is preceded by basic technical data, lists of British Standards and regulations applicable with references to literature and to useful associations. A tradename index is included and the full list of building standards.

When using product information services it should be remembered that none are fully comprehensive. There are over 30 000 manufacturers in the construction industry and few listings cover more than 10 000. Work with the various listings has shown that very rarely do two give the same list of manufacturers for a product and that, except for a few of the largest companies, a manufacturer rarely appears in more than two of the listings for any product. Some products are difficult to locate in one service but not in another. The indexing terms vary and it is often quicker to put a service down and try elsewhere than to persevere with looking for a product in a particular index. Terminology naturally represents more of a problem to students than to qualified architects.

It is also important to realise that the names included in any directory or literature service are selective and depend upon the financial basis of that service. If the manufacturer is charged for entries the large companies can afford to pay and the smaller need such advertisement, but the medium company on a tight budget is not heavily dependent on this form of advertising and may 'opt out'. In some cases both manufacturer and subscriber are charged, but unless there is also a substantial proportion of advertising, subscriptions are likely to remain fairly high.

TECHNICAL DATA

Specification has been described as 'the architect's Bible' and will be found in almost every office. Yet many offices are known to rely on out-of-date editions as the price increases rather than purchase new editions annually or bi-annually. In *Specification* technical information on techniques and materials is combined with model specification clauses and briefly annotated lists of products. Sections appear in SMM work order and each has a bibliography referring to sources of information in published literature, standards, legislation and from related associations. The cost of the publication is borne both by advertisements (confusingly, the pages are numbered separately while maintaining the sequence, i.e. two pages 18) and by purchasers of the volumes. The 1978 and 1980 editions were produced in five slim volumes in an unsuccessful attempt to prevent them falling apart as swiftly as the former two-volume format. The subject index is very detailed and the same volume includes a manufacturer/trade-name index and a list of British Standards. Every edition contains a few current articles at the front of volume one on topics such as 'Rehabilitation' or 'Solar energy' and publication is currently bi-annual.

Barbour Design Library was started in 1979 to provide easy access to technical information by providing on microfiche the full text of every publication referred to in the printed index. This complements a collection of trade catalogues. Coverage is wide, ranging from all the major government departments issuing relevant publications to legislation and regulations, standards, and publications from trade, research and professional institutions. Some local council publications, like the GLC's *Development and Materials Bulletin*, and one or two commercial publications are also included. Up-dated hardcopy indexes with accompanying new microfiche are provided three times a year.

The service is easy to use as the publications required are at the desk. The user searches the printed bibliography volume for the reference number of an appropriate publication before turning to the microfiche. Indexing terms are limited but most topics can be found quickly. Microfiche reference numbers for publications issued in numbered series are listed in the index of contributors at the back of the printed volume to make these easier to locate; for example, CP110 will be found in the list of British Standards at the end as well as by searching through all literature on structural concrete. The success of this 'library' has been followed up by the introduction of a 'Health and Safety Library' on the same lines. Although similar systems have been available in other industries (cf. Ti, p. 44) and internally in the DoE for its trade literature collections, Barbour have pioneered the commercial use of microfiche in the construction industry. Further developments on these lines are inevitable and already include the *Catalogue of British Official Publications not Published by HMSO* from Chadwyck-Healey of Cambridge. This lists all publications from government departments and supplies copies either on request or on standing order in microfiche format.

Technical data supplementing that in the standard textbook such as Barry, McKay and Mitchell's (p. 251) is produced mainly by the government research institutions or by trade and research associations. The latter distribute much literature free or at a small charge. Free literature accumulates on most desks. Specific items will be mentioned by subject in Chapters 11-16. However, a number of important, inexpensive series are of general relevance and should be widely available. While these may be included in the *Barbour Design Library* they will be removed from there when superseded, although a practice may still need to refer to old editions for work-in-hand and for rehabilitation work.

The BRE *Digests* are known to all in both the leaflet form and the cumulated volumes published by Construction Press. The *Digests* reach as many as 78 000 architects, builders, surveyors and engineers. Their re-design was discussed by J. Taylor, 'Processing and communication of research data' (*Architect*, **2**, No. 11, 1972, 73-76), showing how the need for visual information should be accommodated. Although the DoE *Advisory Leaflets* are no longer being up-dated they provide brief, clear guides to practice for site use. The Cement and Concrete Association's *Man on the Job* leaflets fulfil a similar function and were produced in a new edition in 1980. The BRE produce a great number of technical papers, all listed in the free BRE *Information Directory* up-dated by *BRE News*. In 1979 BRE began a series of brief *Information Papers* to communicate the results of reports, mainly the *Current Papers* series, to the many users who failed to read or obtain the fuller version. All BRE series are essential reference material, as are the DoE *Design Bulletins* and other government technical leaflet series, mainly relating to specialized building forms such as hospitals (DHSS Hospital Technical Memoranda, etc.).

The *AJ* Information Programme is designed to provide an overview of technical information and publishes many and varied articles. Unless these are copied, or extracted, for filing with product literature, the abstracting and indexing journals (Chapter 7) remain the main means of access. The bibliographies in *Specification* and *RIBA Product Data* are also helpful in locating technical data.

Trade literature, technical information and standards 149

COLLECTIONS OF TRADE AND TECHNICAL LITERATURE

Only the larger practices can afford full literature collections. Others make do. There are a number of collections around the country which may be consulted by any users. That at the Science Reference Library, Chancery Lane, London, covers *c.* 25 000 manufacturers in all fields, not just construction, and includes sets of Barbour *Index* and *Technical Indexes*. The PSA trade libraries may answer enquiries. The largest collection is at Croydon, and regional offices have standardized but smaller collections cover 1000 manufacturers. Many colleges, polytechnics and universities offering courses in architecture and building will have collections which local businessmen may usually use. In some cases the Small Firms Information Centres can refer enquirers to the nearest collection.

SAMPLES COLLECTIONS

Samples of products are important to specifiers to provide an indication of texture, colours and quality. Collections may vary in number and size. In many practices samples are obtained for specific projects and are scattered through the offices with project documentation. Comprehensive reference collections are not normally maintained, although samples which are easily incorporated into binders and folders may be available with the literature collection. Bricks, blocks, window-frames, etc. are less freely distributed by manufacturers, and present problems in storage, listing and identification. Nevertheless small collections exist, mainly in practices and educational establishments. Unless a local company is very conscientious, up-dating is a problem and a samples collection usually complements the technical data and trade literature collection.

Space to accommodate awkward-sized and shaped samples, and the means of organizing them, are the main difficulties encountered in providing a collection. Where possible, shelving can be spaced at a depth suited to the samples. Stacking should be avoided since it is easy to 'lose' items behind various piles! Drawers can only be used to contain loose fittings samples, i.e. ironmongery, although some manufacturers supply these mounted on display boards. These can be equally difficult to accommodate where wall-space becomes limited unless investment in a display stand is feasible.

The product literature collection must indicate clearly that samples are also held, indicating their location. Users of the samples must also be referred to the location of the relevant literature. This can be done quite simply using a system of labels on the samples bearing the manufacturer's name, product range and CI/SfB reference. Catalogues can bear a gummed label stating 'sample held' and giving its reference number unless samples are organized in CI/SfB order, or in the same order as the literature if CI/SfB is not used.

Exhibitions provide an alternative means for specifiers to see product samples. Permanent displays are maintained at Building Centres and there are regular trade displays at various locations in Britain during the year. They range from specialist trade association exhibitions to the national, biennial building exhibition at the National Exhibition Centre, Birmingham. Lists of current static and travelling displays are regularly published in *AJ* and *Building, RIBA Journal, Building Specification, Building Services Engineer, Current Information in the Construction Industry* and on *Prestel*.

CURRENT INFORMATION

Technology changes fast and it is essential to be up-to-date with new products, new practices and the performance-in-use of products, particularly in the light of the responsibility of the specifier for the satisfactory performance in the completed building of the product selected. Journals reviewing new products were discussed on p. 139. The newsheets in RIBA *Product Data* are an important source of information on current developments. The *AJ* series 'Products in Practice' provides detailed reviews of elements, materials and new developments. A regular survey of the contents of a broad range of journals is not easy to maintain in practice but the use of a service such as the PSA's *Current Information in the Construction Industry* or the DoE/DTP *Library Bulletin* will help to keep abreast of the journal literature before *Architectural Periodicals Index* comes out.

Some manufacturers are offering information services relating to problems which their products may cover. Dow Chemicals announced one such in the *AJ* (24 February 1982) covering insulation problems and especially foams. The service, based in Birmingham, says that if their products are not suitable they will aim to recommend an appropriate source. Others have already been announced, usually operated either by the very large firms or by the trade associations.

FEEDBACK INFORMATION

Some practices compile reference files showing how products used in a particular job performed as an aid to future specifying.

Michael Harries of Alex Gordon and Partners described such an information feedback system in *Industrialization Forum* (1971, No. 4, p. 25+). 'Feedback Information Sheets' were completed on site. He also made monthly, verbal, *ad hoc* requests for feedback from the architects in the practice. These were then integrated with product information in the CI/SfB library. It was found difficult to obtain the information, to classify it and to get it to individuals who did not necessarily refer to trade literature when specifying. Only when information was entered on the standard drawings and the information sheets were also filed with these did that information get used in further projects.

Feedback information should be used to prevent selection of products which have been found defective on previous occasions. Failures may be the result of an inadequate product, a product selected for use in a situation for which it was not designed, a faulty design or poor detailing work, of inadequate information or of cost-cutting, etc. The frightening expense of some failures, combined with recent changes in law and the risks of being sued, make it even more essential in the 1980s to be well informed and aware of new developments.

The BRE is well known for its extensive research and investigations into building failures. It publicized information showing that most, if not all, defects could have been avoided if available information had not been ignored or gone unnoticed. Feedback information in the form of Digests, Information Papers, Current Papers and Reports is published by the BRE. The most significant publications, however, are Defects News and Defects Action Sheets, which both commenced publication in 1982. These come from the new Housing Defects Prevention Unit and provide short, clear notes on specific problems. Most major and some minor failures are investigated by the BRE and reports on events like Ronan Point, the Summerland fire or the Manchester Woolworth's fire usually appear as *Current Papers*.

The *Development and Materials Bulletin* produced by the Materials Information Group of the Department of Architecture and Civic Design of the Greater London Council is printed on separate pages ready for filing with technical information (CI/SfB coded). This bulletin discusses and reports the GLC's own experience of products and services providing a kind of *Which?* guide for other users. It originated from their own efforts to get feedback from building-in-use to designers. It is now widely available and covers a large range of building types and materials.

The Property Services Agency collects feedback information. A selection is published in *Construction* with advice on ways to avoid future problems. The RIBA includes feedback in the 'Construction Notes' in *Product Data*. Some feedback is created as a result of the Agrément Board's work and its publications are discussed in *The Future of Agrément in the UK: The DoE Report of the Agrément Study Group* (HMSO, 1978).

The literature of 'failures' has increased rapidly in recent years, not just as articles but in titles like Scott's *Building Disasters and Failures* (Construction Press, 1975), the National Building Agency *Common Building Defects* (NBA, 1979), *Addleson's Building Failures: A Guide to Diagnosis, Remedy and Prevention* (Architectural Press, 1982). Eldridge's *Common Defects in Buildings* (HMSO, 1976) and BRE's *Building Failures* (research papers, reprinted by Construction Press, 1978) among others. *Building's* series of *Building Failures* sheets is now available in book form.

Though BRE/CIRIA have been cooperating on organizing a method of survey and in Europe a CIB Commission is considering an international data centre for information on building failures, it is the failure to apply internal office information which is of concern to most practices. In all cases it is essential that such performance feedback as is available is kept with or referred to in the trade and technical literature, otherwise it will not be used adequately. Designers will still tend to rely on their heads and those of colleagues.

THE FUTURE

As we look into the 1980s two innovations apear to have great development potential: the *Barbour Design Library (BDL)* and *Prestel*. Both are aimed at getting more current information to a wider audience. Many engineers already rely heavily on the Ti Services and BDL should develop in the same way. In 1976 the PSA reported in the *2nd Progress Report on Data Co-ordination* that the microfilming of trade catalogues for six hundred manufacturers was a means of solving its distribution problems. Microfilm is likely to be used increasingly to communicate this type of data.

In 1972–1973 Barbour Index Ltd reported on their experiment with a computerized product information service. It was not pursued. However, since then developments in computing technology, in particular in the multiple access to databases (see Chapter 4) and the advent of *Prestel* have made the further development of computer information retrieval systems likely. In the 1980s we may see the end of the trade literature collection as we know it. Provided that a centralized database can be developed then access from a network of terminals is feasible. Much of the present printed information is already produced by and is therefore available on computers. Multiple access is only a step away. As David Crawford pointed out as long ago as March 1976, in his survey of the availability and usefulness of catalogues to architects (reported in the *Architect*, 'Product Indexes', March 1976, pp. 31–33); 'Whatever else architects may be short of at times of recession such as the present they certainly cannot complain of any lack of product information services.'

In fact, after the above was drafted several developments along these lines were publicized. The Geneva and Frankfurt divisions of the Batelle Memorial Institute have offered *Buildata* to provide market information on building activities, the demand for products and services. Information will cover Britain, Belgium, France, Italy, Netherlands and West Germany for three years past and three years in advance. Shortly before this, *Building Design* (23 January, 1981) announced that the Building Centre was considering plans for a computerized information retrieval service based on the Centre's manufacturer files.

Standards

Today there are standards relating to every aspect of the building process. These have developed from the application of standards to housing design in rebuilding London after the Great Fire in 1666. In 1774 they were consolidated into the Building Act, and since then have been augmented by various local by-laws, the Public Health Acts of the nineteenth century and, since 1901, coordinated and developed by the British Standards Institution. During the twentieth century the process of standardization development and coordination has extended in many countries, in different ways, towards the wider approach of the European and International standardization movements. As international professional commitments increase so also must the architect's and contractor's awareness of other countries' standards, and the coordinating and rationalizing work of the standardizing bodies described below.

Standardization can be defined as 'the establishment, by authority, by custom, or by general consent, of rules, disciplines, techniques and other defined conditions which have to be followed to enable a society of particular sections of it to function smoothly and efficiently' (Mildren, 1976). As such, within the construction industry topics covered by standards include glossaries, dimensions and measurements, definitions and symbols, methods of test, quality, safety, performance and dimensional specifications, and methods of construction. This is a very wide range and all standards should conform to a familiar structure to enable the user to identify parts and content easily. The aims of standardization have been defined as

a) simplify the group variety of products and procedures in human life,
b) improve communication,
c) promote overall economy,
d) ensure safety, health and the protection of life,
e) protect consumer and community interest,
f) eliminate trade barriers. (BSO: Part 1: para. 3.4)

British standards

The use of standards was developed to prevent the recurrence of failures (e.g. the Great Fire) and is still seen as a means of at least minimizing failures. But the level of quality specified must be recognized for what it is, a minimum level which architects should study before writing standards into specifications (Vandenburg, 1976). Standards also represent a means of communicating with the professions, a vehicle for transmitting research results into practice (BSO: Part 3: 1974, para. 7.4). Standards do not have the force of law, although this is not always recognized. This may, however, be given to them by mention in statutory requirements, as, for example, in the two following statements from the Building Regulations, 1976;

> Section H6(2)(b) 'The balustrade shall be capable of resisting the appropriate load specified in table 3 of CP 3: Chapter V: Part 1: 1967'.
> Section C5(d) '. . . in accordance with the provisions of BS 3462: 1962 or BS 4072: 1974'.

The Public Health and Housing Acts, among others, may specify requirements in similar ways. Only then does a standard have legal force, and yet standards are very closely related to the regulations and need to provide adequate performance specifications if they are to be effective.

In Britain the British Standards Institution (BSI) is the main producer of standards and coordinates all European and International work in this country. Its work covers all the functions outlined above and is outlined in PD 4845: 1977 *The British Standards Institution – Its Activities and Organisation*. BSO: 1974: *A Standard for Standards*, also describes the work of BSI in standardization and the committee network through which all standards pass from inception and drafting towards final approval and publication. Essential to this work are the standards on drawing practice, alphabetical arrangement and SI units. All are presented in conformity with ISO grades and the BSI *Recommendations on Form and Content of British Standards*, 1980/10002. All committees are selected on a basis of expertise in the field and serviced by a secretariat from the Institution. Drafts are circulated to the professions for comment before finalization. This process generates publications with the prefix DD, Drafts for Development, as well as a few of the PDs, a miscellaneous series of publications. The main sequence of publications is prefixed BS followed by number, section, date and title. The only exceptions to this practice are the Automobile (AU), Marine (MA) and Aerospace (A, B,) standards series. Therefore all British Standards publications are immediately recognizable by their unique alphanumeric code – as are those of other countries (see below).

All standards are listed in the annual *BSI Yearbook* which is supplemented bi-monthly by the *Sales Bulletin*, available free to members, and to non-members at £14 in 1981. A numerical list gives full title, date and a brief description of each standard. This is supplemented by a subject index based mainly on titles. Amendments are noted, giving length and price group, as well as recently withdrawn standards and an indication of those endorsed in other countries. All are available from the Sales Office. Currently (1981) prices range from the total of £64 for CP 110 to £5 for CP 3: Chapter IV, but there are few standards left at these lower prices, and recently comments have been made that cost is inhibiting purchase by industry of the standards required (Vandenburg, 1976). It should also be noted that the CP prefix is being phased out, and all new editions are incorporated into the BS series, for example, BS 5250: 1975 *Code for Basic Data for the Design of Buildings: the Control of Condensation in Dwellings*. Reprints of CPs now receive a BS number when reprinted. *Barbour Design Library* now includes a direct reference to this in the index, e.g. CP 211 is now BS 5492. Services are listed in the *BSI Yearbook* also and these include the provision of sets of standards as required by the Building Regulations, England and Wales, at £400 and Scotland at £840 (in 1981). The scope and staffing of BSI is described, as well as the quality assurance schemes, the library, translation and educational services, etc.

Availability of standards is important, and the BSI maintains a full library and information service. Official national and international standards are held there and enquiries can be made by telephone. The *Yearbook* also lists complete reference sets in UK towns (and overseas). However, the BSI does not hold semi-official or industry standards.

156 Trade literature, technical information and standards

All practices should have copies of the free sectional lists covering: Building, arranged in CI/SfB orders is No. 16; Electrical Engineering, No. 26; and Heating, Ventilating, Air Cooling and Refrigeration, No. 42. Most architects will also be familiar with the ring-bound, BS Handbook 3, *Building Materials and Components*. This contains summaries of 1350 construction standards with varying degrees of detail, sometimes rendering it unnecessary to buy the original document. Sixty per cent of the summaries are in sufficient detail for drawings, specifications and BQs. The rest are briefer, because they are of restricted interest or could not be summarized – this applies to most CPs. The three volumes cost £150 in 1981, including a one-year up-dating service which costs £60 thereafter. The content and presentation was heavily criticized on its reappearance (*AJ*, 26 July 1978) after the cessation of publication in 1975, but many were content to see the return of a valuable tool, even if there were criticisms on presentation. Indexes indicate summaries added, lost and revised since the 1975 edition (the last in bound format) as well as providing the traditional subject, Ci/SfB and numerical listings. Other relevant handbooks are now being published which depart from former policy in that their content is not entirely standards, for example, Handbook 21, *Building in London* (1981), containing the entire text of the London building by-laws, which will be followed by Handbook 20, *Building in England and Wales*, containing summaries of the BS specifications mentioned in the Building Regulations. In 1982 Handbook 22, *Quality Assurance* will be published.

The monthly *BSI News* should be used by all professionals to note the new issues and amendment notes. It is the main source of information on new standards. Fortunately for most professionals many journals also publish selective lists of relevant new standards. *Building* lists all new standards once a month as do *AJ* and other specialist journals (see appropriate sections below). Many also carry reports on significant new standards or amendments. The RIBA *Product Data* also notes new ones and both here, in *Specification* and in the *Barbour Design Library* will be found lists of standards relevant to any aspect of construction and materials, giving parts as well as whole standards, unlike the *Yearbook*. These are therefore more reliable sources of specific standards information. Also significant is the monthly *Worldwide List of Published Standards*. In this the BSI lists in UDC order all new British and overseas standards added to their library.

A BRE Design Division team reported to BSI in early 1982 on the presentation and use of standards. The survey commented upon the complex language and dull presentation of British

Trade literature, technical information and standards 157

Standards as well as the number of out-of-date copies found in offices. The high prices were cited as a factor decreasing usage. In future we may see attractive 'packages' of information if the recommendations are implemented (see *Building*, 23 April 1982).

Performance of products and components is important in any process. Quality characteristics and levels of performance are increasingly being specified in such a way as to allow the use and introduction of new techniques, for example, in BS 4873: 1972, *Aluminium Alloy Windows*, requirements are given for materials, component parts, sizes and tolerances, glazing, security and safety with specified performance tests to accommodate climatic conditions in various parts of the country. Testing is also done by the BSI in its laboratories as part of the Quality Assurance Scheme described in the *Businessman's Guide to the KITEMARK Scheme*.

The appearance of the Kitemark symbol or the BSI safety symbol on a product shows that it has been independently tested and approved by BSI according to the relevant standard and that the quality of production has been inspected by BSI. All manufacturers are listed in the annual *Buyer's Guide* with an alphabetical list of the products licensed to bear the symbols. The British Electrotechnical Approvals Board operates a similar scheme and the BEAB symbol also appears on certified, tested products. The shortened BEAB symbol also appears beside any BS summary in Handbook 3 where it has been awarded. A list is available from the BEAB.

Quality testing is closely linked to standardization and to the work of the Agrément Board. There are also other testing laboratories in Britain. A number of these are listed in *House's Guide to the Construction Industry* and include the well-established National Physical Laboratory, parts of the DoE, the PSA civil engineering laboratory and the BRE facilities. There is, however, no national body as in France and West Germany. However, in 1966 the Agrément Board was set up by the government and it now operates in close conjunction with the BRE and the BSI. Originating from the French system of appraisals, its work is expected to be 'accurate and unbiased in giving an independent assessment of materials, products, components and processes' for their performance in use. In France all public works contracts must use Agrément-certified products. The system is based on experience and the development of simulative testing with close inspection of manufacturers' quality control. In the UK the status of the Board is becoming accepted and, despite the recommendations of the Bennett Report (1978) that it should be merged with BSI, its continued independence into the 1980s has been assured.

The Agrément Board tests individual products for manufacturers on payment of a fee. Ten per cent of products fail and 30 per cent are found deficient in some way which is usually remedied before further marketing. The successful products are given a certificate valid for two years, subject to re-testing. These certificates give details of the product, its marketing, its use, the opinion on its assessment, its acceptability under the building regulations and a technical description of its handling and performance. The technical background to these details is set out in MOATS (Methods of Assessment and Test Specifications) and Information Sheets, although where the European Union of Agrément (UEAtc) already has Methods of Test and Assessment these are used. UEAtc also confirms or re-issues certificates in other countries. The scheme is described in the Board's publication *Assessment of Products for the Construction Industry* (1975) and by A. E. Crocker in the 1978 edition of *Specification* (**5,** 187). A list of assessed products and new certificates is found in *Specification*, RIBA *Product Data*, *AJ*, *Building*, the *Architect*, *What's New in Building* and other specialist journals and in the Agrément's Board's own *Newsletter* and publications index volume.

European standards

In his first article in the now established R & D series in *Building* (14 March 1978) George Atkinson surveyed the situation of the

Agrément Board in the light of European practices. Europe also takes part in the wider net of international standardization. However, two years later, the pages of the same journal lamented that there is still very little acceptance 'of other . . . national standards' in the EEC, (19 September 1980, p. 34) and showed the results of some comparative work with American Standards. Such work is essential where overseas contracts are concerned. The BSI offer not only advice and help with foreign standards, including translations, but also assistance with correspondence on American and other standards to professionals through the Technical Help for Exporters service (THE).

The EEC and EFTA countries belong to the European Committee for Standardisation (CEN) to establish common standards. Most of these originate with the ISO (see below), the European Committee for Electrotechnical Standardization (CENELUC) and its Electronic Components Committee (CECC). An agreed standard is prefixed EN and members are obliged to publish or endorse it as a national standard within six months. CENELUC is stricter and members must publish. All these are listed in the *BSI Yearbook* with their BS number or notes of equivalents; many relate to building, e.g. EN 59 and EN 63 on aspects of GRP.

International standards

BSI authorizes the use of all the above and the ISO standards by publication as UK Standards. All are listed in the *Yearbook*. The International Standards Organization (ISO) itself was set up in 1947 after a number of years working towards international cooperation. Progress has been slow in securing agreement on the range of international standards but the development of multinational companies in the 1960s and the growth of overseas work has strengthened the movement. A draft standard is prepared and discussed among the member institutions, by committee, until agreement is reached. The trend towards internationalization is increasing in an effort to unify the many diverse practices, although acceptance is not universal. For example, ISO 6240: 1980: *Performance Standards in Building – Contents and Presentation* was criticized as 'confused and limited' (Martin, 1980). Conformity may also then be limited.

Other countries

A few countries are sufficiently important for their standards work to be briefly described here. A detailed list of countries giving reference codes and publications will be found in Mildren (1976, pp. 105–109).

UNITED STATES STANDARDS

The American National Standards Institute (ANSI) is not a publisher like BSI but a clearing-house for standards publications, maintaining a library of standards from around fifty other countries and publishing a number of listings of American Standards: the annual *Catalog*, a bi-monthly *Listing of New and Revised American National Standards,* a quarterly *Magazine of Standards* and a bi-weekly magazine, *Standards Action.*

The American Society for Testing and Materials (ASTM) also produces standards which are listed in the *Annual Book of ASTM Standards* with an index, in 48 parts in 1981. The sheer volume of standards sometimes makes identification difficult. The annual *List of Publications* covers all other types of ASTM publication, the bi-monthly *Journal of Testing and Evaluation* reports research, while the monthly *ASTM Standardization News* lists additional standards.

There are many other societies concerned with the production of standards in the USA of which the next largest is the National Bureau of Standards. There are also government standards, mainly defence, both of which are listed in either the *Guide to Specifications and Standards of the Federal Government* (1963) with its monthly cumulative supplements, or the Defense Department's *Index of Specifications and Standards*, also with a cumulative supplement, bi-monthly. In Britain the most comprehensive listing of these, other than the BSI library holdings and its *Worldwide List of Published Standards*, is the microfilm service from Technical Indexes Ltd covering all standards from ANSI, ASTM (both of which have construction subgroups), ASCE, ASHRAE, IEEE and NFPA among twenty-eight institutions in the USA. This service also includes other countries.

GERMAN STANDARDS

The Deutsches Institut Für Normung e.V. indentifies its standards with the letters DIN. These are kept and listed comprehensively at BSI. *Catalogue of DIN Standards* lists them annually with *DIN Mitteilungen* up-dating it bi-monthly.

FRENCH STANDARDS

NF Standards are issued by the Association Française de Normalisation (AFNOR) and listed in *Catalogues of French Standards*, the monthly *Bulletin mensuel de la Normalisation Française* and the bi-monthly *Courier de la Normalisation*. French standards

Figure 8.2 (Other countries producing standards specifications)

Country	Title of Organization	Abbreviation	Prefix to standards	Publications
Australia	Standards Association of Australia	SAA	AS	*Annual List of Publications* *Annual Report* *Monthly Information Sheet*
Austria	Österreichisches Normungsinstitut	ÖN	ÖNORM	*Ö Norm* (monthly bulletin) *Annual Catalogue of Standards*
Belgium	Institut Belge de Normalisation	IBN	NBN	*Annual Report* *Annual Catalogue of IBN Standards* *Revue IBN* (monthly journal)
Brazil	Associação Brasileira de Normas Técnicas	ABNT	ABNT	*Boletin* (bi-monthly journal) *ABNT Standards* (in volume form)
Bulgaria	Comité de la Qualité, de la Normalisation et de la Métrologie	KKCM	BDS	*Monthly Bulletin* listing State Standards, approved Amendments to Standards, etc.
Canada	Standards Council of Canada	CSA	CSA	*Standards/Canada* (bi-monthly journal) *CSA Quarterly Review*
Chile	Instituto Nacional de Investigaciones Tecnologicas y Normalización	INDITECNOR	INDITECNOR	*Revista Chilena de Racionalización*
Colombia	Instituto Colombiano de Normas Técnicas	ICONTEC	ICONTEC	*Monthly News Bulletin*
Cuba	Dirección de Normas y Metrologia Ministerio de Industrias	NC	UNC	*NC Bulletin* (issued bi-monthly)
Czechoslovakia	Ufad pro normalizaci a měřěni	CSN	CSN	*Normalizace* (a monthly periodical) *Měrová technika* (a monthly periodical)

162 *Trade literature, technical information and standards*

Figure 8.2 (continued)

Country	Title of Organization	Abbreviation	Prefix to standards	Publications
Denmark	Dansk Standardiseringsraad	DS	DS	*Danish Technical Review* (issued monthly) *Standard NYT* (monthly) *Annual Report* *List of Danish Standards* (issued bi-annually)
Finland	Suomen Standardisoimislitto r.y.	SFS	SFS	*SFS Tiedotus* (a bulletin issued monthly) *SFS Standards* (issued annually)
Greece	Ministry of National Economy	NHS	ENO	An announcement on the publication of each Standard appears in the national press
Hungary	Magyar Szabványügyi Hivatal	MSZH	MSZ	*Lists of Standards* (issued from time to time)
India	Indian Standards Institution	ISI	IS	*ISI Bulletin* (issued monthly) *Standards – Monthly Additions* *Annual Report*
Indonesia	Jajassan 'Dana Normalisasi Indonesia'	DNI	NI	*Berita DNI* (bi-monthly periodical)
Iran	Institute of Standards and Industrial Research of Iran	ISIRI	ISIRI	*ISIRI Bulletin* (issued from time to time)
Iraq	Iraqi Organization for Standards Planning Board	IOS	IOS	*Bulletin* (issued quarterly)
Ireland	Institute for Industrial Research and Standards	IIRS	IS	*Monthly Journal* *Irish Standards Yearbook* (issued periodically) *Annual Report*
Israel	Standards Institution of Israel	SII	SI	*Quarterly Journal* *Catalogue of Israel Standards* (issued annually)

Country	Organization	Abbr.	Publications
Italy	Ente Nazionale Italiano di Unificazione	UNI	*Unificazione* (issued quarterly) *List of UNI Standards* (issued periodically)
Japan	Japanese Industrial Standards Committee Ministry of International Trade and Industry	JISC	
Democratic Republic of Korea	Committee for Standardization of the Democratic People's Republic of Korea	CSK	*Standardization Bulletin* (issued bi-monthly) *Standards Announcements* (issued bi-monthly)
Republic of Korea	Korean Bureau of Standards	KBS	*Quality Control* (monthly bulletin)
Lebanon	Lebanese Standards Institution	LIBNOR	
Malaysia	Standards Institution of Malaysia	SIM	*SIM Standard Yearbook* *Annual Report* *SIM News* (to be issued at regular intervals)
Mexico	Dirección General de Normas	DGN	*Catalogue of Standards* *Annual Report*
Netherlands	Nederlands Normalisatie-Instituut	NNI	*Normalisatie* (issued monthly) *Catalogue of Standards*
New Zealand	Standards Association of New Zealand	SANZ	*Monthly Newsletter* *NZ Quarterly Bulletin* *Index of NZ Standards* (issued annually)
Nigeria	Nigerian Standards Organization	NSO	*List of Industrial Standards* (issued periodically)
Norway	Norges Standardiseringsforbund	NSF	*Annual Report* *Catalogue of Norwegian Standards* (issued annually) *Standardisering* (quarterly bulletin)

Figure 8.2 (continued)

Country	Title of Organization	Abbreviation	Prefix to standards	Publications
Pakistan	Pakistan Standards Institution	PSI	PS	*PSI Standards Bulletin* (issued quarterly) *Annual Report*
Peru	Instituto de Investigación Tecnológica	ITINTEC	INANTIC	
Philippines	Bureau of Standards of the Philippines	KP	PTS	
Poland	Polski Komitet Normalizacji i Miar	PKNIM	PN	*Normalizacja* (issued monthly) *Biuletyn PKN* (official bulletin of the *PKNIM* (issued monthly) *Catalogue of Polish Standards (PN)* *Catalogue of Industrial Standards (BN)* (issued from time to time)
Portugal	Repartição de Normalização	IGPAI	NP	*Standardization Bulletin* *Catalogue of Portuguese Standards* Index cards on definitive Portuguese Standards
Romania	Institutul Român de Standardizare	IRS	STAS	*Standardizarea* (issued monthly)
Singapore	Singapore Institute of Standards and Industrial Research	SISIR		
South Africa	South African Bureau of Standards	SABS	SABS	*Standards Bulletin* (issued monthly) *Annual Report* *Yearbook of SABS Standards and Codes of Practice*
Spain	Instituto Nacional de Racionalización y Normalización	IRANOR	UNE	*Racionalización* (issued bi-monthly)

Trade literature, technical information and standards 165

Country	Organization	Abbr.	Publications
Sri Lanka	Bureau of Ceylon Standards	BCS	
Sweden	Sveriges Standardiserings-kommission	SIS	*Catalogue of Swedish Standards*, with titles in Swedish and English (issued annually) *SIS-nytt* (*SIS News*) (issued monthly)
Switzerland	Association Suisse de Normalisation	SNV	*VSM/SNV Standards Bulletin* (issued monthly)
Thailand	Centre for Thai National Standard Specifications	CTNSS	*CTNSS Annual Report*
Turkey	Türk Standardiari Enstitüsü	TSE	*Standard* (magazine issued monthly) *Catalogue of Turkish Standards* (issued from time to time)
United Arab Republic	Egyptian Organization for Standardization	EOS	*UAR Standards Bulletin* (issued bi-monthly in Arabic and English *Standards Yearbook in Arabic and English* (with yearly supplements)
Venezuela	Comisión Venezolana de Normas Industriales	COVENIN	
Yugoslavia	Jugoslovenski zavod za Standardizaciju	JZS	*Standardization* (issued monthly) *Catalogue of Yugoslav Standards* (issued annually)

Standards organizations have also been formed in the following countries:
Cameroons   Direction de l'Industrie (Service de normalisation)
Ecuador   Instituto Ecuatoriaro de Normalización
Ivory Coast Bureau Ivoirien de Normalisation
Jamaica   The Bureau of Standards
Jordan   Directorate of Standards, Ministry of National Economy
Kenya   Kenya Bureau of Standards
Malawi   Malawi Bureau of Standards
Saudi Arabia Saudi Arabian Standards Organization

have been available on-line since 1976, through a service called *NORIANE*.

OTHER STANDARDS

The numerous countries producing standards publications are listed briefly in *Figure 8.2*. The range of groupings offered by Technical Indexes Ltd (Ti), in addition to the BSI and Defence Standards gives an idea of those considered to be of major importance: Japanese, Canadian and German standards (the latter only in English translation) as well as ISO and NATO standards with Euronorms and EEC technical directives.

Discussion on the publication of standards will be found in more detail in the publications given below. International standards, European standards and some other countries' standards may be obtained from the BSI Sales Office, but not all are held in stock and there may be delays. Delays are also inevitable when purchasing standards direct from the offices of standards institutions abroad. Selective foreign standards are held at some major public libraries and may be consulted there. The British Library may also be able to obtain copies once the reference numbers of those required have been identified. The BSI Library has lists to consult for identification purposes and discussions are in progress on the content and feasibility of an on-line databank of British standards information.

Bibliography

Bullivant, D. (1977). 'The improvement on manufacturers' trade literature to BS 4940: 1973', Paper J6 in *Construction Research International*, K. Alsop (ed.), Vol. 1, Lancaster, Construction Press

Goodey, J. and Matthew, K. (1971). *Architects and Information*. Institute of Advanced Architectural Studies (Research paper No. 1)

Grogan, D. (1976). *Science and Technology : An Introduction to the Literature*, 3rd rev. edn, Bingley, Chapter 16

Martin, B. (1971). *Standards and Building*, RIBA Publications

Mildren, K. (ed.) (1976). *Use of Engineering Literature*, Butterworths

Rogers, C. (1974). 'The handling of trade catalogues in the PSA library service', *CIIG Bulletin*, **4**(1)

Vandenburg, M. (10 Nov. 1976). 'BSI: 75th anniversary', *Architects' Journal*, 877–878

Volbeda, A. (1977). 'Can we harmonise product files?' *Building Research and Practice*, **11/12**, 35

Woodward, C. D. (1972). *B.S.I.: The Story of Standards*, BSI

9
Government publications, legislation and statistics
Charles Rogers

Government publishing

For the past hundred years or so the major role of HMSO has been to act on behalf of Parliament and government departments as the central publishing agency of information which those authorities determined should be put on sale to the public. The exceptions to this general rule are the publications of the Patent Office and certain national museums and galleries, Ordnance Survey maps, Admiralty charts and hydrographic publications. Crown Copyright in all published material is vested in the Controller of the Stationery Office by Letters Patent. The Stationery Office prints and publishes, by direction, whatever is required for the conduct of parliamentary business; it accepts, by agreement, material from government departments for which publication is considered necessary in fulfillment of their obligations and responsibilities to the public. These obligations and responsibilities include making available information on government policy (departmental circulars, for example), information required by industry, commerce and the professions which is only available from official sources (statistics, for example), disseminating the results of research and development work, and providing advice and information, especially where there is an express or implied statutory duty to do so (advisory leaflets, guidance notes on official regulations, for example).

Although the Stationery Office does not commission manuscripts or suggest subjects for possible publications, it has since the

1920s scrutinized the texts passed to it for printing for their own use by government departments to see if any could be published for sale and thus earn some profit to offset costs. At the same time it has always been very aware of the close watch kept on its activities by commercial publishers, and so its official policy has been restrictive. The Stationery Office was founded in 1786 as a central supply organization and the role of government publisher and bookseller was not fully assumed until late in the nineteenth century. (The historical facts in this section are taken with permission from an unpublished Stationery Office document.) Parliamentary papers, which had been on sale since 1836, became the responsibility of the Stationery Office around the same period. In spite of this care not to compete with private enterprise, the appearance in 1939 of *The Principles of Modern Building, Volume I*, written by Robert Fitzmaurice of the Building Research Station – undoubtedly the best-regarded government publication ever produced in the field of construction – led to a protest from the commercial publishing world. A similar protest that the government was encroaching upon commercial publishing territory was made nearly twenty years later about the Ministry of Housing and Local Government book *Flats and Houses 1958*.

The past hundred years have seen a phenomenal growth in the scale of government publishing, reflecting the increasing interest of the state in social and economic life and in science and technology. At the end of the nineteenth century there were about a thousand official, i.e. non-parliamentary, publications, a figure which increased sixfold in the next sixty years. Today between ten and twelve thousand separate items of all kinds are published each year and there are more than 70 000 items currently in print. There are currently about 500 non-parliamentary publications of potential interest to the construction industry available from the Stationery Office.

The past few years have seen changes in the pattern of government publishing and in the availability of documents from government departments. The Stationery Office has been less inclined to publish for departments those items judged to be unprofitable, and such items have often been published and sold by the departments themselves. Also many publications which were formerly issued free by departments are now priced. The move, uncertain though it is, towards what is known as 'open government', which was given a fillip by the Croham Directive (Kellner, 1980), has meant that more documents previously reserved for internal use only are available for purchase from government departments. The problems of bibliographical control and other problems associated with non-HMSO departmental publishing are receiving attention (Rogers, 1980).

Until April 1980 government printing and publishing were financed by the Stationery Office from money voted to it by Parliament. This 'allied service' arrangement has now ceased and each department repays the Stationery Office for the work carried out on its behalf (Thimont, 1981). This change in the relationship between departments and the Stationery Office may have significant consequences in the future. Because the Stationery Office has become commercial in its operations a greater proportion of publications might well be handled by the departments themselves, although the total number of publications will most likely decrease.

It is impossible to give here a full account of all the publications relevant to architecture and building produced by government departments, but attention can be drawn to some important series and a few individual titles. The guides for tracing both HMSO and departmentally published items are described below, but readers unacquainted with the wide range of government publishing might look through the highly selective, briefly annotated list of recent titles from HMSO given in the free booklet *Architecture and Building* (HMSO, 1981, periodically revised).

The various parts of the Department of the Environment are responsible for a large proportion of the official publications on architecture and building. The Building Research Establishment, which comprises the Building Research Station, the Fire Research Station and the Princes Risborough Laboratory (formerly the Forest Products Research Laboratory), has a publishing programme of interest to practical designers and builders as well as to research workers. The BRE *Digests*, published monthly by HMSO, have as their main aim, as seen by BRE itself, 'to make recommendations in the language of the construction industry to assist in the application of the findings of research'. About 150 of the present series are in print; issues are allowed to go out of print or are withdrawn because they have been superseded by new editions, because they are obsolete or for other reasons. Four volumes of BRE *Digests* have been republished by the commercial publishers Construction Press. The four volumes (all second edition, 1977) cover Building Construction, Building Defects and Maintenance, Building Materials and Services and Environmental Engineering.

Papers written by BRE staff, mainly those presented at conferences and meetings or published in journals, are available free from the Establishment in a series of *Current Papers*. During 1979 a new series of *Information Papers*, also free, was introduced with the aim of presenting BRE research results in a more readily usable and compact form (i.e. not exceeding four A4 pages). As a result, fewer *Current Papers* are now published. Those *Current Papers* considered to be long-lasting and of international significance have been brought together in eight edited and indexed volumes published by Construction Press (1978): 1—*Concrete*, 2—*Fibre, Reinforced Materials*, 3—*Foundations and Soil Technology*, 4—*Energy, Heating and Thermal Comfort*, 5—*Building Failure*, 6—*Dams and Enbankments*, 7—*Wind and Snow Loading* and 8—*Fire Control*. BRE papers published in journals only are listed in the BRE *Annual Reports* (HMSO).

BRE's Overseas Division issues publications aimed to help the construction activities of developing countries. The *Overseas Building Notes* are prepared principally for housing, building and planning authorities in countries receiving technical assistance from the British government. A limited number of copies are available free from the Division to those with a professional interest in building overseas. A selection of *Overseas Building Notes* have been republished in a volume entitled *Building in Hot Climates* (HMSO, 1980). The book is divided into the three broad categories of materials, construction and design; there is also a list of building research centres and similar organizations throughout the world.

Some issues of former series, such as the *Fire Research Notes*, FPRL *Technical Notes* and *Timber Papers* are still available from the Building Research Establishment. Information which would have been published in these series now appears in the present BRE series or in technical journals.

Major BRE contributions to construction literature are published as individual BRE Reports (which, in effect, continue the fine earlier series of *Post-war Building Studies* and *National Building Studies*). Most of these reports are of direct value to designers, for example, the information on climatic and other conditions in *Climate and Building in Britain* by R. E. Lacey (HMSO, 1977), *Availability of Daylight* by D. R. G. Hunt (BRE, 1979), *Wind Environment Round Buildings* by A. D. Penwarden and A. F. E. Wise (HMSO, 1975) and *Driving-rain Index* by R. E. Lacey (HMSO, 1976). Libraries for designers should also include *Colour Co-ordination Handbook* by H. L. Gloag and Mary Gold (HMSO, 1978), *Solar Heating Systems for the UK: Design, Installation and Economic Aspects* by S. J. Wozniak (HMSO, 1979), *Results of Fire Resistance Tests on Elements of Building Construction* by R. W. Fisher and P. M. T. Smart (HMSO, 2 vols, 1975 and

1977). *Results of Surface Spread of Flame Tests on Building Products* by R. W. Fisher and Barbara R. W. Rogowski (HMSO, 1976), *Design of Normal Concrete Mixes* by D. C. Teychenne, R. E. Franklin and H. C. Erntroy (HMSO, 1975, reprinted 1979) and the standard works *Handbook of Hardwoods* (HMSO, 1972, reprinted 1977), *Handbook of Softwoods* (HMSO, 1957, reprinted metric edition, 1977) and *Decay of Timber and its Prevention* by K. St G. Cartwright and W. P. K. Findlay (HMSO, second edition, reprinted 1976). The standard work, originated by Robert Fitzmaurice over forty years ago, is *Principles of Modern Building*, in two volumes and frequently revised. Volume 1 deals with the building as a whole and walls, partitions and chimneys (HMSO, latest reprint 1975) and Volume 2 deals with floors and roofs (HMSO, latest reprint 1973). A facsimile reprint of the 1932 edition of R. J. Schaffer's *The Weathering of Natural Building Stones*, still the most authoritative and comprehensive work on the subject, was published by BRE in 1972. It excludes Appendix II, which has been replaced by new material on the external cleaning of buildings and colourless treatments for masonry.

The Property Services Agency (a part of the Department of the Environment) is responsible for the provision of buildings and other construction work for the civil and defence departments of government. Many of its publications give technical and pricing information to contractors and consultants undertaking government work. The Method of Building (MOB) publications are a series of technical guides mainly on building components (PSA Library Sales Office). The PSA Standard Specifications on mechanical and electrical installations (published by HMSO and PSA) are used widely in the construction industry generally. Pricing information is available in the *Monthly Bulletin of Construction Indices* covering building works, engineering works and specialist engineering installations separately (HMSO), the *Schedule of Rates for Building Works 1980* (HMSO, 1981) and the specialist schedules, and other publications such as the *Estimating Handbook for Building Maintenance* (PSA). All the important PSA internal guidance and instruction documents on energy conservation are on sale to the industry at large. The quarterly journal *Construction* (from 1981, No. 35, published by B & M Publications (London) Ltd, Croydon) contains authoritative articles based on PSA experience. The journal includes *Feedback Digest* which reports PSA experience gained during the life-cycle of buildings; defects are analysed and solutions given. The PSA volume *Common Defects in Buildings* by H. J. Eldridge (HMSO, 1976) is a pioneer work in this field.

Government departments produce series of bulletins, notes, memoranda, papers and studies which provide guidance for those concerned with the design and construction of particular building types. These publications also contain much information of wider interest to those with responsibilities for building and the environment. The Department of the Environment series on housing and the environment include *Design Bulletins* (HMSO), *Area Improvement Notes* (HMSO) and the Housing Development Directorate (HDD) *Occasional Papers* (HMSO). For Scotland, the Scottish Development Department issues a series of separate Bulletins which together make up the *Scottish Building Handbook* (HMSO). The Department of Health and Social Security publishes the series *Health Building Notes* (HMSO), *Hospital Design Notes* (HMSO), *Health Equipment Notes* (HMSO) and *Hospital Technical Memoranda* (HMSO). The Architects and Building Branch of the Department of Education and Science series on school and college building consist of *Building Bulletins* (HMSO), *Design Notes* (DES), *A & B Papers* (DES A & B Branch) and *LIU Papers* (DES, Laboratories Investigation Unit).

Two volumes compiled from *Design Bulletins* originally published by HMSO have been published by Construction Press: *Housing the Family* (1974) and *Housing the Elderly* (second edition, 1978). Non-official monographs sometimes contain guidance on official publications, for example Anthea Tinker's *The Elderly in Modern Society* (Longman, 1981) is based on her work in the Department of the Environment's Housing Development Directorate and includes a comprehensive survey of relevant official publications.

Catalogues and lists of official publications

The original attitude of the Stationery Office was that its duty was done if its methods enabled anyone to buy government publications if they went to some trouble to do so. There was no attempt to capture customers until the 1920s, although direct selling to the public through its own bookshops began a few years earlier. The setting up of the bookshops highlighted the need for sales catalogues to replace existing inadequate lists. The computer-based catalogues issued today remain essentially sales tools.

The Stationery Office issues daily, weekly, monthly and annual lists of its publications. Most of the new government publications of any importance to the construction industry are listed at frequent intervals in the professional and trade journals,

Architects' Journal and *Building* for instance. The Stationery Office sectional lists are particularly useful. These lists, revised each year and issued free, are generally restricted to giving details of the in-print non-parliamentary publications of individual departments or, exceptionally, on one subject. Sectional list 61 covers the publications on Construction of the Department of the Environment (including the Building Research Establishment and the Property Services Agency) and other relevant departments. Other Department of the Environment publications are listed in sectional list 5. Details of selected new government publications are put up daily on the *Prestel* viewdata system.

There are several sources for details of the publications issued and sold by the departments themselves. An annual list has been produced since 1971 by the combined Environment and Transport Library Service of all the available departmental (including BRE and PSA) publications, both HMSO and non-HMSO, issued during the year. The Property Services Agency Library issues a catalogue periodically called *PSA in Print* (HMSO, 1980–) which lists all its available publications. The *Information Directory*, issued free each year from the Building Research Establishment, lists all the BRE publications, films and slides packages still current. The quarterly *BRE News* (free) updates the *Information Directory*. Other government departments issue lists either of all their available publications or of their new publications only. For example, all the official publications on health and safety are listed in the annual catalogue of the Health and Safety Executive (HMSO); official publications on farm buildings, fences, hedges, roads, drainage and water supply are listed in the Ministry of Agriculture, Fisheries and Food's departmental catalogue (free from MAFF); details of the official publications issued during the year by the five Scottish departments are brought together in the Scottish Office publications list (free from Scottish Office Library, Edinburgh); and a list of all the Department of Education and Science A & B Branch publications in print can be obtained from the Branch. These departmental lists, except for those issued by BRE and PSA, give basic details and prices only and there are no descriptive annotations to guide selection.

A free list of bibliographical sources of British official publications is available from the British Library's Official Publications Library. The much larger *Directory of British Official Publications: A Guide to Sources* (Mansell, 1981) was compiled by Stephen Richard of the Bodleian Library, Oxford, from returns from government departments. For keeping regularly up-to-date on government publications on building design and construction use might be made of the fortnightly *Current Information in the Construction Industry* and the edited and expanded six-monthly cumulation *Construction References* (both on subscription from PSA Library) and for planning, housing and environmental matters generally the fortnightly *DoE/DTp Library Bulletin* (on subscription from DoE/DTp Library Services).

There is no likelihood in the foreseeable future of a comprehensive catalogue of the non-departmental publications being issued regularly by an official body. The commercial publishing firm Chadwyck-Healey Ltd of Cambridge (Somerset House, Teaneck, NJ in the USA) published a *Catalogue of British Official Publications not Published by HMSO*, beginning with the annual volume for 1980. Thereafter bi-monthly issues (Issue 1, 1981 onwards) will be cumulated into an annual volume. The catalogue includes the publications of most government departments as well as other official and quasi-official bodies. Most of the publications listed in the *Catalogue* will be available for purchase on microfiche from Chadwyck-Healey either as single publications or in subject groups. The subject groups include Environment, Energy and Natural Resources, Health and Safety, Construction Industry and Housing and Planning. The database of the *Catalogue* is designed for on-line searching by subscribers in the future.

Statutes and other legislative information

As has recently been pointed out (Marsh, 1979), the Ten Commandments were straightforward to the point of being blunt but the diffuse and complex nature of British society today requires many thousands of pages of legislative writing to keep it in order. There are more than one hundred and fifty Acts of Parliament (excluding all the Local Acts) concerning such matters as the design and construction of particular building types, arbitration, clean air, boundaries, contracts, employment, the environment, fire, health and safety, historic buildings, insurance, land, landscape, light, management, negligence, planning, pollution, rights of way, sanitation, valuation and value added tax. In addition there are all the official Regulations, Orders, Circulars, Memoranda and guidance notes stemming from the Acts as well as the unofficial legal commentaries, and descriptive, explanatory and critical books, pamphlets and journal articles. The language and logic of legislation is not always easy to follow and recourse to an authoritative explanation and commentary on particular legal matters is to be recommended. The title of an Act is no guide to its application or relevance: the requirement, for example, that all new buildings to which the public are admitted shall, wherever reasonable and practicable, be provided with means of access for disabled people is, along with other building requirements, in the Chronically Sick and Disabled Persons Act 1970 and the Disabled Persons Act 1981, a fact which is not immediately evident.

The processes by which ideas for governing the country become law can be long and complicated and give rise to a variety of published documents. Generally speaking, there is a preliminary stage which may involve publications such as the reports of Royal Commissions, Select Committees of Parliament, Departmental, Advisory and Consultative Committees or other groups, Green Papers providing for public discussion and White Papers expressing the government's intentions. These may be published as Command papers, House of Commons (or House of Lords) Papers or, in some cases, as non-parliamentary publications. A piece of legislation is drafted as a Bill and its numbered provisions are Clauses which can be amended as the Bill moves through Parliament. After the third reading, in the usual case of an ordinary government Bill, it is sent to the House of Lords, where it can be subject to further amendment, and then returned to the Commons. Finally it receives the Royal Assent. A Bill which is passed becomes an Act and its Clauses become sections. The debates in Parliament are published in the daily, weekly and sessional *Parliamentary Debates (Hansard)*.

Many Acts give rise to what is known as subordinate or secondary legislation. Under the powers given them by an Act, Ministers of the Crown make detailed rules and regulations and these are published, in most cases, as Statutory Instruments (SIs). These were called Statutory Rules and Orders (SR & Os) until 1947 and are still called Statutory Rules in Northern Ireland. Government departments send out Circulars to local authorities and these draw attention to legislative changes and give related guidance and information. The tendency towards interdependence between Statutory Instruments (and the Acts themselves) and official and quasi-official publications should be noted. The *Building Regulations 1976* (made principally under the Public Health Acts), published as SI 1976: No. 1676, cite British Standards and Codes of Practice. The Control of Noise Order (SI 1975: No. 2115) designates British Standard 5228: 1975 *Control of Noise on Construction Sites* as the Code of Practice to be followed. Christopher Penn in his monograph *Noise Control* (Shaw, 1979) makes reference to BRE *Current Papers* for definitions of 'noise' and 'equivalent continuous sound level (Leq)'. The final authority on the interpretation of the law, what is 'reasonable' and 'practicable', for example, is a Court of Law.

The Stationery Office publishes Acts singly and in annual bound volumes entitled *Public General Acts and Measures*. The annual publication *Index to the Statutes* lists all the General Acts in force under subject headings, with detailed sub-divisions and cross-references. The companion volume, *Chronological Table of the Statutes*, lists all the General Acts made since 1235 and shows which have been repealed and the effects of later legislation on those still in force. *Statutes in Force* (in progress) consists of the extant general Acts arranged in subject groups in loose-leaf binders. Supplements keep the groups up-to-date. There are, of course, excellent commercial subject guides to the Statutes, such as the multi-volume and supplemented *Halsbury's Statutes of England*.

Statutory Instruments are published individually and in annual volumes. To trace what regulations are in force on a given subject, use could be made of the *Index to Government Orders*. The *Table of Government Orders* is a cumulated chronological list of general Statutory Rules and Orders and Statutory Instruments showing which have been revoked or amended. Both the *Index* and the *Table* are published in revised editions every few years. Although Statutory Instruments are included in the *Daily List of Government Publications*, monthly and annual lists are published separately. The commercial subject guide, parallel to that for Statutes, is *Halsbury's Statutory Instruments*.

Local Acts are those initiated by local authorities to give them powers in their areas in regard to such matters as streets, water supply and public utilities. Except in Inner London, these powers do not extend to building regulations. Local Acts are published individually but there is no published annual volume. They are listed in the annual *Public General Acts* and in the annual booklet *Tables and Index to the Local and Personal Acts*. Local Acts prior to 1967 can be traced in the *Index to Local and Personal Acts, 1801–1947* and the supplementary volume covering 1948–1966.

The Monthly Supplement to the *DoE/DTp Library Bulletin* lists new legislation, circulars, departmental standards and advice notes, as well as the publications issued or sponsored by the two departments. The useful leaflet *Looking up the Laws*, prepared by the Statutory Publications Office, is available free from the Stationery Office.

Legislation, regulations and circulars affecting architectural practice, and commentaries published in the technical press and elsewhere, are recorded and described in the Legislation section of the Index volume of the *RIBA Product Data* files. This regularly up-dated compilation provides a comprehensive survey of relevant legislation enacted before December 1975 as well as more detailed information on subsequent legislation. It covers Scotland and Northern Ireland as well as England and Wales. There are some good general guides to the law as it affects the construction industry. These are listed in the RIBA volume and in *Building Legislation: A Guide to Sources of Information* (PSA Library, 1978). Of special value are *AJ Legal Handbook*, edited by A. Speaight and G. Stone (Architectural Press, 3rd edn, 1982) and *AJ Handbook of Environmental Powers* (Architectural Press, 1976). The annotated bibliography of *Health and Safety in the Construction Industry* (PSA Library, 1980) covers the legislation and associated publications in that field. The indispensible desk reference annual *House's Guide to the Construction Industry* gives general summaries of the major government reports since 1961 still relevant to construction, surveys the legislation affecting planning, design, construction and conservation and examines in detail the Acts of Parliament of particular importance to the industry. Construction Industry Research and Information Association's guide, *Building Design Legislation* (CIRIA, 1982) summarizes and indexes five hundred Acts, Orders and regulations to enable designers to identify legislation relevant to construction. This replaces the Department of the Environment and Welsh Office *Guide to Statutory Provisions* (HMSO, 1972). A short, most useful listing is provided by P. B. Dalloway in 'Building control and associated legislation: a general guide to the Statutory provisions', published in *IBCO: The Journal of the Institution of Building Control Officers* (**XIII**(2), 1981, 30–34).

The most important of all the statutory provisions affecting building design and construction are the Building Regulations. There are separate regulations covering England and Wales, Inner London, Scotland and Northern Ireland. Those for England and Wales are in *The Building Regulations 1976* (SI 1976: No. 1676), the *Building (First Amendment) Regulations 1978* (SI 1978: No. 723) and the *Building (Second Amendment) Regulations 1981* (SI 1981: No. 1338). The Building Regulations are currently being recast and new proposals for building control, set out in a White Paper (Cmnd 8179) in February 1981, are being considered. These new proposals, some of which would require fresh legislation are, in summary; to provide detailed standards for domestic buildings but to rely on a minimum number of functional requirements, supported by a wide range of technical guidance (for instance, British Standards and Agrément Certificates), for the remainder;

to exempt Crown and Local Authority buildings and those of other public bodies, under certain possible conditions, from control entirely; to change some procedures; and to align as far as possible the technical standards for Inner London with those for the rest of England. Consultation letters seeking comments on proposals to amend the Building Regulations are sent out from time to time by the Department of the Environment to over 300 organizations.

Three guidance notes to the regulations have been issued by the Department of the Environment and the Welsh Office: *Structural Fire Precautions* (HMSO, 1975), *Sound Insulation* (HMSO, 1975) and *Conservation of Fuel and Power in Buildings other than Dwellings* (HMSO, 1979). Other guides include *Guide to the Building Regulations 1976* by A. J. Elder (Architectural Press, 1978) and *The Building Regulations, 1976, in detail* by J. Stephenson (Northwood Publications Ltd, 1978) and *The Building Regulations (1st Amendment), 1978, in detail* also by J. Stephenson (Northwood Publications, 1978). *Knight's Building Regulations* by G. D. Binns, J. L'A. Nelson and E. Thompson provides a full text with a legal commentary; it is in loose-leaf form to allow supplements to be incorporated. The RIBA has published the Building Design Partnership's guide to the First Amendment regulations on the conservation of fuel and power in buildings other than dwellings (Part FF). *House's Guide* contains a background survey of building regulations and 'a detailed summary in plain English of the main provisions'.

A series of 'Easiguides' to statutory and other requirements and recommendations, prepared by the National Building Agency, was published monthly as a supplement to the weekly *Building Design*. The series began in March 1969 and now includes guides on gas, stairs and means of escape, electrical installations, water installations, drainage, insulation, lighting, heating and ventilating, roofs, kitchens, brickwork and other topics. The guides aim to set out and clarify the legal requirements and authoritative recommendations and to illustrate them with diagrams, tables and charts. Each guide is well indexed and contains a list of the relevant publications.

Inner London building is controlled by by-laws made under the *London Building Acts 1930–1939*. The *London Building Acts*, being Local Acts of Parliament, are published by the Stationery Office but the by-laws are published by the Greater London Council. The *London Building (Constructional) by-laws 1972* and *1974* were emended by by-laws of 1979. *Building in Inner London* by P. H. Pitt and J. Dufton (Architectural Press, 1976) is a practical guide to the by-laws. The by-law changes are discussed by

Peter Pitt in the *Architects' Journal* (19 and 26 November 1980). The long story of building control in London is told in *The History of Building Regulation in London 1189–1972* by C. C. Knowles and P. H. Pitt (Architectural Press, 1972).

The British Standards Institution published in 1981 its new Handbook No. 21: *Building in London*. The volume contains a consolidated version of the by-laws, 1972–1979 (a convenient but not legally authoritative single text) and summaries of the majority of the British Standards referred to in the by-laws. The summaries consist of extracts from the complete standard, omitting material relating to the control of manufacture of products and verification of conformity, and are intended to be sufficiently detailed for specifying and ordering. An index to the by-laws is included and a supplementary index is provided which relates specifically to district surveyors.

The Building Regulations for Scotland are contained in Statutory Instruments, made under the Building (Scotland) Acts 1959 and 1970, and are known collectively as *The Building Standards (Scotland) Regulations 1971–1979* (SI 1971: No. 2052; SI 1973: No. 794; SI 1975: No. 404; SI 1979: No. 310). The Scottish regulations are administered by the Scottish Development Department which has published through the Stationery Office a series of explanatory memoranda. The government announced that it would

'publish later this year a consolidated edition of the Building Standards (Scotland) Regulations which will include amendments widening the scope of the present exemptions from building control, updating the present fire safety requirements, and extending those aimed at promoting energy conservation. In addition there will be presentational changes aimed at easing the understanding and applications of the regulations'. (*Hansard (Commons)*, 20 May 1981, cols 115 –116)

The Building Regulations (Northern Ireland) 1977 (SR 1977: No. 149), made under the *Building Regulations (Northern Ireland) Order 1972* (SI 1972 No. 1996), consolidate the regulations and bring the technical contents into line with the 1976 regulations for England and Wales. The Northern Ireland regulations are available from the Stationery Office in Belfast. Subsequent *Building Regulation (Northern Ireland) Orders* for 1978 (SI 1978: No. 1038) and 1979 (SI 1979: No. 1709), made under the Northern Ireland Act 1974, allow a more flexible approach and give power to make building regulations in Belfast. New regulations, Part FF, on the conservation of fuel and power (SR 1980: No. 86) match those introduced for England and Wales.

Separate regulations are made under the Education Act 1944 for the standards to which the premises of schools maintained by local education authorities in England and Wales are to conform. The current provisions are in the *Education (School Premises) Regulations 1981* (SI 1981: No. 909) which cover school land (recreation areas and playing fields), school accommodation and structural requirements. The requirements in detail for acoustics, lighting, thermal environment and energy conservation (for new buildings) are set out in *Guidelines for Environmental Design and Fuel Conservation in Educational Buildings*, published in 1981 as Design Guide 17 by the Department of Education and Science.

The *Building Law Reports* (Godwin), published three times a year since 1976, present and comment on selected cases where the decisions are of interest because of their topicality or because of the principles they illustrate. Each volume is devoted to a particular theme or cases of current interest and lists the relevant Statutes and Statutory Instruments. Volume 4 (1977), for example, deals with the obligations and duties of the professional man and Volume 10 (1979) with professional duties and copyright.

Other aspects of the law are comprehensively covered in the series of loose-leaf, regularly up-dated volumes which make up 'The Local Government Library' published by Sweet and Maxwell and obtainable on subscription. The series includes *Encyclopedia of Housing Law and Practice* (4 vols), *Encyclopedia of Environmental Health Law and Practice* (3 vols), *Encyclopedia of Planning Law and Practice* (4 vols) and *Encyclopedia of Land Development* (1 vol.). Each work contains the principal Acts verbatim, with full annotation, and other Acts similarly treated, subordinate legislation verbatim and annotated, and ministerial circulars and similar documents.

Statistics

The word 'statistics', as used here, means the collections, both published and unpublished, of facts about the national economy, industry, commerce and social life presented in the form of numerical tables which are periodically kept up-to-date. The importance of statistics is not just that they show what exists in quantitative terms at any one time but more especially because they can show, by comparison, changes, variations and trends and thus allow for forecasting and planning. It should not be forgotten, however, that statistics are subject to margins of error and that they are open to misuse. On this point reference might be made to

Huff's *How to Lie with Statistics* (Pelican, 1973) and Reichmann's *Use and Abuse of Statistics* (Pelican, 1964). Both these books are described as 'light reading' in Dr D. Edwards' article 'Statistics and maintenance: an introduction to statistics' (*Building Technology and Management*, December 1979, pp. 34–40). Dr Edwards' article is introduced by a quotation from H. G. Wells – 'Statistical thinking will one day be as necessary for efficient citizenship as the ability to read and write'; it this is so, those who have mastered Morris Brodie's *On Thinking Statistically* (2nd edn, Heinemann, in cooperation with the Administrative Staff College, Henley, 1972) will not be at a disadvantage.

The importance of a proper understanding of statistics and their use is demonstrated by the article 'Guide to the use and abuse of statistics' in SHELTER's campaigning housing journal *Roof* (July/August 1980, pp. 106–108). The stimulus for this article is the belief that government and the media succeed in confusing housing issues by exploiting the techniques for using statistics and its purpose is to provide the 'necessary tools' (statistical sources) and guidelines for interpretation.

The major provider of statistics is the Government Statistical Service, but statistics are also collected by local authorities, public corporations, professional, trade and other organizations. Statistical information is made available through official and non-official serial publications, as features, usually regular, in general economic, professional and trade journals, or directly from the collecting body. The Government Statistical Service comprises the statistical divisions of all the main government departments, the Business Statistics Office (BSO), the Office of Population Censuses and Surveys (OPCS) and the Central Statistical Office (CSO).

During 1980 all government ministers reviewed their departmental statistical services and the results were reported briefly in a White Paper. This review was under the general direction of Sir Derek Rayner. The Rayner report itself and the separate reports of the twenty-two departmental detailed examinations were published at the same time (Cmnd 8236). The White Paper stated that, as a result of the review, 'some inquiries have been cut out altogether; some will be made less often; and others will be reduced in size. . . But the Government's statistical operations will still be substantial; the large body of essential economic, industrial, social and other statistics will continue. . . Public access to Government statistics will be maintained but more cost-effectively'. Individual government departments would continue to be responsible for their own statistical services. The Rayner recommendations were subject to public criticism (Townsend, 1981), especially in academic circles, although the effects of implementation are largely for the future.

The best starting point is the annual booklet *Government Statistics: A Brief Guide to Sources*, issued free by the Central Statistical Office. This gives advice on how to find the statistics you want and lists the more important official statistical publications; it also gives the addresses and telephone numbers of the contact points for statistical information within government departments. The *Guide to Official Statistics*, revised periodically by the Central Statistical Office and published by the Stationery Office, is a comprehensive guide to what statistics have been compiled and where they have been published. The *Guide* aims to cover all official and significant non-official sources published during the past ten years. It is the primary guide to sources of information on UK statistics; the first section, which describes general sources, the general classifications used for statistical data and the indexes (of products, place-names, etc.) available should be read by all who have a serious interest in statistics.

The Government Statistical Service publishes important statistical series through the Stationery Office. These include the *Monthly Digest of Statistics* and the *Annual Abstract of Statistics*, which cover a wide range of subjects, and the annual *Social Trends*, which gives information and articles, illustrated by tables and charts, on population, income and wealth, education, health, housing, the environment and other topics. A regular source of economic statistics is *Economic Trends*, published monthly. *Population Trends*, the quarterly journal of the OPCS, contains articles on a variety of population (and medical) topics and regular tables on population and vital statistics. *Regional Statistics*, published annually, provides tables for population, vital statistics, social characteristics; health, housing, economics and other topics analysed by standard region. The weekly *British Business* (formerly *Trade and Industry*) provides the most up-to-date information on such matters as industrial production, prices, capital expenditure and stocks, companies and trade. The *Guide to Public Sector Financial Information* (No. 1, 1979) describes sources relevant to selected topics and provides an annotated bibliography. The quarterly *Statistical News* notes new developments in official statistics. All these publications are described in detail in the *Guide to Official Statistics*, which also lists articles in *Economic Trends*, *Social Trends*, and *Statistical News*. All the official statistical series published by HMSO are listed in its catalogues.

The first comprehensive review of the sources and nature of the immense amount of statistical information available on the construction industry is *Construction and the Related Professions* (*Reviews of United Kingdom Statistical Sources*, Volume XII, Review No. 22) by M. C. Fleming, published in 1980 by the Pergamon Press for the Royal Statistical Society and the Social Science Research Council. This represents the position as it was known at December 1977, although some later revisions have been included, but the most important changes up to July 1979 are noted in an Addendum. (Additions to the statistics published by the Department of the Environment since May 1979 are listed in *Hansard (House of Commons)* Volume 991, No. 234, 30 October 1980, cols 337–338.) The work as a whole is in six parts: Part I, The Construction Industry, deals mainly with the statistics collected by the Ministry of Works 1941–1954 and those collected by the Department of the Environment and its predecessor departments since 1954, production and labour statistics other than those collected by the Department of the Environment and its predecessors, financial statistics, construction costs, prices and productivity, and construction statistics for Northern Ireland; Part II, Construction Materials and Plant; Part III, The Construction Stock; Part IV, The Construction Professions, deals with the numbers, characteristics and employment in the architectural, surveying and engineering professions, the organization and structure of professional practice, earnings and costs, and work undertaken; Part V considers desirable improvements and future developments. These five parts take up a little over half of the volume's 650 pages. A hundred pages are then devoted to a Quick Reference List, which is a descriptive subject-arrangement of the main statistical sources, followed by a key in alphabetical order of title to the publications referred to in the subject list. This is a most valuable reference tool for those seeking current statistical sources. The volume concludes with a full bibliography and appendices showing specimens of the official forms used for collecting data.

The amount of statistical information available is not surprising, since construction is one of the largest industries, providing a major part of national capital investment, is labour-intensive, highly fragmented and a highly significant contributor to the national economy (Fleming, 1980). Other volumes in the 'Reviews' series should be noted: Volume III deals with Housing in Great Britain (Review No. 5) and Housing in Northern Ireland (Review No. 6); Volume VIII deals with Land Use (Review No. 14) and Town and Country Planning (Review No. 15).

The Review volumes are surveys of *sources* and do not include any actual statistics. The two volumes entitled *Statistics Collected by the Ministry of Works 1941–56* (Department of the Environment, 1980), compiled by M. C. Fleming with the assistance of S. R. Rowden, complement to some extent the Review and make much of the data generally available for the first time. The Building Research Station's *Collection of Construction Statistics* (The Station, 1968) brings together conveniently in one volume data for the period 1946–1965. The closest previous approach to a comprehensive survey of construction statistics was made by the former Ministry of Public Building and Works, which produced in 1967 an *Inventory of Construction Statistics* in three volumes. It resulted from an attempt to locate and describe all relevant series. The inventory was not formally published but copies were deposited in the larger public reference libraries. As a by-product the Ministry published a *Directory of Construction Statistics* (HMSO, 1968) as a guide to locating individual tables. Both of these publications are now out of date and have been superseded by the Review volume, but they remain useful sources for specialists.

Of the daunting number of current statistical publications, some should be specifically mentioned. The quarterly *Housing and Construction Statistics* (HMSO), in two parts, contains tables on construction activity and employment, local authority housing loans and sales and slum clearance, housebuilding performance, housing finance and building materials. The annual volume (HMSO, 1980–) of the same title brings together the figures for the previous decade. The *National Dwelling and Housing Survey* (HMSO, 2 vols, 1979–1980) presents the results of a sample survey of housing circumstances and conditions in England. Data collection for this survey is being wound down in 1981. The OPCS publish a yearly *General Household Survey* (HMSO) (also due for reduction), covering such topics as housing, health, education and leisure activities. Sample house prices and mortgage advances are given in the monthly Building Societies Association *Bulletin* and a Housing Cost Index is published regularly in the weekly journal *Building*. Statistics on planning applications and appeals and development control are published by the Department of the Environment. *Planning and Development Statistics* is published by the Chartered Institute of Public Finance and Accountancy (CIPFA). The Business Statistics Office of the Department of Industry publishes a *Business Monitor* series, monthly, quarterly and annually. This series includes the *Report on the Census of Production: Construction Industry* (HMSO, 1977 figures published 1980). The detailed results of the *Private Contractors' Construction Census* carried out by the Department of the Environment in 1978 were published in 1979 (HMSO). The figures are no longer separately published but are included in the quarterly *Housing and Construction Statistics* and also in the annual volume covering the last ten years. Changes in rates of wages and hours of work are published in the Department of Employment's *Employment Gazette* (HMSO, monthly). Construction accident statistics are published by the Health and Safety Executive. *Commercial and Industrial Floorspace Statistics, England and Wales* (HMSO) is published annually. *Commercial and Industrial Property Statistics* (HMSO), published annually, brings together from a wide variety of sources statistics on the activity of the market. Other sources of property statistics are listed in *RICS Abstracts and Reviews (*16(12) December, 1980). The Department of the Environment issues Press Notices on statistics which may up-date published serials; information from the Press Notices is often reported in the periodical press.

Library resources

Most of the publications mentioned in this chapter should be available in private practice libraries; the exceptions would be the larger reference works on legislation and the statistical series, collections and guides, most of which should be in the libraries of the professional institutions. The national reference resource for government publications in general is the Official Publications Library of the British Library in Great Russell Street in London. Government departmental libraries contain all the official publications relevant to their fields of interest. Details of government libraries are to be found in the British Library's *Guide to Government Department and other Libraries* (BL Science Reference Library, every two years). Most departmental libraries allow, by appointment, reference use of their collections by members of the public and they participate in national cooperative schemes.

Good general collections of statistical publications are often kept by academic and the larger public reference libraries. The Statistics and Market Intelligence Library in London is provided by the Department of Industry for public use (Wilson, 1973). The Department's Business Statistics Office Library at Newport, Gwent, in Wales is also open to the public. A commercial information service is offered by the Warwick Statistics Service at Warwick University. The relevant section of the Government Statistical Service can always be contacted for advice if published sources fail. Statistics not readily available elsewhere are sometimes given in answers to Parliamentary Questions and in Ministerial Statements and reported in *Hansard*. References to these statistics are recorded by the House of Commons Library (Englefield, 1981).

References

Cmnd 8179: (February, 1981). *The Future of Building Control in England and Wales*, HMSO

Cmnd 8236: (April, 1981) *Government Statistical Services*, HMSO. This includes details of the Rayner report and the departmental reports and the addresses from which they can be obtained

Englefield, D. (1981). *Parliament and Information*, Library Association, describes the House of Commons Library Public Information Office

Fleming, M. C. (1980), in *The Structure of British Industry*, ed. P. S. Johnson, Granada

Kellner, P. and Crowther–Hunt, Lord. (1980). *The Civil Servants: An Enquiry into Britain's Ruling Class*, MacDonald, contains the Croham Directive. Appendix 4: Sir Douglass Allen's letter on Disclosure of Official Information pp. 324–347. *The Times* published in 1978 (2, 3, 5, 6 and 9 May) a series of five articles on the departmental responses to the open government policy which listed the documents made available. *The Times* of 18 April 1981 reported the Minister of State for the Civil Service as saying 'I can now confirm that departments generally will be able to provide inquirers with information about their own publications either by means of a list or in some other form'. Members of the public should contact the departmental Chief Librarian or Information division

Marsh, P. (1979). *New Scientist*, 15 March

Rogers, C. (June, 1980). 'Government and colleagues' in *Library Association Record*, **82**(6), 269, 271

Thimont, B. M. (May, 1981) 'The Stationery Office Trading Fund' In *Management Services in Government*, **36**(2), 77–81. Mr Thimont is a former Controller of HMSO. Also A. Woolway, 'HMSO – A New Beginning', *Bookseller*, 18 July 1981 pp. 194–195. Mr Woolway is HMSO's Marketing Director

Townsend, P. (1981). *The Guardian*, 15 July. This is just one example

Wilson, M. (1973). *CIIG Bulletin*, **3**(3), Autumn

10
Maps, drawings and slides
Valerie J. Bradfield

Architecture is a visual art. Construction is the technical representation of the design. As such, not all topics on which information may be required are necessarily literary or technical. This chapter, a short, concise one, will try to indicate sources of information in just three of these other areas: maps; draughtsmanship and photography; and slides.

Maps should need little introduction and this section concentrates on the Ordnance Survey and its services, discussing briefly the other types of maps available and the guides to information. Draughtsmanship and photography together represent techniques which all architects try to master. Therefore relevant guides on the development of techniques are included, particularly for students. Slides or photographs are part of an architect's own visual resource. Some collections are available locally or nationally. For use and accessibility, slides need storage and organization. Sources of information are reviewed, giving some basic hints on organizing collections. Most points are also relevant to collections of photographs. At no stage, then, is this chapter intended to be definitive; it provides an introduction in less depth than the sources of information described in later chapters. The sources indicated will lead the interested professional to studies in more depth.

Maps

This section does not describe maps and their availability but indicates some sources of information on British maps with reference to the Ordnance Survey and other producers. The collections of maps available to the public in various locations are indicated, with descriptions of some of the guides available.

Maps are needed locally for purchase or examination. Like books, maps are described, listed and catalogued to provide access to collections and editions. Many guides also discuss the use of maps and the understanding of their symbols and presentation. Since the architect and planner normally require large-scale maps and thematic maps relating to land use, this section will not pretend to cover international maps or atlases.

Source of information

Before looking at the Ordnance Survey and other specific map-producers it will be helpful to refer to the few existing guides to maps. In Brenda White's *Sourcebook of Planning Information* (Bingley, 1971) there is a long chapter on 'Sources of Information on Maps' which looks at all types of land-use maps for the British Isles and indicates where these may be obtained. More recent but less detailed is Harold Nichol's chapter in G. Higgens' *Printed Reference Material* (Library Association, 1980), which also covers atlases and international maps. For those who are interested not only in information but also in the care and storage of maps the same author's *Map Librarianship* (2nd edn, Bingley, 1982) may be helpful. Bowker issues *International Maps and Atlases in Print* at regular intervals (2nd edn, 1976) listing all those currently available in each country covered. When working abroad, lists such as this give a useful indicator of the main map-producers in those countries. Many countries have no equivalent to the Ordnance Survey and are not mapped to the same depth systematically and uniformly.

More specialist lists and guides include the review in the Transport and Road Laboratory report No. 403 (rev. edn, 1976) *Preliminary Sources of Information for Site investigations in Britain*, by M. J. Dumbleton and G. West. This gives detailed bibliographical information as well as checklists and discussion of the availability and value of maps in Britain. A similar review and list was issued as the Appendix to BS 5930: 1980, *Site Investigation*, developing the recent practice of issuing references or bibliographies with some British Standards. This provides one of the most current and succinct coverages of the major sources.

Texts are best found on the local library shelf. They range widely, but Dury's *Map Interpretation* (3rd edn, Pitman, 1967) is still a useful volume and recently Dawsons have published A. G.

Hodgkiss's *Understanding Maps*, (1981), which covers, briefly, the history and development of maps and map-making, regional, nautical and Ordnance Survey maps, town plans, thematic, commercial and private map-making, with a bibliography. Articles on using maps appear in various places (see below). They include such readable and lively articles as Ault's 'Old maps reveal site problems' (*Estates Gazette*, **255,** 20 Sept. 1980, 1087–1089), which might send a site investigator scurrying to the archive office to investigate the existence of old pits, quarries and similar features which, if undetected, could have disastrous effects on the stability of a new building.

Journals

Sources of current news and additional information are important since developments in automation may in future affect all our dealings with graphical information sources, as instanced by Shepherd and Chilton's recent discussion of 'Computer-based enquiries in the map library' (*Cartographic Journal*, **17**(2), 1980, 128–139). *Cartographic Journal* is issued twice a year and not only discusses the use of maps but other points of fringe interest to the architect. For example, the discussion of the perception of information on maps suggests interesting ideas on the interpretation of symbols and of information on all plans and drawings. New atlases, maps and similar ventures are reviewed and collections are sometimes discussed. Reviews of maps and of books on maps appear regularly in both *Geography* and *Geographical Journal*.

Indexing of maps and articles on their use may occur in an indexing service like *API*, where architectural mapping may be found – a rare example is the series of continental town plans showing features of architectural interest which were published in *Architectural Design* during the late 1960s at irregular intervals. *Geoabstracts D: Social Geography and Cartography* mentions some articles and maps. The annual *Bibliographia Cartographica: International Documentation of Cartographical Literature*, originally published in Germany by K. G. Saur but recently taken over by Mansell, lists many new series and items as well as books about maps and mapping. Its comprehensiveness may, however, vary and in the light of the critical review in *Photogrammetric Record* (1976) it should be used with care. The latter journal also notices any new land-use mapping services.

Ordnance Survey

Most readers will be familiar with at least some of the map series from the Ordnance Survey, the official surveyor in Britain.

However, the wide range of leaflets produced and kept up-to-date by the Ordnance Survey give a full description not only of agents and sales points but also of the services available, the digital mapping, the use of coordinates, levelling, control information, metrication and many other topics. The full range of maps produced is listed in the annual *Map Catalogue*. All are available free.

Although the *Map Catalogue* contains reduced index sheets for the 1:250 000, 1:50 000, and 1:25 000 the larger scale index sheets must be purchased to provide an accurate location index for sheets on the scales 1:10 000, 1:2500 and 1:1250. For these last two the SIM (Survey Information in Microform) service makes information available from the Master Survey drawing after every fifty changes using a microfilm copy of the drawing which is only redrawn to normal standards after 300 units of change. Such changes would otherwise not be available to outsiders. The microfilm maps, or print-out paper copies from them, may be purchased. The print-outs are made from the microfilm at the sales agent's offices using special machines. Arrangements can be made to view the Master Survey drawings at any level of change at local Ordnance Survey offices.

In general, when using Ordnance Survey maps it is helpful to remember that the longer the reference number to the sheet, the larger the scale, thus;

TQ 4947 SE refers to 1:1250
TQ 4947 refers to 1:2500
TQ 49 refers to 1:25 000
TQ refers to 1:50 000

A full explanation is given both in the leaflets and in Harley's invaluable manual, *Ordnance Survey Maps: A Descriptive Manual* (OS, 1975). This is essential reading to all trying to understand the use as well as compilation of maps. It has chapters covering the history of the Ordnance Survey, a description of each series and discussion of the accuracy of maps.

Changes in services are usually publicized in *Cartographic Journal* but any which radically affect the output and the types of maps used by architects and planners would be mentioned in the professional journals. Services are extending with developments in tehniques so that computer tapes can be obtained to facilitate the various digital mapping work in progress. These are also discussed frequently in the above journal, which noted the changes proposed at the Ordnance Survey by a government report in the late 1970s. For example, W. P. Smith's article 'The Ordnance Survey: a look to the future' comments on the Serpell Report (*Cartographic Journal*, **17**(2), 1980, 75–82). In 1980 also the *Architect and Surveyor* (**55**(2)) published a useful four-page summary of the Ordnance Survey and its work for the architect. Services were also described by A. Marles of the Ordnance Survey very succinctly in the *Proceedings of the 27th Annual Study Group, Winchester, 30th March – 2nd April 1979*, by A. Pennial (ed.) (LA, RSIS, 1980).

Many users may not be familiar with the Map Users' Conference, a feedback organization aiming to get ideas and comments back to the Ordnance Survey in order that they may react to the needs of the users. The SIM service, giving more up-to-date information, is an example of the results that feedback may produce – as may be the new venture of town maps at 1:10 000 reviewed in *Cartographic Journal* (**17**(2), 1980) and issued initially for Ipswich, Cambridge and Southampton.

Finally, it was announced in April 1982 that the Ordnance Survey maps could be fed directly into the Autotrol AD/380 interactive computer-aided design system. Site planning and layout would thus be not only quicker but also more accurate. Use of National Grid references would make recall and display of features easy.

Institute of Geological Sciences

National geological records are now the responsibility of the Institute which incorporates the Geological Survey of Great Britain, to whom requests for information on wells, shafts and boreholes may be made, enclosing a section of the relevant Ordnance Survey map. Maps published include the solid maps showing main strata and maps showing superficial deposits mainly at 1:63 360, being replaced by 1:50 000. Six-inch maps at survey level are available and 1:25 000 maps are published for some interesting parts of the country, new towns and development areas. These and the descriptive *Memoirs* relating to some, but not all, maps are listed in the IGS catalogue, which is part of the Ordnance Survey Catalogue. Other records are kept at the Institute and information can be checked, although they are not published. Soil maps and memoirs at 1:63 360 and 1:25 000 have been published for many areas and are also listed above. The IGS Global seismologist even has a computer listing of UK earthquakes.

Before leaving the field of official mapping copying of any maps should be mentioned briefly, since the rules laid down in the Copyright Act have not yet been superseded and all Ordnance

Survey maps are copyright. An allowance of 700 cm^2 may be copied for study, research or review under the 'Fair Dealing' provision of the act. Any more, or any other uses, require permission and payment of a royalty fee. Leaflets from the Ordnance Survey describe the procedures for 'Business and Internal Use' or 'Copyright and Other Services – Publishing'. Similar restrictions will apply to any other maps.

Thematic maps

Many maps are compiled by various organizations to illustrate the distribution of features over the land, and these are called thematic, ranging from the DoE atlas to various small local undertakings in the schools and departments of Geography, Land Use or Planning of major universities and polytechnics. The results are listed in the sources of information above and reviewed in the journals. Size and quality varies. The work of the Experimental Cartography Unit is reported by the Cartography Sub-committee of the Royal Society's British National Comittee for Geography in many publications such as *Experimental Cartography: Report on the Oxford Symposium October 1963* (OUP, 1964). Among other publications the unit has produced are *Land Use Mapping by Local Authorities in Britain* (Architectural Press, 1978) which shows how local authority databases can be used to create land-use maps.

Land-use maps of the original and the second Land Use Survey of Britain (begun in 1960) have been prepared to 1:25 000 to show agricultural uses. The maps are retailed through Edward Stanford Ltd (London), not the Ordnance Survey, and are described in *Land Use Survey Handbook* (5th edn, 1968). Land-use work has also been done locally and the nearest institutions should be contacted. Some results have been published, for instance, the University of Sheffield, Department of Geography, *Census Atlas of South Yorkshire* (1974), the *Atlas of London and the London Region* compiled by E. Jones and D. J. Sinclair (Pergamon, 1968) and Patmore's *Merseyside in Maps* (Longman, 1970). Many other small volumes exist.

The major volume is that from the DoE, replacing the MoHLG, *Desk Atlas of Planning Maps*, issued in loose-leaf form since 1953 with revised sheets appearing at irregular intervals. The new volume commenced publication (1977) as *Atlas of the Environment* and sheets are issued when prepared. They are listed in the DoE *Annual List of Publications* each year and a binder is available. Similar is the Welsh Office Atlas, and the Scottish Office is also working on one.

Historical maps range from the Ordnance Survey Maps of Roman Britain, Monastic Britain, etc. to those preserved in many local archive offices and collections which are described below. Lists have been made locally and in Skelton *County Atlases of the British Isles 1579–1850* (Carta Press, 1970). Other lists can be traced in the sources of information already listed.

Town plans can often be found most quickly in the RAC book of *UK Town Plans* (1979) and in the major road atlases from both British motoring organizations, the Reader's Digest and similar producers. On a larger scale the publications catalogue of Geographia Ltd gives a wide range of detailed town plans, conurbation marketing maps and others such as the survey of manufacturing industry based on the 1961 Census of Production. Plans for the professional are produced by C. H. Goad of Hatfield, showing the location of amenities, services and traffic flows within urban areas. They were described in a brief article in *Property Journal* in 1979 ((**1**), 10–11). Several other firms provide such services, for example Market Location Ltd of Leamington, but their plans are aimed mainly at the market research companies and can be expensive if not available in the local library.

Air photographs

While not strictly speaking maps, air photographs can be useful and are available for a large part of the country through two sources. The Ordnance Survey takes, or commissions, a wide range to cover mapping areas and prices of these are given in the SIM/SUSI price list where they can be purchased. Enquiries should always be made to the Ordnance Survey for the existence of such photographs. Alternatively, the DoE Central Register of Air Photography of England and Wales has details of all maps available and will answer any enquiries for surveys of a particular area according to its holdings, referring enquiries on to the holders of the photographs where they are not held centrally. This may entail going to the commercial firm who did the work.

Collections

Not all collections are open to the public but enquiries may be made by telephone or post to the Ordnance Survey and the DoE above. The DoE and the Scottish Office have Map Libraries which should be contacted and may permit access. The Scottish Office publishes *Catalogue of the Map Library*. Many local libraries have collections relating to the area, or the maps are held at the archive office. Practice varies. Few have collections like that at the Guildhall library in London. Collections in Britain (27) are included among the 300 listed with information on their holdings and accessability in *World Directory of Map Collections* (W. W. Ristow (ed.), comp. International Federation of Library Associations (IFLA), Verlag Dokumentation, 1976). The British Library Reference Division in Bloomsbury is listed as having 1 250 000 map sheets, 12 250 manuscript maps, 20 000 atlases and 50 globes. The holdings of the Map library of the Royal Geographical Society in Kensington and of the University of London at the Senate House, Bloomsbury, are also considerable.

The British Library has published the *British Museum Catalogue of Printed Maps, Charts and Plans* in fifteen volumes (1967), with supplementary volumes since. However, a distinction should be noticed here in that these refer to 'printed' maps, and many local collections will include manuscipt maps and plans such as estate maps which never have been printed but were commissioned and used for local, private and land-management purposes. J. B. Harley produced a guide to these for local historians, *Maps for the Local Historian: A Guide to British Sources* (National Council for Social Services, 1972). Local collections often have their own lists as the many brief college guides indicate, as well as those like Birmingham Public Libraries' History and Geography Department's Bibliography No. 1, *Sets of Maps and National Atlases in the Map Room* (1979).

Both the Public Record Office and the Scottish Record Office have extensive map collections and publish guides. These mainly cover the historical part of the collections. City and County record offices are also repositories for maps, current and historical. Many publish guides like P. G. M. Dickinson's *Maps in the County Record Office, Huntingdon* (Huntingdon, Imray Laurie Norie and Wilson Ltd, 1968) which in its 72 pages indexes contents likely to have been moved since the redesignation of county boundaries in 1974.

More recently, *British Library and Information Work 1976 –1980* (Library Association, 1982) included an article on 'Map libraries' by David Ferro summarizing developments in Britain and North America. A useful chapter by G.R. P. Lawrence on 'Maps, atlases and gazetteers' is included in Butterworths' *Guide to Sources of Information in Geography* (forthcoming in the same series as the present guide).

Conclusion

Little more remains to be said on sources without going to the level of detail in White. However, in closing it might be appropriate to make a few notes along the lines to be followed in the section on slides since preservation, storage and access to maps often presents similar problems and that section aims to give advice as well as sources of information.

Plan chests with many drawers for flat storage of maps always present problems where size varies and insertion and removals damage the maps just as rolling or folding does. Although hanging cabinets are a less damaging alternative from which removal is easy and painless (to the maps), time is required on receipt to attach hanger strips which also come off if not treated with care. Advice will be found in Nichol's book above and in Calderhead's *Libraries for Professional Practice* (Architectural Press, 1972). Modern methods involve the use of microfilming, where financially viable, for maps, plans and drawings which are not in regular use as an economical and space-saving alternative to plan chests. The possibilities are outlined succinctly by Tony Morgan of the GLC in *Local Government Chronicle* for 23 March 1979 (pp. 324–327), and earlier by P. McAllister in 'Uses of microfilm in architecture' (*Architect* (Perth), 4(111), August 1973, 98–99). Only the sophistication of the equipment and the willingness of professionals to accept alternative formats for sources of information have changed since then. Digital mapping and the wider availability both of computer graphics equipment in offices and of tapes and disks containing mapping information may change the scene radically in the next ten years.

Further advice can be sought from the librarians or custodians at the map libraries mentioned. Considering the importance of maps and their availability to many sectors of industry and the professions, there are remarkably few guides and handbooks available.

Draughtsmanship and photography

Drawing

So essential is drawing to the architect that it might even seem strange to include it in a guide to sources of information. But techniques change and develop. Some need to learn from scratch what the professional is able to do instinctively – hence the inclusion of a brief section here mainly covering texts and journals. Practice varies, but principles remain the same. Recent discussions have laid an emphasis on presentation of work in publications whether for the practice or on a wider scale, and suggestions for procedures have been outlined, on both sides of the Atlantic in *AJ* and *Architectural Review*, and in *Architectural Record, AIA Journal* and *Progressive Architecture*. Many American texts are cited below because in this sphere there are few guides, lists or bibliographies and not a great many post-war books in English in comparison with the wealth in other topics.

Fraser Reekie's *Draughtsmanship: Drawing Techniques for Graphic Communication in Architecture and Building* (3rd edn, Arnold, 1976) must be on many professional bookshelves. It remains a 'standard'. There are others, however, and many of the texts mentioned below have come from the Architectural Press, filling a professional need where other publishers have perhaps trodden more warily. Most up-to-date are Porter and Goodman's *Manual of Graphic Techniques, 2* (1982), and Wang's *Plan and Section Drawing* (1979), a descriptive manual, complementing Ching's earlier *Architectural Graphics* (1975) on technique. Earlier British texts also include C. Martin, *Architectural Graphics* (Macmillan, 1970), C. Kemmering, *Graphic Details for Architects* (Pall Mall, 1968) and P. Hogarth, *Drawing Architecture: A Creative Approach* (Pitman, 1973). Those wishing to take a simpler approach might look at one of the texts written for builders, especially at HNC/HND levels and the more recent TEC course instruction texts. F. Hilton, *Building Geometry and Drawing*, metric edn (Longman, 1973) is aimed at this level. Less technical is Don Davy's *Drawing Buildings* (Batsford, 1981), which looks at perspective, textures and shading with sketchbook examples.

Among the American books, Goodban and Hayslett, Architectural Drawing and Planning (McGraw-Hill, 1972), has reached a second edition, takes a very different approach to British texts and covers quite a lot more, with a long bibliography and much data for different aspects of drawing. More basic, but with 'execrable' freehand drawings (according to the *AJ* review of 4 October 1978), is R. Dagostino, *Contemporary Architectural Drawing* (Reston, 1977). Dudley Leavitt, *Architectural Illustration* (Prentice-Hall, 1977) might be mentioned.

During 1976 and 1977 the *AJ* produced a *Working Drawings Handbook* (*AJ* 7 July 1976 – 3 August, 1977) compiled by Daltry, Crawshaw and Styles. Published by Architectural Press in 1982, this covers aspects such as the media, conventions, symbols, lettering and procedures with which the architect should be concerned, as well as illustrating basic types of drawing and referring to other works, both texts and manuals.

These naturally include BS 1192: 1969, *Building Drawing Practice*, which many regard as inadequate, but despite discussion and reports in the press in 1978 of its revision there is, as yet, no alternative or new edition. PD 6479: 1976, *Recommendations for Symbols and other Graphic Conventions for Building Production Drawings*, should be read with BS 1192, as should BRE Digest 172 on working drawings which resulted from the work of Crawshaw and Daltry reported in BRE CP 18/73, *Working Drawings in Use*, and CP 60/76, *Coordinating Working Drawings*. These two were complemented by two BRE slide/note sets, *A Critical Look at Working Drawings – Lessons from Practice* (1973) and *A Sample Set of Architects' Working Drawings – A Systematic Arrangement* (1976). Systematic arrangement has been of concern to the DoE, and proposals covering the whole of the construction project were put forward in *Structuring Project Information* (HMSO, 1972), while the above papers from the BRE suggested the use of CI/SfB as explained in a long section on drawing coordination in *CI/SfB Construction Indexing Manual* by Alan Ray-Jones and D. Clegg, (3rd edn, RIBA Publications, 1976). However, another useful exposé on this theme which is still recommended is P. Scher's 'Working drawings: analysis and recommendations' (*RIBA Journal*, November 1971, 496–503). Incidentally, he has written the up-date on drawings for the *AJ* 'Annual Review', whose bibliography changes little with the years.

Working and Design Drawings is the title of an international text by R. Prenzel (Stuttgart, Erasmus, 1980), which tries to show techniques, as does McHugh's *Working Drawing Handbook: A Guide for Architects and Builders* (Van Nostrand, 1977), which consists mainly of checklists with few drawings. Two complementary texts from Wiley in 1977 also follow American practice , Wakita and Linde, *The Professional Practice of Architectural Detailing* and Liebing and Paul, *Architectural Working Drawings*.

Theory

There are many discussions in general of design theory which are not the province of this book but two recent books should assist the development of competency in drawing skills. They are Lawson's *How Designers Think* (Architectural Press, 1980) and Porter's *How Architects Visualise* (Studio Vista, 1979).

Rendering

The Thames and Hudson Manual of Rendering in Pen and Ink (1973) and H. Jacoby, *New Techniques of Architectural Rendering*

(Thames and Hudson, 1971), cover this specific aspect of draughtsmanship, while A. O. Halse's *Architectural Rendering* is in its second edition (McGraw–Hill, 1972).

Perspective

Walters and Bromham's *Principles of Perspective* (2nd edn, Architectural Press, 1976) is a reference book, which will certainly help the student with definitions of the different types of perspective and, unlike the many texts on the library shelves, it covers buildings specifically rather than incidentally, as in the art textbooks. There is no shortage of explanations of basic perspective, with some descriptions like Doblin, *Perspective: A New System for Designers* (Whitney Library of Design, 1956) offering alternative methods of expression. Anne Tyng discusses *Perception and Proportion for Architects* in the Pigeon Audio-visual presentation (1980).

Modelling

Although this is not a technique peculiar to architects a greater use of the model as a method of design presentation is found in architecture than in many other fields. Hints on preparation and new techniques appear in *AJ* and frequently in the American journals but, for the student, texts exist such as Renoir's *How to Make Architectural Models* (Studio Vista, 1973), T. Hendrich, *Modern Architectural Models* (Architectural Press, 1957), R. Janke, *Architectural Models* (Thames and Hudson, 1968) and Dutton's *A Student's Guide to Model Making* (Pergamon, 1970). The same emphasis is seen in the United States, with J. Cleaver, *Constructing Model Buildings* (Academy editions reprint of New York edn, 1973), J. R. Taylor, *Model Building for Architects and Engineers* (McGraw–Hill, 1971), S. Hohauser, *Architectural and Interior Models* (Van Nostrand, 1971) or the Australian, H. J. Cowan, *Models in Architecture* (Elsevier, 1968). The latter is perhaps nearer to British practice.

Symbols

Architectural graphics involves the use of labels and symbols and the PD was mentioned above (p. 197). The theory is covered in Broadbent, Bunt and Jencks, *Signs, Symbols and Architecture* (Wiley, 1980), with information on design and designers in Follis and Hammer, *Architectural Signing and Graphics* (Whitney Library of Design, 1979). Many dictionaries also exist. The handbooks mentioned in Chapter 6 give the relevant ones for each aspect of construction. The British Standards for specific areas also give both British and International standardized symbols.

Presentation

With the opening of advertising to the architect in Britain there have been suggestions recently that more attention should be paid to the presentation of all information, and, in particular, drawn work. Louis Dezart has followed up his *AJ* article, 'Marketing 3: Presentation' in the 'Aids to Practice' series (16 April 1980, pp. 783–790) with a book, *Drawing for Publication* (Architectural Press, 1980) which covers aspects of printing, reductions, lettering, etc. which, it is claimed, have never been readily available before, although they have been in the many manuals and texts for graphic designers and printers but not necessarily specifically directed at the architect. However, such techniques are essential to the effective production not necessarily of books but rather of practice leaflets and presentations.

An American text, W. W. Atkin, *Architectural Presentation Techniques* came out in 1976 (Van Nostrand), reflecting the earlier interest in this field, However, for those wishing to venture further, texts on lettering, printing methods and their prerequisites, layout and design are abundant. There are also manuals and handbooks in which it is possible to locate assistance, *Creative Handbook* for instance. *Writers' and Artists' Year Book* (Black) gives background facts and hints for any publishing work, including references.

Presentation matters, in particular when entering for competitions through which individuals gain recognition and practices may gain work. The first guide to 'winning' competitions, with an indication of the regular ones which exist was Judith Strong's *Participating in Architectural Competitions* (Architectural Press, 1976). She was Competitions Secretary at the RIBA and therefore in a position to give guidance. She was also linked with the production of *Architectural Competition News* at the RIBA. It is easy also to find out about competitions in the pages of *AJ* each week and in the front inserts to *Current Information in the Construction Industry* every other week. Some competitions are regular but will still be announced in these sources, e.g. the Wiggins Teape and *AJ* Measured Drawings competition advertised on 3 March 1982. In 1979 a similar American text was published, *Design Competitions* by P. D. Spreiregen (McGraw-Hill), and the AIA was due to publish its *Handbook of Architectural Competitions* in August 1981.

Photography

In keeping with the rest of the chapter, this will be a brief guide. Both professional and amateur have their favourite texts and journals. There are general texts like Sheppard, *Photography for Designers* (Focal Press, 1971), A. Feininger, *Principles of Composition on Photography* (Thames and Hudson, 1973), and *A Manual of Advanced Photography* (new edn, Thames and Hudson, 1970), J. Hedgecoe, *Photography; Materials, Methods* (OUP, 1971) or the *Kodak Handbook for the Professional Photographer*. The list could be endless. A few selected titles should suggest the range of texts provided specifically for architects. De Maré produced *Photography and Architecture* (Architectural Press, 1961) and *Photography* (Penguin, 1980). Also from Architectural Press more recently (1978) was J. Schulman, *The Photography of Architecture and Design*, which represents a detailed study of exterior and interior photography in both natural and artificial lighting. For those who appreciate that photography can only be shown in photographs there is the Pigeon Audiovisual slide/tape by J. Donat, *Architecture through the Lens* (1980), discussing how to solve some photographic problems.

Two useful reference works, from Focal Press, are the *Focal Encyclopedia of Photography* in two volumes (1965), which includes a list of authors on photography and Spencer's *Focal Dictionary of Photographic Technologies* (1973), which covers a wide range of techniques to achieve special effects as well as giving standards and a subject bibliography. From abroad there are J. Giebelhausen, *Architectural Photography* (Munich, 1965), two more of the same title by Veltri (New York, Amphoto, 1974) and Molitor (Wiley, 1976) and Burden, *Architectural Delineation* (McGraw-Hill, 1971), which is principally about photography.

Photogrammetry as a branch of this is covered on page 221. Ross Dallas' two articles in *AJ* (30 January 1980, pp. 249–255, 20 February 1980, pp. 395–399) should be added to this.

Journals

The architectural journals will sometimes review new texts in photography. All keen photographers are aware of the main photographic journals. Many articles appear in a very wide range of journals and the use of indexing and abstracting journals is sensible to locate information on specific problems. Journals like *Design* are indexed in services like *API* and *Design Abstracts International*. *API* has headings for Drawing, Competitions and Photography with at least a few articles on each appearing every year. Articles relating to draughtsmanship and photography may be indexed in *Art Index, Artbibliographiesmodern* and *British Humanities Index*.

For photography there is also *Photographic Abstracts*, published by the Royal Society since 1921 (bi-monthly). Useful information will be found in wider sources like *Chemical Abstracts* and *Physics Abstracts*, which will be found in many large academic libraries.

Conclusion

Like all parts of this chapter this is brief but it is also more like a selected bibliography than others, simply because that is the way of this type of literature. Yet any student researching into the area further will find not only many texts covering all aspects of drawing but also articles, brief hints, discussion and ideas in many of the design and general theory books.

Collections of drawings and photographs may be visited for further information. A few have published lists of holdings like the RIBA *Catalogue of the Drawings Collections* (RIBA publications, various dates). The RIBA also has a large photographic collection, not fully accessible, which does not duplicate the architectural photographic collection of the National Monuments Record to any great extent. The latter may be visited. The Royal Photographic Society have compiled a *Directory of British Photographic Collections* (J. Wall (ed.), Heinneman, 1977) which not only provides a listing describing collections but also subject, owner, location, photographer and title indices, a bibliography and background information on use of the collections, fees and copying, etc. Many exhibitions are held and are usually referred to in *AJ* if they are likely to be of architectural interest. Guidance publications in this area are few. The handbooks listed indicate the location of useful collections, most of which are aimed at the writer, advertiser and journalist. The *Picture Researcher's Handbook* (H. & M. Evans, Saturday Ventures, 1979) gives guidance on contacting more of these and on locating specialists.

Slides

Slides, small but essential tools, accumulate, and demand considerable attention if they are to be of future use. This section will aim to indicate the sources of information which discuss their organization, their commercial availability and to indicate the collections accessible to architects. Some brief hints on the organization of collections will be added, since these have been requested on a number of occasions.

Sources of information

Most architects and practices keep records of work and these are usually either slides or photographs, stored either in boxes in the order in which they were taken – hoping that retrieval will be possible when needed – or roughly organized in an attempt to make them retrievable. Sometimes someone writes briefly to one of the journals about his system and technique, and, although these articles are noticed by others, the copies are invariably 'lost' in the filing 'system', or the good intentions work only until time becomes occupied with masses of other jobs. A list of references follows this section to give access to the main literature on the use of slide collections. It is not definitive and, as it will inevitably date, it should be up-dated using *API* or *Library and Information Science Abstracts* (LISA). The new Library Association Handbook on *Picture Collections* (1981) should provide some hints on organization but the only major British surveys of practice which give ideas on effective organization are White (1967) and Bradfield (1976). The most useful text is Irvine, which presents a number of options, all of which will bear investigation but reflect US practice. However, her bibliography reflects the state-of-the-art in 1974 and is extensive.

Much of the literature available is aimed at the librarian and the architect will possibly be more interested in Harris' description of Ove Arup's system and the descriptions of some practice collections in White. Naturally, the articles in *CIIG Bulletin* also reflect the architectural practice needs rather than those of academic collections.

Commercial slides

Anyone visiting a country house, public building, zoo or other location in the UK or the world has seen slides for sale. Many collections hold such sets as well as making their own from books, prints and actual buildings. Publishers' lists are available from firms such as Visual Publications, Slide Centre and Focal point. There are many, and the first attempt at listing them by the Library Association's Audio-visual Group is due for publication at the end of 1981. Some are given in the list available through the

Scottish Council for Educational Technology prepared by the Scottish branch of the above group.

The Pigeon Audiovisual branch of World Microfilms produces cassette/slide programmes discussing various aspects of architecture both modern and historical. Each year a series of six or seven talks is produced with titles like *Lesson of Milton Keynes* (Derek Walker, 1980), *Water* (Peter Shepherd, 1980), *The Architecture of Urban Landscape* (Denys Lasdun, 1980) and *A Question of Scale* (Philip Dowson, founder of Arup Associates, 1979). Incidentally, the same company has issued microfilms reproducing the *RIBA Transactions and Proceedings 1835–93*, the British Architectural Library *Drawings Collection* (selections), the British Architectural Library *Unpublished Manuscripts* (various miscellaneous papers described in brochures), the RIBA *Comprehensive Index to Periodicals 1956–1972*, and the British Architectural Library *Microfilmed Collection of Rare Books*, including *English Pattern Books, Cottage Architecture, Country Houses and Palaces, Ancient Civilisation* and *Architectural Treatises and Works on Perspective*.

Sussex Video issue video tapes in preference to slides, but the Commonwealth Association of Architects issues slide-lectures on topics ranging from *Human Settlements and Disasters* to *Introduction to Structural Mechanics, Historic Towns and Buildings in Tropical Areas: An Introduction to Conservation, Fire and the Architect, Windows and Environmental Design, The Appearance and Lighting of Buildings,* and *Landscape Architecture*.

The BRE have issued a number of slide sets, with notes, on topics like *Effect of Wind Loading on Typical Buildings* (1973) and *Keeping out the Rain* (1974) as well as a number of films. All are listed in *Information Directory*. C & CA slide sets are listed in *Concrete in Print*. All such productions, films in particular, can be traced in the *British National Film Catalogue*, which has regular supplements and indicates whether items are for hire or purchase. The most useful guide, however, is the *Film Guide to the Construction Industry* (Construction Press, 1979), compiled by the British Industrial and Scientific Film Association.

Slide libraries

Most practice collections are not available to the public or other professionals except as clients or friends, but many of the collections belonging to university, polytechnic and college schools of architecture or libraries may be used by local professionals. The BBC Hulton Picture Library relates mainly to photographs but has some slides, and is described, along with many others, in Evans, *Picture Researchers' Handbook: An International Guide to Picture Sources and How to Use Them* (2nd edn, Saturday Ventures, 1979).

After the announcement of its closure the V and A slide collection was reprieved in 1981 and many may have first learnt of its existence during the campaign to keep it open as the major public collection in Britain. It has a good architectural section. Others do exist, but nothing like the same scope is achieved by those at public libraries such as the Audio-visual Department of Birmingham Public Libraries.

The Architectural Association and the RIBA collections are only available to members. The AA has recently revised and developed its already large collection which is available for loan. *Landscape Design* in February 1982 announced that Cliff Tandy's extensive and completely indexed collection had been bequeathed to the AA and would be kept intact. The Courtauld Institute in London also has a good collection with many architecture slides, but permission must be sought to use it. The best guide to collections for the architect is that in Ruth Kamen's *British and Irish Architectural History: A Bibliography and Guide to Sources of Information* (Architectural Press, 1981).

Organization

Lengthy manuals could be written on techniques for organizing slide collections in practices – Irvine's goes beyond architectural collections and the items in the bibliography show how others organize since there is no one agreed and standardized system. Calderhead mentions equipment for slides in passing (*Libraries for Professional Practice* (Architectural Press, 1972)) but not organization.

Some points to remember initially are that listing, paperwork, etc. should be kept to a minimum, that the system of organization (Classification) should, as far as possible, reflect the usual way in which slides are required, i.e. if one always knows the job number and never uses the slides for any other purpose then keep them that way with no other records: above all the simpler the better. Merrett's recent article on computerized indexing is exciting and remains simple but the indexing still requires much effort, the time for which is not always readily available.

The basic points to consider are:

The listing on receipt of what is held;

The mounts in which the slide is kept, and remounting if necessary;

The means of identification, for use, memory and storage;
The means of description of the image, its date and features;
The means of viewing and of browsing, for retrieval;
The means of storage for retrieval, space conservation;
The organization of that store;
Any policy of duplication for security or for dual retrieval.

These will be amplified, but only briefly.

ACQUISITION

As slides arrive it is a good idea to record briefly what is received, job, site, date taken and the subject, to form a record of holdings which is especially useful if further action is delayed, as is often the case. Visual identificaion is not as easy as with a photograph or other picture due to size; therefore this deficiency must be partially made up in writing. Numbers can be allocated at this stage and written on mounts or labels as permanently as possible to ensure identification later, and they may be needed for the system of retrieval or organization chosen. They are then ready for use.

MOUNTS

White's survey discussed when and why the mounts in which slides are received from the commercial processors were kept or destroyed. Slides may be remounted in more permanent plastic mounts with glass protection for the image. The use of these depends on time, finance and the degree of permanency required, but should also take account of the fact that, if not done well, remounting can also have a deleterious effect since 'Newton's rings' can form within the glass and damage the slide. Everything needs labelling, but some card mounts can be written on, thus obviating the need for labels which, if not small enough or adequately attached, can jam the projector.

IDENTIFICATION

This will vary with the system of retrieval used, but basically it must be sufficient to identify the slide either at once or by using its code to refer to a list or index. The latter takes longer but is neater, even when small-face typewriters are used for labelling. The identification should also indicate exactly where the slide belongs within the system for re-filing and to whom it belongs. Any code should be capable of quick and easy interpretation, preferably using mnemonics. Some code systems using half-words like the BBC's have been found difficult to file in practice as inaccuracies are higher than with numbers and inaccuracies lead to losses.

DESCRIPTION

Memory is not adequate to recall information. Each slide needs to be described succinctly. Location, date and architect are essential features. View or angle from which the slide was taken may be significant, as may be many close-ups of features.

VIEWING

Holding a slide to the light may sometimes be adequate for identification purposes but it does not show features clearly. The use of box viewers is time-consuming. A light-box with light projecting from behind onto a flat surface on which slides may be laid is ideal for selection purposes before loading projector magazines. Plastic wallets may be laid directly on the light-box without removing slides.

RETRIEVAL

A variety of options are open depending on the types of use to which collections are to be put. The usual ways in which a slide is likely to be required should be analysed to decide how many means of access are necessary. Are slides just required by location (specific buildings can always be found with reference to their location), or by architect with the occasional reference to a particular type of building or to features? Or are they always required by features? In this case a complex system of indexing becomes necessary to permit all means of access, perhaps using the computer system described, or optical-coincidence cards or even the microform-holding edge-notch cards which also store the slides. Each of these requires a lot of input work. Card indexing may seem a cheaper alternative and require only the same input effort and, although currently treated as outmoded, it does not require expenditure on equipment to the same extent. If only a few points of access are required then the original register order should be carefully selected to try to reflect one order, leaving the storage order to reflect one, if not two, further options. For example, the job number might reflect date, order in the year and region (79/6/SE) with the order in the store being by type, then architect, or by architect, then type. A key list should be maintained giving all architect's names used and the building type headings used. There are many alternative permutations possible according to need; see those listed in White, Havard-Williams and Bradfield, and see also Chapter 6, pp. 115–123.

STORAGE

Order reflects organization for retrieval, but the physical media should be chosen according to the need to be able to browse, the space available and the finance or existing equipment. Almost every alternative has been tried from 5×3 catalogue drawers with central dividers, to the boxes in which the slides arrive from processing, to larger boxes either commercially available or especially made, or to plastic folders either hanging in filing cabinets or in binders and to folders of various sizes and types, and even to commercially available cabinets holding 1000–2000 slides (a few will hold 5000), having integral light-boxes for viewing. These, being based on larger frames full of slides, are mostly cumbersome and expensive. It has to be remembered that box-storage means excessive handling of slides during selection, and inevitable removal to examine each slide whether selected or replaced. Also the time spent in flipping through and re-filing is longer than with the plastic holders, which do protect the slide from handling to a certain extent.

DUPLICATION

In some circumstances it has been found cheaper and easier to duplicate a slide to locate it in the retrieval system according to several features than to index in detail or to employ alternative means of retrieval. However, before opting for this seemingly easy answer it is essential to remember that every duplicate needs time spent on labelling, mounting, accessioning and filing, and will take up store space. Is it worthwhile?

Conclusion

Hopefully, these brief notes will form an adequate starting point for anyone wishing to organize slides and will indicate the lines of enquiry to follow in depth while at the same time indicating some alternative sources of information. Much of what has been said throughout this section, including the sources of information and collections' guidance, is also applicable to photographs, remembering mainly that description of content is less vital but identification of photographer and date remains important, and that storage may require mounting and must take account of preservation, especially of colour.

Bibliography

Bradfield, V. J. (1976). *Slide Collections: A User Requirement Survey*, British Library (R & D report 5309)
Bradfield, V. J. (1978). 'Slides and their users: thoughts following a survey of some slide collections in Britain', *Art Libraries Journal*, **2,** No. 3, 4–20
Caldicott, E. L. (1956). 'Running the lantern slide collection', *Architectural Association Journal*, **LXXi,** No. 998, 160–161
Harris, S. (1977–1978). The organisation of slide libraries', *CIIG Review*, No. 2, 223
Harvard-Williams, P. and Karling, S. A. (n.d.). *Rules for the Cataloguing of Slides in the Liverpool School of Architecture*, mimeo
Havard-Williams, P. (1960). 'The slide collection at Liverpool School of Architecture', *Journal of Documentation*, **16,** No. 1, 11–14
Irvine, B. J. (1974). *Slide Libraries*, Libraries Unlimited
Keaveney, S. S. (1975). 'Report of the slides and photographic session, CAA meeting, 1973', *Worldwide Art and Library Newsletter*, **1,** Nos 1–2
Merrett, C. E. (1980). 'Computerized information retrieval from a slide collection for architects', *South African Libraries*, **47,** No. 3, 103–106
Ministry of Public Building and Work (1963). *Notes on the MoPBW Photographic Library*, mimeo
Roberts, M. (1970). 'Slide collections: some retrieval problems and their solution', *CIIG Bulletin*, **1,** No. 1, 5–12
Rush, J. (1974). 'Slide and photography libraries', *CIIG Bulletin*, **4,** No. 2, 3–4
White, B. (1967). *Slide Collections: A Survey of their Organisation in Libraries in the Fields of Architecture, Building and Planning*, Edinburgh, the author
White, B. (1966). 'The SfB system: classification for the building industry', *Library Association Record*, **68,** 428–432

11
Developing a design

It was stated earlier that information is needed throughout the construction process. Four sections follow which relate directly to each stage in the design, planning, construction and finishing of a building. The first section aims to cover, in some detail, the sort of information which the architect will need to gather together in the early stages of a project while developing the brief. Initially, 'design data' covers precedent studies, user studies and ergonomic and anthropometric data as related to any specific building type. This is then developed to look at other 'fringe' topics which are of importance not only to the architect but to the other members of the construction team whether or not they specialize in these areas. Thus the site survey and the land use and planning information relating to any area are both covered here. Finally the sources of climatic data, its value and uses, are discussed with relation both to Britain and the rest of the world.

Design data

Valerie J. Bradfield

Those architects who have specialized in several types of building will have kept up-to-date with the current examples and will have, or should have, related information at their fingertips. When they come to tackle something new – a new aspect or another type of building – then user needs must be investigated and new data assembled. Others may vary their workload and need to perform such searches more frequently. New techniques develop, and an architect may be requested to use them by clients or contractors. Information must be found. New inventions like computers and their installation in many different types of building necessitated an understanding of their requirements in ventilation and floor loading. Later generations of computers then appeared with less stringent environmental requirements. Solar heating methods require investigations in a similar way.

There are basic information needs for any types of building:

(1) The precedent study;
(2) The study of the users and their normal activities, i.e. workflow (sometimes described in the brief but not adequately);
(3) Special requirements of equipment, users and structures;
(4) Standard technical, product and systems information.

The last-mentioned is dealt with elsewhere. The first usually requires reference to the architectural journals, studies of modern architecture, *AJ* and *Building* analyses of building, etc., which can usually be located quickly using the *Architectural Periodicals Index*. But information on specific aspects of building types is frequently to be found in the literature of the related subject. Thus for schools and their changing needs the education literature should be used, for the crown courts the law journals, and computer-user needs will be discussed in the literature of management and computers.

Indexing and abstracting services are always the quickest source of background information and can be located fairly easily in major educational or institutional libraries. Most subject areas have at least one relevant service while many have also a related database (see p. 64) which can speed the search considerably, since it will almost always be easy to define the information needed fairly distinctly:

> Today there is less need for illustration of construction details. Manufacturers increasingly distribute technical information which can be filed in uniform office systems: and

with telephone line and video display unit an office can reach vast computerised and regularly revised data banks. To make sense of this mass of information the architect now needs even clearer guidance on the principles and bases of design. (Neufert, 1981, foreword)

This section will go on to look at the resources providing this guidance at the start of any project, outlining the basic resources and pointing the way to locating those which will assist the more obscure lines of enquiry. This will mean discussing the texts and reference handbooks available before noting some of the most helpful indexes, abstracts and associations. Other information needs mentioned by Neufert above are covered in Chapters 4 and 7 respectively.

For the basic building types the *AJ* 'Annual Review' has established not only a bibliography with notes on new pamphlets and articles but also a review of the year's work and developments. These are worth keeping, since the subsequent issues add to the early ones and condense earlier lists of references into the newer bibliographies. Although some items omitted in succeeding years have genuinely been superseded, others have only been omitted for space reasons.

Supplementing this, the newer *AJ* 'Buildings Update' aims to discuss recent developments in a particular building type in greater detail and in the second of each two-part feature gives further sources of information.

Handbooks

The usual starting point for information is the desk reference book. At least one of the following should be readily available to every designer. Two may prove more expensive to maintain in currency but will complement each other if selected with care. Some articles in the front of *Specification* will prove helpful, but in Britain either the *New Metric Handbook*, Mills' *Planning* or Neufert's *Architect's Data* are the standard handbooks. All require familiarity for effective use, the cheapest and easiest to use being the *New Metric Handbook*.

Before considering each of these a brief mention should be made of *House's Guide to the Construction Industry* (8th edn, House Information, 1981), which summarizes various regulations and indexes their contents along with other relevant legislation. Many questions concerning the minimum legal provision of facilities can therefore be answered from here.

The original *AJ Metric Handbook* has been revised, almost completely rewritten by contributors and edited by Patricia Tutt and David Adler as the *New Metric Handbook* (Architectural Press, 1979). Information on metrication is less important after the familiarity of ten years' work with the system and the content now provides a larger volume of basic data on a wide range of building types and environmental and structural design in forty chapters, extending from the layout of roads to the appendices of conversion data and tables for design calculations. Treatment of most subjects is fairly brief while attempting to provide adequate basic information. References to further reading are given at the end of most chapters but are limited, both in number and scope. By a happy coincidence, the buildings covered complement rather than duplicate the coverage of Mills and Neufert. Naturally, information given here does not overlap more than necessary with that in other *AJ Handbooks* listed in Chapter 6, p. 101, and those refer to information on building types where relevant to the structure, etc. as part of the design decision-making process. For example, the *AJ Handbook of Building Enclosure* refers to basic sources of dimensions in the MoPBW/DoE series of publications on dimensional coordination (listed in *PSA in Print*) such as DC7 (1967), *Recommended Intermediate Vertical Controlling Dimensions for Educational, Health, Housing and Office Buildings and Guidance on their Application*.

Planning, edited by Edward Mills, used to be one large volume of basic design data relating to both general needs for circulation, work, design and specific building-types, but the ninth edition has changed this; a five-volume format, where the first volume covers general data, circulation, fittings, anthropometrics and conversion factors while each of the others deals with groups of building types; *Planning: Buildings for Education, Culture and Science; Planning: Buildings for Health, Welfare and Religion; Planning: Buildings for Administration, Entertainment and Recreation; Planning: Buildings for Habitation, Commerce and Industry* (Butterworths, 1976–1977). Each discusses the range of buildings within its scope and provides reference drawings and data as well as lists of significant buildings, references to articles, texts, standards and legislation. The volume of references is varied, but careful use of the text will often reveal more than those listed in the basic bibliography at the end of each section.

Mills is also currently the editor of a further series for Butterworths on specific building types. Volumes issued so far are *Design for Leisure Entertainment*, by Wylson (1980) and *Design for Health Care* by Cox and Groves (1981). Hopefully, further

Developing a design   213

volumes will not duplicate other single-volume works published by Architectural Press such as Duffy, Cave and Worthington's *Planning Office Space* (1976), Falconer and Drury, *Building and Planning for Industrial Storage and Distribution* (1975), Gosling and Maitland, *Design and Planning of Retail Systems* (1975), Lawson's *Hotels, Motels and Condominiums* (1976), *Principles of Catering Design* (2nd edn, 1978), *Conference, Convention and Exhibition Facilities* (1981), Ham's *Theatre Planning* (1977), Stone's *British Hospital and Health Care Buildings* (1980), Thompson's *Planning and Design of Library Buildings* (2nd edn, 1977) and Perrin's *Sports Halls and Swimming Pools* (Spon, 1980). This list could go further, but suffices to show the activity generated by the need for design data for building types – the *AJ Factory Design Handbook* was published by Architectural Press at the end of 1981 as *Factories: Planning, Design and Modernisation*, edited and revised by Jolyon Drury. A four-volume revised edition of the *AJ Handbook of Sport and Recreational Building Design* was published by Architectural Press in conjunction with the Sports Council Technical Unit in 1981 (eds. G. John and H. Heard).

Naturally, these date, as do all handbooks, and recently the second edition of Neufert's *Architect's Data* (Granada, 1981) has been published. The original German edition of 1936 was published in English in 1970 (with revision) and became yet another 'standard'. However, the new edition is more international than its predecessor. It is much more expensive and no larger than the *New Metric Handbook* which it complements rather than duplicates. Data is given, however, without reference to the country of origin and some of the printing is very small. Although the publisher's blurb states that all dimensions are metric at least one reviewer has pointed out that they are not (Herzberg, *AJ*, 24 and 31 December 1980). Indexing proved inadequate to locate floor space requirements for flats – but the information was found through careful reading of the text. The bibliography covers British and American publications and standards in one sequence referred to by numbers in the text and therefore not easily followed for references on any one type of building.

A number of British architects also refer to the two American volumes of data similar to the above, De Chiara's *Time-saver Standards for Building Types* (2nd edn, McGraw–Hill, 1980) and Ramsey and Sleeper's *Architectural Graphic Standards* (7th edn, R. T. Packard, Wiley, 1981). This is the second edition to be prepared in association with the American Institute of Architects and is a compilation of information from a large number of contributors, mainly firms. This concentrates more on technical data than the British volumes – in Britain we rely more on the *AJ Handbooks* for this type of information – but it includes anthropometric and design data. This latter volume has been described as the 'architect's Bible'.

However, some basic data will be better located in an engineering handbook such as *Kempe's Engineers' Yearbook*, or the British Constructional Steelwork Association's *Structural Steelwork Handbook* (2nd edn, 1978) or by using the references in the *Barbour Design Library (BDL)*, which has in some ways cut out the need for intermediary handbooks. Although only housing is included as a building type in the *BDL* there are many references which relate to very specific buildings, like hospitals or junior schools, under specific structural problems and materials. At other times an association will have to be contacted from those given in *BDL* or by using one of the directories listed in Chapter 6, or the sources discussed at the end of this section.

Anthropometric data

People use buildings; people complain about buildings designed for non-humans by architects who are humans. As a result much work has been done on the science of anthropometry, 'the measurement of the human body' (*OED*), to investigate the 'average person' and data as well as to discuss the differences between the various data books available and their use to provide adequate design data. It may sometimes seem incredible that two different design texts can give different data for the average human reach! MIT's *Humanscale* portfolio of calculators, charts and drawings give basic data and means for calculating varying human dimensional needs in a novel way likely to appeal to many architects. Studies of the space needs in buildings are not numerous. H. Dreyfuss, *The Measure of Man: Human Factors in Design* (Architectural Press, 1967) remains one of the standard texts. Sommer's *Personal Space* (Prentice-Hall, 1969) discusses personal needs and the ways of gathering data rather than actually presenting that data. The Land Use and Built Form Study Group at the University of Cambridge School of Architecture has worked on the *Environmental Evaluation of Buildings* (Working paper, 28, 1970) and Croney's text *Anthropometrics for Designers* (2nd edn, Batsford, 1980) was fairly basic. More recently Panero and Zelnick have published *Human Dimension and Internal Space* (Architectural Press, 1980), 'a unique new source book of standards for designers in every discipline', with anthropometric tables relating to not only different types of person and of activities but also to the ways in which needs affect interior design. The elderly and the disabled are also included. From another point of view *Housing Climate and Comfort* by M. Evans (Architectural Press, 1980) presents clear applied information to one particular building type.

Ergonomic data

Complementary to anthropometrics is the study of the efficiency of persons in their environment, whether at work, play or doing the chores, how they perform tasks and the best ways in which to provide for effective task performance. Hence for the designer thought is not necessarily only required about human dimensions but about the best layouts for various purposes. Although many people prefer personally designed spaces to work in, there are recommendations which can be followed in numerous different situations, but not all are readily locatable. Works like Inchbald's *Bedrooms* (Studio Vista, 1969) and Kira's *Bathrooms* (Studio Vista, 1969) should be referred to in the handbooks, as should other fairly well-known ones like the University Grants Committee's *Kitchen Planning* (HMSO, 1972) in the *University Building Notes* series. Unfortunately some will only be identifiable after consulting a number of bibliographies, handbooks, the *AJ* 'Annual Review' and *API*, and may only then be locatable in the larger libraries.

General texts do exist such as P. Tregenza's *The Design of Internal Circulation* (Crosby Lockwood Staples, 1976), which has a particularly long bibliography covering many building types. McCullagh's *Physical Working Conditions* was published by Gower for the Industrial Society (1969) and gives much data on various working situations but is no longer current and will not include more modern tasks – although such basic data usually only dates in its presentation and many tasks can be broken into component actions. Imperial measurements in the 1960s have now given way to fully metric presentation in the 1980s. Singleton's *Measurement of Man at Work* (Taylor and Francis, 1971) and Grandjean's *Ergonomics of the Home* (Taylor and Francis, 1973) are both in similar vein. The list could be endless, very specific and very varied as two more examples will show; Gooch's *Sports Ground Construction Specifications* (2nd edn, NPFA, 1975) and the DES *Building Bulletin 52, School Furniture; Standing and Sitting Postures* (HMSO, 1976). Almost all have useful bibliographies. The United States Department of Commerce published *Building for*

People, by Rubin and Elder (1980, NBS Special publication No. 474) to try to emphasize the importance of this type of study, and all aspects of design application are included in Huchingson's *New Horizons for Human Factors in Design* (McGraw–Hill, 1981). So many recent publications after a lull reflect a revival of interest in designing for human needs.

British standards sometimes provide this sort of data, e.g. BS 5940: Part 1: 1980, *Specification for Design and Dimensions of Office Work Stations, Desks, Tables and Chairs,* among others.

Those interested in this area of investigation, and in all building types, should be aware of the work of the Ergonomics Information Analysis Centre at the University of Birmingham Department of Engineering Production. They have been gathering information since 1959, although only operative to the public since 1968. Enquiries can be answered and bibliographies are available. Charges may be made if work is undertaken. They publish *Ergonomics Abstracts*, in which a wide range of periodical articles are indexed regularly, from journals in the arts, life sciences, sciences and technology and managements fields. The only other source for abstracts of periodical articles on ergonomics is the more specialist *Design Abstracts International* (ceased 1981).

The disabled and the elderly

Although not necessarilly usually grouped together, modern society is increasingly showing its concern with these two groups of persons, and all architects should be aware of the legislative requirements for access to buildings and circulation within buildings (see p. 177) which often apply equally to both groups. Now in its third edition, Selwyn Goldsmith's *Design for the Disabled* (RIBA Publications, 1976) has long been recognized as the basic handbook and contains not only a wealth of data but an extensive bibliography, relating not just to purpose-built buildings but to needs in all other buildings. So vastly has the information and data now available in this specific field increased that the third edition is double the second in size. Still valuable, although dating now, is Bayes and Francklin's early volume, *Designing for the Handicapped* (Godwin, 1971), which deals with various types of disablement and has good lists of references and resources.

The *AJ* 'Annual Review' maintains a separate section on the handicapped and the Centre on the Environment for the Handicapped produces many notes and leaflets giving data for use in specific instances as well as a *Bibliography/Information Sheet* series which includes No. 4, *Designing for Elderly People* (CEH,

1976). Anthea Tinker used to work for the Housing Development Directorate of the DoE, and *The Elderly in Modern Society* (Longman, 1981) provides good references on accommodation for the elderly – as do the DoE *Design Bulletins*, although some are now aged themselves.

The concentration on housing is also reflected in the numerous *AJ* analyses of new homes both for handicapped and elderly people, and volumes such as Penton's *A Handbook of Housing for Disabled People* (London Housing Consortium West Group, 1981). There is also BS 4467, *Anthropometric and Ergonomic Recommendations for Dimensions in Designing for the Elderly*.

Journals

So much has been published during the 1970s in this area that the periodical indexes and abstracts are essential in this field. Material published for architects and designers will be found in *API*, but it will also be worthwhile to consult *British Humanities Index* and *Social Services Abstracts*. A number of indexing and abstracting journals have already been mentioned, like *Ergonomics Abstracts*, which also has an 'Application' index to assist users in locating information related to their specific situation, and *Design Abstracts International* from the International Council for Societies of Industrial Design (ICSID). *Current Technology Index* has a number of references to anthropometrics and ergonomics in buildings, including examples such as 'task lighting'. *Psychological Abstracts* will also prove useful for detailed study, although sometimes more difficult to use. A few references will be found to specific situations under the building types headings in *API* as well as the *Construction References* and *International Building Services Abstracts*. However, information from the people using the buildings will come from their own journals indexed in services like *Hospital Abstracts, British Education Index* or the ERIC database (education) and *Library and Information Science Abstracts* (also available on-line), for example. In the same way all the architecture journals carry the occasional articles and brief notes, while the only journal in this field is *Ergonomics* from the International Ergonomics Association (Taylor and Francis, monthly, 1957–).

Associations

The directories in Chapter 2 indicate the relevant-interest organizations according to building type with their current addresses. Until the *Handbook of Sport and Recreation Buildings* was published in 1981 the National Playing Fields Association with the Sports Council were always the main source of data on sports buildings requirements. The Society of Motor Manufacturers provide data for use in relation to cars and buildings. The list is endless.

The Design Council studies of human needs in various situations are usually published in book form or in their journal, *Design*, and they can sometimes supply information if contacted. Various government departments with special interests will be located in *Technical Services to Industry* (DoI, 1979). The DES and DHSS provide many leaflets on requirements in various situations, as well as the names of contacts, and many bibliographies are available from their respective libraries.

Special-interest societies such as that for the handicapped have been mentioned and will be found in the *Directory of British Associations* along with many local societies who are more geared to caring for, than to developing data on, the needs of the handicapped and the elderly in particular.

The potential sources already indicated are numerous. This is the type of data or information which, along with structures' and materials' data, is the most amenable to databank storage and retrieval systems such as the French *ARIANE* (see p. 66). The possibilities were discussed by W. J. Mitchel in *Computer-aided Architectural Design* (New York, Petrocelli-Charter, 1977), showing how such databanks could also be used by the computer for the production of drawings. In particular, the bibliography (pp. 515–560) should be mentioned, although it is only slightly more up-to-date than the DoE *Bibliography on the Application of Computers in the Construction Industry 1962–1971* (DoE, 1971) with its various supplements. It may not be long before some larger practices have large in-house databanks of basic design data to which additions are made when required by the diversification of work.

Site survey

Andrew McDonald

The site survey enables the location of a construction to be set on the ground and basically involves measuring a small area of the earth, with its boundaries and features, and representing it to some suitable scale on paper. The surveyor uses various techniques and instruments to measure particular quantities such as distances, heights and angles to an appropriate degree of accuracy, and this inevitably entails some practical mathematical knowledge.

The architect may wish to conduct relatively simple surveys using techniques such as chain surveying, levelling and tacheometry, or he may wish to understand a survey commissioned from a professional surveyor.

Developments in the use of calculators and computers have brought highly mathematical techniques within reach. The application of electronics to surveying instruments has simplified many measurements such as electromagnetic distance measurement. Techniques relevant to other sciences and other branches of surveying have become increasingly important in land surveying.

Hence it is a professional asset to be aware of the books and reference works relevant to simple surveys, of resources such as periodicals for keeping abreast of current developments, of the retrieval tools such as abstracting services and of the specialized organizations able to provide expert services and advice.

Basic texts

There are a number of relatively non-mathematical textbooks which explain the basic techniques and instrumentation, and some describe how to tackle a basic site investigation and survey. The early chapters of the more advanced books can also be helpful. Remember that some of the practices referred to in the American books are different from those practised in this country.

Basic Metric Surveying, by W. S. Whyte (2nd edn, Butterworths, 1976).
Elementary Surveying, by R. C. Brinker and P. R. Wolf (6th edn, Harper and Row, 1977). American.
Elementary Surveying, by A. L. Higgins (3rd edn, Longman, 1970).
Fundamentals of Survey Measurement and Analysis, by M. A. R. Cooper (Crosby Lockwood Staples, 1974). Advanced.
Guide to Site Surveying, by R. Hewitt (Architectural Press, 1972). Good, practical and written with architects in mind.

Land Surveying, by R. J. P. Wilson (2nd edn, MacDonald and Evans, 1977). Good and practical.
Plane and Geodetic Surveying, Volume 1: Plane Surveying, by D. Clark (6th edn, rev. by J. E. Jackson, Constable, 1972).
Practical Field Surveying and Computations, by A. L. Allan, J. R. Hollwey and J. H. B. Maynes (Heinemann, 1968). Advanced.
Principles and Use of Surveying Instruments, by J. Clendinning and J. G. Olliver (3rd edn, Van Nostrand Reinhold, 1969). Advanced.
Principles of Surveying, by J. G. Olliver and J. Clendinning (2 vols, 4th edn, Van Nostrand Reinhold, 1978). Advanced.
Site Investigation, by C. R. I. Clayton *et al.* (Granada, 1982). Broad coverage and recent.
Surveying, by A. Bannister and S. Raymond (4th edn, Pitman, 1977).
Surveying, by R. H. Dugdale (3rd edn, Macdonald and Evans, 1980).
Surveying for Construction, by W. Irvine (2nd edn, McGraw–Hill, 1980).
Surveying for Engineers, by J. Uren and W. F. Price (Macmillan, 1978). Good.
Surveying for Young Engineers, by S. W. Perrott, rev. by A. L. Allan (3rd edn, Chapman and Hall, 1970).
Urban Surveying and Mapping, by T. J. Blachut, A. Chrzanowski and J. H. Saastmoinen (Springer-Verlag, 1979). Canadian and good.

Two audio-visual presentations can be recommended; *Preparing a Site Plan using Chain Surveying and Levelling Techniques*, by R. W. A. Dallas (Commonwealth Association of Architects, 1979), cassette/slides with booklet, and *Surveying for Construction*, by F. Shaw (Audio Visual Aids Unit. Loughborough University, 1978–), a series of cassette/slides with booklets.

There was a good series of supplements to the *Architects' Journal*, October-November 1965, called *Guide to Site Investigation* (Information Sheets 1338 to 1360). Although written with civil engineers in mind, *BS 5930: 1981 Code of Practice for Site Investigations* (British Standards Institution, 1981) is both detailed and practical, and it contains sources of information and a good bibliography. Section five of *BS 5606: 1978 Code of Practice for Accuracy in Building* (Building Standards Institution, 1978) deals with setting out on-site. Accuracy is also covered in Building Research Establishment, Digest 234, *Accuracy in Setting Out* (HMSO, 1980). Other relevant Building Research Establishment

Digests are 202, *Site Use of the Theodolite and Surveyor's Level*, (HMSO, 1977) and 63, 64 and 67, *Soils and Foundations* (HMSO, 1965, 1965 and 1966).

Some of the books mentioned in this section give details or point to sources of information about the practical problems which can be encountered in a site investigation such as soil testing, rock classification and tree identification. They also introduce important resources such as the Ordnance Survey, the Geological Survey and Soil Survey Maps and *Memoirs* (now incorporated within the Institute of Geological Sciences), Admiralty charts and hydrographic publications of the Hydrographic Department of the Ministry of Defence, the Meteorological Office and sources of hydrological information, the Central Register of Air Photography of England and Wales, which is maintained by the Department of the Environment, and the Global Seismology Unit of the Institute of Geological Sciences (see p. 193).

Photogrammetry

Photogrammetry is a technique usually applied to mapping large areas, but it has applications to site surveying where suitable up-to-date air photographs exist or can be commissioned. Two useful basic texts are *Elementary Air Survey*, by W. K. Kilford (4th edn, Pitman, 1979) and *Elements of Photogrammetry*, by P. R. Wolf (McGraw-Hill, 1974).

More advanced texts are *Mapping from Aerial Photographs*, by C. D. Burnside (Crosby Lockwood Staples, 1979) and *Photogrammetry*, by F. H. Moffitt and E. M. Mikhail (3rd edn, Harper and Row, 1980). The *Manual of Photogrammetry* (4th edn, American Society of Photogrammetry, 1980) is both comprehensive and advanced and it contains a good, up-to-date dictionary of the terms and symbols used. Two much older dictionaries are the *Photogrammetric Dictionary* (Elsevier, 1961) and *Standard Definitions of Terms used in Photogrammetric Surveying and Mapping* (National Mapping Council of Australia, 1963).

Two multilingual dictionaries, although rather out of date, may be of use when dealing with foreign-language material. *Dictionar Poliglot de Geodezie, Fotogrammetrie si Cartografie: Englezā, Romānā, Germānā, Franceza, Rusa*, by G. Marton (Editura Tecnicā, 1976) and *Multilingual Dictionary for Photogrammetry*, International Society for Photogrammetry (6 vols, Argus, 1969), which covers English, French, German, Italian, Polish and Swedish.

The technique of photogrammetry is also used in architecture for recording facades and monuments and is important for conservation work. This is covered in *Architectural Photogrammetry*, by R. W. A. Dallas (2nd edn, Commonwealth Association of Architects, 1978), cassette/slides with booklet, and *Photogrammetric Surveys of Monuments and Sites*, by J. Baedekas (Elsevier, 1976).

Periodicals

Information relevant to site surveying can sometimes be found in architecture and building periodicals such as the *Architects' Journal* and *Building*. Although few of the periodicals published of interest to the surveyor are of real interest to the architect they do provide a means of keeping abreast of developments in professional issues, thinking and practice and of developments in surveying techniques and instrumentation. Most of the relevant periodicals are published by the professional bodies and learned societies in surveying and so provide details of society activities, members and publications, advertisements for equipment and services, conference reports and announcements, useful bibliographies and book reviews.

The 'general professional interest' periodicals are excellent sources for information about professional news and developments and they often also include contract news, equipment reviews and details of educational and professional opportunities. The *Chartered Surveyor* is such a periodical, published monthly by the Royal Institution of Chartered Surveyors, but since it covers all aspects of surveying, the land surveying content is very limited. Apart from very readable topical articles, regular features deal with property, housing, market intelligence, investment, estate agency, parliament, coming events, RICS news and library notes. *Chartered Land Surveyor and Chartered Minerals Surveyor* evolved from the *Chartered Surveyor* as a quarterly periodical concentrating on slightly more technical papers on land and minerals surveying. The contents page gives useful summaries of the articles. Abstracts of articles from other periodicals are included. The *Surveying Technician* is a slim monthly published by the Society of Surveying Technicians.

There are also a number of periodicals which publish original research and review papers. They are often highly mathematical and technical, and are largely of research interest: *Australian Journal of Geodesy Photogrammetry and Surveying* (University of New South Wales, half-yearly), *Australian Surveyor* (Institute of Surveying, Australia, quarterly), *Canadian Surveyor* (Canadian Institute of Surveying, quarterly), *New Zealand Surveyor* (New

Zealand Institute of Surveying, six-monthly), *Photogrammetria* (International Society for Photogrammetry and Remote Sensing, bi-monthly), *Photogrammetric Engineering and Remote Sensing* (American Society of Photogrammetry, monthly), *Photogrammetric record* (Photogrammetric Society, half-yearly), *South African Survey Journal* (Central Council of Land Surveyors of the Republic of South Africa, three p.a.), *Survey Review* (Directorate of Overseas Surveys of the Foreign and Commonwealth Office, quarterly) and *Surveying and Mapping* (American Congress on Surveying and Mapping, quarterly).

The contents pages of *Photogrammetria* and *Photogrammetric Engineering and Remote Sensing* appear in the current-awareness services *Current Contents, Physical, Chemical and Earth Sciences* and *Current Contents, Engineering Technology and Applied Sciences*.

Abstracts and indexes

Some periodicals such as *Chartered Land Surveyor/Chartered Minerals Surveyor* and *Photogrammetric Record* contain abstracts of articles from other periodicals and sources. There are no abstracting or indexing services which concentrate solely on surveying, although a useful English-language-based service is *Abstracts and Reviews*, produced monthly by the Royal Institution of Chartered Surveyors (RICS) Library Information Service, regularly abstracting some four hundred periodicals. The Reviews Section contains an article with references or a bibliography emphasizing recent references on a topical subject. The back cover lists up-to-date statistics such as the DoE construction indices. Cumulative subject indexes have been produced irregularly since 1965.

Bibliographia Geodaetica is a monthly abstracting service of more interest to geodetic surveyors but it contains sections on surveying and photogrammetry produced from the International Federation of Surveyors and the Technical University of Dresden, respectively. The papers are predominantly German, with some in Russian, French and English, but all foreign-language papers are also given in English. They are arranged by subject (Universal Decimal Classification) with a monthly author index and an annual subject and author index.

GeoAbstracts Part G – Remote Sensing, Photogrammetry and Cartography abstracts not only the primary periodicals but also other important sources of information such as discussion papers, conference and symposia papers and patents. Part G, which started in 1974, now has sections on surveying, measurement,

224 Developing a design

photogrammetry and mapping and is one of the seven parts of *GeoAbstracts* which are published six times a year by GeoAbstracts Ltd, University of East Anglia, Norwich NR4 7TJ. In the issues you must use the contents page to find an appropriate section and inspect the abstracts given. Subject and author indexes are published annually and a cumulative index for Part G is published every five years. The coverage of photogrammetry has recently been extended by the inclusion of the *ITC Bibliography (International Bibliography of Photogrammetry)*, which was produced by the Institute for Aerial Survey and Earth Sciences (ITC) in Holland. Previously this was a card index arranged by subject using the Universal Decimal Classification, covering all aspects of photogrammetry in English, French and German with author and subject indexes.

References can also be found in the multidisciplinary engineering services *Engineering Index* (Engineering Index Inc., monthly), the more general *Current Technology Index* (previously *British Technology Index*) (Library Association, monthly), the interdisciplinary science and technology service *Science Citation Index* (Institute for Scientific Information, bi-monthly) and the multidisciplinary service specializing in report literature *US Government Reports Announcements and Index* (National Technical Information Service, bi-weekly).

Databases

Although *GeoAbstracts* is available on *DIALOG*, the on-line services do not hold any other databases with very much material relevant to a site survey. The odd relevant reference can be retrieved from the large number of databases available, which would be very time-consuming to search manually and have not been indexed with the architect or surveyor in mind. Such databases are *COMPENDEX* (Engineering Index), *INSPEC* (includes Physics Abstracts), *NTIS* (US Government Reports Announcements), *Conference Papers Index, Comprehensive Dissertation Index,* and *SCISEARCH* (Science Citation Index).

References from about 1970 are available from these databases. Developments in telecommunications and the ever-increasing number and range of databases available point to an important future for on-line techniques as a retrieval tool.

Prestel

The Royal Institution of Chartered Surveyors (RICS) was one of the first professional bodies to provide information to *Prestel*. The

RICS pages are all free of frame charges and provide details of the service a chartered surveyor can offer, how to locate one, fees, the work of the RICS and property facts and figures. In conjunction with *The Estates Gazette* there is a property advertising and intelligence service. Some RICS booklets can be ordered on *Prestel*.

The range of potentially useful information on Prestel is very large, from details of recently published surveying books provided by the British Library to the weather forecasts provided by the Meteorological Office. There is an information index and an Information Provider index both on *Prestel* and in the associated printed official directory available in the magazine *The Prestel User Viewdata and TV User* (Adprint Ltd, quarterly).

Equipment

The basic texts describe simple equipment and many periodicals review and advertise new equipment. Details of equipment available in the UK is given in *The Surveying Equipment Buyers Guide* (Drawing Office Material Manufacturers Dealers Association, 1978). A number of periodicals published from the various equipment manufacturers are very useful sources: *Bulletin Kern*, Kern & Co. Ltd, Switzerland, *MOM Review*, Hungarian Optical Works, *Surveying News* (Vermessungs-Informatioen), VEB Carl Zeiss Yena, East Germany, *Wild Reporter*, Wild Heerbrugg Ltd, Switzerland and *Zeiss Information*, Carl Zeiss, West Germany. Some libraries have good collections of trade literature.

Conference proceedings

The proceedings of the conferences and symposia of bodies such as the International Federation of Surveyors (FIG), the American Society of Surveying and Mapping, the International Society of Photogrammetry (ISP) and the Conference of Commonwealth Surveyors can be valuable sources of up-to-date research information.

Institutions

The Royal Institution of Chartered Surveyors is the main professional body in the United Kingdom for surveyors with a membership of some 56 000. RICS can always help you locate a chartered surveyor or a specialist whether in surveying practice or in the academic world and the Institution publishes a number of useful directories. Survey firms in the UK with chartered surveyors on their staffs and details of their services, equipment, personnel and experience gained abroad are given in the *Directory of Land and Hydrographic Survey Services* (2nd edn, RICS, 1981). The *Yearbook* (RICS, annual) gives details of officers and members and lists organizations employing RICS members.

Professional and technical enquiries should be addressed to the Secretary of the Land Survey Division. Enquiries from members for information from published sources should be referred to the Library Information Service.

The Library has an up-to-date and comprehensive collection of publications of professional interest and includes books, periodicals, EEC publications, law reports, statistics, land tribunal decisions, maps, British Standards and the Barbour Index of trade literature. It can borrow from other libraries and provide photocopies. The Library Information Service aims to keep subscribers aware of developments and produces a number of services. The *Weekly Briefing* is a digest of news selected from the press and government statements. The monthly *Abstracts and Reviews* abstracts some four-hundred periodicals with selective bibliographies and reviews of topical subjects and a statistical summary. A cumulative index has been published irregularly since 1965. The *Digests of New Legislation* are produced in collaboration with the *Municipal Journal* and summarize new legislation in non-legal language.

The Photogrammetric Society operates from the Department of Photogrammetry and Surveying, University College, London. Its organ is the *Photogrammetric Record*. The Society of Survey Technicians operates from Aldwych House, London, and publishes the periodical *The Surveying Technician*.

Universities and polytechnics which are engaged in the teaching of and research into surveying, architecture or building will have supporting libraries and often specialized staff and enquiry services. The *Directory of Research and Development Activities in Surveying and Related Fields*, by I. J. Dowman (3rd edn, Surveyors Publications Ltd, 1982), lists organizations in the United Kingdom involved in research and development.

Organizations concerned with land surveying in the countries of the International Federation of Surveyors are listed in *Organizations for Land Surveying*, by J. R. Hollwey (International Federation of Surveyors, 1968) and the RICS publishes the *Directory of International Practices* (2nd edn, RICS, 1981).

Land use

John Barrick

The system of town and country planning is concerned with balancing the various and competing uses of land resources for the benefit of the community. This section includes references to background information on the development of the planning system but concentrates on land-use techniques and those areas of the system of most interest and relevance to practising architects, that is, matters of law, development control, planning permission and applications, site investigation, appeals and environmental impact analysis. Useful journals, abstracting and indexing publications are also mentioned as sources of further information.

Sourcebooks and guides

Sourcebook of Planning Information by Brenda White (Bingley, 1971) is a thorough examination of the types and sources of information available. In particular, pages 449–456 describe land-use information sources. Sources for maps, plans, aerial photographs, statistics, development plans and reports are also discussed. In 1974 a more concise volume entitled *Urban and Regional Planning* was published. This lists regional and local plans. As both of these are some years old now, they should be used in conjunction with later sources.

Town and Country Planning in the Department of the Environment's Information Series (Lib/Inf./6, 1979) is a guide to sources of information listing the names and addresses of organizations where information can be obtained. It lists government, official and non-official bodies, giving an indication of the work of each and the final section on reference works enumerates various guides to sources of advice, research in progress and bibliographies.

The *Annual List of Publications* of the Departments of the Environment and Transport, Library Services, lists all publications issued by these organizations, and by HMSO for them, including the Building Research Establishment, the Property Services Agency and the Transport and Road Research Laboratory. There is a detailed index of subjects, authors and issuing agents, that is, all persons and organizations with responsibility for the Departments' publications. Since many of the publications issued by the government have a direct bearing on practice, this is an essential tool for keeping abreast of current advice.

Directories

Contact is often necessary with officials at local and national levels and there are various reference books available to assist in identifying names and addresses of relevant personnel.

The *Directory of Official Architecture and Planning* (Godwin, annual) gives the names of staff in architecture, planning and related departments such as environmental health, industrial development, surveying and housing. It also lists local authority consortia, gas, water and electricity authorities and staff architects to commercial and industrial firms. There is a brief section on information sources for the construction industry and in the 1980/1981 edition there is a legal survey of the last decade. At the end a long list of useful institutions and organizations is given in both subject and name order and should be used with the sources given in Chapter 2

Municipal Yearbook (Municipal Publications, annual) covers government departments, county councils, district councils, Greater London government and the development corporations. The section on town and country planning provides information on economic planning machinery in the regions, industrial development, organizations concerned with town and country planning administration and the regional organization of local planning authorities. The first part also gives an up-to-date account of the functions of the various tiers of local government.

The *Planning Directory and Development Guide*, edited by G. Holt (Ambit, 1981), also attempts to define and describe organizations in the UK concerned with planning. It lists central and local government departments, development corporations, non-governmental organizations and planning consultants. *Where to Find Planning Advice* (produced by the Royal Town Planning Institute) lists firms of planning consultants. These firms are prepared to act on behalf of, and give advice to, clients on a wide range of planning matters.

Texts

PLANNING SYSTEM

While the history and development of the planning system might not be of immediate relevance to architects working on specific jobs, the following books illustrate the present system and its evolution.

Cullingworth's *Town and Country Planning* in Britain in its most recent edition (8th edn, Allen and Unwin, 1982) is a useful standard study of the development and function of the British planning system. It describes the evolution of town and country planning, the role of central government, the local planning machine, the legislative framework and the control of development. There are also chapters on the various forms of land use, such as leisure, traffic, land values and new towns. It must be remembered, though, that books of this kind are always a little out of date as far as current practice and legislation are concerned. Therefore they must be used in conjunction with journals such as The *Planner* and *Planning*, which give up-to-date coverage of current developments.

The Evolution of British Town Planning by Gordon Cherry (Leonard Hill, 1974) is a lucid account of the origins and developments of the British planning system.

Remaking Cities by Alison Ravets (Croom Helm, 1980) analyses the development of urban planning since 1945. Its essential point is that the 'clean-sweep' style of planning has caused much damage, and it argues for a new system with an awareness of power and exploitation and a belief in personal responsibility at its heart.

PLANNING TECHNIQUES

A useful compendium is Robert's *An Introduction to Planning Techniques* (Hutchinson, 1974) which examines design, implementation and evaluation in a clear direct manner. The book also considers different land-use techniques such as population, housing, transport and shopping.

The planning and Transport Research and Computation (International) Co. Ltd, or PTRC as it is more commonly known, produces a series of reports each year based on its summer annual meeting. Many of these papers are by planners in local authority departments and give a good idea of current practice. The range of subjects covered is wide. For example, in 1979 subjects included planning for employment and economic development, retailing, local planning policy analysis, strategic and structure planning practice.

In 1980 the weekly journal *Planning* produced a series of concise information sheets aimed at architects and others (not necessarily planners) involved in assessing any particular site. This *Handbook of Site Planning* (R. Evans (ed.), 18 January 1980 onwards) provided not only a checklist of useful points but also an informed list of references on each topic. These topics include organization of site survey, townscape, user behaviour, site management and usage, environment, subsurface and microclimate.

Written in a straightforward way for those engaged in the development process is *Building, Planning and Development* by E. H. Green (Macmillan, 1981). It covers subjects such as receiving instructions and preliminary investigations, site appraisal and analysis, residential development, shop development, town centre development and renewal, industrial development, services and landscaping. Articles such as 'Making a planning application', an *AJ* 'Technical Study' of 20 September 1978–4 October 1978 by Waters and Robinson of the Boisot Waters Cohen Partnership reflect experience and sometimes present a bibliography.

LAND-USE TECHNIQUES

Land Policy in Planning by N. Lichfield and H. Daren-Drabkin (Allen and Unwin, 1980) reviews the evolution of land policy in Britain up to the 1970s but it is more than a simple historical survey. Sections 2 and 3 in Part 1 on the implementation of development plans and the development process in planning provide a valuable description which practising architects should find most useful. Section 8 in Part 2 and section 9 in Part 3 consider some new land policies for Britain. An interesting appendix contains an international survey of land policy measures and a useful bibliography completes this up-to-date survey.

Rhind and Hudson's *Land Use* (Methuen, 1980) describes, in a straightforward way, the complicated subject of land use. It has sections on history, techniques, applications, models and the framework within which land-use planning functions. The sections on obtaining land-use data, handling and analysing it are likely to be most useful.

Derek Lovejoy's *Land Use and Landscape Planning* (2nd edn, Leonard Hill, 1979) gathers together articles on a wide range of topics, including applied analysis and evaluation techniques, land use and agricultural change, forestry, leisure, communication in the landscape, uses of derelict land and of computers. The long lists of references and the bibliographies to each section are especially useful. It is complemented by the more practical manuals of Weddle and Tandy. *Landscape Techniques* by A. E. Weddle (2nd edn, Heinemann, 1979) describes data collection, site surveying, presentation of information, site-use factors, costs, maintenance, timing and elements of the plan. It then considers such subjects as types of surface, enclosures (walls, fences, bollards, etc), outdoor fittings and furniture, planting techniques, turf, trees and conservation. Although a further chapter on professional practice relates to landscape architecture the discussion of the client's conditions of engagement, drawings, vetting the contract, management and supervision, and negotiations and legislation may be relevant to any site work. Compiled in conjunction with the Landscape Institute and aiming to cover large spaces, the advice and techniques are often equally appropriate to smaller spaces in site finishing.

Originally published in the *Architects' Journal*, Tandy's *Handbook of Urban Landscape* (Architectural Press, 1972) reviews techniques that might be applied in the urban landscape. It also examines, although in less detail than Weddle, such procedural techniques as surveys and contract management, checklists, site investigation, specifications, estimates, procedures and control. Also included are information sheets on parks and open spaces, recreation, gardens, housing estates and elements of landscape construction.

LANDSCAPE RECLAMATION

Landscape Reclamation Practice by B. Hackett (IPC, 1977) considers in detail administrative procedures, survey information, design and layout, landform, drainage and financial control. *The Restoration of Land* by A. D. Bradshaw and M. J. Chadwick (Blackwell, 1980) is subtitled 'the ecology and reclamation of derelict and degraded land', and provides a detailed guide to the problems of derelict land and the appropriate measures for dealing with these problems. There is a great deal of information about soils, vegetation and improvement techniques and, when involved with a local authority, section 2.6 on planning requirements and financial support is useful. However, practitioners should also consult Part ix of the Local Government Planning and Land Act, 1980 which includes an essential definition of a minerals application, and Part xiv involves reclamation grants.

Lanscape towards 2000: Conservation or Desolation, edited by Douglas Smith for the International Federation of Landscape Architects (Landscape Institute, 1979), is a collection of papers on different conservation problems and techniques. The problems which are examined include inner city rehabilitation, historic landscapes, rural landscapes and coastlines and special techniques such as environmental impact analysis, environmental monitoring and ecological conservation.

LAW

Because planning law changes all the time it is important to remember that all the sources in this section must be used in conjunction with journals such as *Planning* and *The Planner*, which will give details of any legislative changes, and the legislation notes in the RIBA *Product Data*. At the time of writing (January 1981) the Local Government, Planning and Land Act has received the Royal Assent and the various clauses in it will be introduced gradually. Part ix on Town and Country Planning, Part x on Land Help by Public Bodies, Part xi, which repeals the Community Land Act, and Part xiv, which deals partly with reclamation grants, are relevant to practice. For a comprehensive examination of the various clauses see the series of articles in *Estates Gazette* by B. Denyer-Green (10 January 1981, onwards).

Sir Desmond Heap's *An Outline of Planning Law* (Sweet and Maxwell, 1982) is perhaps the best-known of the general descriptions of planning law. Currently in its eighth edition, it examines the making of development plans, development control enforcement, inquiries, compensation, compulsory purchase and local authority powers.

The seventh edition of R. N. Hamilton's *Guide to Development and Planning* (Oyez, 1981) has been revised in the context of the 1980 Act and looks at all aspects of the development process, including administration, development plans, control of development and planning permission, appeals, compensation, development land tax and investigation of planning title. His complementary *Planning Procedure Tables* (4th edn, Oyez, 1981) enable the user to follow the steps necessary in the various planning procedures, showing where and how these steps should be taken. It examines development plans, permission, controls, mineral working, enforcement notice procedure and conservation areas among other subjects, and is especially useful for those who are not legal specialists.

Awareness of changes in legislation is vital when, in any one year, a large number of circulars and statutory instruments are issued. A subscription to the *Encyclopedia of Planning Law and Practice* (Sweet and Maxwell) also covers an up-dating service for all new circulars and statutory instruments, Acts of Parliament, appeals and decisions. Architects should find the detailed index especially useful and the 'definitions' of terms used in legislation. There are four loose-leaf volumes.

When considering the question of appeals and applications it is particularly important to remember changes in legislation, and references in this section should not be used without referring to changes in the law since their publication. The *AJ* usually features significant appeals.

The Royal Institution of Chartered Surveyors has produced a series of pamphlets giving step-by-step instructions on how to

Developing a design

apply for permission, etc. There are seven of these Practice Notes (RICS, 1977), i.e.

(1) Investigations of a local authority's planning proposals;
(2) The need for planning permission;
(3) The making of a planning application;
(4) Enforcement of planning control, surveying, valuation and planning investigations;
(5) Grants for the repair of historic buildings;
(6) The impact of traffic management schemes on the use and enjoyment of property;
(7) The making of section 52 agreements.

Information about past decisions on planning appeals can be an important factor in current practice when decisions have to be made or advice given. A number of publications contain information of this kind. The three-volume set, *Planning Appeals* (Ambit Publications, 1976 and irregular) lists and comments on a wide range of appeals, including housing, shops and offices, transport, industry and warehousing, caravans, minerals and leisure. The same organization also issues *Planning Appeals Monthly*, the purpose of which is to enable users to identify cases on which information is required and to give the relevant reference numbers, sources of decision and availability. There is an annual index. Blundell and Dobry's *Planning Appeals and Enquiries* is now in its third edition (Sweet and Maxwell, 1982).

While architects in practice will not necessarily have much contact with compulsory purchase, the two items worth noting are Boyton's *Compulsory Purchase and Compensation* (4th edn, Oyez, 1977) and *Compensation for Compulsory Purchase*, an Occasional Paper from the *Journal of Planning and Environment Law* (1975).

The 1980 Act abolished the Community Land Act but the development land tax is still in operation, and architects wishing to understand how the system works, the terms, intentions and functions of the legislation should consult the *RICS Handbook of Community Land and Development Taxation* (Kluwer-Harrap, 1976) and the *Encyclopedia of Planning Law and Practice; Land Development Series*, Volume A1 (Sweet and Maxwell). Both are loose-leaf with regular supplements and consist of explanatory essays with copies of the acts, rules, orders and circulars. A clear guide is *Development Land Tax: A Practical Guide*, by C. Joseph (2nd edn, Oyez, 1980).

Journal of Planning and Environment Law appears monthly and contains articles on aspects of planning law with regular features on parliamentary news, notes of cases and ministerial planning decisions. Some articles are of particular interest. For example, the two articles by J. N. Hawke, 'Planning agreements in practice', in January and February 1981, look at the legal status of planning agreements and how these are used as a means of development control.

DEVELOPMENT CONTROL

The development control system is concerned with granting or withholding of permission to develop land or to change the use made of that land. The 1980 Act and subsequent circulars, such as *Circular 2/81: Town and Country Planning: Development Control Functions*, have recently affected the system described in most texts. 'Development control: the influence of political, legal and ideological factors' by M. L. Harrison (*Town Planning Review*, **43**(3), 1972, 254–274) presented a considered examination of the factors influencing the evolution and functions of the system.

Speculation about the future of the system may well be proved wrong by actual as opposed to imaginary changes, but the following publications contain enough thoughtful material to make them at least worth a glance. The 'Policy forum: the relevance of development control', edited by H. W. E. Davis (*Town Planning Review*, Papers of **51**(1), 1980, 15–24) questions some of the assumptions about development control. *Development Control – Thirty Years On* (Sweet and Maxwell, 1979) contains conference papers on specific aspects of development control legislation, conditions and agreements from the local authority and developer viewpoint, enforcement, the role of the courts and the role of the ombudsman. John Alder's *Development Control* (Sweet and Maxwell, 1979) examines the philosophy of development control and includes many case studies.

Development Control in the 1980's is a report from a working party on development control established by the Royal Town Planning Institute (1979), in five sections, the aims and objectives of the system, policy framework, participants in the planning process and new directions in both major and minor development proposals.

ENVIRONMENTAL IMPACT ANALYSIS

Environmental impact analysis, the assessment of the environmental consequences of development, is already established as a planning technique, but its importance will increase if current EEC proposals to make some form of EIA compulsory succeed.

Chapter 3 of Lovejoy and pages 32–41 of Smith above give concise descriptive examinations of EIA techniques. For further reading and information there is an exhaustive bibliography with abstracts by B. D. Clark and others in *Environmental Impact Assessment* (Mansell, 1980). The various sections of the bibliography deal with critiques and reviews of EIA, EIA and other aspects of planning, EIA in selected countries and information sources.

SITE USE

A recent article in *Estates Gazette* (**255**(6002), 20 September 1980) pointed out how important maps can be in determining previous uses of a site where such uses are likely to affect new buildings, for example, former quarries. In showing the difficulties Mr Ault also gave a very clear guide as to how to go about finding information from maps and locating those old maps. Sources of information on site use such as rights of way, trees, etc. are given in Aldridge's *Registers and Records* (3rd edn, Oyez, 1976), a regularly up-dated and useful list of names and addresses to contact on all such queries.

Research

The results of research projects can be helpful, and the Department of the Environment's annual *Register of Research* is useful, as is the British Library's *Research in British Universities, Polytechnics and Colleges*, both of which give addresses and brief descriptions of the projects themselves. The *INLOGOV Register of Research Projects in Research and Intelligence Units* by A. G. Bovaird (University of Birmingham, Institute of Local Government Studies, 1977) is a descriptive list of projects being carried out in local authorities.

Journals and abstracts

With constant changes the most useful way of keeping up-to-date is to consult the relevant professional journals and the various abstracting publications. The *Journal of Planning and Environment Law* has already been mentioned as particularly good for keeping abreast of changes in the law. *The Planner* (bi-monthly) is the journal of the Royal Town Planning Institute and is aimed at the practising planner, containing articles on current developments and aspects of planning practice which an architect might find useful. It also has book reviews, research reviews and, perhaps of most interest to architects, a review and analysis of recent plans, reports and studies. *Planner News* (monthly) contains articles and notes on professional and practical developments in the planning system, also from the RTPI.

Planning is a very useful weekly newspaper for the practitioner, containing news items, book reviews, comment and items on professional practice. The briefer *Planning Bulletin* also provides a weekly digest of news and publications in readable form.

Town Planning Review is more academic but often contains useful, well-written, articles. For example, in the April 1980 issue there was an interesting article on the future of development plans.

The *Architects' Journal* will be known to architects already but its usefulness is worth mentioning again, especially the legal and technical supplements.

Abstracting journals are very important in keeping up-to-date, and in this context the most useful is the Departments of the Environment and Transport *Library Bulletin*, with sections on planning, transport, housing and environment. Issued with the bulletin is a monthly supplement of government publications, legislation, circulars and technical memoranda issued or sponsored by the Departments.

RICS Weekly Briefing digests news items on energy, housing, conservation, professional practice, planning and development while *RICS Abstracts and Reviews* also has a planning section. *Urban Abstracts* has lengthy coverage of planning techniques, development issues and public participation. These all index a wider range of planning journals than the *API*, which has a section on planning also.

Conclusion

While all the foregoing items will be of use and interest to the practitioner it is also useful to make direct contact with the various organizations which are concerned with planning matters. The Royal Town Planning Institute, which is the professional institute for Chartered Town Planners, produces a range of publications, including working party reports, conference proceedings, consultation memoranda and bibliographies. A publications list is available from 'Publications Despatch' at the Institute. The Town and Country Planning Association is a pressure group on environmental matters and is willing to offer advice to groups and individuals. There are many other pressure groups in the environmental area offering help on such matters as legal problems and funding. The May/June 1981 issue of *The Planner* has a useful list of these organizations, giving their name, address, and what they can offer to the enquirer.

The need to make documents accessible has been recognized by many information services, and Capital Planning Information launched its *Urbandoc Microfile* in 1982. Documents are distributed on microfiche with an index and back-up service like that provided for the *Barbour Design Library*. It will concentrate on local authority publications complementing the Chadwyck-Healey service for *British Official Publications not Published by HMSO*. However, its value lies in the availability of essential documents at the deskside, improving awareness and accessibility.

Climatic data

Bob Frommes

The importance of climatic data in planning and building

Any building, any neighbourhood, any town is under the influence of climate and of all its elements, be it temperature, humidity, radiation, wind, etc. Any building, any neighbourhood, any town alters climate, by absorbing or reflecting received energy or water, by creating turbulences, by furthering or hindering normal air flows, for example.

Applied climatology in building and planning activities must permit the creation of the best possible indoor comfort with minimum use of costly energy and with minimum harm to the outdoor climate. Observation of the rules of applied climatology avoids spoiling indoor and outdoor climate and contributes to reduced investment and operating costs.

Consequences of ignorance

It is not possible, of course, and would be out of place to give here a digest of the theory of applied climatology. But as so few planners seem to know about it, and as so few universities and schools of architecture provide such knowledge to students, it seems essential to give some practical statements on how climatic conditions can be spoiled by mistakes in planning and building.

Towers and other high-rise buildings cause air turbulence at the ground level which can be dangerous to pedestrians. In Sweden an expensive underground access had to be built at one site to make a residential building accessible without any risk for the pedestrians. In seven new towns in Britain the pedestrian precinct had to be covered afterwards as the inhabitants refused to go shopping there, although in the mind of the architects it had been planned to please and to attract the pedestrians. In a new housing scheme in West Germany, in a warm, sticky river valley, the huge, long residential buildings were wrongly located, preventing the nightly downwind from cooling the area. These buildings are extremely dense, in concrete painted in dark colours; only some 15 per cent of the ground-surface is covered with vegetation. As a result of the maximum heating of concrete volumes and surfaces in daytime (they reach up to 63°C in summer), and in the absence of nightly cooling, the air temperature goes up to 10°C higher than some 400 feet away at the edge of the forest. The high skin temperature of the huge buildings even provokes an updraft of the warm air from the valley below, thus carrying the dusty polluted air of the highway to all windows. At night-time in summer, indoor temperature is often up to 10°C higher than outdoor temperature.

Glass architecture gives insufficient heat insulation in winter, low superficial temperature inside and therefore low comfort. In summer, heat irradiation by the sun and the absence of sufficient thermal capacity of the buildings make the rooms uneasy to live in. Tremendous quantities of energy are wasted in heating in winter and even more for cooling (conditioning) in summer. Plated glass can, of course, slightly reduce the irradiation and thus the necessary cooling energy in summer. This needs more heating energy in winter while keeping off the sun irradiations which would be very welcome as complementary free heating energy. Such examples could be continued by the dozen.

Interest of applied climatology

To each negative example, of course, it is possible to give a positive one, and since the ensuing damage has been pointed out, the positive application of climatologic rules leads inevitably to the avoidance of such irretrievable damage and thus to a valuable benefit. One example above all is worth mentioning here. In Zurich an interdisciplinary group – an architect, a climatologist, a physiologist and a specialist in air conditioning – cooperated in 1976 in planning a polyvalent building (shops, offices, flats). The orientation of the building, the dimensions of windows, the use of appropriate materials, the heat insulation value and thermal capacity of walls and ceilings let them do without air conditioning and heat the building with a minimum of energy. Incidentally, the investment cost for the heating and ventilating system of such a building could be reduced by 67 per cent, and the overall yearly operating costs of the whole building by 71 per cent, not to mention the significance of energy savings in terms of national economy.

Information needed in the field of climatology

To plan with correct consideration for the climatic problems we need:

(1) A basic knowledge of meteorology, climatology and applied climatology;
(2) Knowledge of detailed problems of climatology; and
(3) Specific information concerning the meso-and micro-climate (meteorologic data).

BASIC KNOWLEDGE

Applied climatology is related to a wide range of disciplines, starting with meteorology and climatology, hydrology, and even mineralogy and botany. It pre-supposes a certain understanding of biologic and physiologic phenomena, since an optimal indoor climate for the needs of the human body should be reached. The architect and planner cannot, of course, be a professional in all these disciplines, but his comprehension must be sufficient to prevent him from making dangerous mistakes. The problem is to know exactly how much he ought to know in each discipline.

There are a number of excellent handbooks, ranging from an absolute but efficient minimum, Sealey's *Introduction to Building Climatology* (Commonwealth Association of Architects, 1979), to more scientific manuals, often so scientific that a busy architect can hardly find time for the profound study of the whole. In this field it is best to start with a simple and easily understandable digest like the above and proceed to V. Olgay, *Design with Climate* (Princeton, 1963), and B. Givoni, *Man, Climate and Architecture* (Applied Science, 1976). One could also mention here *Applied Climatology* (1978), a brochure edited by the Standing Committee Urban and Building Climatology of the International Federation for Housing and Planning (IFHP), Luxembourg.

A word of warning is necessary here about some misuse of the term 'bio-climatology' which formerly, quite clearly, meant climatology for human life. Recently it appears more frequently as a symbol of some pseudo-science, with so much success that in one country even ministries give it financial support.

Knowledge of detailed problems

Whenever you have to look at more specific problems of climatology, for example, precipitation, radiation, air humidity, sun-protection, etc., there is no better way to find sources than in bibliographies. The number of publications is increasing rapidly and bibliographies become more and more important. While only some twenty publications originate before 1900, some 120 were issued between 1900 and 1940, 500 from 1940 to 1960, 1000 from 1960 to 1970, and 2500 from 1970 to 1980. However, in the field of climatology, bibliographies are not very numerous. They differ mostly by the number of quoted publications. Two questions are essential:

(1) How far should bibliographies include related sciences?
(2) Should they include an appreciation of the quoted publications?

Developing a design   241

If bibliographies are to be a real help to users they should include scientific publications on each discipline connected with climatology but only in so far as the knowledge is indispensable for the understanding of climatologic problems. They therefore should not only include essays and articles on climate and meteorology, on elements of climatology like radiation, temperature, moisture, precipitation, wind, etc. but also, for example, on geophysics, biology, physiology, building properties, energy, alternative energy, energy conservation, physics (heat flow, heat insulation, thermal capacity, moisture, etc.).

There is much discussion about the question of whether alternative (soft) energy and environmental pollution should be included or not. In the author's opinion they both should. As to the first, all energy comes from the sun, and alternative energy includes many climatologic problems. As to the second, it is doubtless a problem of climatic alteration.

Should a bibliography include an evaluation of the quoted publications? Everyone would certainly appreciate it if that could be done. But any appreciation is subjective, and hence not free of doubt. It depends on the accidental state of knowledge of the evaluator. Where would one find the scientist who is competent in several hundred specialized fields of research? Furthermore, how could anyone have the necessary time to read and evaluate thousands of publications? It is definitely not the role of a bibliographer to judge the quality of his colleagues. No-one should dare to be that presumptuous.

There remains therefore the risk that bibliographies name, side by side, good publications and less good, even erroneous ones. There exist some selective bibliographies but they are, of course, far from being complete. They may represent a good guide to the user, but they are not real bibliographies.

The major bibliographies on problems of urban and building climatology are T. J. Chandler's *Selected Bibliography on Urban Climate* (World Meteorological Office, 1968), Frommes' *Bibliography on Urban and Building Climatology* (IFHP, 1979), Griffiths and Griffiths' *A Bibliography on Weather and Architecture* (US Dept of Commerce, 1969) and J. T. Peterson's *The Climate of Cities: A Survey of Recent Literature* (US Dept of Health, 1969). A list of more detailed bibliographies dealing with special problems of climatology is appended to this section.

Databases

These considerations would not be complete without mentioning the possibility of computerized bibliographies. Their value for the user depends on their inner organization and on the choice of their keywords. Although it is less troublesome to consult them, and although their answer comes faster, the user has no keyword index under his eyes and must be able to imagine all possible keywords fitting the question he has in mind. That, for instance is why one such computer-bibliography gave out but two titles under the keyword 'building climatology'. Computerized bibliographies are therefore more appropriate to experienced users with access to the appropriate thesauri either in print or on-line. Although some of the databases mentioned in Chapter 4 may include climate, the only specific one is *Meteorological and Geoastrophysical Abstracts* (MGA) (1950–, monthly) from the American Meteorological Society. This is also available as a printed service.

The Meteorological Office provides information on weather through the British *Prestel* service. Actual weather reports and forecasts cover the United Kingdom in detail and worldwide figures with long-period weather averages, shipping and general weather forecasts.

Local climate

In order to locate a building and construct it correctly we need information about the local climate. It is the role of meteorology to give such information. *Requirements to be Met by Climate Data Books*, produced by the Standing Committee Urban and Building Climatology (IFHP) in 1979, indicated what climate data books should include. Up to now most of the meteorological statistics available do not quite coincide with these recommendations.

Furthermore, statistical data applies only to those points of those territories where measurements are taken. In many cases, an extrapolation will be necessary. For important building tasks one therefore should take the advice of a climatologist who normally has a better ability to find the right comparable data and to interpret it. Professor J. K. Page of Sheffield University has worked out a computer program to provide us with the meteorological data for any point in the world. This is quite extraordinary. But, of course, such computer data cannot be more accurate than the general meteorological data on which it is based. In Britain the Meteorological Office will provide specific data on a particular location for a small fee. Services are described in the pamphlet *Weather Services for Builders* (MO, 1980). Most data for Britain is published in the *Monthly Weather Report* (HMSO) and all current publications are listed both in HMSO's Sectional List No. 37, which is regularly revised, and in the Meteorological Office's own publications list (both free). The publications of the Meteorological Office are too numerous to mention here. Many are discussed in *Climate and Building in Britain* (below) and they include such items as *Maps of Hourly Mean Wind Speed over the UK, 1965 –1973* (MO, 1976), *Maps of Mean and Extreme Temperature over the UK, 1941–1970* (MO, 1975), *Tables of Surface Wind Speed and Direction over the UK* (MO, 1968). 'Weather forecasting for construction sites' was discussed recently by M. S. Prior, giving some useful references to further information (*Meteorological Magazine*, **110,** No. 1310, September 1981, 260–266).

R. E. Lacy's work at the BRE resulted in his *Survey of Meteorological Information for Architecture and Building* (CP 5/72, BRE, 1972), and latterly in a comprehensive analysis of data, its use and sources entitled *Climate and Building in Britain, A Review of Meteorological Information Suitable for Use in Planning, Design, Construction and Operation of Buildings* (HMSO, 1976). This includes much of the data itself with discussions on the reliability of the various figures available. In the same year he also produced *Driving-rain Index: Annual Mean Driving Rain Index in the United Kingdom with Proposed Revised Rules for Assessing Local Exposures* (HMSO, 1976). Also from the BRE is D. R. G. Hunt's *Availability of Daylight* (HMSO, 1979), giving British data based on current figures for balancing energy conservation with lighting.

A number of BRE *Digests* cover climatic data and its uses, for example, Nos 42 and 42, *Estimating Daylight in Buildings* (1969 and 1970) updated by *Sunlight and Daylight* (HMSO, 1972) and the associated protractors; No. 110, *Condensation* (1972) discusses internal/external temperature; No. 119, *Assessment of Wind Loads* (1970) gives a wind-speed map; No. 210, *Principles of Natural Ventilation* (1978) gives principles of wind-speed calculation, a map and references. Further work is reported in Current Papers such as CP70/74, *The Measurement of Wind Pressures on Two-storey Houses at Aylesbury* (BRE, 1974). George Atkinson has attempted, in the 'R & D Round-up' in *Building*, to bring this type of data to the notice of designers and builders, for example, 'The weather report' (*Building*, 8 September 1978, pp. 99–100), and 'Questions of degree' (*Building*, 27 March 1981, p. 52). The BSI included a survey of literature and data availability in DD 67: 1980, *Basic Data for the Design of Buildings: Sunlight*.

Many of the handbooks include brief references to basic data requirements. Section 1 of the *AJ Handbook of Building Environment* covers climate, IS8 and IS9 in Section 4 of the *AJ Handbook of Factory Design* cover climate and wind (*AJ*, 28 June 1978, pp.

1271–1273, and 13 September 1978, pp. 501–503). The CIBS *Guide* Section A2 *Weather and Solar Data* (1982) gives a brief survey of British data and refers the user to other more detailed sources, as does A10, *Moisture Problems*. In discussing 'Microclimate' in the Ove Arup Partnership's *Building Design for Energy Economy* (Construction Press, 1980) R. Emmerson points out that neither the CIBS not the ASHRAE information publications give sufficient data and refers to the BRE work. Weddle and Tandy (see p. 230) mention the climatic survey of a site.

Numerous texts discuss the British climate. The standard is Chandler and Gregory, *The Climate of the British Isles* (Longman, 1976) but among the useful newer texts are M. Evans, *Housing Climate and Comfort* (Architectural Press, 1980) and Aynsley's chapter, 'Available climatic data and how to use them' in H. J. Cowan, *Solar Energy Application in the Design of Buildings* (Applied Science, 1980). For those working on foreign contracts the Meteorological Office publishes *Tables of Temperature, Relative Humidity and Precipitation for the World*, in six parts covering all the continents (the Americas in two parts) and other publications, especially covering coastal regions for the benefit of shipping. The standard text is Landsberg's *World Survey of Climatology* (Elsevier, various dates) in fifteen volumes with various authors; Volumes 1 to 3 are general discussions and the rest give details on all regions, Volume 5 covers north and west Europe. Comparable tables to the Meteorological Office ones can be obtained for many countries, either via the Meteorological Office Library, the embassy or through direct contacts if there is time. Addresses can be obtained from the Meteorological Office Library.

In Britain there is a lot of public interest in climate and many local groups, colleges and individuals collect more localized data than is available from the Meteorological Office. Although its reliability needs to be carefully assessed, such records can be obtained from local sources. The local public library or college may be able to provide addresses. The Polytechnic of the South Bank's Institute of Environmental Science and Technology publishes some of its work in this field, for example, *Annual Frequency of Occurrence of Hourly Values of Outside Air Conditions at 23 Meteorological Stations in the United Kingdom* (1981). The need for guides to this information may be filled when Mansell publish P. B. Wright's *Keyguide to Information Sources in Meteorology and Climatology* (in preparation, mid-1981). Therefore, in conclusion, we can see that although climatology has a very important role to play in planning and building its application in practice still creates many problems.

Bibliography

Barbey, G. and Gelber, Ch. (1973). *Rapports entre l'environnement construit et le comportement humain: ètude bibliographique et analytique*, Lausanne, Ècole polytechnique fèdérale, IREC

Centre scientifique et technique du bâtiment. (1955). *Étude bibliographique du confort thermique*, Nantes, Éstablissement de Nantes

Engineering Societies Library. (1951). *Bibliography on Domestic and Industrial Applications of Solar Heating*, New York, The Library

Gertis, K. (1973). *Litteraturzusammerstellung Baulicher Sonnenschutz*, Stuttgart, Fraunhofer Gesellschaft

Harmon, R. B. (1980). *Climatological Factors in Architecture: A Selected Bibliography*, Monticello, Illinois, Vance Bibliography, Architecture Series, No. A166

Ingeniorsvetenskaps Akademien. (1964). *Bibliography on International Literature about Energy*, Stockholm, The Academy

Jones, M. E. (1968). *Wind Turbulence and Buildings: A Literature Review*. Building Research Station, CP85/68

Joubert, S. P. (1951). *The Resistance of Thin Walls to Rain Penetration: A Review of the Literature*, Pretoria, South African Council of Scientific and Industrial Research

National Research Council. (1953). *Tropical Housing Bibliography*, Washington DC, The Council

Page, J. K. (1955). *A Selected and Classified Bibliography on the Measurement of Radiation in USA*, Sheffield, UK, no publisher

Pearce, D. C. (1951). *A Bibliography on Snow and Ice*, Ottawa, National Research Council

Pelle, W. J. (1964). *Bibliography on the Planning Aspects of Air Pollution Control, Summary and Evaluation*, Washington, DC, Public Health Service, USGPO

Ross, H. D. and Grimsrud, D. T. (1978). *Air Infiltration in Buildings: Literature Survey and Proposed Research Agenda*, US Dept of Energy

Rydell, C. P. and Schwarz, G. (1968). 'Air pollution and urban form: a review of current literature', *Journal of the American Institute of Planning*, **34**, 115–120

Schriner, R. D. and Cohen, M. (1973). 'Bibliography on solar power', *Professional Engineer*, October

Tibbetts, D. C. (1969). *A Bibliography on Cold Weather Construction*, Ottawa, National Research Council

12
Executing a design
Valerie J. Bradfield

Introduction

In such a small compass this chapter cannot hope, and will not try, to be comprehensive in providing lists of all sources of information. Rather it will try to provide a selection showing the types of resource available in each sphere and will attempt to give a brief qualitative assessment of some of those resources combined with some hints on usage. This contrasts with information in Chapters 1–10, which was often quantitative and which should be referred to for more detailed information on some of the titles mentioned in this chapter.

It should also be noted that no list of texts can be complete. A selection indicates the range available. This applies also to the handbooks and reference texts.

Some resources will be referred to frequently throughout since an understanding of the range of the work at the Building Research Establishment (BRE), for instance, is essential and it is frequently the first sensible contact point for advice and information on structures or materials. However, the first point of contact for cost and specification information may be the National Building Specification Ltd (NBS) or the Property Services Agency (PSA) of the Department of the Environment (DoE), which also has wide interests in all aspects of construction covered.

The *Barbour Design Library* (*BDL*) has in two years established its usefulness in locating information at every turn in the construction process and should be referred to constantly for texts and lists on all points covered in this chapter, although it may not be mentioned specifically at every instance. Repetition grows tedious.

Structures

Structures and their detailing are the main scope of this section. In large buildings the designer will not proceed himself but will make the decision as to which specialist to call in to do the structural or civil engineering side of the design once the type of structure required has been indicated.

The specialist is located from experience, from known firms which the practice 'always uses' and from friends willing to recommend consultants. Where none is known, local contacts can be found in the lists of members of institutions such as the Institution of Civil Engineers, the Institution of Structural Engineers, the Royal Institution of Chartered Surveyors and the Chartered Institute of Building. The annual *Building and Contract Journals Directory* lists most contractors in this field. The RICS issued a *Directory of International Practices* (1981) with separate coverage of surveying and mapping, land administration and construction and also with a geographical listing. Other directories of organizations are given in Chapter 2.

Much work has been done in the many problem areas of structures: there have recently been numerous articles and reports of research on flat roofs but, as Chapter 8 points out, work on different types of failures and their causes has shown that much of the information was known and available earlier but not sufficiently widely disseminated. Professionals can no longer rely on the few texts which they have had for years to keep them out of trouble and their structures foolproof.

Inevitably in this section there will be overlap with some of the following sections (for example, the Brick Development Associations' *Low-rise Construction in Brick* (3 vols, BDA, 1979) and discussions on structural steelwork overlap with the materials section), but this will be kept to a minimum as far as possible. As with the other sections of this chapter, a standardized format is normally adopted.

Trade and technical

When gathering information initially the bibliographies in *Specification* and the RIBA *Product Data* are a good starting point – always check these with the up-dates to the BSI *Yearbook* and *Barbour Design Library* for any changes since the date of these bibliographies. Usually the manufacturers' catalogues will be current while most texts should be used with care. One unique example of a text which has more references than usual and should be used at this stage is Rich's *Principles of Element Deisgn* (Godwin, 1977) was the NBA for a second edition published in 1982. This is a collection of checklists or data sheets designed to give designers up-to-date references on each element using texts, BSs, CPs, regulations, digests, etc., at the same time as presenting design information. Originally published in *Building* (17 May 1974 to 31 December 1976) the references were up-dated for publication. Coverage extends from foundations through floors, walls and roofs to doors and windows.

Most practices use their own files of *BRE Digests*. The printed volumes *Building Construction* (2nd edn, Construction Press, 1977) and *Building Defects and Maintenance* (2nd edn, Construction Press, 1977) are useful, especially because their more detailed indexing enables the user to find specific points, but such volumes do not up-date regularly and do not include the more recent digests which often take account of particular current problems. The *Information Papers*, produced by BRE since late 1979, to try to disseminate information more widely, are useful and usually relate to structure or materials, while the output of *Current Papers*, reporting research results, has declined drastically in 1980 and 1981 to around ten a year from fifty or more in earlier years. The most significant of these were published in book form by Construction Press in 1978 as *Building Research Series*. The relevant titles are *Foundations and Soil Technology, Building Failure, Dams and Embankments* and *Wind and Snow Loading*. Indexing is only in the annual BRE *Information*, which is an essential desk-reference pamphlet. *BRE News* was still free in 1981 and the best way of keeping abreast of technical developments if used in conjunction with the journals. Unfortunately, it is not indexed in great detail for information retrieval, although articles of significant length will appear in the bibliographies and indexing journals. The BRE checklists of design features (in progress 1981) will be useful when published.

In 1980 the PSA *Advisory Leaflets* ceased publication but the PSA *Method of Building* pamphlets give technical guidance on every aspect of the building structure from basement, concrete, claddings, windows and doors, to partitions, etc., with a library of working details (including instruction manuals). A few appear in the *Barbour Design Library* and all are listed in *PSA in Print*, (HMSO), items 215–241, with a price range from 30p to £4.60 each in 1980.

Trade literature has already been discussed (Chapter 8) and is relied upon heavily for technical detail, especially where structural systems are involved, and for detail drawings. Some catalogues are full and clear, Bison and Trent in the large structures, and Astrawall provides working drawings for its cladding systems in a detailed booklet. Marley Technical Manuals (roofing and flooring in particular) are more like texts. Conder issued a student handbook in 1979 which is also of a very high standard and has been revised once already. These are the larger firms with finance for large publications – there are many others of varying quality – but some are very useful and extend even to the provision of full floor plans for housing, as with the leaflets from the Swedish–Finnish Timber Council, giving examples of the uses of their products in housing. The list is endless – and sometimes the detail sheets in RIBA *Product Data* will be adequate. The *Barbour Compendium* and the RIBA *Directory of Manufacturers* need to be exploited to the full for further literature. When using a CI/SfB-organized literature system some structural design leaflets will be located at the comprehensive numbers since, if the leaflet covers doors and windows, or floors and roofs, it will be put into the inclusive number (3–) or (2–) rather than with one element. Because of this, the larger catalogues can be temporarily difficult to locate.

Trade association leaflets are also essential tools here. The BCSA technical series have superseded the old BSA ones and remain very useful and, while they are often obtainable free, many are in the *Barbour Design Library*. TRADA's pamphlets are similar, and they issues technical manuls on timber structures, the *Timber Frame Housing Manual* (1980) and *Timbers of the World* (2 vols, 1979–1980). Those from the Concrete Society and Cement and Concrete Association provide technical information with precision on narrower topics.

DETAILING

Catalogues are used for detailing but detail books are still in use and range from the PSA standards details already mentioned above (*Method of Building*) to the most frequently consulted Boyne and Wright, *Architects' Working Details* in fifteen volumes (reprinted, Architectural Press, 1977), which include British and foreign examples representing solutions to numerous problems. These are supplemented by K. Gatz, *Detail* (5 vols, Iliffe, various dates), which covers brick, concrete, timber and steel construction, curtain walls, surface structures, and internal details, etc. By the same publishers the *Architects' Detail Library* covers various

250 Executing a design

elements in separate volumes, for example, *Windows and Window Walls* (No. 2, 1966), *Entrances and Staircases* (No. 5, 1967), *Exterior Detailing in Concrete* (No. 6, 1967). Handisyde's *Everyday Details* (Architectural Press, 1976) is useful and concise as is the NBA's *External Works Detail Sheets* (Architectural Press, 1977). The GLC Department of Architecture and Civic Design has issued items from its reference files of recurring details as *GLC Good Practice Details* (Architectural Press, 1980). These refer to the external fabric of simple building types, while *Detailing for Building Construction* (Construction Press, 1980) covers every sort of work and is also from the GLC files. Northwood issue more basic *Builder's Detail Sheets* in SI metric (1st series, 1973; 2nd series, 1977). Very much more specific is Duell and Lawson's *Damp-proof Course Detailing* (2nd edn, Architectural Press, 1983).

Handbooks and texts

Most architects and constructors will possess their own working copies of the *AJ Handbook of Building Structure* (2nd edn, Architectural Press, 1980) and the *AJ Handbook of Building Enclosure* (Architectural Press, 1974) which provides checklists for each space but which needs up-dating bibliographically. They will also have the relevant parts of others such as the *Handbook of Factory Design*. The new *AJ* series have already been mentioned and will no doubt augment the above as they develop, forming another handbook which will be up-dated in rotation. It is this up-dating which is a constant problem in all technical matters as the rate of change and development increases. Therefore, first, texts and handbooks such as those below must be used with care, and second, a section on current awareness has been included here to indicate the quickest ways of keeping abreast of change.

There are far too many texts to do more than mention a few here: omission is purely for space reasons, as this is not a bibliography. Bibliographies will be found in the BRE, PSA, C & CA and CIRIA series as well as from many departments of the United States government and by using the indexing and abstracting services.

In addition to the standard building dictionaries J. A. Barker has produced a *Dictionary of Soil Mechanics and Foundation Engineering* (Construction Press, 1981). Few others exist.

Handbooks and reference works specifically for the construction industry and this aspect of it are not numerous. They present detailed standard information, figures such as load tables and references. Apart from the *AJ* ones those relating to structures, which are not heavily American, are Black's *Builder's Reference Book* (11th edn, Northwood, 1980), Blake's *Civil Engineers' Reference Book* (3rd edn, Newnes–Butterworth, 1975) and *Kempe's Engineers' Yearbook*, which has already been mentioned. Those cited as general reference books in lists such as the Building Bookshop's are, in fact, specific to one or two topics or of the type covered in Chapter ?. House building has been mentioned above (TRADA) and there are two manuals, Powell's *Housebuilder's Reference Book* (Butterworths, 1979) and the *Registered Housebuilders' Handbook* from the National House Building Council (1974) in loose-leaf form (also on BDL). These both give detailed guidance on principles for the whole process including basic summary data – very much like the *New Metric Handbook* only in greater depth, and with some useful checklists. Most directories are covered on p. 262 but the annual *British Systems Yearbook* (System Builders Section of the NFBTE) relates purely to structural systems in building.

Standard texts vary according to preference but the BRE (MoPBW) *Principles of Modern Building* (3rd edn, 2 vols, HMSO, 1959 and 1961) is still in current use and most architects have one or more editions of Mitchell on their shelves. The latest revisions of this have been published by Batsford as single volumes with different authors, although with a series title of *Mitchell's Building Construction* (Mr Mitchell ceased working on revising his texts long ago; cf. many law texts). The relevant ones were, in 1981, J. S. Foster's *Structure and Fabric* (2nd edn, 2 vols, 1977 and 1979), giving many references throughout, and H. King's *Components* (2nd edn, by D. Osborn, 1979), which has now separated from Everett's *Finishes* (2nd edn, 1979) (formerly King and Everett, *Components and Finishes*). Some prefer to use McKay's *Building Construction* in four volumes (metric edn, Longman, 1971). Simpler is Barry's *Construction of Buildings* in five volumes (various edns and dates, Crosby Lockwood Staples). The development of TEC courses in construction technology has resulted in a number of new texts for these courses which can also be useful at an elementary level. The main ones are those by Bowyer, *Building Technology* (3 vols, Butterworths, 1978–1980), Chudley, *Construction Technology* (4 vols, Longman, 1973–1977), Clark, *Construction Technology* (3 vols, Northwood, 1981), Grundy, *Construction Technology* (3 vols, Arnold, 1978–1981), King and Nield, *Building Techniques* (2 vols, Chapman and Hall, 1976 and 1980) and Reid, *Construction Principles: Function* (Godwin, 1973).

Texts on specific aspects abound, but certain standards always appear to the fore, like Morgan's *The Elements of Building*

Structure (2nd edn, by I. G. Buckle, Pitman, 1977), Morgan and Hamilton's *Student's Structural Handbook* (2nd edn, Butterworths, 1973), Salvadori and Levy, *Structural Design in Architecture* (Prentice-Hall, 1967), Salvadori and Heller, *Structure in Architecture* (Prentice-Hall, 1975), Rosenthal's *Structural Decisions* (Chapman and Hall, 1962) and *Structure* (Macmillan, 1972). Each takes a different viewpoint and those by Salvadori, apart from being American, are design-oriented rather than purely technical.

Beckett and Marsh's *An Introduction to Structural Design: Timber* (Surrey University Press, 1974) is well known and there are an increasing number of texts on concrete structures. Faber and Alsop's *Reinforced Concrete Simply Explained* (6th edn, Oxford University Press, 1979) and Faber and Johnson's *Foundation Design Simply Explained* (2nd edn, Oxford University Press, 1979) are still standards, and in 1981 the Concrete Society published a *Reinforcement Detailing Manual* by R. Whittle, aimed at providing a standard basis for communication between design engineers and detailers to CP 110:1972. Others which should be mentioned include Reynolds, Kent and Lazenby's *Structural Steelwork for Building and Architectural Students* (Hodder and Stoughton), now in its fourteenth edition, while Ghali and Neville's *Structural Analysis* (Chapman and Hall, 1978) is now in its second edition. Two new texts for architects from the USA may prove useful, Laver's *Structural Engineering for Architects* (1981) and *Engineering for Architects* (1980) both from Architectural Record. There are now designer's manuals for concrete, masonry, steel and timber: P. Abeles and B. K. Bardhan-Roy, *Prestressed Concrete Designers' Handbook* (3rd edn, Viewpoint Publications, 1981); W. G. Curtin and others, *Structural Masonry Designer's Manual* (Granada, 1981); the *Steel Designer's Manual* (4th edn, Crosby Lockwood Staples, 1972) and Ozelton and Baird, *Timber Designer's Manual* (Crosby Lockwood Staples, 1976) with the *Structural Steelwork Handbook* from the BCSA (2nd edn, 1978).

While some architects and authors are influential for a brief period, works like Frei Otto's *Tensile Structures* (2 vols, MIT, 1967) stay with us. His work and its influence has now been listed by L. Doumatio in *Frei Otto's Tensile Structures: A Selected Bibliography* (Vance Bibliographies, Architecture Series, No. A142, 1979).

More precise texts are listed below and in sources like the *AJ* 'Annual Review' bibliography. Texts like Marsh's *Air and Rain Penetration of Buildings* (Construction Press, 1977) should be used in conjunction with items like the PSA *Flat Roofs Technical Guide*

(2nd edn, PSA, 1982), which has a bibliography, and with the practical recommendations in others listed in BRE *Information*.

The sections of the Building Bookshop *Catalogue* and the *RIBA Booklist* will augment these with new literature in print, but not all standard, good texts remain in print, so it is necessary to use bibliographies as well. Where the professional continues to use his college texts he should be aware that lecturers have their biases and preferences; sometimes their own knowledge of what is available may not be complete; they may also rely on their colleagues' works.

The developments in new techniques and reviews of old ones are often not published in texts but in journals (see below) and frequently in conference proceedings, which should not be overlooked as the papers published may often be in greater detail than the original presentation – and they need not be read in full, but scanned for relevant data. Examples might be *Design for Movement in Buildings: Proceedings of a One-day Symposium. . . 14th October 1969*, edited by I. N. Guy (Concrete Society, 1969), which presented much information which has now been integrated into texts, and *Thin-walled Structures: Recent Technical Advances and Trends in Design, Research and Construction: Proceedings of the International Conference at the University of Strathclyde, Glasgow, 3–6 April, 1979*, edited by J. Rhodes and A. C. Walker (Granada, 1980), which is a large volume of 796 pages and has not yet had time to be fully assimilated, but includes bibliographies and was sponsored by the Institution of Structural Engineers and Constrado. (For information on locating conference proceedings see p. 47.)

Published feedback on problems often goes unheeded and problems goes recur. Failures have been mentioned (see p. 151) and a glance at the publications available will show the importance of the literature, ranging from the Open University, 'Materials under Stress' course team, *Designing against Failure* (Open University Press, 1976) to the *AJ Guide to Building Failures* published from 30 March 1977 onwards. The range of publications on failures from the government, its research establishment, independent organizations, conference and journals is very wide, and is usually referred to in *Construction*.

Journals

So many journals cover these fields that it is only possible to mention a few of the most important – omitting those covered elsewhere. Detailed information on structures is rarely given in *AJ*

254 Executing a design

or *Building* but rather in *Structural Engineer*, now in two parts; 'A' appears monthly and includes book reviews, lists of additions to the library, news of meetings etc., while 'B' presents academic papers and appears quarterly. *Proceedings of the Institution of Civil Engineers* usually has some useful articles in the separate *Part 1: Design and Construction* similar to that of the American Society of Civil Engineers' *Journal of the Construction Division* and *Journal of the Structural Division*. Articles in the latter are frequently relevant to British Practice despite their expression in American standards and imperial measurements. (America is metricating its construction industry in the 1980s.)

Building Specification frequently discusses structure in relation to specific products and buildings. The new *Construction Papers* from the CIoB (1981–) promises to provide useful scholarly articles and it is good to see that the very clear and informative *Construction* from the DoE is to continue publication in 1981 under commercial publishers after a lapse in publication following issue 34, when government funding was withdrawn. Feedback and failures were a feature in this journal, which originated as a means of internal dissemination of information. Another internal journal which turned commercial is the *GLC Development and Materials Bulletin*, which also covers structures and is indexed at intervals, but is designed to be separated and filed with a literature collection (discontinued 1982). Other useful journals are *Building Research and Practice* (CIB), *International Journal of Solids and Structures* (Pergamon), *Computers and Structures* (Pergamon), *Materials and Structures* (RILEM, France) and *Building Science* (Pergamon).

Indexes and abstracts

Construction References, formerly Building References, from the Property Services Agency, and their many predecessors, cover structures well. In recent years the indexing has improved in detail, making it easier to locate information needed – not all of which is either British or in periodical articles since this does cover all types of pamphlets, books and government literature.

Building Science Abstracts, its main rival in the field, has unfortunately been defunct since the end of 1976 pending its reappearance as a database from the BRE, which has not yet occurred. Until then, and when (if ever) it reappears this was, and may again be, the best source of information on structures in Britain for those in the construction industry. The BRE has continued the indexing work on which the service was based, and it is to be hoped that it will resurface. However, the older volumes may still have a value in certain situations when older structures are being investigated.

The civil engineering aspects of structures are covered in the Institution of Civil Engineers' *ICE Abstracts* (monthly) and in *ACE: Articles in Civil Engineering* from the University of Bradford Library also. This has abstracts rather than just index entries as in *Current Technology Index* (known as *British Technology Index* until January 1981). The scope of the latter is wide and only British journals are indexed. Information is gathered which does not appear in the ICE or ACE services. It is also up-to-date and easy to use quickly. Very similar to this is the American *Applied Science and Technology Index*.

Engineering Index spreads over the whole range of engineering and provides abstracts but is more difficult to use because of its American terminology. The *Subject Headings in Engineering* (*SHE*) volumes should be consulted when using this. Although produced in the USA, a wide range of languages and publications of other countries are indexed. Structures is well covered.

The only other useful resource is *Geodex*, which is not as widely available as the others. It will often be located in the libraries of institutions with civil engineering courses and offers a structural information service as well as geological and foundation engineering ones. It is basically an abstracting service and, like *Engineering Index* (*COMPENDEX*), is available on-line as a database.

Current awareness

Keeping abreast of new developments is vital as laws and standards change and new products come onto the market. Journal reading can be helpful but there are other ways: for example, the Selective Dissemination of Information services mentioned in Chapter 2 may be available from the practice, or other, library and, as research has shown, American engineers who feel they can rely on this sort of system can halve their reading time.

The digests in circulation on various topics ranging from the *BRE Digests* and 'Information' papers to the 'R & D' and 'Techalert' notes in *Building*, the *Building* 'Catalogue' and the *AJ* 'Publications File' provide potted lists of new information. For example, they will mention research on a topic like flat roofs (BRE *Library Bibliography* 258, 1976) and a later 'Techalert' may refer to a similar item such as *The Upside Down Roof* by B. A. Peterson (BS95/T80 4470, 1980) reporting Swedish research into flat roof construction. RIBA *Product Data's* 'Construction' section provides quick resumés of new information with a reference to the full report and each is indexed in the full index so that it will be located with the relevant data sheets in a search for information.

In 1982 *Building Design* began a two-page weekly *Easibrief* section prepared by Haverstock Associates and Gerry Thompson (ex-NBA) to present new and changed technical information quickly and clearly with appropriate references in handy form. However, finding or filing these when needed may prove difficult and a number of corrections have been printed to data originally printed wrongly.

Although not a construction journal *New Scientist* reports recent events over a wide range of interests – often covering structures and materials in some detail. The US equivalent has the same wide scope – *Scientific American*. A useful summary article like 'Putting data on tap' (M. Phillips, 2(9) 1976, 37–42) was included in *Construction News Magazine*, which is not regularly read by structural designers.

The more frequent of the indexing and abstracting services discussed above will keep the professional up-to-date – *Current Information in the Construction Industry*, appearing fortnightly, is geared to that and is only later cumulated into *Construction References*. There is no need to read the whole, just the relevant UDC numbers, in this case the 624s and 690s. There is also *Current Contents in Engineering, Technology and Applied Sciences*, published weekly by ISI, giving contents lists from the journals issued the previous week, whether they were weeklies, monthlies, quarterlies or anything else. Items of interest should be recognized easily and sent for. This does, however, have an American slant.

Conferences may provide useful information. Many have published proceedings such as those of the *First International Conference on Composite Structures 1981* (Applied Science, 1982) edited by I. H. Marshall. Also recently published is *Plastics in Material and Structural Engineering: Proceedings of the ICP/RILEM/IBK International Symposium, Prague, June 23–25, 1981* (Elsevier, 1982). Sources to locate other such publications are given on page 47, but these give an idea of the range of topics.

Associations and enquiries

Enquiries arise frequently, and for structures and materials questions the BRE Advisory Service can offer assistance. CIRIA tends to be more sympathetic to members' questions, although information is available on a fee-paying basis. Both the ICE and the ISE can answer enquiries from outsiders and all the materials associations will cover the structural problems relating to their materials (see p. 267). But results of some work are published, for example, in the joint DoE/CIRIA Piling Development Group's six papers on piling methods (listed in *Construction* (DoE), **32,** 1980, 4).

Some of the larger commercial firms are using their expertise to set up advisory services, and those like Laing and Ove Arup can undertake investigation into specialist problems for a fee. Bovis announced a consultancy service called Construction Engineering Management Ltd, launched in 1981.

Services like the Farm Buildings Information Centre at Stoneleigh, Warwickshire, are almost unique. This offers an enquiry service (with a scale of fees) as well as some publications on this specialized group of structures. Others may follow. Specialist trade associations cover elements and materials like the Aluminium Window Association, the Dry Lining and Partitioning Association and the Steel Window Association. New ones are sometimes set up like the Bituminous Roofing Council in 1981 offering *Technical Information Sheets* and a Flat Roof Advisory Service.

The National Building Agency publications may be useful and they may be contacted for advice on consultants. (After this was written the government withdrew its support (September 1981) and they ceased operating in February 1982). The Building Centres also act as referral agents passing enquiries which they cannot handle onto appropriate organizations. Their addresses are found in the guides listed in Chapter 2.

Most recently many professionals are concerned with computers and their programming, and this inevitably means bringing in outside assistance both from the manufacturers and the retailers of specialized programmes or from practices like the Design Office Consortium, Cambridge, or Hutton and Rostron, Guildford, who have specialized in this field. The latter have also published catalogues of programs, *Computer Programs for the Building Industry* (2nd edn, Architectural Press, 1979) as have the Chartered Institute of Building, *Programming in Construction* (1981). Those interested in this sphere should contact the specialists mentioned in these or firms such as GENYSYS of Loughborough for assistance.

Materials

Materials form the major part of any building and of all the elements within it, and it is difficult to isolate related information. Thus this section cannot be read and used in isolation and its use must be linked with a thorough understanding of Chapter 8 on

Executing a design

Trade and Technical Information and Standards. Information given there will not be repeated here. This section will try to look at the other principal sources of information and suggest some points to note. Fire has been singled out for inclusion here, as that very important aspect of materials has not been covered elsewhere.

Trade and technical

The *Barbour Design Library* covers many of the publications and trade associations mentioned below but does not include even the more substantial trade catalogues. The *RIBA Product Data* directory includes many references to standards and literature as does *Specification*. This section will add to those bibliographies although, when used in conjunction with each other, they should be adequate to most situations. These bibliographies are fairly lengthy and each lists trade and research associations as well as manufacturers. The old *Building Documentation UK* will remain useful for a few years until all the information is out-dated, and the brief data sheets in the *Barbour Compendium*, with their illustrations, provide a useful indication of the appearance of many materials, although there are very few of these in relation to the number of manufacturers listed.

Up-dating any of these are the *AJ* sections on 'Products in Practice' which should be detached and kept with the relevant catalogues. Good catalogues abound. They overlap with the previous section in the Marley's Series, Roofing, Flooring, Waterproofing, Insulation, also need mentioning here along with Cape, ICI and similar 'big' names whose literature resembles texts. Lytag and Pilkingtons have also produced very clear and detailed manuals. The list is endless, and the best are selected for mention in the *AJ* 'Trade Literature' file regularly and annually in their 'Guide to Sources of Information' as part of the *Annual Review*.

Companies like Crown Paints operate a Technical Advisory Service from their headquarters at Darwen (Lancs) with experts available to advise and, if necessary, to visit sites. Ibstock Products Ltd also offer a design centre service for consultancy and stated, when the service was announced (*Building Trades Journal*, 5 December 1980), that consultants could be called in and seminars would be held regularly both in London and Manchester. Other companies have, or are starting, such services and these are usually mentioned in their literature or, when launched, an announcement may be found in *AJ, Building, Building Specification* or *Building Trades Journal*.

House journals from many manufacturers and trade associations are worth obtaining and scanning, very quickly, both for new products and application information, for warnings and for examples of products-in-use. However, they rarely contain very detailed information. *Cem-fil News* from Fibreglass Ltd, of Pilkingtons, mentions new publications such as John Young's *Guide to GRC for Architects* (Architectural Press, 1978) as well as applications and was issued to coincide with the last of the *AJ* articles on GRC (19 April 1978).

Brick Bulletin is almost in a class on its own rather than representing association journals and includes articles on application mainly, but is not as learned as those from the C & CA (see p. 264). Although not a house journal, the GLC *Development and Materials Bulletin* reports on uses and performance of materials.

Technical literature from trade associations is very extensive, including descriptive information as well as applications but ranges very widely in reliability, scope and volume. It should always be remembered that such information is likely to be heavily biased in favour of the type of product but not to the extent of inaccuracies, only by using innuendo. For example, 1981 saw campaigns by both TRADA and a grouping together of the BDA, C & CA, Aggregate Block Association and Autoclaved Aerated Concrete Products Association to influence the construction industry and the house-buying public in favour of specific materials for house construction. Literature produced in conjunction with such campaigns should only be used with extreme care.

TRADA is not the only producer of timber information and data sheets – there are many from the Council of Forest Industries of British Columbia (COFI), with a different approach, for example, *Timber-frame Construction: A Guide to Platform Frame*, or *Nailed Plywood Beams*. The British Plastics Federation's *Plastics in Building: Index of Applications and Suppliers* (1981) was compiled in conjunction with ICI, whose 1977 publication it replaced, to indicate to users which manufacturers can be consulted for specific types of specialized plastics applications, usually made to order.

Technical information sources have been quoted elsewhere. The *AJ* has published, in serial form, the handbooks on Hard Landscape (in brick, concrete and stone). The *BRE Digests*, either in hardback or the individual sheets, are essential. The relevant reprints of important *Current Papers* by Construction Press under the main title of *Building Research Series* are *Concrete, Fibre Reinforced Materials* and *Fire Control* (1978).

Current awareness

There is very little to add here which was not mentioned on p. 255 (Structures). Much information on materials is available free and it will always be useful to maintain a collection of the annual publications lists from associations which, together with the annual *Building Bookshop Catalogue, RIBA Booklist* and *BRE Information*, and, less frequent, *PSA in Print*, should form a formidable desk-side information resource.

Building Specification, What's New in Building and *Building Trades Journal*, while not always regular reading for architects, are strong not only in their coverage of products but in their brief articles about various materials and their uses, thus supplementing the advertising in *AJ, Building* and *Building Design*, etc.

Journals

While products are advertised in the majority of journals (see p. 138) the *RIBA Journal* and *Architectural Association Quarterly* have included regular product sections in recent years, gathering together advertisements and a few articles (brief ones) on particular products. The Building Materials Producers have their own journal and *Monthly Statistical Bulletin* but the only other British materials journals are the C & CA's *Concrete Quarterly* and *Magazine of Concrete Research*, Construction Press's *International Journal of Cement Composites* (quarterly, 1979–) and *International Journal of Lightweight Concrete* (2 p.a., 1980–). Also useful, however, is *Acier/Stahl/Steel:* although published in Belgium it is mainly in English. Most other journals in this area are localized by state or country and, since few manufacturers are international, they are of little value. The occasional useful article will be found by using the indexes.

Journals and texts on building science stress the importance of an understanding of the chemical and physical properties of materials in their proper usage in construction. The texts available are limited and do require an elementary knowledge of these two subjects. Fairly elementary and readable articles are published quite often in journals like *Nature, New Scientist* and *Chemistry and Industry*. Examples might be Birchall's 'Flexural strength and porosity of concretes' (*Nature*, **289**, No. 29, Jan. 1981, 388–390), J. Benstead, 'Effects of surface area upon early hydration of Portland cement' (*Chemistry and Industry*, 18 April 1981, p. 293) and Urang's 'How mature are polyurethane foams?' (*Chemical Business*, 29 June 1981, 55, 57–58). Any such articles can be located using *Chemical Abstracts, Physics Abstracts* and *Engineering Index* as well as from trade association publications with which offprints may be circulated. Sometimes questions relating to materials are complex and, if they can be expressed with precision, the on-line databases associated with these abstract services may be useful, i.e. *CASEARCH, INSPEC* and *COMPENDEX* to which could be added more specific ones such as *WELDASEARCH* and *METADEX* (see Chapter 4).

Indexes and abstracts

Materials and their performance used to be well covered in *Building Science Abstracts*, but since its demise in 1976 there remain the PSA's *Construction References, Engineering Index* and *Current Technology Index*, which latter benefits from its wide coverage of technology and science journals. There are abstracting services for specialist materials, although *Zinc Abstracts* and *Lead Abstracts* have now ceased and *Copper Abstracts* is continued as *International Copper Bulletin*, covering applications and building use as well as properties of copper. *Chemical Abstracts* and ISI's *Science Citation Index* can be used for matters concerning materials science, their composition, reaction, corrosion, etc.

Some databases related to these were mentioned above and there are others which may be useful such as *NONFERROUS METALS ABSTRACTS, RAPRA ABSTRACTS, SCISEARCH, SURFACE COATINGS ABSTRACTS, WORLD ALUMINIUM ABSTRACTS* and *WORLD TEXTILES* (polymer and fibre-based materials). Each of these has a printed service, but any search required by architects and others in the construction industry is likely to be so specific that it will be best performed on-line to save time and energy.

Handbooks

Data on strengths of materials and their properties is generally available in handbooks such as N. Jackson, *Civil Engineering Materials* (2nd edn, MacMillan, 1980) which covers uses, defects and behaviour in service for all main materials. *Kempe's Engineers' Yearbook*, Parrish, *Mechanical Engineer's Reference Book* (11th edn, Butterworths, 1978) and the American, Brady and Clauser *Materials Handbook* (11th edn, McGraw–Hill, 1971) also cover this ground, while Sax, *Dangerous Properties of Industrial Materials* (5th edn, Van Nostrand, 1979) should be consulted if in any doubt. The most substantial of the directories associated with materials is the *Concrete Yearbook,* which contains some basic technical information but is mainly devoted to manufacturers and suppliers. In this vein also are titles like *Adhesives Directory* (Richmond, Surrey, O'Connor, annual), *Adhesives Handbook* (2nd edn, Butterworths, 1976), *Building Board Directory* (Benn, annual), *Buyer's Guide for Reinforced Plastics* and *Buyer's Guide to Plastics Additives* (British Plastics Federation, annual), *Woodworking Industry Buyers' Guide* (Benn, annual) and *Construction Industry Buyers' Guide* (Biggar, annual). The *Directory of Precast Concrete Products* from the British Precast Concrete Federation uses a grid system to indicate regional availability of products. There are also *Carpet Annual* (Haymarket), *Contract Carpeting* (Benn, annual) and *Where to Buy Building, Construction and Maintenance Plant* (Where-to-buy, annual). The list is endless, and new or current editions can always be checked in *Current British Directories* (see p. 140). New titles are sometimes mentioned in reviews, for example, *What's New in Building* described *Tiling Index 1981* (Giddings Business Journals) as covering data, contractors, manufacturers, retailers, importers and distributors in October 1981 (p. 111), also pointing out that it covers standards and adhesives information. The *Wood Book* (annual) is an American version of the TRADA *Timbers of the World* (2 vols, 1979 and 1980). In 1979 Thomas Corkhill compiled *A Glossary of Wood* (Stobart) from his many years of work with dictionaries.

Handbooks of textbook style are mentioned below and include the materials sections of the *AJ Handbook of Building Structure,* which includes most appropriate everyday tables, those mentioned above and ones like S. Murray, *Brickwork and Blockwork: SMM6 Practice Handbook* (Godwin, 1981), which is the first of a series to cover all sections of the Standard Method of Measurement.

Textbooks

Everett's *Materials* (2nd edn, Batsford, 1978) refers to the standard texts throughout. Lyall Addleson's *Materials for Building* in four volumes, *Physical and Chemical Aspects of Matter and Strength of Materials; Water and its Effects 1 and 2; Heat and Fire and their Effects* (Iliffe, 1972), are essential. Others like H. J. Eldridge *Properties of Building Materials* (MTP, 1974) or G. D. Taylor, *Materials of Construction* (Longman, 1974) supplement these. Most other texts refer to one or more materials.

BRICK

Texts from the BDA have already been referred to and appear in their publications list, in particular Handisyde's *Bricks and Brickwork* (1976) and Bidwell's *Conservation of Old Brick Buildings* (1977) should be mentioned. The BDA concentrates on design information with series of *Design Guides, Design Notes, Practice Notes* and *Technical Notes*.

McKay' *Brickwork* (Longman, 1974) is a handy brief guide as is S. Smith, *Brickwork* (2nd edn, Macmillan, 1975). Murray has been mentioned above, and there are a number of bibliographies like the now rather dated BRS Library bibliography 206, *References to Prefabricated Brickwork and Blockwork* (1968) and the British Ceramic Research Association's *A Review of the Literature of Reinforced Brickwork* (1979).

CONCRETE

Design and Blockwork by Gage and Kirkbride is now in its third edition (Architectural Press, 1980), which is an indication of its value. Orchard's *Concrete Technology* (2nd edn, Applied Science, 1976) and P. H. Perkins, *Concrete Structures: Repair, Waterproofing and Protection* (Applied Science, 1976) represent different aspects of the material. Reynolds and Steadman, *Examples of Design of Buildings to CP110* (C & CA, 1978) should be useful to the architect. But Wadell's *Concrete Construction Handbook* (2nd edn, McGraw–Hill, 1974) must be used with care as it represents American practice. There are perhaps more texts on concrete and its properties than any other material – some of them representing the reports of conference proceedings, like Neville's *Fibre-reinforced Cement and Concrete* (2 vols, Construction Press, 1980), reporting the 1975 RILEM conference and Swamy, *Testing and Test Methods of Fibre Cement Composites* (Construction Press, 1980), reporting the International Symposium at the University of Sheffield in 1978. Cembureau (France) issued a *World Directory of Cement and Concrete Organisations* in 1982 to provide addresses and contacts for those requiring information.

While the United Nations Industrial Development Organization (UNIDO) published *Information Sources on the Cement and Concrete Industry* (2nd edn, 1977) the Cement and Concrete Association publishes many of the detailed texts in this field. Items like *Principles of Thermal Insulation with Respect to Lightweight Concrete*, appropriately published in 1978 when the new thermal insulation regulations were published, and W. Monks, *Visual*

Concrete: Design and Production (1980) a less technical publication and the first in a series entitled *Appearance Matters*. All are listed in *Concrete in Print* which is published annually. However, it was announced late in 1981 that the C & CA textbook and journal publishing was to cease. Technical publications from the Information Division rather than the Publications Division will continue. The journals *Concrete, Precast Concrete* and *World Cement Technology* have been taken over by Eyre and Spottiswoode.

STEEL

This has been covered under Structures.

TIMBER

TRADA publications are numerous and authoritative and are listed in their annual publications list. The older *Guide to Timber Subjects* has unfortunately not been re-issued, but there is a UNIDO *Information Sources on Building Boards* from wood and other fibrous materials (1974). TRADA Library still publish bibliographies such as *Timber Frame Construction Literature 1976 –1980* with 250 references but no index. TRADA also operate a quality assurance scheme, details of which can be obtained from them.

The BRE *Strength Properties of Timber* (HMSO, 1969) and *Timber Selection by Properties*, by Webster (HMSO, 1978) are useful and new editions and titles are reported in *News of Timber Research* from the Princes Risborough Laboratory of the BRE which researches on timber properties and problems such as weathering – problems which were discussed by G. Atkinson in 'It won't stop raining' (*Building*, 28 March 1980, p. 53). The *Timber-frame Housing Design Guide* has been revised by the NBA and TRADA and published by Construction Press as *A Manual of Timber-frame housing: A Simplified Method* (1980), giving a bibliography, mainly referring to standards, in the appendix and also mentioning alternative materials. Essential also to working with timber are texts like B. A. Richardson's *Wood Preservation* (Construction Press, 1978) and booklets from firms like Rentokil.

OTHER MATERIALS

Texts on other materials do exist, ones like G. Brand, *Principles of Glazing* (Essential Structures Research Association, 1977) or the Lead Development Association's *Lead Sheet in Building* (1978), which was originally issued free. Some other examples which users are less likely to know are J. Young, *Designing with Glass Reinforced Cement* (Architectural Press, 1978), I. Berkovitch, *Hazards of Asbestos in Construction Practice: A Review of UK Sources of Information and Advice* (CIRIA, 1976) and the British Ceramic Tile Council's *Guide to the Choice of Wall and Floor Surfacing Materials: A Costs-in-use Approach* (Hutchinson, 1976). All of these can be located by using tools such as those mentioned above or bibliographies which are relatively easy to locate as shown in Chapter 3. These include titles like the BRE Library Bibliography 247 (revised), *Long-term Weather Resistance of Plastics* (1975). Some bibliographies are published by the RILEM Committee on Materials and Structures (for an example, see, 8(44), 1975, 131–144). Bibliographies on high alumina cement concrete were published after the problem was brought to public notice and those from the ICE (1974) and the ISE (1974) and appearing in RICS *Abstracts and Reviews* R336 (1974) should be mentioned. These have recently been augmented by a very comprehensive review of the situation by Safier, 'HACC – appraisals, the problems and some findings' (*Structural Engineer*, 58A(12), 1980, 381–385).

While the papers and books quoted above may seem to present a very mixed picture the bibliographies already referred to in *Specification* and the RIBA *Product Data* present a good starting-point and will be revised more frequently than this guide. Those above should give some idea of the range and diversity of what is available to those who take the trouble to find out. If it is revised in the near future the CIRIA *Index of Technical Publications* (1970) should once again be useful.

Fire

Information on fire will often be found with any of the trade and technical information relating to specific products. Taylor and Cooke's *Guide to the Fire Precautions Act in Practice* (Architectural Press, 1978) is a standard text supplemented by Underdown's *Practical Fire Precautions* (2nd edn, Gower, 1979) and the older *A Complete Guide to Fire and Buildings* by Marchant (Construction Press, 1972) with the many articles in the *AJ* and *Fire Prevention*. *BS 4422: Glossary of Terms Associated with Fire* in five parts, 1969–1976, should be used to ensure correct terminology. A number of other standards refer to fire (see either the BDL or the BS *Sectional List* at (K)).

The Home Office's *Future Fire Policy* (HMSO, 1980) prompted several reviews of the problem (*AJ*, 17 September 1980 and the

'R & D Round-ups' for 13 February 1981 and 6 March 1981 in *Building*). Many refer back to the work of the BRE at the Fire Research Station, Boreham Wood, formerly the Joint Fire Research Organization. The BRE publications are too numerous to identify particular items but they are listed in BRE *Information*. The numerous *Fire Research Notes* are listed regularly until the last in 1977, No. 1979, the final summary. Since then, work on fire has been published together with other BRE papers in the *Current Papers* series, the *Information Papers* and single publications. These are also listed in DoE *Annual List of Publications*. The research papers were brought together into *Fire Control* (Construction Press, 1978). Added to these are the many references given in the BDL and the Home Office Fire Department publications, *Fire Prevention Guides* and *Guides to the Fire Precautions Act 1971*.

The Fire Protection Association publishes many booklets, *Fire Prevention Design Guides* and its journals, *Fire Prevention* and *Fire Prevention Science and Technology*, which report recent research. The Building Regulations naturally cover fire and the GLC issued *Code of Practice: Means of Escape in Case of Fire* (rev. edn, GLC, 1976). Summer's *Handbook of Industrial Fire Protection and Security* (Trade and Technical Press, 1981) may be useful in conjunction with some of the ideas from the American manual *Fire Protection Handbook* (15th edn, Boston, National Fire Protection Association, 1981). Other useful publications include the appropriate part of Addleson's *Materials for Construction*, Butcher and Parnell's *Smoke Control in Fire Safety Design* (Spon, 1979) and the second part of the BDA's *Low Rise Domestic Construction in Brick* (1978).

Conferences are held regularly by the major associations and the government. Research is reported in journals and more general volumes of proceedings, cf. 'Fire and buildings' in Alsop, *Construction Research International* (Construction Press, 1977). Synchrome Ltd have a Fire Alarm Information Service (with a fee), as have other manufacturers of equipment.

The most important source of detailed information must, however, be the BRE *Fire Science Abstracts* (1981–), formerly *References to Scientific Literature on Fire:* full wide-ranging indexing service issued twice a year, originally free but priced since 1976. Since 1948 this has provided not just technical and highly scientific references but also many useful design articles. There is also an American abstracting service produced three times a year in Washington, DC, by the National Research Council's Committee on Fire Rescue, called *Fire Research Abstracts and Reviews*.

Naturally, further information on any problems is available from Boreham Wood, the Fire Protection Association or the local Fire Officers.

Associations

The most important associations have been mentioned continuously throughout this section but others in fields less frequently used can be found using the CIRIA *Guide to Sources of Information, House's Guide to the Construction Industry*, the *AJ Guide* in the 'Annual Review' or any others of those given in Chapter 2. Most will assist with enquiries, although on various terms and sometimes, when trade associations, according to whether the products involved come from associated manufacturers. All have a range of publications which are usually listed in their own leaflets but are not always available free or to anyone requesting them without evidence of their potential uses.

All sections of the BRE will give advice on materials but in particular the Princes Risborough Laboratory covers timber, and their publications appear with those of the BRE in the DoE *Annual List of Publications*, and are reviewed in the BRE *Annual Report* and *BRE News*.

Energy

Introduction

All services contribute either to the supply or demand for energy. After years of free use of energy the later 1970s have seen a changed attitude towards conservation, qualitative assessment of usage and new methods of achieving the requirements for heating, lighting and ventilating of buildings. 'There is still a sparsity of literature about quality' (Croome and Roberts, 1981). Also there has been more stress laid on the role of the services engineer and his contribution towards the environment and its design to ensure that structure and services are compatible and in harmony for conservation. (As discussed by Lush, 'Getting it together' *Building Services*, **3**(8), 1981, 9–30.) The CIBS and BSRIA are developing their publications and publicity, with notes such as A. Bowyer's *Space Allowances for Building Services – Outline Design Stage* (1979). Adding to the already large volume of general information, which is far greater than in some aspects of building design, are reports on developing sources of alternative energy in journals such as *Alternative Technology*, which sometimes have a very

Executing a design

different style to the usual professional press. Thus as the available information becomes increasingly voluminous it becomes more difficult to isolate items of value for a coherent discussion, as Croome and Roberts point out in the introductory chapter to their *Air Conditioning and Ventilation of Buildings* (2nd edn, 2 vols, Pergamon, 1981).

The starting point for this section is less clear than for others and it will aim to indicate some of the sources of information in terms of technical literature, journals and handbooks before discussing some indicative works on a highly selective variety of topics but without presuming to provide more than ideas to follow through when requiring information – not providing a full bibliography.

Trade and technical

Many of the manufacturers of heating, lighting and ventilation equipment produce large, glossy handbooks, often including a great deal of technical data and pictures for the interior designer. Few are as plain as the fact-packed *Phillips Lighting Handbook*, but many are very useful, like Pilkington's well-produced range of leaflets and booklets. They and many others responded to the Thermal Regulations Part FF with informative promotional pamphlets showing how the new requirements could be met without lessening areas of glazing substantially. Thorn Lighting gives another example of such a handbook with full tables, diagrams and explanations. All these are usually reviewed in the trade literature sections of *AJ, Building* and *Building Design*, but especially in *Building Services Engineer* and *Building Services and Environmental Engineer*. Each of these not only lists new products but reviews good literature. Both also give all new standards, amendments to standards, ISO and IEC standards regularly with reports from abroad in 'Techalert'. The *Building Documentation UK* volumes on *Heating*, and *Air-conditioning and Ventilation* are still useful and may be up-dated when the new service is announced.

The *BRE Digests* cover energy, and the *Services and Electrical Engineering* volume (MTP) was issued in a second edition in 1978.

Information is published in a variety of forms by the nationalized industries. These range from the Solid Fuel Heating Advisory Service's *Solid Fuel Heating* (1980), an extensive handbook costing £12, and giving basic design guide information, construction details, regulations and equipment available, the *British Gas Directory of Energy Saving Equipment* (1981), with 646 items listed, compiled by Cambridge Information and Research Services at £6.50, to the CEGB Information Service Bibliographies and

Electricity Boards' Technical Information Sheets on various building types and to booklets for popular use like *Moulds in the Home* (1980), from the Electricity Council Research Centre.

The *New Metric Handbook* covers Thermal Insulation, Light and Sound, giving references, while the *AJ Handbook of Building Environment* is being up-dated in *AJ*'s new programme of information sheets by those on 'Services for Buildings'. Their 1977 sheets form the *Guide to Domestic Heating Installations and Control* (Architectural Press, 1977). The CIBS *Building Services Manual* is a loose-leaf binder containing all their *Commissioning Codes, Technical Memoranda, Practice Notes, Energy Notes, Group Study Reports*, miscellaneous documents and, most importantly, the parts of the *CIBS Guide*. This has been published in pamphlet format since 1975, each item's number reflecting the numbering of the sections in the former *IHVE Guide*. This format is now under review and it may become loose-leaf. Currently the booklets are;

A1	Comfort
A2	Weather
A3	Meteorological data
A4	Air infiltration
A6	Solar data
A8	Assessment of indoor temperature in summer
A9	Estimation of plant capacity
A10	Condensation and moisture problems
B2 and B3	Ventilation and air conditioning
B5	Fire protection systems
B8	Sanitation and waste disposal
B10	Electrical power
C1 and C2	Properties of humid air, water and steam
C3	Heat transfer
C5	Fuels and combustion
C7	Units and miscellaneous data

The current cost-consciousness led BMCIS to introduce in March 1981 the *Energy Cost Index* as a regular feature, calculating the costs from the individual indices for gas, electricity, oil and coal. Full details are given in their R & D paper of March 1981.

Reports covering energy in buildings are best located either in the sources on p. 47, via the *INSPEC* database or using the 'Techalert' sheet published most months in *Building Services Engineer*. This is not the same as the one in *Building*, but a more specialized one for energy. Microfiche copies of most reports mentioned are available for between £1.50 and £3. This journal also carried some useful building types studies such as that of the services design in the police headquarters at Croydon, 'Services to crime' by D.C.M. Loverack (*Building Services Engineer*, **3**(8), 1981, 20–23). BSIRIA *Product Profiles* are now published in one volume (1982). Advice on some products is available.

Journals

'Building services: planning accommodation' appeared in *AJ* (5 April 1978, pp. 648–661) while a 'Directory of alternative technology' appeared in *Architectural Design* (Nov. 1974, April and May 1975), and 'Inflation ban' in *New Scientist* (7 May 1981, p. 336) with 'Cavity insulation: key point for house sales' by J. Baker in *Building Trades Journal* for 6 March 1981 (pp. 28–29). The range of journals is wide, but these tend to be less technical articles. The main journal is *Building Services Engineer*, the journal of the CIBS (containing 'degree-day' data each month) to which was added *Building Services Engineering Research and Technology* in January 1980 to publish full papers, technical notes and literature reviews complementing those in *Building Services Engineer* and *Lighting Research and Technology*. All are now from the CIBS. *Building Services and Environmental Engineer* is a free, controlled distribution journal of value for keeping up-to-date with brief notes of research products and technical literature. Many recent pages of the 'R & D Round-up' in *Building* have discussed energy, its conservation and the development of solar and other sources, heat pumps, etc.

The BSRIA publishes a list of *Library Periodicals* annually which cannot be rivalled as a list of the journals available in this field, internationally. There are around 335 entries in the 1981 edition, giving some idea of the number relevant to energy and services. Some British ones which might be mentioned include the *International Journal of Ambient Energy, Energy and Buildings, Applied Energy, Building and Environment, Domestic Heating Engineer, Electrical Review, Energy Digest, Energy Manager, Energy Trends, Energy World, Heating and Air-conditioning Journal, Heating and Ventilating Engineer, Insulation, International Journal of Energy Research, Journal of Institute of Energy, Noise and Vibration Control, Plumbing, Solar Energy, Solid Fuel, Sun at Work in Britain* and *Sun World*.

Indexes and abstracts

To locate specific information in all the periodicals above the indexing and abstracting services become essential. As well as the general ones which cover all construction, *Current Technology Index, Engineering Index, Construction References, API, Applied Science and Technology Index* and the *DoE Library Bulletin*, the most important source is *International Building Services Abstracts*, which is produced at BSRIA. Formerly called *Thermal Abstracts*, this has international coverage and not all papers are in English, but every item should be available through inter-library loans at BSRIA. Its database, *IBSEDEX*, is now available on-line. Also produced at the same address, but in the Air Infiltration Centre's offices, is the *Air Infiltration Data Base*, available as a published bibliography with regular supplements and on computer at the centre. Also on computer, on *Prestel*, are the Building Services Group frames, again under the auspices of BSRIA.

Energy and its applications will be covered in the abstract journals of *INSPEC*, also available on-line. These are *Physics Abstracts, Electrical and Electronic Abstracts* and *Computer and Control Abstracts*. Science Citation Index can also produce useful items if the names of workers in the field are already known, although it is much quicker to use on-line (*SCISEARCH*).

Two foreign services might be mentioned. The US Department of Commerce, National Technical Information Center began *Current Energy Patents* and *Synthetic Fuels Update* in 1981, both abstracting and reviewing current literature. In Australia the *Building Services and Environmental Engineer* (November 1980) reported that CSIRO was opening an 'energy information system' covering surrounding countries providing a database on 'insolation, shading, photovoltaics, radiation on materials, biomass, wind, geothermal, ocean and hydroelectric'. This would cover data as well as documents.

A guide to information in book form was published by the New York Environment Information Centre, entitled *Energy Index: A Select Guide to Energy Information since 1970* (1973).

Bibliographies

Some of these are listed below, but the major institutions publish a large number of bibliographies in this field, some quite specific, like the BSRIA ones covering services in specific building types. The CEGB and PSA are equally prolific and the CIBS supplements these (see below, Energy Conservation).

Handbooks

Most of the reference texts are similar to those cited above, or from the manufacturers and their associations. Only the *Electrical*

272 Executing a design

Engineers' Reference Book (M. G. Say (ed.), 13th edn, Butterworths, 1973) and the *Mechanical Engineers' Reference Book* (Parrish (ed.), 11th edn, Butterworths, 1973) with the *Mechanical and Electrical Equipment for Buildings* edited by McGuiness and others (6th edn, Wiley, 1980) can be added to those on p. 261.

McGuiness is American in units and case studies but covers standard information on techniques giving charts etc. In 1981 the Grosschen-Verlag, Dortmund, published the EEC's *Solar Radiation Atlas*, giving maps showing the extent of solar radiation over Europe at different times of the year.

A new venture in 1981 is the *International Dictionary of Heating, Ventilating and Air Conditioning* (Spon), giving terminology in ten languages, English Dutch, French, German, Hungarian, Italian, Polish, Russian, Spanish and Swedish, with the main entries in English order giving translations and nine indexes for the other languages which refer to the English sequence. The English section also gives US terms where they differ.

Heat Recovery Systems and Directory of Equipment and Techniques by Reay (Spon, 1979) includes a bibliography and manufacturer's index and is one of the few trade directories not produced by a trade association. *Heating, Ventilating, Refrigeration and Air Conditioning Yearbook*, from the Heating and Ventilating Trades Contractors' Association, gives some technical information and a full product directory, as does the *Electrical Contractors Association Yearbook and Directory*, among the others to be found in the pages of the *Current British Directories* or the lists of associations.

Texts

This section will cover a number of different topics after giving a brief mention of the major texts which can be updated using the *AJ* 'Annual Review' pages or the *RIBA Booklist*. Burberry's *Environment and Services* (2nd edn, Batsford, 1978) in the Mitchell's series is still current and volume 5 of Barry's *Construction of Buildings* is *Engineering Services* (Granada, 1978). Longman published F. Hall, *Building Services and Equipment* in 1978 as a standard text but the standard longer texts remain Faber and Kell, in its sixth edition, with P. L. Martin, *Heating and Airconditioning of Buildings* (Architectural Press, 1979) and Croome and Roberts (*op. cit.*), which aims to provide information on the design and practice of comfort in buildings, being both a text and a reference book for practising engineers, with companion volumes in the series which include T. C. Angus, *The Control of Indoor Climate* and the forthcoming *Energy and Buildings*, with the 1977

Noise, Buildings and People mentioned below. Bibliographies and references are given. Also worth mentioning are Hall, *Heating, Ventilating and Air Conditioning* (Construction Press, 1980), McQuistan and Parker, *Heating, Ventilation and Air Conditioning: Analysis and Design* (Wiley, 1977), Marsh, *Thermal Insulation and Condensation* (Construction Press, 1980) and Shaw's fourth edition of *Heating and Hot Water Services* (Granada, 1980).

ENERGY CONSERVATION

The interest of recent years in energy and its conservation is shown by the very wide range of bibliographies issued since 1975. They range from the Departments of the Environment and Transport *Information Series, 31, Energy: Sources of Information* (1979) through the following: Birmingham Public Library, *Wind Power: A Select Bibliography 1970–1975* (188 refs, 1975); BSRIA, *Heat and Power from the Sun* (3rd edn, BSRIA, 1978); Council of Planning Librarians, Exchange Bibliographies No. 742 *Energy Situation: Crisis and Outlooks: An Introductory Non-technical Bibliography* (1975) and No. 776, *Energy for the Future: A Selected Bibliography on Conservation* (1975); DoE, PSA Library Service, *Current Information on Energy Conservation*, a continuing bibliography with new editions every few years, in the following sections, *District Heating, Total Energy, Solar Energy, Energy Conservation in Building Design, Thermal Insulation in Building Design, Systems and Systems Control in Buildings, Boiler Plants for Domestic, Commercial and Industrial Use;* DoE, PSA Library Service, *Total Energy: Energy Conservation and Consumption in Relation to Building and Services, An Annotated Bibliography* (1975) with sections covering, Comfort, Consumption and Conservation, Air Conditioning, Lighting and Applications in Office Buildings; DoE, PSA, *Energy Conservation in Building Design: A Bibliography* (2nd edn, 1980); *Energy Conservation: New Techniques*, a bibliography in the Construction Notes section of RIBA *Product Data*, No. 76/54; B. and D. Harrah, *Alternative Sources of Energy: A Bibliography of Solar, Geothermal, Wind and Tidal Energy, and Environmental Architecture* (Scarecrow, 1975); A. F. Haseler, *District Heating* (PSA, 1975); D. E. Morrison, *Energy: A Bibliography of Social Science and Related Literature* (Garland, 1975); *Solar Energy for Domestic Heating and Cooling: A Bibliography with Abstracts and a Survey of Literature and Information Sources* (Pergamon, 1979).

To these must be added the references given in texts. The theory given in Banham's *Architecture of the Well-tempered Environment*

(Architectural Press, 1969) with the texts cited above, and Handisyde's *Thermal Insulation of Buildings* (HMSO, 1971) is becoming superseded by newer volumes like P. Marsh, *Thermal Insulation and Condensation* (Construction Press, 1979) and A. F. G. Sherratt (ed.), *Air Conditioning and Energy Conservation* (Architectural Press, 1980). Burberry's *Building for Energy Conservation* (Architectural Press, 1978) and Ove Arup Partnership's *Building Design for Energy Economy* (Construction Press, 1980) include basic text and checklists.

One publisher (Applied Science) has recently published Weller, *Thermal Energy Conservation: Building and Services Design* (1981), Fisk, *Thermal Control of Buildings* (1981), Lebens, *Passive Solar Heating Design* (1980), Cowan, *Solar Energy Applications in the Design of Buildings* (1980), B. P. Lim et al., *Environmental Factors in the Design of Building Fenestration* (1979), Muncey, *Heat Transfer Calculations for Buildings* (1979), Harkness, *Solar Radiation Control in Buildings* (1978) and finally Sherratt's *Energy Conservation and Energy Management in Buildings*. A formidable list.

Architectural Press are also publishing in this field, and Diamant and Kut's *District Heating and Cooling for Energy Conservation* (1981) covers a wide range of energy sources. To these can be added the numerous periodical articles, some summarized by G. Atkinson in 'Energy saved in practice' (*Building*, 14 November 1980, pp. 56–57) and formalized by the new *CIBS Energy Code* being published in parts (1 – 1979, 2a – 1981, 2b – 1983), giving targets for total energy and methods of calculating design solutions. To keep up with this volume of publishing, bibliographies and indexes are essential.

Useful handbooks from the other side of the Atlantic have been publicized. In Britain, H. E. Marshall's *Energy Conservation in Buildings: An Economics Guidebook for Investment Designs* (US National Bureau of Standards, Ref. Techalert BS98) details techniques for evaluation conservation, while solutions are described in the same author's *Simplified Energy Design Economics* (US Center for Building Technology, Ref. Techalert BS96). The Royal Architectural Institute of Canada has produced *Energy Conservation: Design Resource Handbook* (The Institute, or Commonwealth Association of Architects, 1981), summarizing basic data and systems, with international contributors. Freeman Insulation Ltd has started a series of technical papers on energy conservation. The RIBA has brought out a calculator for energy work and an 'Energy Package' for designers (see *RIBA Journal*, January 1981).

Executing a design 275

Among other useful sources of information, many available in the *Barbour Design Library*, are the DoE Directorate of Mechanical and Engineering Services *Mechanical Data Book* in various parts from the PSA (e.g. Parts E and F, 1980) and an *Energy Conservation Checklist* (1979) and *Checklist for Design Teams* (1979). The Department of Energy's *Energy: A Register of Research, Development and Demonstration in the UK, Part 1: Energy Conservation* (HMSO, 1980) will help those seeking advice, as will the Building Centre's *A Product Index for Energy Conservation* (1979/1980). Some practical installations have been described in product literature such as the heat pumps brochure from Lennox Industries and Colt Solar Control's description of the Turret Press office systems. Many conferences have been reported and research is summarized regularly the CIB symposia. Thus 'The environment within buildings and the services that provide it, both from a design and an engineering viewpoint' reports latest developments (K. Alsop (ed.), *Construction Research International*, Construction Press, 1977).

Energy conservation measures do have side-effects, and standard texts like the DoE *Condensation in Dwellings* (2 vols, HMSO, 1970 and 1971) should not be forgotten. The best way of checking that all such standards have been remembered is, as previously, to use the bibliographies in *Specification*, RIBA *Product Data* and *Barbour Design Library*.

LIGHTING

The essential texts for lighting work remain the current editions of the IES *Code for Interior Lighting*, although the IES has now merged with the CIBS, and the Lighting Industry Federation's *Interior Lighting Design*. The DoE *Sunlight and Daylight*, in two parts with its protractors, is also essential, with the Institution of Electrical Engineers *Regulations for the Electrical Equipment of Buildings* (14th edn, IEE, 1969) and Miller's *Guide* to these (2nd edn, Peregrinus, 1972). Hopkinson's *Environmental Physics: Lighting* (HMSO, 1963) has long been a useful aid to understanding the principles of lighting. The Lighting Industry Federation has begun a series of *Factfinders* from 1980 with titles such as *Dimming, Lamp Guide, Lighting and Energy*, and one on the benefits of certification of equipment. The CIBS also publishes a number of technical leaflets such as *Lighting Guide: Sports*, and the Electricity Council covers some specific situations, for example, *Lighting for Hotels and Restaurants* (1977). BSRIA bibliographies cover light and *Building Specification* devotes an issue to light at irregular intervals. Books like I. D. and E. J. Collins, *Window Selection: A Guide for Architects and Designers* (Butterworths, 1978) are rare but useful.

NOISE

Most work on noise is reported at conferences and in journals, but the following should be consulted: W. S. Atkins, Research and Development, *The Control of Noise and Ventilation: A Designer's Guide* (Spon, 1977), Beranek's *Acoustics* (McGraw–Hill, 1954), D. Croome's *Noise, Buildings and People* (Pergamon, 1967), H. R. Humphreys' *Sound Insulation in Buildings* and the DoE booklet of the same title (HMSO, 1971), J. O. Knudsen, *Acoustical Design in Architecture* (Chapman and Hall, 1950) with Parkin and Humphreys' *Acoustics, Noise and Buildings* (3rd edn, Faber, 1979). Sound Research Laboratories have produced a film, *We'll Never Sleep Again* in conjunction with the NBA, giving case studies of noise in buildings, and three texts from Spon, *Noise Control in Industry* (1976), *Practical Building Acoustics* (1976) and *Basic Vibration Control* (1978).

SOLAR ENERGY

The great interest generated by solar energy in the 1970s has resulted in a large number of texts, only a few of which can be mentioned – even the bibliographies are out-of-date within a year, although the Pergamon one cited above is vast in its range. The references in the texts and articles in the specialized journals such as *Solar Energy, Helios, Sun World*, etc. must be used. Many, however, refer to other countries and climates. D. Oppenheim's *Small Solar Buildings in Cool Northern Climates* (Architectural Press, 1981) brings Britain into the picture, with Wozniak's *Solar Heating Systems for the UK* (HMSO, 1980), although others do consider British problems. Szokolay's handbook, *Environmental Science Handbook for Architects and Builders* (Construction Press, 1980) and his earlier *Solar Energy and Building* (2nd edn, Architectural Press, 1979) are useful. Some others might include H. J. Cowan, *Solar Energy Applications in the Design of Buildings* (Applied Science, 1981) and Franta and Olsen, *Solar Architecture* (Ann Arbor, 1978), which report on symposia held in Australia and America but discuss solar energy in an international context. Harkness and Mehta in *Solar Radiation Control in Buildings* (Applied Science, 1978) reviewed past work and tried to present a working basis for designers. *Passive Solar Design Handbook*

Executing a design 277

(NTIS, 1981), by B. Anderson and D. Balcomb, with *A Survey of Passive Solar Homes* (National Solar Heating and Cooling Information Center, Rockville, Md, 1981) by the AIA Research Corporation with HUD, present a picture of further developments in solar research applications in the USA which may have relevance in Britain. Turrent and Ferrari reported to the Energy Technology Support Unit on *Passive Solar Housing in the UK* in 1980. A long list is given in the *Building Bookshop Catalogue* and specific reports and technical publications are integrated with the bibliographies in *Barbour Design Library*. The 1981 Homeworld exhibition at Milton Keynes was well reported and emphasized solar energy as did the 'Solar energy in the 80's' conference at Birmingham, September 1980, reported in *Building Services and Environmental Engineer* and organized by the UK section of the International Solar Energy Society. In Britain their work is supplemented by that of the Solar Trade Association, the Centre for Alternative Technology and the Natural Energy Association, among others. Solar energy articles are indexed in most of the indexing and abstracting sources above.

Early in 1982 the BL, SRL, received one of the first volumes from the US Patent and Trademark Office indicating patents activity in the field of *Solar Energy, 1963–1979*. This is one field where the registration of patents can act as a useful source of further information and ideas (see Chapter 4).

U-VALUES

The emphasis on conservation and insulation has led to an increase in publications covering the various U-values. A succinct article by W. I. Robbins 'The new energy conserving requirements of the building regulations' (*Surveying Technician*, **9**(2), 1980) listed a number of sources including Roberts' articles in *AJ* 7 February 1979 and 4 July 1979 and Pitt's in the 16 May 1979 issues, with the *Guide for Specifiers* from the Aluminium Window Association and the Fibre Building Board Development Organization's *Design Data Sheet DD/3*. To these should be added more specifically the *CIBS Guide A3*, the tables in the 1981 *Insulation Handbook* (Comprint) and the Structural Insulation Association, *U-values for Building* (n.d.), which has a bibliography. Eurisol–UK's *U-values Manual* (1981) is substantial and they also publish *Facts about Insulation*, covering a description of the association's *Domestic Insulation, R-values, Terminology, Condensation, Physical Properties of Mineral Fibre Insulation* and *Brick Spalling and Thermal Insulation of Cavity Walls*.

Similar lists can be built up for any related topics using the types of source mentioned but there is neither space nor context to cover everything in these pages.

Associations

Throughout this section a large number of associations have been mentioned by initials and these tend to be very well known in the profession, although not all architects have caught up with changes like the merger of the Institution of Heating and Ventilating Engineers with the Illuminating Engineering Society to form the Chartered Institute of Building Services. Many may not be familiar with the work of BSRIA (Building Services Research and Information Association), which now also houses the Air Infiltration Centre at Bracknell, and published a wide range of information, listed in its *BSRIA in Print*. This covers *Application Guides, Laboratory Reports, Information* and *Technical Notes*, bibliographies and a miscellaneous group of other publications. Its *Statistics Bulletin* and *Omnibus*, a house journal covering recent developments, are also available to members. Technical advice, design aid and site visits can be offered and are described in a pamphlet outlining the work of the association.

Some work on energy is carried out at the BRE, and the Building Centre in London has a special advisory unit on energy, aiming to give advice to the profession. The National Physical Laboratory works mainly with acoustics but there are other governmental sources of assistance which are best located in *Technical Services to Industry* (see p. 30).

The many trade associations are too numerous to list. Some have been mentioned earlier as producers of handbooks or directories and others are very specific but easily locatable in the usual directories (Chapter 2). Finally in this area there are once more the nationalized industries, almost all of which have information services of some description and are also listed in *Technical Services to Industry*. The less official societies may also be able to offer information and advice, but not always with the same authority – they too are numerous, especially in the area of alternative technology including places like the Centre for Alternative Technology at Machyllneth. It should by now be fairly obvious that, whatever other information may be lacking in this field, there is no shortage, but the abundance may sometimes lead to difficulties in locating the right information at the appropriate time.

Costs

The architect looking at sources of cost information should turn first to the texts and to A. Ashworth's articles on 'Sources of cost information' in *Civil Engineering* (December 1980, pp. 24–25) and 'Source, nature and comparison of published cost information' in *Building Technology and Management* (**18,** No. 3, 1980, 33–37), which are both succinct and critical and represent one of the few instances where this guide can refer to other guides of a very precise nature. To these might be added, as sources of basic references and current texts, the *Building Bookshop Catalogue* and the *RIBA Booklist* with Burt's *A Survey of Quality and Value in Building* (BRE, 1978), the CIT Agency *Cost Contract and Quantity Surveying Literature 1979* (CIT, 1981) which is to be an annual survey, and Flor-Henry, *Quantity Surveying Development: An Annotated Bibliography* (PSA Library, 1978), which covers price data in section 10, fluctuation in section 11 and analysis in section 12. *A Decade of Quantity Surveying* by Harlow (CIOB, 1980) was compiled mainly from *Building Management Abstracts*.

This is a formidable recent output, reflecting the concern with costs during a period of recession. At the beginning of 1981 when the *AJ* stated its new policy on information publications, papers on costs with comparative cost information and forecasts were to figure regularly. The *Handbook of Building Enclosure* (Vandenberg (ed.), Architectural Press, 1974) had pointed out that 'in the use of published cost analyses it is essential to interpret reasons for differences in elemental costs', checking the quality achieved and required, and giving the basic principles to follow. Many articles discuss this, and these will be found indexed in *Construction References, API,* and the *CIOB's Building Management Abstracts.* The information given in this section will look first at the texts available, then discuss the various price books and cost indices published before looking at cost analyses for designers and specifying information. There will not be separate sections on indexes, associations, etc. since these are less relevant here – several have been mentioned already, and the section will conclude with reference to the associations not already mentioned.

Texts

Among the many British texts some can be singled out, ranging from Stone's classics, *Building Design Evaluation: Cost-in-use* (3rd edn, Spon, 1980) and *Building Economy* (2nd edn, Pergamon,

1976), through Geddes, *Estimating for Building and Civil Engineering Works*, revised by G. Chrystal-Smith (7th edn, Butterworths, 1981) with Chrystal-Smith's own *Estimating for Repairs and Small New Works* (4th edn, Northwood, 1981) to Ferry, *Cost Planning of Building*, in its fourth edition, with P. Brandon (Hart-Davis, 1980). Bathurst's *Building Cost Control Techniques and Economics* (2nd edn, Heinemann, 1980), which emphasizes the influence of economics on the construction industry, should be remembered as well as Bailey, *Principles of Builder's Estimating and Final Accounts* (4th edn, Crosby Lockwood, 1971), Seeley, *Building Economics* (2nd edn, Macmillan, 1976) and C. Wilcox, *Measurement of Construction Work* (2nd edn, Godwin, 1980). Articles such as the early ones by Nisbet in the *AJ*, 'Cost planning and cost control' (3, 10 and 24 November 1965) still have a relevance in the statement of principles.

Cost indices

Cost information is essential but, except in very large firms where in-house information from accounts can be kept and analysed with the assistance of computerized systems of accounting, it is more usual to rely on published data. These vary according to the compiler and their view of the 'average' (see references on pp. 279 and 281). Comparison of several sources may reflect a more accurate rate or cost than acceptance of just one set of data, especially as rates vary throughout the country. *Building Specification* states clearly when it is publishing 'London measured rates' (alternative issues). The fullest source of data is the BCIS (below), although many periodicals now publish cost indices on a limited basis. These are up-to-date and therefore useful in conjunction with the fuller sources below if adjustment techniques are used with the indices.

Building Specification 'Cost Index' covers all-in rates, excavation and earth-work, concrete work, brickwork, block partitions, damp-proof courses, roofing, carpentry, joinery, glazing, painting and decorating and drainage. *Building* 'Cost File' covers analysis of all-in rates for building and plumbing operatives, materials prices, measured rates. occasionally plant-hire rates and discussion of the building market. In July 1981 *Building* announced that this service would now be available on *Prestel* from A + B Ltd. *Building* also publishes the *NEDO Price Indices* for use with the *Price Adjustment Formulae* for both civil engineering and building works. They are available also as a separate monthly pamphlet from the NEDO and their use is described in the National

Consultative Council's *Price Adjustment Formulae for Building Contracts (Series 2): Guide to Application and Procedure* (HMSO, 1977) and *Price Adjustment Formulae for Building Contracts (Series 2): Description of the Indices* (HMSO, 1977) as well as many articles and pamphlets such as Barnes, *The Serviceability of the Building Price Adjustment Formula: Report on a Study . . .* (NFBTE, 1975), Sims, 'NEDO Price adjustment formulae', *Building* (**227**(6859), 22 November 1974, 97–98), Osbourne, *NEDO Price Adjustment Formulae for Building Contracts* (Chartered Surveyor, **106**(9), 1974, 259–260), Goodacre, *Formula Method of Price Adjustment for Building Contracts* (CALUS, 1978) and a new method of use in described in Grimes, 'Programmed calculation of NEDO price adjustment' (*Quantity Surveyor*, **37**(4), 1981, 74–77). A comparison between the first and second series is given in an appendix to Porter's *Building Contract Conditions* (Godwin, 1980). 'Estimating Supplement' to *Building Trades Journal* forms a quarterly pull-out supplement with changes published in intervening months. 'Rehabilitation of older houses' is covered separately by G. Chrystal-Smith, while P. Stronach edits up-dating notes on 'Current Prices' which give rates quoted by specific firms as well as average rates for materials, elements and equipment. The 'Provincial measured rates' section covers all basic work sections from excavation to finishing, followed by wage rates.

The *QS Weekly* used to publish data on a rotating basis until the issue of a new monthly service, *Cost Data File for the Building Industry* in January 1980. They cover Labour, Materials and Measured Rates in accordance with SMM6 and in more detail than the former guides can do, taking account of comparative work done by Ashworth and cited earlier. However, at £100 p.a. this is not a cheap service, although papers are included discussing costs.

In 1981 OCM Publishing commenced the *National Schedule of Rates* from the Society of Chief Quantity Surveyors in Local Government and the NFTBE. With quarterly reviews it is compiled to meet the needs of Part III of the Local Government Planning and Land Act 1980. Although based on the home counties and housing work, it can be adjusted for other areas and types of work.

Measured rates are also published regularly in *Civil Engineering* as prepared by Davis, Belfield and Everest, thus supplementing Spon's (below).

As inflation rates vary so do costs, and BRE work recently published in *Current Paper 7/80* discusses *A Method of Predicting Changes in Building Costs*. Much research will be reported in *Construction References* as these lines are followed.

BUILDING COST INFORMATION SERVICE

Originally on limited circulation, BCIS became more widely available a few years ago when it was already firmly established as the major source of cost data and information. A service from the RICS, it supplies not just the basic costs for works of all kinds but cost analyses, brief and lengthy, for various types of buildings supplied by subscribers and printed without reference to the name or location, just the type of building, organized by broad CI/SfB categories. Statistical information related to costs and trends is up-dated regularly and short papers are published. Abstracts of other relevant literature are also circulated with the loose-leaf sheets for insertion in the binders. The index is constantly updated to ensure ease of reference. The *Chartered Quantity Surveyor* reported in August 1980 (p. 21) that a microcomputer was being used to up-date the information and the future might see the availability of the data itself in machine-readable form. *Computer Talk* (11 July 1979, p. 1) also reported developments in computerized output of price information, this time from the Stock Exchange, and if and when organizations can develop systems then it may be that cost data will be available on *Prestel*, since it is the type of regularly up-dated, factual information which is ideally suited to this service.

In 1981 the BCIS commenced publication of a *Quarterly Review of Building Prices* (at £60) giving average building prices for 140 building types taken from information on 3000 tenders, and giving locational variations by county for England and Wales, and by region in Scotland. It also includes the tender price index and building cost index from 1974 with forecasts and current reports.

Estimating information service from the CIOB complements the data services as it consists mainly of papers discussing costs and methods. Papers from the service with a review of technical literature were published separately by the CIOB as *The Practice of Estimating* (1981).

PRICE BOOKS

Spon, Laxton, Griffiths, Hutchins and Savory Milln are all variations on the price book principle, and the first textbook discussing their use in conjunction with the above was published by Spon in 1981, B. A. Tyson, *Construction Cost and Price Indices: Description and Use*. Most are revised annually and there are slight variations in their coverage as Ashworth points out:

> Each of the price books incorporate information dealing with materials prices, measured rates, approximate estimating,

professional fees, daywork, etc. In addition 'Spon's provides some comparative prices for work in the European Economic Community and 'Laxton's' has a section dealing with minor projects. Both 'Griffiths' and 'Hutchins' provide data for the man-hours allowed in the analysis of measured rates and 'Hutchins' has the added advantage of being able to be purchased in individual sections (*Civil Engineering*, Dec. 1980, p. 24)

Spon's Architects' and Builders' Price Book, edited in its 107th edition in 1982 by Davis, Belfield and Everest, is complemented by *Spon's Mechanical and Electrical Services Price Book* edited by the same firm and both annual. *Spon's Landscape Price Book*, edited by Derek Lovejoy and Partners, is less frequent, with a new edition available in 1981, the first since 1977, when the new book was launched. *Laxton's Building Price Book*, the 152nd edition in 1981 (Kelly's Directories) is also annual, edited by N. R. Wheatley. It gives prices for specific items according to the usual unit of measurement under subject headings with an index. *Griffiths' Building Price Book* (Barton) is also annual, in its 27th edition in 1981, and gives wage rates, prices of materials and measured rates and prices for spot items. *Hutchins' Priced Schedules*, edited by G. Chrystal-Smith and first published in 1946, followed the layout of a standard bill of quantity and is available separately as Trade schedules, Excavation, Brickwork, Carpentry, Plasterwork, Plumbing, Decorating, Masonry, Roofing, Sundries, Improvement Grant Work and Repairs, Drainage, Sewers and Public works, as well as in one volume. *Savory Milln's Building Book* and quarterly *Building Bulletin* are more concerned with prices and costs in the building share market and summarize cost information. The analysis by Ashworth in *Building Technology and Management* should be consulted for a comparison of content.

DESIGN COST ANALYSES

The *AJ* 'Cost Analyses' are very familar to most architects but they are by no means the only ones available, since *Building* issues similar ones less frequently and some of these for 1979–1980 have been reprinted in *Building Dossier*, compiled by A. Williams (Builder Publications, 1980). Some *AJ* ones have been republished in the various handbooks or studies of building types published by Architectural Press, and are referred to in Mills or the *New Metric Handbook*. Others can be located in *API*.

Specifying

Texts are fewer in this field although they are often linked with costing. The most important are Willis, *Specification Writing for Architects and Surveyors* (7th edn, Crosby Lockwood Staples, 1979), which covers the development of specification writing, and Bowyer's *Practical Specification Writing* (Hutchinson, 1981) and *Small Works Supervision* (2nd edn, Architectural Press, 1979), which is actually about specification. *Specification* itself does not discuss writing clauses but provides model clauses for most stages of work, up-dated every alternate year.

Standard clauses are now available from the GLC in *Preambles to Bills of Quantities* (GLC, 1978). However, there are two standard libraries. Fletcher and More, *Standard Phraseology for Bills of Quantities* (4th edn, Godwin, 1979) is regularly revised and in loose-leaf format with an *Introduction* published in 1980 for the first time. The *Manual of Headings and Specifications for Levels 2 & 3: Standard Phraseology* was published in 1981 (Godwin). This has been developed by computer and can be used with computerized systems. Similar to this is Monk and Dunstone, *Standard Library of Descriptions of Building Works* (3 binders, 2nd edn, Estates Gazette, 1978). However, since its introduction in 1973 emphasis must be laid on the *National Building Specification* (NBS) developed with the RIBA but since put on an independent commercial basis. There were very varied reports of its use and value on publication but since then a *Small Works Version* has been issued and a set of sample applications to a church building, *Example Project Docments: Church* (NBS, 1974). The *NBS Small Jobs Book* is also available as a separate book without up-dating in CI/SfB or SMM order.

On its introduction the *AJ* looked at its value to practice (**159**, 3 April 1974, p. 743) and published a study 'NBS for beginners' (10 September 1973, pp. 535–537) while in April 1975 (16 April 1975, p. 811) future plans were outlined and followed by S. Hendy's 'NBS in practice' (*AJ*, 2 March 1977, pp. 407–413). At the same time R. Stevens commented in *Building* that the NBS showed how to reduce words (22 April 1977, pp. 97–99). The *Pocket Book*, also published by NBS, provides a succinct account of using the NBS, and of specifying too. As long as there are volumes of standard specifications available, many professionals will use one or all rather than labour with compiling their own versions.

A few examples of specialized texts exist; for instance, Levitt, Bernstein and Richardson, *Specification Clauses for Rehabilitation and Conversion Work* (Architectural Press, 1981).

Further information

This section has been briefer than some others as there is a finite amount of information needed in this field and it is therefore more readily listed. Further sources of information will normally be the institutions concerned, including the offices of the BCIS at the RICS, the Institute of Quantity Surveyors and the Chartered Institute of Building, with the experts at the NBS and possibly those concerned with the compilation of the schedules and specifications above. Certainly the practices involved will be able to undertake consultancy work. Although perhaps less active in this area, the work of the BRE and the PSA, Quantity Surveying Directorate, should not be forgotten and some information published by them is listed in *PSA in Print* and DoE *Annual List of Publications*. As with so many aspects of construction, the DoE has its own standard indices and specifications akin to those of the largest of firms. However, usually the architect will be working with a quantity surveyor rather than on his own in this sphere, and if further information is needed it can be gathered from the sources mentioned at the beginning of this section.

Maintenance

Why should the architect look at maintenance and its information sources since he is concerned with the design and erection of the building rather than its later upkeep? But this is a fallacy. The buildings should endure, probably for many years and should do so in good condition. Maintenance of our older building is often called conservation or preservation and both form part of the architect's workload. This section should therefore be read with Chapter 15 and with articles such as Farrel and Grimshaw's in the *RIBA Journal*, 'Buildings as a resource' (**83**(5), 1976, 171–190). The cost of maintenance is being viewed as a design criterion and the new science of terotechnology has developed and will be outlined below.

BRE *CP 3/78* reported a colloquium discussing the ways in which management costs influence design considerations and the system developed by SSHA, Princes Risborough Laboratory and Peterborough Development Coporation. Other aspects of information on maintenance relate to the section on materials – it has often been pointed out that the Greeks and Romans understood better than the modern generations the use of maintenance-free materials like marble, which also contributed to the maintenance of comfort within the building!

Texts

The main texts relating to maintenance are ones like Lee, *Building Maintenance Management* (Crosby Lockwood Staples, 1976) and I. Seeley, *Building Maintenance* (Macmillan, 1976), with others such as Gibson, *Developments in Building Maintenance* (Applied Science, 1979), Hutchinson, Barton and Ellis, *Repair and Maintenance of Buildings* (Butterworths, 1975) which is intended as an examination textbook, Melville and Gordon, *Maintenance and Repair of Houses* (Estates Gazette, 1973), Mills, *Building Maintenance and Preservation* (Butterworths, 1980) and the two volumes of the recent *SLASH Housing Maintenance Manual* (SLASH, 1980-1981).

The volume of BRE Digests entitled *Building Defects and Maintenance* (2nd edn, Construction Press, 1977) deals with remedy on discovery of defect or failure. Many lists link the two and one should therefore refer to the literature of failures discussed elsewhere on pages 151. To these may be added Richardson, *Remedial Treatment of Buildings* (Construction Press, 1980). The GLC *Development and Materials Bulletin* turns its attention to maintenance sometimes and in 1974 in a series of articles on 'Avoidance of building failures' pointed out that the inadequate use of feedback on completed buildings has meant that maintenance has not always been related to design. The 'Feedback Digest' in *Construction* brings one to the same conclusion. Perhaps the current sets of checklists for the building surveyor would be helpful to those involved in maintenance and in assessing design needs. They are P. O'Keeffe, *Building Surveying Checklists* (House Information Services, 1981) which cover dwellings, and S. Staveley, *Structural Surveys* from the CIOB Maintenance Information Service (Paper 15, 1980).

Although it has not produced texts in this field the government has been involved in the cost aspect of maintenance, and the DoE *Annual List* should be consulted, with BRE *Information*, for a full list of publications. Linking with the previous section and with economics of buildings generally are the two PSA publications, *Costs in Use: A Guide to Data and Techniques* (HMSO, 1972), showing how to present and use available data in maintenance and design, with *Costs in Use: Elemental Tables* (PSA, 1977). The same year they also published their own *Estimating Handbook for Building Maintenance* in loose-leaf format with illustrations of the various tasks, and shortly after an article by B. Smith pointed out the 'Costs in use reduction needs government lead' (*Building Maintenance and Services* No. 7/8 1976, 15-16). The same journal

Executing a design 287

also carried a description of the PSA's computerized operation of maintenance at USAF bases (No. 3, 1976, 11–12).

BUILDING MAINTENANCE COST INFORMATION SERVICE

A companion service to the BCIS already discussed (p. 282), is the BMCIS, although this is not linked with the RICS in the same way. It is run on a commercial subscription basis and depends on feedback information from subscribers. Included in the service are cost indices, cost analyses of work executed, design performance data, case studies of the organization, financing and physical results of maintenance work and a publications digest covering recent articles with a back-up photocopy service to supply those articles on request. Some papers describing techniques are included in the regular mailing of sheets. Also included is a brief, regular, newsheet which gives notes on current information and highlights such new features as the *Energy Cost Index* introduced in March 1981. Also published in 1980 was the BMCIS *Building Maintenance Price Book*, giving current prices for maintenance work in trade order with labour constants in hours and all-in labour costs for basic trades. Other brief cost guides exist from the CIOB or the RICS mainly, like *Definition of Prime Cost of Building Works of a Jobbing or Maintenance Character* (2nd edn, 1981), produced by the RICS with the NFBTE.

Most of these can be found through the publications lists of the PSA, RICS, CIOB and NFBTE in conjunction with the *RIBA Booklist* and the *Building Bookshop Catalogue* and the references in the texts cited. The journal indexes also ensure that users are aware of most new publications – and the Publications Digest from BMCIS is valuable.

Journals

Maintenance in design is covered in all the major journals very sporadically, but the feedback aspect is covered best in the two mentioned above, GLC *Development and Materials Bulletin* and *Construction* (DoE). *Building Research and Practice* reports include maintenance sometimes and *Plant Engineer* frequently covers design in buildings as relating to services. *Building Maintenance and Services, Building Maintenance* and *Cleaning and Maintenance* with *Building Technology and Management* are useful.

There are no specific indexing journals either, but the CIOB *Building Management Abstracts* has a section on maintenance and

Current Information in the Construction Industry cumulating into *Construction References* will usually refer to articles, new books, pamphlets and government papers. *RICS Abstracts and Reviews* published a review of literature on 'Structural Surveys' (R453 in August 1981) and also has a regular section on maintenance.

Bibliographies

While there are not many of these, the PSA Library service has a continuing *Current Information on Maintenance* which covers *Cleaning Buildings, Design and Maintenance, Management and Economics, Building Services and Engineering, Deterioration and Weathering of Materials* and *Preservation and Restoration of Buildings*. An Foras Forbartha, the National Institute for Physical Planning and Construction Research, in Dublin, produces many bibliographies, among which is No. 100, *Building Performance* (1977). Occasionally others will be found among those from trade associations.

Handbooks

The annual *Manual of Building Maintenance* (Turret) is intended to provide a collection of products and companies involved in maintenance with some information on topics such as Practical Building Management and Maintenance Management. The Building Centre has issued the loose-leaf format, A4, *Building Centre Maintenance Manual and Job Diary* (4th edn, 1981) by J. Blacker, covering the sources of information, general maintenance requirements and services maintenance requirements for buildings with the intention that this should form a basis for a manual to be prepared for each building on completion. *Maintenance Manuals for Building* from the Ministry of Public Building and Works (HMSO, 1970) discussed the contents and preparation of such manuals. A procedure for doing this has also been suggested in the USA (W. Rosenfield, 'An as-built project manual', *Progressive Architecture*, June 1981, p. 122) to provide a guide to the finished building and the way in which it was designed to be maintained. This is partly linked with terotechnology. Advice on completing such manuals should be taken from the checklists in the texts and the Report Writing section above.

Terotechnology

It could be argued that architects do not need a new science and name to express a concept which has been preached, if not practised, for a number of years. The definition quoted in Croome and Roberts is full and clear:

> Terotechnology is described as a combination of management, financial engineering and other practices applied to physical assets in pursuit of economic life cycle costs; it is concerned with the specification and design for reliability and maintainability of plant, machinery, equipment, buildings and structures, with their installation, commissioning, maintenance, modification and replacement, and with feedback information on design performance and costs. It aims to promote improved understanding and co-operation between the user, designer, contractor, operation and maintenance staff, and other professional advisers concerned with buildings, structures, sites and services in order to achieve the most satisfactory use of resources. (Carpenter, *Building Services Engineer*, **42**, 1974, A18)

Since all aspects of engineering are concerned, the information sources for terotechnology as a whole are considerably wider than those expressed here, which relate specifically to buildings. The Committee for Terotechnology of the Department of Industry published many pamphlets and documents in the mid-1970s such as *Design Aspects for Terotechnology* and *Maintenance Aspects for Terotechnology* (The Committee, 1975) and *Terotechnology Handbook* (HMSO, 1978), all of which can be located through the Department's list of publications or library, and *Government Publications* from HMSO. *Building* for 25 April 1975 looked at its impact on buildings and the origin of the new interest after, or during, the 1973 oil crisis. In the same year *Building Services Engineer* devoted a whole issue (**43**(7)) to various aspects of design and planning for maintenance. At this time many articles were published like 'Building care starts before drawing board' by J. Ware (*Building Maintenance*, **9**(5), 1975, 18, 21, 23) and 'Planning tells me everything' by S. Henderson (ibid., **9**(3), 1975, 9–11, 13, 15) in which the system of planned preventive maintenance is described as it is operating at Cherry Knowle Hospital, Sunderland. It is under the term 'planned preventive maintenance' that further references will be found, as the use of the word terotechnology seems to have faded a little, so that in 1980 the RICS produced *Practice Note 4, Planned Building Maintenance*. Quite an extensive bibliography can be accumulated from the pages of the *Building Management Abstracts*, usually under this heading. One text from America deserves mention; E. B.

290 Executing a design

Feldman's *Building Design for Maintainability* (McGraw–Hill, 1975), which has many references and clear checklists of points but is broad rather than deep in its coverage.

Further sources

Maintenance is a topic which is readily discussed and, as such, many conferences and seminars have been held, covering various aspects of the building fabric and will be found either through the brief reports in the pages of *Building, Building Services*, etc. or the indexes to Conference Proceedings given on p. 47. That at the Polytechnic of Central London's School of the Environment was reported in *Building* (20 February 1976, pp. 63–64) and *Building Maintenance* reported a BMCIS seminar, 'Responsibility for the built environment from inception to demolition' (**7**(1), 1973, 12–14). The DoE published the papers of the Building Maintenance Conferences, e.g. *4th National Building Maintenance Conference*, London, November 1975, which covered Structure of Building Obsolescence, Challenge of Lifetime Care and Costs. The British Council of Maintenance Associations published *Optimising Maintenance by Computer, Papers Presented to a Conference, London, October 1974*.

Sources of advice remain ill defined. Most of the associations mentioned above will be found in *Directory of British Associations*, and the CIOB *Maintenance Information Service* is the only specific source in this country. Although the Building Centre may be able to refer enquiries onwards, it does not, like its Dutch equivalent, Bouwcentrum, operate a consultancy service on building maintenance and cleaning (see G. Atkinson, 'Long distance information', *Building*, 12 June 1981, pp. 52–53).

13
Finishing a design

Landscape

Shirley Herbert

Landscape design is, like architecture, one of the branches of environmental design. Many architects erroneously believe that it is concerned with the ornamental planting of gardens and spaces around buildings – a kind of 'exterior design' analogous to interior design – both fields which lie within their own area of professional competence.

In fact, even in mainly urbanized countries like Britain, the natural components of the environment greatly exceed those added by constructional activity, buildings only occupying a small percentage of the surface area of the land. The analysis and modification of plant communities, soils, water bodies, landforms and local climates, and their adaption to the needs of society is properly the concern of landscape designers. It is therefore important, in all but the most limited scope of development, that their skills should be included in the design team's composition right from the outset.

The Landscape Institute is the professional body for landscape architects, and is now expanding to include professional members and practitioners in the allied fields of ecology, geomorphology and land management. The Institute has a library for the use of members.

Periodicals

Landscape Design is the quarterly journal of the Landscape Institute. It consists of articles in depth on landscape construction and plant materials, and is a most useful bibliographical tool with its book reviews and 'Bibliography', a subject list of new books added to the Institute Library and references to articles.

Architects' Journal has several items each year of great interest to the landscape profession. C. C. Handisyde wrote a series of articles between 9 July 1975 and 3 March 1976 on 'Hard landscape in brick'; 'Rural settlement and landscape' appeared in the issues of 21 and 28 January 1976. In September 1973 there was an article about 'Office landscaping', and on 17 May 1978 twenty pages on 'Interior planting'. The 'Annual Technical Review' includes a section on landscaping. In addition, when discussing new housing estates there is often criticism of the landscaping of the sites.

Anthos is published quarterly in Zurich by the Swiss Federation of Landscape Architects on Behalf of the International Federation of Landscape Architects. There are parallel texts in English, French and German.

Landscape Architecture is the journal of the American Society of Landscape Architects. It is published bi-monthly in Louisville, Kentucky, and covers regional and land planning, landscape design and construction.

Landscape Planning is published quarterly by Elsevier, Amsterdam. Articles are on scientific aspects of landscape, and it is a useful source of book reviews and abstracts from other journals.

Landscape Research News is published three times per annum, from Manchester University, Department of Town and County Planning.

Garten und Landschaft is published monthly in Munich by the German Federation of Landscape Architects. The text is in German, but English summaries are included.

Journal of Garden History, an international quarterly, was first published in 1981 in London (Taylor and Francis). It is planned to cover not only the architectural history of garden design but also the relation of gardens to the history of landscape taste.

Landskap is the organ of the Danish Landscape Architects and is published in Copenhagen eight times per year.

Indexes, abstracting and current-awareness services

The *Architectural Periodicals Index* includes landscape architecture and is the main source of articles. The *Index* is arranged

Finishing a design 293

alphabetically by subject, and there is an index of architects and landscape architects.

The Property Services Agency has produced two useful guides to landscape: the first one is *Landscape: The Space around Buildings: An Annotated Bibliography* (Property Services Agency, 1975). This is a bibliography of the subject and also includes all relevant British Standards for landscape, and lists of photographs of buildings in their landscapes. The second PSA booklet is *Landscape: Guide to Sources of Information* (Property Services Agency, 1978). As well as giving some bibliographical information this guide also includes a list of almost one hundred associations of interest to landscape architects, together with addresses, telephone numbers and a description of the activities and resources of the associations concerned.

Current Information in the Construction Industry and its six-monthly cumulation, *Construction References*, are prime sources of current awareness for landscape architects, including most of the books and pamphlets on landscape which appear in the English language. The coverage is good on practical manuals, and although they include some historical material, they are less complete on the historical landscape side. Books on environmental impact analysis also appear in this category, and, of course, most major periodical articles in the field of landscape architecture are also listed. The arrangement of these journals is by UDC order, so it is easy to pick out the books and articles of interest to landscape architects.

There is no abstracting journal of specific interest to landscape architects, but particular aspects are covered by specialist abstracts such as *Ecological Abstracts*, Norwich, University of East Anglia, *Geo Abstracts* (6 times p.a.); *Forestry Abstracts* Slough, Commonwealth Agricultural Bureau (monthly); *Horticultural Abstracts*, East Malling, Kent, Commonwealth Bureau of Horticulture and Plantation Crops (monthly); and *Biological Abstracts*, Philadelphia (semi-monthly).

Spon's Landscape Price Book, Derek Lovejoy and Partners (ed.), (2nd edn, Spon, 1981) is a prime sourcebook for landscape architects and, after sections on legislation and fees, has specifications for items required by landscape architects. These cover items such as groundworks, seeding, turfing, planting, fencing, hard finishes, playground equipment, water features and street furniture, materials' prices and measured work prices together with approximate estimates for contractors' works'. The final section covers international landscape contracting in many European countries, the USA, India, Hong Kong, Canada and New Zealand.

General Monographs

Some of the most noteworthy landscape architects are women and these ladies have proved to be very good at writing about their subjects. Dame Sylvia Crowe and the late Miss Brenda Colvin were both pioneers of the art in the 1940s and 1950s, and Miss Nan Fairbrother, Mrs Susan Jellicoe, and Miss Elizabeth Beazley were all writing in the 1960s and 1970s.

Examples of their works include B. Colvin, *Land and Landscape: Evolution, Design and Control* (2nd edn, John Murray, 1970), which concentrates on rural landscaping; S. Crowe, *Tomorrow's Landscape* (Architectural Press, 1956) (this early book covers urban landscaping and the problems of industrial blight); N. Fairbrother, *New Lives, New Landscapes* (Architectural Press, 1970): this book studies the pattern of Britain's landscape and how it has evolved, and it considers present and future land use and the problems of reconciling new developments with rural conservation and landscape architecture. Susan and Geoffrey Jellicoe have together produced a very well-illustrated book, *The Landscape of Man: Shaping the Environment from Prehistory to the Present Day* (Thames and Hudson, 1975). As the subtitle tells us, they trace the evolution of the landscape through the ages, including the ancient cultures of Mesopotamia, Greece, Rome and the Muslim world, the medieval cultures of Europe, India, China, Japan, old America and the post-Renaissance West. Elizabeth Beazley's book *The Design and Detail of the Space between Buildings* (Architectural Press, 1960) is essentially a practical approach to such problems as fencing, street furniture, car parks and preservation of the landscape. Ian Laurie's *An Introduction to Landscape Architecture* (Elsevier, 1975) gives useful information on landscaping, planning, ecological analysis and conservation, whilst W. G. Hoskins has written several books on the historical evolution of the landscape, of which probably the best is *The Making of the English Landscape* (7th edn, Hodder and Stoughton, 1970). This book explains the features of the landscape and is based upon fieldwork as well as historical documentary research.

Landscape Techniques

Professor A. E. Weddle edited *Techniques of Landscape Architecture* (2nd edn, Heinemann, for the ILA, 1979), and this book is one of the basic texts covering subjects such as the design of open spaces and the preservation of the countryside.

In 1973 Derek Lovejoy edited *Land Use and Landscape Planning* (Leonard Hill), and this covers survey, assessment, analysis and classification. A fully revised and up-dated second edition came out in 1980. It includes a chapter on environmental impact analysis and has several case studies illustrating successful applications of the methods described.

Two guides to design were published in 1981. Lane L. Marshall's *Landscape Architecture: Guidelines to Professional Practice* (American Society of Landscape Architects) and Leroy Hannebaum's *Landscape Design* (Reston), covering the private garden mainly. The former covers a wide range of practice and services.

Landscape analysis

A *National Land Use Classification* was published by HMSO for the Department of the Environment in 1975 with the aim of producing a national hierarchical classification. *Site Planning* by Kevin Lynch (2nd edn, Massachusetts Institute of Technology, 1971) gives a good introduction to site planning and shows how to apply the principles to shopping centres, urban renewal, housing and industrial estates and public utilities.

Landscape planting and maintenance

Plant books for the landscape architect seem to fall into two categories – ones about trees and shrubs and ones about plants. In the first category, the main encyclopedic work is the recently revised four-volume work by W. J. Bean, *Trees and Shrubs Hardy in the British Isles*, edited by Sir George Taylor (8th edn, John Murray, 1970–1980). As well as describing the species botanically, methods of cultivation and distribution are described. Another excellent book is published by the nurserymen Hillier and Sons in Winchester: *Hillier's Manual of Trees and Shrubs* (5th edn, 1981). This is a guide to trees and shrubs available for sale, and includes some 8000 species. Brenda Colvin's *Trees for Town and Country: A Comprehensive Selection of Trees Suitable for General Cultivation in Britain* (4th edn, Lund Humphries, 1972) was first published in 1947 and describes, with the help of pictures and detail drawings, trees best suited for particular conditions. The Forestry Commission, amongst many helpful booklets, have No. 20, *Know your Broadleaves*, (1975) and No. 15, *Know your Conifers* (1970) both by H. L. Edlin. These are identification manuals with clear photographs and line drawings. Rather elderly, but still important as a standard work, is K. Makins, *Identification of Trees and Shrubs* (Dent, 1952).

General planting is described and catered for very well in Brian Clouston's *Landscape Design with Plants* (Heinemann, and the Landscape Institute, 1977). It explains varied conditions and is well illustrated. The Horticultural Trades Association list of plants is a basic work for all practitioners. It is now produced under the title *Joint Council of Landscape Industries Plant List of Trees, Shrubs and Conifers* (Reading, HYA, 1977). It lists about 1300 plants and is a combination of the lists of the HTA with the former Institute of Landscape Architects. *Plants for Ground Cover* by G. S. Thomas (Dent, 1970) surveys flowers and shrubs which are ornamental but which require minimum work because of their growth habits.

A new style of guide was described in *Landscape Architecture* in March 1982 (p. 91). The *AVIS–ARID* Vegetation Information System is a database designed to help choose the right plant for the right soil/site. Plant information in the database covers everything from growing preferences to height, leaf shape, colour and size, and can be retrieved according to most variables.

Landscape maintenance

G. E. Brown's *The Pruning of Trees, Shrubs and Conifers* (Faber, 1972) is a major work on this specialized subject. It includes the pruning and tree surgery requirements of most species. A. S. Conover's *Grounds Maintenance Handbook* (3rd edn, New York, McGraw–Hill, 1977) was originally written for use within the TVA, and covers horticultural and civil engineering maintenance in both small- and large-scale projects. It includes some particularly useful charts giving solutions to maintenance problems with plants, pests and soil types. In J. D. Fryer's two-volume *Weed Control Handbook* (7th edn, Blackwell, 1973) the second volume gives recommendations for dealing with the weeds once they have been identified from Volume 1.

Specialized landscaping

For gardens A helpful handbook by J. Brookes is *Room Outside: A Plan for the Garden* (Thames and Hudson, 1969). This is useful for planning and creating smaller gardens, and includes sections on plant selection for site conditions, planting, hard-surfacing, special features and garden furniture.

For hospitals P. R. Thoday's *Hospital Grounds Maintenance: An Investigation into their Layout, Organisation, Staffing and Mechanisation* (Bath University, 1973) was commissioned by the DHSS and was based on a survey of the landscape maintenance of thirty-five Devon hospitals.

For industrial sites   One of the most useful books in this area is *Landscape of Industry* by C. R. V. Tandy (Wiley, 1975). It is concerned with the impact of industry on the landscape in the past, present and future. It suggests ways of putting right the damage which industry has done to the environment.

For parks   Elizabeth Beazley's *Designed for Recreation: A Practical Handbook for all Concerned with Providing Leisure Facilities in the Countryside* (Faber, 1969) was written as a guide for planning authorities on the provision of camping and picnic sites, information centres, signs, footpaths, etc. and covers such features as public lavatories, shelters, swimming pools and marinas.

For playgrounds   Lady Allen of Hurtwood was a great campaigner for the cause of children's playgrounds in the 1960s. She is the author of *Planning for Play* (Thames and Hudson, 1968) in which she pleads for planners to relate the scale of individuals to the buildings. Types of play areas such as adventure playgrounds, playparks and incidental play areas are described and details are given. Play areas required for abnormal children are also discussed. The Department of the Environment's Design Bulletin No. 27, *Children at Play* (HMSO, 1973) considers the importance and pattern of play, and the problems of providing for play-needs in inner cities and new housing estates.

For playing fields   The Department of Education and Science's Building Bulletin No. 28, *Playing Fields and Hard Surface Areas* (HMSO, 1966) gives guidance on the layout, construction and maintenance of playing fields.

For roof gardens   One of the best writers on this subject is a German, G. Gollwitzer, and he has written two books on the subject: *Dachgarten und Dachterrassen* (Roof Gardens and Roof Terraces) (Munich, Callwey, 1962) and *Dachflachen* (Roof Surfaces: Lived, Enlivened, Planted) (Muchich, Callwey, 1971). Both books are in German but are very well illustrated by photographs and design details.

Burolandschaft – Office landscaping   Office landscaping was an innovation brought in in an effort to improve the working conditions inside rather drab offices. It is particularly in vogue in open-plan offices and can include large banks of flowers and shrubs, often maintained on a self-watering principle. It is difficult to find good literature on the subject, but the *Architects' Journal* produced a series of articles on interior planting starting with the issue for 17 May 1978, **167,** No. 20, 963–982, 'Interior planting' by S. Scrivens and J. Bell. Case studies appear in Volume 169 of 1979, Nos. 11, 13, 15, 17 and 19, dated fortnightly from 14 March 1979 to 9 May 1979, and cover planting schemes in leisure centres, banks, offices and showrooms.

STREET FURNITURE

This is the composite name given to all the signs, notices, litter-bins, lamp-posts, seats, planting boxes, etc. found in the open spaces of roads and pedestrian areas. The most useful guide to this external furniture is published by the Design Council: *Street Furniture: List of Designs included in Design Index* (7th edn, Design Council, 1977). Specifications and pictures of street furniture currently available are given, providing a wide range of choices in all areas for landscape architects, as well as offering design ideas. Another useful source of information is the trade catalogues of the manufacturers of the items concerned.

HARD LANDSCAPE

The Architectural Press has produced three technical studies on hard landscape, all of which originally appeared in the *Architects' Journal*. *Hard Landscape in Concrete* by M. Cage and M. Vanderbilt (Architectural Press, 1975) covers the general areas of urban design including roads and pedestrian precincts, play areas and street furniture. *Hard Landscape in Brick* by C. C. Handisyde (Architectural Press, 1977) specializes in retaining walls and free-standing walls, pavings and steps, and also covers tree surrounds, sculptures and play areas. In addition the *Architects' Journal* of 19 May 1976, pp. 1005–1009, has a 'Technical study: hard landscape in stone' by J. Ashurst, describing the selection, durability, road finishes, landscape walls and patterned pavings and does some costings on the use of stone as a landscape material.

Interior design

Anthony J. Coulson

The completion of any large-scale architectural project or conversion of premises normally involves an interior designer to ensure that the finished building fits the needs and tastes of the client. The interior designer may be part of an architectural partnership or in practice by himself. In either situation his specialist design expertise demands a substantial and diverse input of information.

Professional bodies

Interior design is a profession in its own right with a central institute, the British Institute of Interior Design, which has its own qualifications, publications, library and information service. Many interior designers also hold qualifications awarded by the Society of Industrial Artists and Designers. The Interior Decorators and Designers Association Ltd is a trade association which maintains a directory and issues its own publications. In a broader way, the Design Council is deeply concerned with many aspects of interior and product design through its magazine *Design* (monthly), its growing range of monographs, specialist services and committees. The interior designer needs to have publications by all these bodies together with detailed files on their services and activities.

Besides these central bodies there are many other national and international organizations which may need to be contacted for current information and codes of practice. Conveniently many are listed in *World Design Sources Directory: Répertoire des sources d'information en design*, edited by the Centre de Création Industrielle, Centre Georges Pompidou, Paris, for ICOGRADA (International Council of Graphic Design Associations) and ICSID (International Council for Societies of Industrial Design) (Pergamon Press, 1980).

Information sources in the practice

Most successful interior designers tend to develop specialities or particular interests and, as designers move from one practice or group to another fairly often, their knowledge and experience is the main source of fresh information on problems and solutions. To support them, most practices maintain detailed and (often within very tight financial and space constraints) comprehensive libraries of samples, information sources, general reference works and records of completed projects. Although few practices have a full-time librarian or information officer, most interior designers are well aware of the range of sources and materials they need.

ARCHIVES AND PAST RECORDS

Once a practice has been established for some time with a number of regular clients, or clients in a particular field, reference to past jobs becomes an important part of planning new work. Detailed and carefully filed records of contracts, suppliers, particular site difficulties, colour schemes/coordination, samples of material and special conditions demanded by the client are essential to prepare the designer adequately. As nearly all models and detailed presentation plans are lodged with the client as part of the contract, the practice will need to retain details of as many of these decisions as it can within its own resources. For ease of retrieval and re-filing the archives are probably best kept according to the established system of recording a contract and samples. Detailed photographic records (prints and slides) provide essential reference materials for negotiations with current and new clients. These archive materials provide the core of the library/information service.

SAMPLES

Next to its own records, the collection of samples is probably the most heavily used resource – both for making up sample boards for clients and for more general reference. Ideally the designer will want to draw on as many examples of materials *that are available for contract* as possible to show colour, texture and other physical characteristics. This bulky and easily disorganized resource normally includes samples of carpet and other floor coverings, furnishing material (for curtains, drapes, wall hangings), ceiling boards and panel samples, paint colour cards, plastics, tiles and ceramic finishes, light fittings, switches and handles, wood and metal samples, glass (for interior divisions), wallpaper and plaster samples, leather and textiles for furniture, lettering and graphic signs. It can be quite difficult ensuring that this collection only includes material available but many practices deal with this problem by encouraging representatives and agents of contractors and suppliers to remove obsolete material when delivering fresh samples and new price information. Other samples collected on a more occasional basis are carefully dated, to be discarded or replaced after a set period (rarely more than three years).

Finishing a design 301

It is hardly ever possible to keep samples of larger items, such as furniture, available, and so the designer has to rely on a full range of catalogues and promotional literature systematically weeded and up-dated on the same period basis. Multiple copies are useful to allow for cutting up for interior sample boards. In the case of imported items or pieces made to order only it is essential to keep a careful note of estimated fabrication/delivery times. Unfortunately this information changes constantly and often without warning, and so most practices need to keep a careful note with the samples/leaflets of contacts (agents, shippers and manufacturers) from whom up-to-date information and news can be obtained rapidly and accurately. Few contracts can tolerate long delays or uncertainties. If the materials cannot be made available fairly easily, they cannot be used.

TRADE LITERATURE AND DIRECTORIES

As well as this assorted collection of samples and leaflets to be cannibalized for sample boards, the interior designer will need access to as full a range of manufacturers' catalogues and price lists as possible for instant reference. Maintaining this collection is time-consuming and up-dating by contractors and sales representatives is vital. It also needs to be supported by a detailed range of current address books and directories or provide prompt access to product and supply information elsewhere. These reference books include telephone directories (alphabetical and yellow pages), local street directories, such as *Kelly's Post Office London Directory*, as well as company and product directories such as *Kelly's Manufacturers' and Merchants' Directory*, *Kompass Register of British Industry and Commerce*, *Key British Enterprises*, *UK Trade Names*, and *Stubbs Directory* (see Chapter 8, p. 140).

Local directories of all sorts are useful and overseas trade directories (such as the Kompass directories for individual European countries and other developed countries) are valuable if the practice is involved with overseas contracts. In the case of foreign suppliers and contracts a detailed index of contracts, telephone numbers and addresses is necessary. Many of the commercial attachés in London embassies and trade delegations can be very helpful in providing information that is more up-to-date than printed sources. A card index of names, times and numbers can save a lot of time. Dealings with a wide range of statutory and advisory bodies occur in the course of any work and general reference works such as *Councils, Committees and Boards: A Handbook of Advisory, Consultative, Executive and Similar*

Bodies in British Public Life, edited by I.G. Anderson (4th edn, Beckenham: CBD Research Ltd, 1980) provide addresses, contact names and information about the bodies listed.

These general reference works will need to be supplemented by more specific directories aimed at potential clients and contractors such as the British Carpet Manufacturers' Association, *Index of Quality Names* (three per year). The problem is that there are so many associations, companies and organizations involved in the building and allied trades, and the interior design practice is normally very short of space. The most convenient solution is probably to invest in a directory covering these specialist organizations, such as *Directory of British Associations, Directory of European Associations* or *Trade Associations and Professional Bodies of the United Kingdom* rather than pile up data that may only be used occasionally (see Chapter 2, p. 28).

STANDARDS AND ERGONOMIC DATA

In the execution of any contract the designer pays careful attention to the great range of standards, regulations and specifications that bear on the products and materials to be used. Apart from the local and national building and planning regulations that have been discussed earlier in the book (see Chapter 8) the designer needs access to current individual standards. To answer this need, the information service includes many British Standards Institution publications, particularly *British Standards Yearbook, Annual Report, BSI News* (monthly) and *BSI Buyers' Guide* as well as individual standards that bear directly on work in progress, such as *BS 4875: Strength and Stability of Domestic and Contract Furniture, Part 1: 1972 Seating, Part 2: 1977 Tables and Trolleys, Part 3: 1978 Cabinet Furniture*. Individual foreign and international standards may also be necessary but are usually kept selectively as space is at a premium. In practice it may be cheaper to subscribe to the monthly BSI *Worldwide List of Published Standards* and develop a more thorough knowledge of the main BSI Library and local libraries holding complete sets of British Standards (see Chapter 8). Many other organizations, such as the British Carpet Manufacturers Association, apply their own standards and grading schemes, and information on the bases of the schemes and how widely they are applied is necessary. The body concerned is the only reliable source of this data. Publications of consumer organizations, such as *Which?* (Consumers Association, monthly), and materials testing organizations, such as the *Annual Book of ASTM Standards* (American Society for Testing and Materials, Philadelphia) are useful. The potential range of this material is enormous and the limited selection held locally provides for immediate needs and special interests.

To supplement this data more general texts on ergonomics help with some of the spatial and functional aspects of interior design, e.g. J. Panero, *Anatomy for Interior Designers* (latest edition, Architectural Press, 1978), J. Panero and M. Zelnick's *Human Dimensions of Interior Space: A Sourcebook of Design Reference Standards* (Architectural Press, 1980), J. Croney's *Anthropometry* (Batsford, 1980) and H. Dreyfuss, *The Measure of Man: Human Factors in Design* (latest edition, Architectural Press/Whitney Publications, 1978). The selection will depend on the particular interests of designers. Interior designers particularly interested in this aspect of design may up-date their knowledge with subscription to *Applied Ergonomics* (IPC Science and Technology Press, quarterly) and *Ergonomics Abstracts* (Taylor and Francis, quarterly).

JOURNALS

For more general current information and visual ideas heavy use is made of journals. The importance of both features and advertisements has already been noted earlier in this book and this is particularly important in this type of design. As well as the regular interior design features in such journals as the *Architectural Review* a lot of useful ideas are gained from advertisements in more general architectural magazines. More specifically tailored to the UK interior designer are the two monthlies, *Interior Design* and *Decor and Contract Furnishing* (both, Morden, Surrey: Westbourne Journals Ltd) and the annual *Decorative Art and Modern Interiors* (Studio Vista). Some of the important journals published in other parts of the world assist the professional to keep up to date with new developments.

America *Interior Design* (New York: Whitney Communications Corporation, monthly), *Interiors for the Contract Design Professional* (New York: Billboard Publications, monthly), *Residential Interiors* (New York: Billboard Publications, bi-monthly), *Sourcebook for Interior Planning and Design* (Los Angeles: Design World Productions, monthly), *Contract: The Business Magazine of Commercial Institutional Design, Planning and Furnishing* (New York: Gralla Publications, monthly), *Architectural Digest: The International Magazine of Fine Interior Design* (Los Angeles: Knapp Press, nine per annum) and *Interior Decorators Handbook* (New York: Columbia Communications, semi-annual).

Canada *Canadian Interiors* (Toronto: Maclean-Hunter Ltd, monthly).

Scandinavia *Interior* (Stockholm: Swedish Furniture Manufacturers Association, (semi-annual), *Nye Bonytt/Design for Living* (Oslo: Forlaget Bonytt AS, ten per annum) and *Design from Scandinavia* (Copenhagen: World Pictures AS, annual).

Italy *Interni: la rivesta dell'arredamento* (Paderno-Dugnano: Gorlich Editore SP, monthly).

Germany *M.D.* (Leinfeldin-Echterdingen: Robert Kohlhammer Verlag, Monthly) (formed from the merger of *Innenarchitektur* and *Mobel & Decoration* with text in English, French and German) and *Design International, Issue A* (Koenigswinter: Design International, bi-monthly) (text in English and German).

Belgium *Decoration-Ameublement/Woningrichting* (Brussels: Union Professionnelle Nationale de la Décoration et de l'Ameublement de Belgique, eight per annum).

France *Architecture intérieure* (Paris: Societé d'Edition et de Presse, bi-monthly), *Art et décoration: la revue de la maison* (Paris: Charles Massin (ed.), seven per annum) and *Répertoire C.A.I.M.* (Paris: Syndicat National des Créateurs d'Architectures Intérieures et des Modèles, bi-monthly).

Japan *Japan Interior Design/Interia* (Tokyo: Interia Shuppan, K., monthly) and *GI/Global Interior* (Tokyo: ADA Edita, irregular).

Only the largest practices will be able to afford many of these and so many of the smaller practices opt for the more lavish and easily obtainable general overseas architectural journals: *Domus: architettura, arredamento, arte* (Rozzana, Italy: Editoriale Domus, monthly). *Casabella: rivista di urbanistica architettura e disegno industriale* (Milan: Editoriale Electa S.p.a., monthly), *Abitare* (Milan: Editoria Segesta, ten per year) or the more popular domestic journals: *Homes and Gardens* (IPC Magazines, monthly), *House and Garden* (Condé Nast, monthly), *Ideal Home* (IPC Magazines, monthly) and *House Beautiful* (New York: Hearst Magazines, monthly).

Apart from the indexes to architectural journals already mentioned elsewhere in this book (see p. 127) there are no really adequate indexes to this rich body of journals. The quarterly *Design Abstracts International* (Pergamon) had very limited application for the interior designer. However, as a lot of information is obtained from advertisements and chance visual combinations, regular browsing is more important than searching through indexes even though to a librarian, this is not a particularly efficient way of exploiting a journal file.

Specific elements of interior design

Up to this point the information sources discussed have a fairly general application, but within each practice there will be need for more specialized material on key elements of design. As I have suggested earlier, the balance will depend on the special interests and needs of the individual designers. Emphases and the nature of designing vary considerably from practice to practice. Information needs and sources for structural problems and services have already been discussed earlier (see Chapter 12) and in this section I will try to survey some of the materials available to support more detailed investigation of lighting, colour, furnishing materials, furniture and fittings.

LIGHTING

A number of important codes for lighting particular interiors have been developed. These have important functional and national differences. As well as general documents, such as the *Code for Interior Lighting* (Illuminating Engineering Society, 1977), access is needed to the publications and specialist information services of the most important national bodies in the field, notably the Lighting Industry Federation, its regular *Interior Design Handbook* and the more specific *Better Office Lighting, Lighting for Shops, Stores and Showrooms, Interior Lighting Industry* (D. W. Durrant (ed.), 4th edn, 1973), and the more technical Illuminating Engineering Society, which now has merged with the Chartered Institute of Building Services.

For more general current information the interior designer may well pick up useful ideas from *International Lighting Review* (Eindhoven: Phillips, quarterly) and *Lighting Equipment News* (Maclean-Hunter, monthly). Fortunately there are now a number of handy textbooks, such as J. L. Nuckolls, *Interior Lighting for Environmental Designers* (Wiley, 1976) and P. R. Boyce, *Human Factors in Lighting* (Applied Science, 1981) as well as a growing number of studies of lighting for particular effects, such as S. Wells, *Period Lighting* (Pelham, 1975) and F. Basham and B.

Ughetti, *Neon* (Plexus, 1980). A. Duncan, *Art Nouveau and Art Deco Lighting* (Thames and Hudson, 1978) might prove useful as a general reference.

COLOUR

As with lighting, the variety of colour systems, terminology and practices has given rise to a considerable and often confusing literature. Standards are gradually being published, e.g. BS 4800: 1972 *Paint Colours for Building Purposes*, and BS 4727: Part 4: Group 02: 1971 (1980), *Vision and Colour Terminology*. The Building Research Establishment publications make a very important contribution to the vital aspects of coordination: *The Coordination of Building Colours, BRE Digest 149* (HMSO), H. L. Gloag and M. Gold, *Colour Coordination Handbook* (HMSO, 1978). As regards dyes and colouring the publications of the Society of Dyers and Colourists provide the most useful guide in the large form of the *Colour Index* (3rd edn, 1971), five volumes with quarterly supplements, *Colour Index Additions and Amendments*. Nevertheless the literature of colour is extremely specialized and complex. For a lot of very detailed technical data it is wisest to develop the information collection with the aid of the following specialist bodies in this field and their publications.

Manufacturers and research British Colour Makers Association, Oil and Colour Chemists Association and Colour Group (Great Britain) of Bowater Technical Services Ltd.

Paint Paint Research Association (publishers of the monthly *World Surface Coatings Abstracts*) and the Paintmakers Association of Great Britain Ltd.

On a more general level, wide-ranging studies, such as T. Porter and B. Mikellides *Colour for Architecture* (Architectural Press, 1976) and F. Birren *Colour for Interiors: Historical and Modern* (Wiley, 1963), might be stimulating and useful.

FURNISHING MATERIALS

In selecting information on the properties and design of individual materials one is on the edge of an immense range of technical literature. The retail/contract aspect is conveniently treated by *Decorating Contractor Annual Directory* (London: International Trade Publications) and the work of the British Contract Furnishing Association Ltd).

Some of the many specialist central bodies that have emerged over the last hundred years provide more technical information about likely performance and suitability of materials.

A key source of information on textiles is the Textile Institute. As well as its more technical publications, the *Journal of the Textile Institute* (monthly), *Textile Progress* (quarterly) and many monographs, the Institute publishes two very useful guides – to terminology, *Textile Terms and Definitions*, edited by C. A. Farnfield and P. J. Alvey (4th edn, 1975), and to sources of information, *A Guide to Sources of Information in the Textile Industry*, compiled by C. A. Farnfield (1974). Together with a few basic texts on textile design, such as W. Watson, *Textile Design and Colour*, revised by E. G. Taylor and J. Buchanan (7th edn, Butterworths, 1975), I. Winget, *Textile Fabrics and their Selection* (7th edn, Englewood Cliffs: Prentice-Hall, 1976) and A. J. Hall, *Standard Handbook of Textiles* (8th edn, Newnes-Butterworths, 1975), they will provide a concise nucleus of technical information. Those with a particular interest in the technical performance of specific fabrics should acquire the publications of other specialist textile associations: Cotton, Silk and Man-Made Fibres Research Association at the Shirley Institute, which publishes *World Textile Abstracts* and *Digest of English Language Textile Literature*; Lambeg Industrial Research Association (Linen) at the Research Institute, Lisburn; International Wool Secretariat.

Probably the textile form that most concerns the interior decorator is the carpet. For current information and developments there are the regular journals *Carpet Review Weekly* (London: Haymarket Publishing), *Carpet Review Export* (London: Haymarket Publishing, quarterly) and the annuals, *Carpet Annual* (London: Haymarket Publishing), *Contract Carpeting* (London: Benn), but for more detail access is needed to the publications of the British Carpet Manufacturers Association, particularly its *Technical Bulletin* and research emenating from its Technical Centre. For more general information a standard general work, such as G. S. Robinson, *Carpets and Other Textile Floor Coverings* (2nd edn, Manchester, 1972) might be useful but in practice there is usually more concentration on problems of availability rather than technical issues. I briefly touched on synthetics earlier and information on plastics helps in judging the performance and suitability of these common but extremely diverse materials. As well as general surveys in the nature of S. Katz, *Plastics: Design and Materials* (Studio Vista, 1979) some useful journals include *European Plastics News* (IPC Industrial Press, monthly), *Plastics and Rubber Weekly* (Croydon: Maclaren) and *Beetle Bulletin* (house journal of British Industrial Plastics Ltd). For more detailed technical information turn to the publications of the Rubber and Plastics Research Association, particularly *RAPRA Abstracts* (bi-weekly) and *New Trade Names in the Rubber and Plastics Industry* (annual) together with the technical leaflets of the Plastics and Rubber Institute and Plastic Coating Research Company Ltd.

If the practice can only carry a very small collection of this data, there is a useful directory: E. R. Yescombe (ed.), *Plastics and Rubber: World Sources of Information* (Applied Science, 1976).

FURNITURE AND FITTINGS

There has probably been more published about furniture than on any of the preceding topics but fortunately there are two well-established and highly regarded current British journals: *Cabinet Maker and Retail Furnisher* (Benn, weekly) and *Furniture Manufacturer: The International Journal for the Furniture Manufacturer* (Oxted, Surrey: Magnum Publications, monthly) and the annual *Directory to the Furnishing Trade: Cabinet Makers' Directory* (Benn). For more technical issues it may be useful to obtain some of the publications of the Furniture Industry Research Association, like *FIRA Bulletin* (quarterly) and the general cumulation, *Furniture Literature* (1975) with later supplements, and there is the detailed but compact United Nations directory, *Information Sources in the Furniture and Joinery Industry* (Vienna: United Nations Industrial Development Organization, 1977).

As well as these factual sources it may be helpful sometimes to have available a few historical studies and more general surveys to give an idea of range, shape and the effects of different materials and settings, e.g. C. Meadmore, *The Modern Chair, Classics in Production* (Studio Vista, 1974). This clearly depends on the tastes and interests of the designers concerned. Similarly, when considering the information to be collected on the minor pieces of furniture (knobs, handles, switches) it is best to try to estimate the depth of interest before going beyond trade literature and materials readily available from 'knobs and knockers' retailers. If there is a clear interest it will be worth seeking out specialist associations such as the British Blind and Shutter Association, and its quarterly *Blinds and Shutters*. *Kompass* and *Directory of British Associations* are convenient starting-points for these special groups and companies.

Designing for particular functions and problems

Designing for a specific range of functions – restaurants, shops, hotels, offices, hospitals, exhibitions – pose distinct combinations of problems and so has generated separate ranges of information sources. Broadly, it is possible to categorize each range into handbooks and manuals, e.g. J. Pile, *Open Office Planning: A Handbook for Interior Designers and Architects* (Architectural Press, 1978), *The Structure and Design of Tomorrow's Office: A Report*; prepared by Urwick Nexos Ltd in Collaboration with Francis Kinsman Associates (1980), F. Lawson, *Conference and Convention Centres: A Handbook of Planning, Design and Arrangement* (Architectural Press, 1981), D. Mun, *Shops: A Manual of Planning and Design* (Architectural Press, 1981), A. Rattenbury, *Exhibition Design: Theory and Practice* (Studio Vista, 1971), F. Lawson, *Principles of Catering Design* (Architectural Press, 1978); standards, by-laws and publications of official bodies in the field concerned, e.g. British Institute of Management; 'show-case' books or books of examples, e.g. *Interiors 2nd Book of Hotels,* H. End (ed.), (Architectural Press, 1978). *Interiors Book of Shops and Restaurants* (Architectural Press, 1981), *Interiors 3rd Book of Offices* J. Pile (ed.), (Architectural Press, 1978), E. Brown, *Interior Views* (Thames and Hudson, 1980); journals in the field concerned – aimed at the practitioner rather than designer, e.g. *Hotel Catering and Institutional Management Association Journal* (fortnightly).

There are also recurrent problems in all schemes of rooms that have to meet a limited but particular range of uses. Bathrooms and lavatories are perhaps the clearest examples. Detailed research may have been done such as Alexander Kira's work on bathrooms, *The Bathroom* (enlarged edition, Penguin, 1976), and T. Conran, *The Bed and Bath Book* (Mitchell Beazley, 1978), which should be used with the former *Architects' and Specifiers' Guides: Bathrooms and Kitchens* (Builder Group, annual until 1980), *Ceilings and Partitions* (Builder Group, annual until 1980) and sanitary regulations discussed in an earlier chapter (see p. 215).

There are also particular types of design problem that affect all schemes and every designer will need to be aware of the issues. Ensuring that the interior layout can meet the needs of handicapped and disabled is now more important than ever before. Consequently the designer will probably need to consult both a general text, such as S. Goldsmith, *Designing for the Disabled* (3rd edn, RIBA, 1976), and the publications of the specialized agencies, particularly the Disabled Living Foundation. Less easily identifiable are the issues that stem from restoration and adaption which may call for detailed knowledge of historical materials and fire regulations.

A final word

I hope that the preceding pages show that the interior designer can fruitfully draw on almost as large a range of information sources as the architect. The emphasis is different, as the interior designer is generally an assembler and modifier rather than a constructor. His sources need to be used much more selectively and vary enormously from one contract to another. In practice the interior designer tends to specialize much more than is realized at first glance.

14
Managing the design and the office

Contracts
Ken Turner

Contract procedure

It is probably true to say that no two architectural firms carry out contract procedures in the same way; there are minor differences in one way or another. However, there are certain standard practices to be observed and the main elements or parts of the procedure will most probably be common to all architectural practices. What is certainly required by all firms is a smooth running of the contract with proper observation of the duties and obligations of the parties to it.

Basic procedures are very well set out in two books produced by the Aqua Group; *Precontract Practice for Architects and Quantity Surveyors* (6th edn, Granada, 1980) and *Contract Administration for Architects and Quantity Surveyors* (5th edn, with supplement on the JCT 1980, Granada, 1981). The former deals with the first stages of the contract, through approximate estimates and cost control, drawings, schedules, specification notes, bills of quantities, sub-contractors and suppliers to obtaining tenders. The latter covers all aspects from the placing of the contract through to completion and the final account. Additional chapters also deal with delays and disputes and with bankruptcy. Both are up-to-date and take into account current practice requirements.

The basis for the present-day management of building contracts was set out in the report published by HMSO in 1964, entitled *Placing and Management of Building Contracts for Building and Civil Engineering Work: Report of the Committee*. It was produced for the then Ministry of Public Building and Works under the chairmanship of Sir Harold Banwell. Since this report the National Economic Development Council has, through the Economic Development Committee for Building, published *Action on the Banwell Report: A Survey of the Implementation of the Recommendations of the Committee...* (1967).

A more recent report of the Joint Working Party Studying Public Sector Purchasing under the chairmanship of Sir Kenneth Wood, *The Public Client and the Construction Industries,* published by HMSO in 1975, dealt with public sector activities and made recommendations for good contract practices and procedures.

The *Handbook of Architectural Practice and Management* (4th revised edn, RIBA, 1980) offers far more than contract procedure in its pages. The section dealing with job procedures covers management of projects as well as contract procedure. It also contains the *Plan of Work for Design Team Operation* which can be obtained as a separate booklet.

Publications of the national Joint Consultative Committee for Building which are published by the RIBA include *Management of Building Contracts (1972)* and *Code of Procedure for Single-stage Selective Tendering (1977)* which are both relevant and should be noted. In 1981 the RICS published guidance on *Tendering a Contract: Procedures for Small Firms*. Two standard textbooks which, although covering fairly wide fields, deal in some detail with contract procedure are *Architectural Practice and Procedures: A Manual for Students and Practitioners* (6th edn, Batsford, 1974) by H. H. Turner and *The Architect in Practice* (6th edn, Crosby Lockwood Staples, 1981) by A. J. Willis and W. N. B. George. Sections are well presented and the indexes are good. Brian Armstrong's *The Programming of a Building Contract* (Northwood, 1981) discusses planning techniques for projects.

Forms of Contract

The standard forms for building contracts can be grouped into three categories; the standard form of building contract; government contracts; civil engineering contracts.

THE STANDARD FORM OF BUILDING CONTRACT

This is published by the RIBA for the Joint Contracts Tribunal (JCT) and is sanctioned by the RIBA, RICS, NFBTE and key local authority and contractors organizations. The latest edition is 1980 and consists of the following six main forms:

Local authority, with quantities
Local authority, without quantities
Private, with quantities
Private, without quantities
Local authority, with approximate quantities
Private, with approximate quantities

Additional documents to be used in conjunction with the above are:

Sectional completion supplement
Fluctuation clauses for use with the local authority editions, with quantities, without quantities and with approximate quantities (clauses 38, 39 and 40)
Fluctuation clauses for use with the private editions, with quantities, without quantities and with approximate quantities (clauses 38, 39 and 40)
Tender NSC/1: Standard form of nominated sub-contract tender and agreement
Agreement NSC/2: Standard form of employer/nominated sub-contractor agreement
Agreement NSC/2a: Agreement NSC/2 adapted for use where tender NSC/1 has been used
Nomination NSC/3: Standard form for nomination of a sub-contractor where tender NSC/1 has been used
Nominated sub-contract NSC/4: Standard form of sub-contract for sub-contractors who have tendered on tender NSC/1 and executed agreement NSC/2 and been nominated by nomination NSC/3 under the Standard form of building contract (clause 35.10.2)
Nominated sub-contract NSC/4a: Sub-contract NSC/4 adapted for sub-contractors nominated under the Standard form of building contract (clauses 35.11 and 35.12)
Fluctuation clauses for use with NSC/4 and NSC/4a
Formula rules for use with clause 40 of the Standard form of building contract and with clause 37 of NSC/4 and NSC/4a
Agreement for minor building works with supplementary memorandum

Practice note M1 to agreement for minor building works and supplementary memorandum
JCT design and build contract

In addition, the various standard forms, certificates and instructions to be used with the contract documents can be obtained from the RIBA. Another important related form is that produced by the National Federation of Building Trades Employers: *The Sub-contract Conditions for Use with the Domestic Sub-contract DOM/1 Articles of Agreement 1980*. This replaces the former conditions of NFBTE sub-contract.

The *JCT Guide to the Standard Form of Building Contract 1980 ed. and to the JCT Nominated Sub-contract Documents* published by the RIBA on behalf of the JCT should be read as an explanation to the JCT publications. Further useful commentaries which have been produced are *A New Approach to the 1980 Standard Form of Building Contract* by G. P. Jones (Construction Press, 1980); this is set out in the form of flow charts for each clause: *Guide to the JCT Standard Form of Building Contract 1980*, by R. F. Fellows (Macmillan, 1981); *Building Contract Conditions* by R. Porter (Godwin, 1980): this examines the main points, features and changes in the Standard Form, and also covers government and minor forms of contract. All the main forms are listed in Appendix 1 of the book. Notes on the JCT and practice notes issued for use with contracts forms are included. The *Standard Form of Building Contract 1980 JCT Form* by J. Parris and O. Luder (Granada, 1982) examines the role of the architect as well as the provisions of the form. This is appropriate, since Owen Luder was president of the RIBA in 1982.

A very detailed standard work which is in loose-leaf form and can therefore be up-dated with the supplements issued from time to time is *Standard Form of Building Contract*, by Sir D. Walker-Smith and H. A. Close (C. Knight, originally published 1974). More specific guides to particular forms are being published and *Contractors' Guide to the Standard (Non-nominated) Form of Building Contracts* by V. Powell-Smith (IPC, 1980) is worthy of note, as is the RICS *Manual for Use with the JCT Form of Agreement for Minor Building Works* (1980).

GOVERNMENT CONTRACTS

There are two forms: *General Conditions of Government Contracts for Building and Civil Engineering Works – GC/Works/1, Edition 2* (HMSO, 1977) and *General Conditions of Government Contracts* for *Building and Civil Engineering Minor Works – GC/Works/2, Edition 2* (HMSO, 1980). The Institute of Quantity Surveyors have issued a document in connection with GC/Works/1 entitled *A Report by the Civil Engineering Committee of the IQS on Procedure in Connection with General Conditions of Government Contracts for Building and Civil Engineering Works from GC/Works/1 Edition 1 1973 and Edition 2 1977.*

Notes are included in the *Quantity Surveyor* from time to time and in other professional journals.

CIVIL ENGINEERING CONTRACTS

The principal form is issued by the Institution of Civil Engineers, the Federation of Civil Engineering Contractors and the Association of Consulting Engineers – *Conditions of Contract and Forms of Tender, Agreement and Bond for Use in Connection with Works of Civil Engineering Construction, 5th Edition Revised* (ICE, 1979). A complementary 'International' form, approved by the principal international organizations, is also available.

A number of commentaries and explanatory guides to the ICE form exist, of which the chief ones are *The Fifth Edition Explained: Notes for Guidance on the ICE Conditions of Contract (5th edition – revised 1977)* (2nd edn, 1979), produced by the Association of Surveyors in Civil Engineering: *A New Approach to the ICE Conditions of Contract*, by G. P. Jones (2 vols, Construction Press, 1975–1976). This is similar in treatment to the same author's book on the *Standard Form of Building Contract* in that flow charts are employed to guide users through the detail of each clause; *ICE Conditions of Contract, Fifth Edition: A Commentary*, by I. N. D. Wallace (Sweet and Maxwell, 1978) is a detailed standard work. Abraham's *Engineering Law and the ICE Contracts* (4th edn, Applied Science, 1979) is also a standard.

Few of the texts on contract yet take account of the 1980 Standard Form but important ones which should be noted include *Enden's Building Contracts and Practice* in its eighth edition, edited by S. Bickford-Smith and E. Freeth (Butterworths, 1980) (the second volume is loose-leaf to allow up-dating). D. Keating's *Building Contracts* (4th edn, Sweet and Maxwell, 1978) includes the ICE as well as the JCT. Jack Bowyer's *Small Works Contract Documentation* (Architectural Press, 1976) will need up-dating now and I. Duncan Wallace provides a standard work on all contracts in *Hudson's Building and Engineering Contracts* (10th edn, Sweet and Maxwell, 1974, with supplement, 1979) and on the international FIDIC civil engineering contract, *The International*

Civil Engineering Contract (Sweet and Maxwell, 1974, with supplement, 1980). Cases affecting contracts are published in the appropriate volumes of *Building Law Reports* (Godwin).

Current information

As this is written publishers and authors are writing new guides such as Bob Greenstreet's *Legal and Contractual Procedures for Architects* (Architectural Press, 1981). This not only has a useful bibliography but it also lists addresses to contact for further information. The best way to keep up-to-date with cases and minor alterations is by reading the half-page 'Contract' section weekly in *Building* or by scanning the 'Construction Notes' issued to RIBA *Product Data* Subscribers. The *AJ* usually publishes notes or editorials on recent changes or decisions.

To help track down this literature the CIT Agency published *Cost, Contracts and Quantity Surveying Literature 1979*, in 1981. It is hoped that this will become an annual survey and the next issue is needed quickly. Similarly, some assistance may be found in the CIOB's compilation entitled *A Decade of Quantity Surveying – Review of the Literature 1970–1979* (CIOB, 1980), which covers contract thoroughly, if a little dated already. A new edition is necessary, but it has been followed by P. Harlow's *Contracts and Building Law: A Review of the Literature 1977–1980*, Vol. 2 (CIOB, 1981), although this is mainly a summary of *Building Management Abstracts*.

The *AJ* 'Annual Review' discusses contract developments under the heading 'Law' each January while the *AJ Legal Handbook* (2nd edn, Architectural Press, 1978) covers all aspects of law for architects.

The indexing and abstracting services cover contract – in particular the *Architectural Periodicals Index* has a sub-heading 'Contract' which brings together useful articles in the architectural press while the CIOB's *Building Management Abstracts* cites useful references from the wide range of other journals, including titles such as the *Contract Journal* and *Quantity Surveyor*. For information published recently *Current Information in the Construction Industry* is useful and contract in its wider sense is well covered in *Index to Legal Periodicals*. The CIOB publishes several series of occasional papers. The Surveying Information Service covers such titles as the *1980 JCT Standard Form of Contract* (Paper 2, 1980).

Legal matters are influenced by changing conditions and interpretations. *Building Law Reports* and news items in *AJ* will assist the professional in keeping abreast of developments. Leonard Fletcher's *Construction Contract Dictionary* (Spon, 1981) will help those unsure of the meanings of legal phrases and texts.

Advice and assistance will always be obtainable from the appropriate professional institute. The main institutions are listed in Porter (above). But this is an area where, if there is any shade of doubt, legal advice should be sought.

Working abroad

Margaret Hallett

International work is increasing. A possible shortage of work in the United Kingdom may have influenced practices to increase foreign contracts. Ventures abroad often require different types of research and forethought at the early stages. The RIBA Overseas Affairs Section may be able to assist a practice with detailed information, but much of the required information is only available outside these shores. The necessary information which is available in Britain is scattered.

However, a valuable starting point is the series of articles by the *Architects' Journal* entitled 'Architecture for Export'. Although compiled in 1978, the list of contacts provided in the first part of the series 'How to go about it' (published along with part 2, 'Climate', in *AJ*, 23 August 1978) is still invaluable as an intitial list. Part 3 covers 'Design factors' (*AJ*, 30 August 1978) and part 4 'Countries with opportunities' (*AJ*, 6 September 1978). The *AJ* list of contacts, besides covering those organizations which can provide technical information or basic advice on living and working abroad, details the various international development and funding agencies, most of whom hold registers of practices willing to act as consultants for various projects. The agencies who advise on export opportunities are also detailed here. The precise terms of reference of some may have changed slightly since then, but this can be checked in one of the directories mentioned. However, the Export Intelligence service of the British Overseas Trade Board are evergreen in their remit. The various United Nations' organizations also maintain registers of consultants interested in working for the UN agencies.

Information on projects financed by multilateral development agencies can be obtained from the World Aid Section of the Projects and Export Policies Division, Department of Trade. Many guides are available from libraries. For European information an example is Gay Scott's *A Guide to European Community Grants and Loans 1980* (Euroinformation Ltd, 1980). Methods of applying for funds are given with addresses and availability. Euroinformation Ltd itself provides an information service and many other guides for businessmen. On-line services via *Euronet* (see Chapter 4) can be used for some business information in Europe and American databases offer much company, financial and market information.

Sources of information

More detailed research may be carried out by turning to any of the organizations mentioned in the *AJ* article quoted above and to the main documentation centres: the RIBA Library; the Technical Help to Exporters, which is part of the British Standards Institution; the Overseas Division of the Building Research Establishment; the Department of the Environment Central Library; and the British Overseas Trade Board.

The RIBA Library holds a variety of information collated from indexing foreign architectural magazines, publications on specific aspects of a country and practice documents received from architectural institutes abroad. The Overseas Affairs Section of the RIBA can also provide information of the latter type on various countries along with contact addresses, such as local institutes, government ministries and registration boards. As the service is free (except for some copying charges) the Institute cannot offer a more comprehensive service.

Technical Help to Exporters (THE) on the other hand, does make a charge for the information provided and covers a wide field including professional practice, codes of practice, standards (where they exist) or, in the case of developing countries, the standards most commonly used. For example, in the eastern half of Saudi Arabia it is more likely that work is undertaken to American Standards. The Engineering and Consultancy Division of THE issue *Structural Data Sheets* on some countries. These include, amongst other information, building regulations, meteorological data, standards and codes of practice. In addition THE can send a specialist to obtain the required information or can prepare tailor-made reports – the great advantage being that they have all the necessary contacts and therefore reduce the time spent on research. Quotations for the cost of reports are made in advance as fees vary according to the complexity of the enquiry and service provided. THE also maintains a library and document retrieval system, and aims to cover all countries including the EEC member states.

The Overseas Division of the BRE issues a series of *Overseas Building Notes*, a selection of which were published under the title *Building for Hot Climates* (HMSO, 1980). The objective of the Overseas Division is to assist developing countries in the field of technical information, research and advice and to offer British consultants, especially to countries receiving aid from the British government or agencies sponsoring projects. The service includes, for example, information on design, use and construction of buildings in hot climates. George Atkinson discussed BRE work aboard, indicating opportunities and giving references, in 'Trade winds overseas' (*Building*, 10 April 1981, pp. 47, 49).

The DoE Central Library provides information on legislation and practice in other countries as well as on housing and planning. The Library also acts as a source of information on EEC construction information.

The British Overseas Trade Board collects information on opportunities for export from British diplomatic representatives abroad and operates a subscriber service. Overseas marketing information is also gathered and disseminated through regional as well as national offices. A useful series of general booklets entitled *Hints to Exporters* cover basic information required when working overseas: addresses, office hours, methods of doing business, climate, currency, import and export control regulations. Its work was recently described in the new *AJ* column entitled 'Opportunities'; a 'column which identifies sources of finance and assistance, building competitions and areas of new work'. Both in Britain and abroad, free frames on *Prestel* describe BOTB services (index frame 20461).

The commercial department of the British Embassy, High Commission or Consulate is an essential contact and can provide introductions, advice on local conditions and, if given advance warning, may help considerably in achieving the aim of a visit to another country. Further sources will be found in the directories discussed on p. 35.

Language can present a problem unless a member of the practice, or a contact, is fluent or has a good command of the local language. Misunderstandings arising from confusion over technical terminology should be avoided. It may be necessary to have certain documents (certainly documentation for registration purposes) and contracts translated. There are agencies who specialize in construction translation: the Technical Help to Exporters and the Construction Industry Translation Unit at the Building Centre are just two. Translators at the SRL will scan documents and read the content to enquirers but cannot provide written translations although both the SRL and ASLIB, among others, maintain lists of qualified translators for commissions.

Background information

Publications on working abroad are few but the *AJ* 'Aids to Practice' have included items such as 'The lesson from working abroad' (*AJ*, 13 February 1980, pp. 351–356). The *Architectural*

Periodicals Index does not list 'Working Abroad' as a specific section but under 'Architectural Practice' many of the sub-headings such as contract, practice and management do index any articles which have appeared relating to practice in other countries – often from their own local journals rather than British journals. *Willings Press Guide* now includes sections listing some major newspapers and periodicals in Europe, the USA, the Middle East, Australasia and the Far East.

A bibliography on quantity surveying literature from the Chartered Institute of Building (see p. 279) recently contained quite a lengthy section on working abroad. Various aspects of the management of overseas projects can be discussed with the relevant departments of the CIOB, RICS, IQS and the Institution of Civil Engineers, etc. as well as the RIBA.

To familiarize yourself with the financial health of the country the *Financial Times* reports are the most readily available source. Their Business Information Service will provide information on business and practices all over the world. Their information consultancy will undertake specialized reports at a cost in 1982 of £35 per hour for research. Information on foreign companies can be gained from the Extel and McCarthy's services for other areas (see p. 142). The British Overseas Trade Board or the Bank of England should be able to provide the relevant currency regulations. Some nations only permit a percentage of fee income to be withdrawn from that country.

Statistical data is available for all countries in similar series to the British ones discussed in Chapter 8. The services of the University of Warwick Statistics Collection or of the Statistics and Market Intelligence Library may be consulted and hold many overseas publications. The UN *Statistical Yearbook* and some of the EEC statistics publications are fairly widely available. Chadwyck-Healey have recently started production on microfilm of retrospective volumes of statistical data for countries of Europe (including the USSR), Africa, Latin America and the Caribbean. The extension of such a service to current volumes will greatly increase availability.

Background on the construction industry in European countries will be found in *Construction Europe* (House's Information, irregular) but for other countries the directories like the *Statesman's Yearbook* and the *Europa Yearbook* will give standard data and are revised annually. Most major addresses are given and they are widely available. Climatic information can be found in the major atlases. The *Daily Telegraph* has a publication called *Working Abroad* (G. Golzen, (ed.), Kogan Page, 1982), with

322 Managing the design and the office

related publications on various countries. Professional institutes like the British Institute of Management and the Institute of Directors have also published guides. Business International SA issue weekly management reports on various countries. The US Department of Commerce has issued a guide to *Foreign Business Practices* (NTIS, UK Service Centre, 1981). The Department of Employment should be able to provide information on labour permits.

Practice requirements

Along with the basic background research about a country it may be a stipulation of local law that an associateship be formed. Information about forming such an associateship with local practice may be obtained from the local arcthitectural society if there is one (addresses are available from the Overseas Affairs Section of the RIBA or, failing that, from the Trade Attaché at the British Embassy). Even if it is not a legal requirement to employ a local practice to handle the project, either the title or function of the architect may be protected by law.

Obviously, precise requirements for registration as an architect overseas vary considerably. Many countries have a Registration Act similar to that of the United Kingdom with an independent registration body. In others the registration body and professional institute are combined and do not directly relate to any UK organization. Some nations operate a federal system of registration, the law varying substantially in some cases from state to state. For example, some states will demand a certain period of residence in that state, others that a professional practice examination be taken, some ask that the architect virtually undergoes his entire architecture course again, while others are more lax in their approach.

There is one reciprocal recognition agreement in which the UK is involved. This is the National Council of Architectural Registration Boards of the United States of America (NCARB) and the Architects' Registration Council of the United Kingdom. ARCUK sign and maintain the agreement and it should be this body that comments on its effectiveness.

Through the Commonwealth Association of Architects, the Commonwealth Board of Architectural Education operates a system of Visiting Boards to Commonwealth Schools of Architecture in CAA member states. The CBAE makes recommendations only as to whether a School of Architecture should be recognized. These decisions are not incumbent upon CAA member-institutions, although most do follow the recommendations.

The European Economic Community has a long-term commitment under the Treaty of Rome to establish the right of free movement for all professionals. The Directive (which, if agreed within the Community, will become law in the UK) for the free movement of architects has been under discussion for many years within the various EEC committees and with the Commission. The stumbling-block on agreement has been the Article within the Directive covering the minimum required length of architectural courses. Until agreement is reached, the existing arrangements for registration as an architect in EEC member-states stand.

Details of registration laws can be obtained by approaching the appropriate national architectural institute or registration body. Again the Overseas Affairs Section of the RIBA can provide most of the relevant addresses and more detailed information for some countries.

The local architectural institute may be contacted for information on the method of practice, which can differ sharply from the UK. For example, in Spain the Colegios collects the architectural fee, retaining a percentage for the practice's subscription to the Colegios and any other required amounts, handing the remainder back to the practice.

Conclusion

Working abroad, whether it be to handle a one-off project from the UK or to establish an office abroad, is not something to be taken lightly if only with regard to the costs and time involved. It requires a substantial outlay of both, with no guarantees of a job at the end or of a financially viable career. But those practices who are firmly established abroad seem to enjoy working overseas and are loathe to cease.

Running the practice
Ken Turner

An architect in practice, in addition to being proficient in the design and construction of buildings, should also have a good understanding of business principles. On the one hand, he should be aware of the problems of managing and motivating a group of people and the systems that need to be set up in order to make the firm operate successfully. On the other hand, he must concern himself with the many detailed techniques and practices required both by law and by office practice. The lessons to be learned from Creswell's *The Honeywood File* (Faber, 1962) and *The Honeywood Settlement* (Faber, 1950), although now relating to past days, have been essential reading for many years and have recently been augmented by A. J. Elder's *The Rubicon File* (Architectural Press, 1980), Watson's *The Complete Surveyor* (Estates Gazette, 1973) and A. I. Nellist, *Pippitt, Dotterell and Others* (Construction Press, 1978).

Management of practices

Undoubtedly the most important publication in existence is the *Handbook of Architectural Practice and Management* (4th rev. edn, RIBA Publications, 1980). Written for the architect, this covers in great detail the professional and business activities with which he must concern himself. A useful list of further references (for reading) appears at the end. As a complement to it, and dealing with legal matters, is the *AJ Legal Handbook*, edited by A. Speaight and G. Stone, (3rd edn, Architectural Press, 1982). The coverage is wide and, because of this, the detail is perhaps sometimes less than one would wish. However, precise sources are quoted which the user can follow up quickly when amplification is needed. It has a good bibliography.

From time to time, the *Architects' Journal* in its 'Aids to Practice' produces articles dealing with a wide range of topics, including many aspects of office administration. Each January the 'Annual Review' has a sub-section 'Practice', which reviews the developments of the past year as well as giving references to essential reading under the main headings: Economics, Regulations, Management, Law.

Handbooks can never be completely up-to-date and two services in *RIBA Product Data Service* are the *Legislation Notes*, which list and abstract legislation and government circulars relating to architecture, and the *Practice Notes*, which summarize information, up-dating key documents such as the *Handbook of Architectural Practice and Management* and the *Conditions of Engagement* among others and provide references to new articles, reports and other events. Both series are up-dated three times a year when new sheets are inserted.

The *Architect in Practice* by A. J. Willis and W. N. B. George (6th edn, Crosby Lockwood Staples, 1981) includes some general information about office practice, partnership and management principles, although it concentrates on taking the architect through the stages of managing a project. Essential references are given throughout and this edition includes the 1980 contract.

All the management aspects of the professional work of the architect and building surveyor are outlined in Philip Bennett's *Architectural Practice and Procedure* (Batsford, 1981), the latest addition to the Mitchell's series. The range of information covered is wide.

Another 'standard' text is Turner's *Architectural Practice and Management* (6th edn, Batsford, 1974). This covers very similar ground to Willis in that it deals with office practices first and then follows through all the stages of contract management, insurances and other needs. Oxley and Poskitt's standard text, *Management Techniques Applied to the Construction Industry* (Granada, 1980) is now in its third edition. Coxe's *Managing the Architectural Practice* (Wiley, 1980) is written in a chatty style and has few references, but some advice is relevant to British practice.

Partnership

The information in the *Handbook of Architectural Practice and Management* and in Willis is supported by a detailed analysis of the law in *Law of Partnership* by C. D. Drake (2nd edn, Sweet and Maxwell, 1977). D. H. Harrowe's guide to greater efficiency in *Managing a Partnership Office* (Butterworths, 1978) should be useful.

Group Practices

The Guide to Group Practices and Consortia (RIBA Publications, 1965) gives general guidance for architects.

Finance and insurance

The standard work, *Financial Management and Policy*, 4th edn, by J. C. Van Horne (Prentice-Hall, 1977), provides a detailed treatment of this subject. Financial control in offices is covered by *Resources Control: RIBA Management Handbook Guide* (RIBA Publications, 1976). The most recent book to explain the range of protection available to the construction industry – *Insurance for the Construction Industry* by F. N. Eaglestone (Godwin, 1979) – treats every aspect exhaustively. Guidance to taxation may be found in *The British Tax System* by J. A. Kay (OUP, 1978). Information publications from the Inland Revenue should always be obtained to give guidance on the current position and are usually available free. A list of publications can be obtained. See *Technical Services to Industry* for addresses.

Office procedures

STAFF ADMINISTRATION AND EMPLOYMENT

The *Handbook of Architectural Practice and Management* provides extensive coverage of staff administration. Two books which support it and offer up-to-date guidance on the statutory requirements of employment are

Guidance to Employment Conditions, 2nd edn, by R. Porter (Godwin, 1977), and
Modern Employment Law: A Guide to Job Security and Safety, 2nd edn, by M. Whincup (Heinemann, 1978).

The former is presented in a very practical way as its author is a member of the construction industry. The publications of the Institute of Personnel Management will always be useful, in particular the annual *Personnel and Training Management Yearbook and Directory* (Kogan Page) and guides such as Alastair Evans' *A Guide to Manpower Information* (IPM, 1980), indicating where to seek assistance with various personnel problems and giving a current bibliography.

ARBITRATION

An important document on procedures is the *The Architect as Arbitrator* in its revised edition (RIBA Publications, 1978). Since it was published, however, the Arbitration Act 1979 has appeared. A book which takes this Act into account but which has been directed at the builder is *Arbitration for the Builder*, by P. J. Lord-Smith (Northwood, 1980).

MARKETING

Although written with the smaller practice in mind, *An Architect's Guide to Marketing the Smaller Practice* (amended edn, RIBA

Publications, 1975) will be of value to all. Those larger organizations who might take professional advice on public relations will find the information useful. Many brief articles have appeared in *Progressive Architecture* in recent years and the *AJ* 'Aids to Practice' series covered marketing on 12 and 26 March 1980 and 16 April 1980.

Management principles

Many books have been written on the subject of management. Two which give sound practical information are *Management: Tasks, Responsibilities and Practices* by P. F. Drucker (Heinemann, 1972) and *Corporate Planning: A Practical Guide*, by J. Argenti (Allen and Unwin, 1978). They deal with business organizations in general and are not directed at architects. However, others do look at professional practices, like M. Allsopp's *Management in the Professions* (Business Books, 1980) and C. Lorenz, *Investigating in Design* (London, Anglo-German Foundation, 1979). Both the latter are recommended by the *AJ* 'Annual Review'.

CURRENT INFORMATION

Following from the establishment of newsheets in the RIBA *Product Data* the *RIBA Journal* in April 1980 announced a 'round-up of news, information and advice essential to the smooth running of architectural practice' as a regular feature. This covers technique as well as practice management and is therefore indexed in *Architectural Periodicals Index* with many other references to 'Architectural Practice'. Other professions encounter similar situations, therefore the advice and references from sources like the PSA bibliography, *Quantity Surveying Development* (PSA Library Service, 1978) with sections on the profession, insurance, claims and insolvency, can be useful. The RICS *Abstracts and Reviews* has a regular section for references on 'Practice Procedure' and has issued reviews (bibliographies) on topics such as *Professional Negligence* (Review 449, March 1981). In the same way *Building Management Abstracts* should be reviewed occasionally. Any management principles will be discussed in the management as well as the construction press and thus the section in *Anbar Abstracts* on the 'Professions', with a subsection for 'Architects', as well as the general sections on personnel, finance, management principles, work study, etc. will be useful. The subscription to this particular service also includes a postal supply service for copies of references, unlike other services. Lists of recent additions to the RIBA and the RICS libraries are published, and these will always note recent texts as they are published.

Conclusion

Practice management is often a neglected aspect of professional resource provision and the paucity of sources in this survey reflects this. However, additions are appearing continuously as methods and regulations change. For example, in 1981 R. A. Reynolds published *Computer Methods for Architects* (Butterworths), which not only covers all aspects of design, calculation and management uses but also has a section on sources of information and a good bibliography. As far as the architect is concerned this is also an area in which books tend to be more important and the continuing sources of information limited in volume, but they may extend into the management literature, which is too voluminous to attempt to cover. Reference should be made therefore to the guides which already exist, in particular, M. J. Campbell *Business Information Services* (Bingley, 1974) and K. D. Vernon, *Literature of Business and Management* (Butterworths, 1975).

Information in the office

Jacqui Ollerton

Information services need to be understood and 'actively subscribed to' in the whole establishment with continual evaluation towards modification and responsiveness to change and development. In this sense the whole of a study like Broadbent's on design (p. 2) is reviewing, assessing and evaluating, critically and constructively, information about the work of others in order to present a methodology for the present. It is noticeable that such reviews in the last ten or fifteen years have included quite clearly a role for information, its organization and analysis, which was either assumed or ignored formerly.

A clearly defined policy on obtaining relevant information can produce savings of time, labour and money, and improve quality in the office by getting better results. There are, however, difficulties in the use of information. The architect may face the following types of problem:

> He may not know whether the information needed exists;
> The information may exist but he does not know where to find it;
> Searching can be abandoned if it becomes too difficult, expensive or too time-consuming;
> The information exists in the wrong format;
> The information found is inconclusive or gives conflicting advice.

In a typical office of medium size, information may be organized and sought in a variety of ways.

Internal information

In a working office dissemination of internal information is a vital method of communication, whether it is to convey office policy or to make staff aware of good practice. Offices may issue information in many forms, e.g. bulletin, newsletter, notes, handbook, information files, or as a house journal. The type of information to be conveyed is usually

> News, new projects, job progress or completion, staff changes;
> Office organization and policy, guidance of organization, services, etc. which may be recorded in a handbook, manual or as standing instructions;

Good practice, the results of experience, perhaps by trial and error, may be communicated and encouraged by producing technical bulletins, design notes, approval lists, specifications or standard details. Technical bulletins can provide a current-awareness service for the office by covering such topics as materials supply, economic factors or feedback and advice on problems.

Office feedback

Some offices disseminate information internally. Records need to be kept and fed back. The RIBA *Plan of Work* defines the purpose of feedback as 'to analyse the management construction and performance of the project by means of analysis of job records, inspection of the completed building and studies of the building in use'. Therefore feedback is seen as a continuous process. Larger offices may appoint a technical officer to specialize in research and advice and may devise special systems or standard forms for the collection of information. 'Whilst documentation is most valuable in making designers aware of likely problems, it is thought that the greatest benefit is obtained by there being an individual or a central section which has responsibility for the collection and transfer of technical experience throughout an organisation' (NBA, 1977).

As far back as 1962 the RIBA pointed out that 'more serious attempts should be made to record design decisions and job history in a systematic way and integrate these records with the office information system for future use'. Examples of performance-appraisal by means of checklists are given in the RIBA *Architects' Job Book*, but there is still a need for reviewing office feedback procedures. The sensitive nature of recording failures and the need for confidentiality can cause difficulties in the collection of such information. The range of information in job records will vary but will usually include the following:

Details of the job, e.g. location, client;
Personnel involved, e.g. quantity surveyors, engineers, contractors, suppliers and outside consultants;
Cost information, e.g. elemental breakdowns, certificates and fee records;
Job reports, summaries and analysis of performance;
List of material produced, e.g. drawings stored or microfilm.

Job records may then form the basis for other information, e.g. list of contractors, sub-contractors with details or reference to costs, completion dates, other jobs tendered for, etc. Feedback should prevent an office from repeating mistakes from one job to another.

Colleagues and personal contacts

Person-to-person communication is known to be a preferred method of searching for information and advice. Personal contact has advantages over written documentation in that it may help to clarify thinking, generate ideas and provide instant feedback. Contacts are made selectively. Colleagues are used most frequently. Whilst recognizing the value of personal contacts the user may still use written documentation to verify facts. Sometimes personal contact may not be the most satisfactory method, wasting expensive staff time in information searching and duplication of effort, resulting sometimes in the use of out-of-date or inaccurate information.

Personal contacts are formed in working situations, maintained from previous working situations, and made at conferences, lectures, exhibitions, through friends and professional colleagues. At work some people prefer to discuss a product with a manufacturer rather than to locate and read through data sheets or literature. Telephone directories and address book then become vital tools.

Larger organizations, recognizing the value of personal contact and subject knowledge, may compile an 'expertise index' which 'explicitly identifies persons knowledgeable in particular subjects or having specific skills. It is therefore potentially useful as a means of identifying appropriate persons to deal with problems or tasks requiring specific expertise and as an aid to manpower resource management' (Hoey, 1978). Even in a small practice it may be worthwhile maintaining a directory of specialist knowledge internally and locally.

Private information collections

Most designers like to keep basic desk-top reference material of a collection of working documents to hand. The main problem arises in maintaining such a collection (unless there is a link with the Information Officer/Library or servicing on a commercial basis) and in keeping the collection adequately organized to locate information when it is required. 'The hypothesis that researchers set up their own collections in order to become independent of libraries must be rejected. At the very least most researchers will rely on libraries to up-date their own collections' (Rowley and Turner, 1978). The way in which the information is kept together reflects the attitudes to it and its use by differing persons and offices according to a survey of 'Architects' personal and office libraries' which asked 'how useful are they in practice?' (*AJ*, 28 August 1968, pp. 407–420).

If a collection grows beyond the basic reference materials there is a danger of relying on incomplete, inaccurate, out-of-date or even incomprehensible material. If the collection is not properly organized time will be wasted in trying to retrieve material.

Journals such as *AJ* are designed to have the data sections, building studies and technical informatin torn out and filed in the office. Technical information has also been issued in separate supplements, with magazines like *Building Design* containing the NBA *Easi-guides* to the Building Regulations. But, on the whole, the designer cannot spend enough time reading and scanning to keep abreast of new developments, and there is a tendency to hoard too much information unread. Some offices issue working documents on specific projects which can be maintained by the Information Officer/Librarian and then returned to the central collection when the job is completed.

Office libraries and library services

An Information Officer should be willing and able to be actively involved with users to provide a satisfactory information service. An active approach is necessary to develop an awareness of demands and to anticipate the needs and problems of the office. The Information Officer will not necessarily provide all the answers from the office's resources but will know and be able to exploit external sources and contacts. The skill required to assess the economics of providing information from in-house sources and obtaining it externally should not be underestimated. The RIBA *Plan of Work* describes the information needs at the design stage(A to E) and information dissemination at the contract stage (F to M). To derive full benefit, Information Officers should be given the opportunity to contribute to a project as a member of the design team. By keeping in touch with office projects in this way information needs can be anticipated. Some of the ways in which such an Information Officer can become more involved are by:

Sitting in on design meetings;
Being aware of new projects;
Maintaining a regular liaison with a professional member of the team who may act as a technical adviser;
Being involved in the production of internal information circulars.

It may be necessary to discuss and question the problem in order to define specifically what is required. Therefore, as far as possible it is better to make an enquiry personally to allow for interchange and to cut down the modifications which can occur when information passes through many people (see Chapter 2).

Some enquiries or requests for information may be straightforward and are answered quickly from standard sources. A detailed record of enquiries, perhaps on standardized forms, may save time when a difficult question is repeated.

The type of library or information service will be governed by the size and function of the office. Selection of material is vital, as no office can hold or afford all the information it may require. Office libraries have developed as partners recognized the contribution that they can make to the economy and efficiency of the practice. Information will be collected, organized, displayed and disseminated, and should be easy for employees to use. Browsing can often be a valuable method of locating information.

When setting up or organizing an office library it may be cheaper to subscribe to a commercial service than to employ a librarian. An assessment should be made of how far a commercial service fulfils the office's special needs and how much information still has to be obtained elsewhere. This assessment will be based on the work of the office. For example, the manufacturer of a product is a basic source of information about that product and a prime information-supplier. The specifier may have to select a product from a vast range of non-standardized information.

Though trade literature is gradually improving since the introduction of BS 4940: 1973 the vast amount of changing product information means that many specifiers are unable to keep up-to-date. 'To understand the information users' problem it is necessary to realise that up to 10 000 manufacturers supply the construction industry with, according to DoE about 360 000 different products and a considerable variety of services' (DoE/PSA, 1979). There have been many proposals in the past to establish a central commodity file but so far this has never really become a viable proposition. This need for help and for organized product information services has established and developed the commercial product information services. The commercial service has to balance the needs of the specifier who requires concise technical data against the needs of the manufacturer or supplier who wishes to sell a product (see p. 146).

A variety of services such as published directories, data sheets, indexes and back-up enquiry services are provided by organizations like Barbour Index Ltd, the Builder Group and RIBA

Services (see Chapter 8). These are the few survivors from the larger number of services offered in the 1960s. Recently, Barbour Index Ltd and the Builder Group have announced a link-up to combine the resources of the two organizations.

A clear policy on product information is required in an office – even if an office subscribes to a commercial service, trade representatives will still call in and literature will be collected individually by office staff. The office may wish to ban products found unsatisfactory. Trade literature often seems to be a cheap way of obtaining information but is not really *free* if you take into consideration the cost of staff time, phone calls, etc., and the fact that some manufacturers are even making a charge for some of the more substantial catalogues.

Guides to specialist sources of information are described in Chapter 2. Unfortunately none are comprehensive and there is a degree of overlap. Currency is important.

Information Brokers

A fee-based information service can be provided by an information broker. 'The overall aim is to provide access to information by a single telephone call' (White, 1980). Information brokerage is well developed in the USA though not in the UK, where information brokers are only slowly being accepted as necessary specialists. The services of an information broker usually include on-line computer searches and may also cover information consultancy work such as current-awareness services, document delivery, indexing, system design and installations, contract research, translations, organizing seminars, etc. More detail can be found in Boss and Maranjian's *Fee-based Information Services: The Commercial Sector* (Bowker, 1980). With the ever-increasing problems of locating and obtaining information, the information broker may provide a vital service for those who do not have information expertise.

Computers

Direct on-line use of a computer through a terminal/typewriter device is increasingly being used all over the world to give a direct response in information searching, providing relevant references, actual data, order and document delivery services for the material located. As computers are used in design for their capacity to access data and apply it to complex problems, so their use for other types of material becomes more acceptable. For a variety of reasons the UK construction industry has not yet made much use of on-line searching. 'The activities of large sections of the construction industry are likely to remain based upon "low" rather than "high" technology' (NBA, 1977). There has always been a significant gap in the provision of on-line databases in the UK which cover architecture and construction (Siddall, 1982). However, there are now signs that this will change as major construction information providers are planning on-line and view-data information services. This will significantly change the management and use of information in the office of the future.

References

Some useful reading is included here with items referred to in the text.

Boss, R. W. and Maranjian, L. (1980). *Fee-based Information Services: the Commercial Sector*, Bowker

DoE. (1979). *General Information: Towards the Better Use of Existing Construction Industry Information Resources. Final Report of the General Information Group of the National Consultative Council of the Building and Civil Engineering Industries*, DoE

DoE/PSA. (1979). *Better Trade Literature*, PSA

Hoey, P. (1978). *Guidelines to Setting up an Expertise Index*, Report No. 5519 to the British Library Research and Development Department on Project SI/OPA/069

National Building Agency for the National Consultative Council Standing Committee on Computing and Data Co-ordination. (1977). *Benefits of Data Co-ordination: A Survey and Evaluation*, NBA

National Building Agency. (1981). *Videotex in the Construction Industry*, by I. Fraser. Report No. 888/040A on project No. 24(L)1621, NBA

Rowley, J. and Turner, C. M. D. (1978). *The Dissemination of Information*, André Deutsch

Siddall, P. (1982). 'Gaps in UK database provision', *Journal of the RSIS*, **2**(2), 8–9

Stern, A. (1980). Information and documentation within housing, planning and building: a kind of state-of-art report, Swedish Institute of Building Documentation, Stockholm, *Housing Science,* **4**(2), 75–79

White, M. S. (1980). 'Information for industry – the role of the information broker', *Aslib Proceedings*, **32**(2), 82–85

Setting up an office information unit
Ken Turner

The decision to set up an office information unit or library should not be made without careful thought. Hasty action may result in a great deal of money being spent with subsequent disappointment or dissatisfaction from the user. Moreover, the information officer cannot happily perform in a situation where the requirements of the organization have not been defined and the unit itself not developed to meet them.

A number of questions must be asked before any action is taken. Briefly, answers should be sought to the following questions:

> What are the information needs of the organization?
> What sort of material will be required?
> How should the material be arranged and indexed?
> What sort of accommodation will be needed?
> How much will it cost and what staff will be necessary to run it?

Some of the questions may be difficult to answer but without a basic idea of the direction in which one wishes to travel the unit will not function effectively.

The information needs of the organization

The requirements of users can be many and varied. On the one hand, high-quality and precise data may be needed sometimes; on the other, very general information may also be wanted. At all times a user will want

(1) Access to information when a need arises either by knowing who to ask or where to go and look for it;
(2) To be kept informed of new facts either generally over an unspecified period of time or at a particular point in the course of his work.

Some indication of the nature of the organization that the unit will serve must first be ascertained:

(1) How many and what kinds of staff are there?
(2) What are the kinds of information they require?
(3) What sort of service would they like or do they need?

STAFF TO BE SERVED

If the organization is spread over several different locations rather then being in one building, problems of staffing availability and extra expense or duplication must be resolved. Equally, if there are a number of different disciplines or professions to serve, consideration must be given to this.

KIND OF INFORMATION REQUIRED

This will indicate the subjects on which the unit will have to store information and also the forms in which it will have to be (e.g. trade literature, reports, pamphlets, samples, slides, etc.). Information needs will be important in determining what should be acquired or purchased for the unit and what should be borrowed from outside organizations. It will also help decide how big the storage area should be and the kinds of furniture and equipment which will be needed.

KIND OF SERVICE

Many kinds of service are possible. One or more of the following may be given remembering that the more services one gives the higher the cost.

(1) Referral: this is the most basic. It entails simply keeping up-to-date directories and yearbooks and having a person whose job it is to put the enquirer into touch with the appropriate source whether it be person, library, organization, etc.
(2) Storage and display: this involves establishing a collection of material or a library, organized systematically. For this, three things are needed; space for storage and possibly reading or reference; indexes to enable material to be located; staff to organize the collection.
(3) Receiving and distributing documents: the main activities here are circulating periodicals and other regular publications; distributing books, pamphlets, trade literature, etc.; lending from the collection or borrowing on inter-library loan from other libraries.
(4) Producing indexes, bibliographies and bulletins: these are compiled from internal and external sources as guides to availability of information and to keep clients up-to-date on specific topics.
(5) Enquiry answering: this is probably the most skilled of the services which could be offered and much depends upon the training and abilities of the person who is running the unit.

Choice of material for the unit

The information unit can expect to hold only a part of the resources likely to be needed by its users. Therefore selection is necessary and an attempt must be made to select the right types of publication. In a small organization it will be possible to see each potential user personally and to discuss requirements with them. However, in a large organization it may be necessary to be more formal, employing such methods as arranging special meetings with particular groups of users, attending project meetings and reading reports of the organization's work, and even sending out questionnaires.

The subject-needs of the users will determine the publication form of information required. In many technical libraries books do not play such an important role as reports and periodicals. Trade literature, standard specifications and codes of practice are often the key publications. In addition, photographs, slides and maps are often of considerable value. Assessing the value of different materials, ensuring that there is little, if any, duplication of stock, acquiring the material from the most economic sources and in the most efficient manner are all important aspects of selection. Finally, ensuring the renewal of publications is a key activity, i.e. 'self-renewal', which takes place when new editions replace or modify earlier ones should be an automatic process, and 'planned renewal', which the librarian or information officer undertakes by checking the stock and the publishers for new additions and formats.

Arranging the material

In any collection of documents it is vital that one should be able to locate items quickly. It is quite impractical to search through the whole collection to find relevant items. In an organized collection of material there are two important issues to consider; first, the physical storage of the items themselves on shelves or in cabinets, and second, the indexes that are necessary to locate items which the physical arrangement fails to reveal.

There are three principal systems of physically organizing material; in classified subject order, in name or author order, or in sequential order.

Classified subject order is the arrangement of items according to their subject (see p. 115). A small collection may not require a great deal of detail and broad headings may suffice. However, if a large collection is involved, perhaps one having several thousand items, a standard classification should be used to organize it. There are three principal schemes which should be considered: Dewey Decimal Classification (DC), which is most widely used in public libraries; Universal Decimal Classification (UDC), based on the DC, and used in the libraries of many firms and institutions; *CI/SfB Construction Indexing Manual*, produced for the construction industry, which also has international origins like the two preceding schemes. The RIBA is the UK agency.

Name or author order means the person or organization responsible for producing the documents. Organizations such as the British Standards Institution and the RIBA are examples of corporate authors as indeed are the names of manufacturers where trade literature is concerned. Name or author can be a useful method to use, but it lacks the obvious retrieval potential that a subject arrangement has, and therefore usually makes subject indexing essential.

Sequential order is a very basic method where items are assigned a number in sequences as they are acquired. The items are arranged in numerical order, but unless users know the number that has been assigned to the item it is difficult to locate it. However, when used with a coordinate index it can be quite effective.

INDEXES

The purpose of an index is to provide a description of a particular item together with an indication of where it may be found. In information units indexes frequently produced are names of people, places and organizations; titles of items; subjects. The type of index needed depends mainly upon the order of items in the collection.

The arrangement of items on the shelves in classified order can be regarded as a first level of subject indexing since the items are in a subject order. With suitable shelf-labelling some information can be located merely by browsing. However, an alphabetical subject index, which is an alphabetically arranged list of all the subjects represented in the collection showing the appropriate class numbers, will be necessary if full and specific access is required. In addition, if access to the names of persons, organizations and titles of items is required then an index for these must be produced. Similarly, if resources are organized according to names and titles then a subject index is necessary unless reliance is placed on the use of bibliographies and lists to identify items required for work.

Sequential order requires an index, known as a coordinate index (see p. 53). The subject matter of each item is converted into a number of simple terms, each of which is used as an index heading. Each entry card is composed of a heading under which are listed a series of item numbers. If the user requires references concerning hospital floors, the index entries for hospitals and floors must be consulted. Each card will show the numbers of items dealing with the subject. Numbers common to both cards indicate items which deal with the composite subject. The process may be repeated for any combination and number of headings to increase precision. The main drawback of sequential order is that no browsing is possible.

Indexes should be chosen to meet the needs of the users. Questions which should be asked are

(1) Who will use the material? Information unit staff or architects?
(2) What kind of questions will be asked?
(3) What kind of material will be involved?
(4) What will be the size and scope of the collection?

The answers to these should indicate the kind of system, the level of sophistication and details in the indexing required. This must be weighed against the time and finance necessary to provide more complex forms of index.

Accommodation

It is not always possible to have the ideal accommodation for the information unit but, whatever the situation, it is useful to consider at the outset

How much space will be required?
How should the space be planned?
Should there be an allowance of room for expansion?
Where should the unit be located within the organization?

A great deal of information will be found in *New Metric Handbook* prepared by P. Tutt and D. Adler (Architectural Press, 1979) and in Patricia Calderhead's *Libraries for Professional Practice* (Architectural Press, 1972).

Space standards for material, furniture and equipment are given as well as basic configurations. The space requirements for books and other material, for work activities and for consultation must be carefully calculated. Noisy, high-activity areas must be separated from those where reading or research is carried out.

Budgeting and staff

Budgeting is needed for three reasons: to ascertain how much money is required to establish the service; to indicate the annual sum required to maintain and develop the service; and to control expenditure.

If the information unit is to function properly then not only must the initial funding be well prepared but also the maintenance fund. It is pointless setting up a unit which is not adequately sustained. Intitially money is required for new material and equipment, but, as time goes by, a greater proportion will have to be spent on maintaining the content of the unit.

A budget should cover the three main areas of staff, resources (books, periodicals, etc.), equipment and stationery. Staff costs are likely to be the largest element where permanent staff are engaged. The type of service to be given will influence number and quality but, in any event, over 60 per cent of the finance will be required for this.

Information unit duties can be divided into two areas for staffing purposes; clerical and the Information Officer or Librarian. In a small unit offering a basic service a clerical person may be adequate to undertake the work. An existing member of the professional staff may be responsible for directing the information unit with a clerical person to deal with routine activities of acquiring and labelling items selected by the professional, circulating periodicals and other material, issuing, receiving back and reshelving material, and typing.

In a larger unit, and particularly if a more sophisticated service is to be introduced, then a librarian with information skills and some subject knowledge may be required. If a person of this calibre is appointed then he or she cannot be expected to carry out clerical functions as well, and thus clerical support staff will be needed either as a full-time post or part-time from among the existing practice establishment.

Conclusion

In addition to the guidance in the *RIBA Handbook of Architectural Practice and Management* (4th edn, RIBA, 1980) which sets out the main considerations clearly, detailed advice on setting up a practice library was given in Patricia Calderhead's *Libraries for Professional Practice* (Architectural Press, 1972). The basic concepts have not changed, although the books lists, suppliers and addresses are now dated. The former can be up-dated using the *AJ*

'Annual Review', while the Library Association can supply advice on the latter. The *Aslib Handbook of Special Librarianship and Information Work* is revised regularly and provides a guide to all the services and considerations involved. Aslib may also provide a consultancy service.

Members of CIIG vary in size, from large practice libraries in both architectural and engineering practices to some quite small units run by non-professional staff and with several sites. Many are willing to discuss their experience in running such a unit with others. The *CIIG Review* sometimes contains articles on the issues arising.

15
Conservation
John Smith

Conservation is such a wide-ranging field that its sources of information extend much further than would be expected. Architects, conservators and students investigating any of its aspects will, at an early stage, be directed to literature, people or specialist bodies far removed from what at first sight would appear to be architectural conservation. Even if at one end the planning aspects of conservation, or at the other, the wider field of environmental or nature conservation are excluded, the range of information needing to be consulted is extremely wide.

In common with other practical disciplines there are two approaches to seeking information in conservation: one is through the expert practitioner or specialist body or society, the other is through the literature of the subject via, perhaps, the specialist library and its librarian, or one of the various bibliographies in the field. The two approaches are complementary: the advantage of the former and its personal contact is that there is the chance of producing a solution tailored to the peculiarities of a specific problem, and if the expert has already tackled a similar problem himself, the possibility of a great saving in time and energy. The literature, on the other hand, is usually more easily to hand, can often provide a more detailed and thoughtful follow-up to a personal interview, and in most cases is an essential preliminary to a meeting with an expert. A careful study of the bibliographies and their author indexes can also direct the enquirer to the right expert.

In this chapter literature will be considered first, starting with bibliographies. In the absence of a nearby specialist library, they will probably form the first and easiest entry to the subject. Unfortunately, bibliographies are obsolescent the moment they are completed, so this is followed by a section on methods of up-dating and supplementing the information they contain. A survey of current periodicals carrying a significant number of conservation articles, ranging from the general to those produced by learned and professional bodies, will also be included at this point. This is followed by a brief discussion of the types of specialist library available. A brief description of the sources of architectural history relevant to the architect and conservator is then given, followed by a final section on the identification of the various specialist advisory bodies.

Bibliographies of conservation

Generally, bibliographies are much-neglected tools and are grossly under-used by all except librarians. This is a pity, as they can be extremely valuable in giving direction to the search for information.

Conservation bibliographies come in different types: some attempt to cover the whole field of architectural conservation, some touch on it while dealing with a related subject area, and others are specialist, dealing with one small facet of the subject. It is well to be aware of this when using them.

There have been a number of small general bibliographies of conservation published over the last ten or fifteen years (for example, the very useful 'Conservation of old buildings: a select bibliography' by John H. Harvey, *Transactions Ancient Monuments Society*, Vol. 16, 1969, pp. 115–144 offprinted), but the major bibliographical survey of the whole field of architectural conservation is *A Critical Bibliography of Building Conservation: Historic Towns, Buildings, their Furnishings and Fittings* by John F. Smith (London: Mansell, 1978). This work is worth considering in a little detail, as the boundaries defined by its classification of conservation are those adopted for this chapter.

This classification scheme, based on a descending scale of elements from towns to buildings, their parts and their contents, includes sections on the history and philosophy of building conservation, legislation, towns and villages, buildings – fabrics, materials, installations, furnishings and fittings – historical gardens, tourism, archaeology in building conservation, the organization of conservation, and conservation abroad. The final section acts as a guide to other sources of information by listing indexes to the periodical literature and directories, giving information on advisory and grant-giving bodies. The references have been selected 'to give details of all aspects of the conservation of historic towns, buildings and their contents, particularly the practical problems encountered during their conservation. Topics also include the background history, details of techniques, and information related to the work of specialist consultants' (author's preface). Perhaps the most useful feature of the bibliography is that it is critical: most entries carry a brief note detailing the work's contents, assessing its relevance and placing it in context.

There are a number of other general conservation bibliographies, but they are mostly quite small and selective, and are often only semi-published with a restricted circulation. It would be impossible to list such items here, but they may be worth enquiring after locally.

General bibliographies in English but published abroad can also be useful, but, naturally, their emphasis will lie more in the country of origin. F. L. Rath and M. R. O'Connell's *A Bibliography on Historical Organization Practices. Vol. 1, Historic Preservation* (Nashville: American Association for State and Local History, 1975) covers the general field from a North American viewpoint and is part of a five-volume revision of the authors' earlier work, *Guide to Historic Preservation, Historical Agencies and Museum Practices: A Selective Bibliography* (Cooperstown, NY: New York State Historical Association, 1970). Volumes 2–5 are mainly concerned with museum practices. *Architectural Preservation in the United States, 1941–1975: A Bibliography of Federal, State and Local Government Publications* (New York: Garland Publishing, 1978), by Richard Tubesing, also shows the keen North American interest in building conservation. Large international bibliographies comprising entries in different languages tend to be less useful, as a lack of familiarity with a particular national scene and with the idiomatic use of language can affect the selection of titles. The bibliographies published in *Monumentum*, the journal of the International Council of Monuments and Sites (ICOMOS), though of some use, have in the past suffered from this drawback.

The conservation aspects of planning go beyond what any one general bibliography of conservation can encompass. Smith includes almost eight hundred titles on urban conservation, but more specialized information will have to be sought in one of the guides to the planning literature. Brenda White's bibliographical review of the literature of planning, a *Sourcebook of Planning*

Information (Clive Bingley, 1971) is still very good (see p. 227). A more recent, but much slimmer, volume is *Sources of Information on Town and Country Planning* by John Barrick (see p. 227). Brenda White's *The Literature and Study of Urban Planning* (Routledge and Kegan Paul, 1974) and *A Guide to Sources of Information in Planning* by G. M. K. Beck and G. M. Snowball (Information Paper No. 12, Centre for Environmental Studies, 1973) may also be worth considering. Also of note are the lists of town and village conservation reports issued by local authorities, compiled by Robin Bloxsidge, which have appeared annually since 1975 in the October issue of the *Town Planning Review*. They form a very useful supplement to the three hundred or so reports of a more permanent nature listed in Smith (see Chapter 13 above).

Special-subject bibliographies dealing with one small facet of conservation abound, and these may be the most useful type for the architect, practitioner or student faced with a practical problem. Smith, in his *Critical Bibliography*, gives details of over fifty of them and the following selection of subjects gives an idea of the range noted there: brick, damp-proof courses, industrial archaeology, modernizing old dwellings, mortar, paint, slate, stained glass, stone, damage by tree roots, vaults, roofs and arches, a number devoted to urban problems, vernacular architecture, vibration and wood. Some official bodies in Britain produce special-subject bibliographies, notably the Department of the Environment Library and the Building Research Establishment Library. The Library Service of the Property Services Agency of the Department of the Environment produces six bibliographies under the general title *Current Information on Maintenance* and the last in the series, entitled *Part F: Preservation and Restoration of Buildings: A Bibliography* (Croydon: DoE/PSA, 1976) is the one obvious conservation title in the series. Three of the others, *Part A: Cleaning Buildings*, *Part B: Design and Maintenance*, and *Part E: Deterioration and Weathering of Materials* (1977) also include titles of relevance. Parts A–D are in their third edition and produced from 1977 onwards, parts E and F are still in their second edition. The *Library Bibliographies* produced by the Building Research Establishment at Garston are much more academic in approach and most have a limited relevance to conservation. However, a few of them are worth combing for sections or individual titles of relevance. Number 235, *Concerning the Application of Damp Proof Courses to Existing Buildings* and its supplement is obviously one of these, and others on such subjects as *Vibration* (numbers 252 and 253) and the *Long-term Weather Resistance of Plastics* (number 247) can also yield useful information. These bibliographies are not widely available (BRE research being disseminated mainly through its more orthodox publications) but some architectural and building libraries keep them. An up-to-date list of the titles can be obtained from Garston.

Non-government organizations also produce specialist bibliographies reflecting their particular concern. These can be specifically concerned with conservation or be relevant to some branch of it. A very useful series on the scientific and technical aspects of conservation dealing 'specifically with the technical examination, investigation, analysis, restoration, preservation and technical documentation of objects and monuments' are the *Art and Archaeology Technical Abstracts* (New York University, Institute of Fine Arts, 1955–) produced by the International Institute for the Conservation of Historic and Artistic Works. These are issued twice a year and are divided into sections on methods and techniques, paper, wood, textiles, paint and paintings, glass and ceramics, stone and metal. Each volume has a supplement devoted to one topic, for example, stone preservation (1966), deterioration and conservation of stained glass (1973), and these can be very valuable. The bibliographies produced by the Association for Preservation Technology in their bulletins and newsletters are very much concerned with the nuts and bolts of conservation, covering topics such as adobe, brick, 'historic hardware', mortars, paint and paint colour research and slate. These come from the other side of the Atlantic and are published 'for Canadian–American Preservationists', but are extremely useful over here and are held by good architectural libraries. The Council of Planning Librarians (publishing from Monticello, Illinois) has produced a number of specialist conservation bibliographies, though they tend to be slanted towards North American usage. Recently their name has changed to Vance Bibliographies, Architecture Series, and Public Administration Series. One or two architectural libraries in the UK hold them. As an example of the sort of thing they produce, the *Architectural Preservation in the United States* bibliography by Richard Tubesing referred to above started life as a Council of Planning Librarians' *Exchange Bibliography*.

Frequently the architect, conservator or student may be faced with a building the literature of which, if it exists, would best be sought in a more general bibliography covering studies of a class of building rather than in a conservation bibliography. For example, aspects of the conservation of vernacular buildings might best be sought in something like R. de Zouche Hall's *A Bibliography on Vernacular Architecture* (Newton Abbot: David and Charles,

1972), or its supplement *A Current Bibliography of Vernacular Architecture, 1970–1976* (D. J. H. Michelmore, Vernacular Architecture Group, 1979); whereas information on industrial buildings would perhaps be best sought in the annual review of the literature of industrial archaeology and history to be found in each November issue of *Industrial History*, or in the *Industrial Archaeologist's Guide* (edited by N. Cossons and K. Hudson, Newton Abbot: David and Charles, up-dated and reissued at intervals). For buildings of archaeological importance or the conservation of which has archaeological implications, the *Archaeological Bibliography for Great Britain and Ireland* and *British Archaeological Abstracts*, published annually and bi-annually respectively by the Council for British Archaeology, will be of the greatest help. Unfortunately, many classes of buildings, including that large and very important class, churches, do not have specific bibliographies or lists devoted to them and advice on them will have to be sought from one of the specialist institutions. These may be identified via the sources listed in the final section of this chapter (see p. 359 and Chapter 2.)

Up-dating bibliographies

Having consulted a bibliography and failed to find a suitable reference, the task is then to supplement or up-date the information it contains. In seeking this information, a general warning must be given with regard to the use of up-dating lists, indexes and catalogues: it would be very unwise to restrict the search for information to the sections of the lists headed 'Conservation'. In many cases, works of the most direct relevance to the subject are not included there or do not even merit a cross-reference. It is sensible as a matter of course to look always under related section headings: for example, topographical lists, type of area, type of building, type of work carried out, techniques or equipment used, or any other feature important to the topic being sought.

The general official sources of information are described in more detail in Chapter 6. *Sectional List 61, Building* (HMSO) and *Information Directory*, issued annually by the Building Research Establishment, give up-to-date information. The fortnightly *Current Information in the Construction Industry*, cumulated at six-monthly intervals in *Construction References* (see Chapter 7), and the *DoE/TP Library Bulletin* all contain references to current and recently published conservation book and pamphlet material. However, it can be a tedious operation extracting the conservation references from such a large number of general ones, particularly in those lists published at very frequent intervals. The *Accessions List* of the British Architectural Library (issued by RIBA Publications Ltd) is perhaps the best library list to consult for conservation references, though if only an introduction to the subject is needed, the much more basic annual *RIBA Book List* (also issued by RIBA Publications Ltd) might suffice. The *AJ* 'Annual Review', which usually appears in the January issue of the *Architects' Journal*, is also an extremely valuable source for conservation material.

In the absence of any of the foregoing lists from specialist libraries or agencies the *British National Bibliography* can be a help and is held by most libraries. This has the advantage of being arranged according to subject by the Dewey classification. Conservation references are therefore relatively easy to find if the various subject headings are used sensibly. This, together with frequent up-dating, makes it more useful than the better-known *Books in Print*, which is arranged alphabetically in author and title order.

If a more selective approach is required a study of the lists of those publishers which tend to specialize in the field of conservation, such as the Architectural Press or Butterworths, will help, but perhaps a more useful exercise is to look through the book review columns of the most relevant professional journals. The value of this is that they will not only reveal relevant titles but will also give some idea of content and worth. By far the quickest way to make an acquaintance with the most recent conservation literature is to visit a good architectural library, explore its shelves, use its accession lists and subject catalogues and take advantage of the expertise of its librarian. Naturally in doing this one is entirely dependent upon the quality of the library, its staff, and the scope of its purchasing policy and funds.

Periodical literature

Seeking out the most recent periodical literature presents a different problem. Its bulk is far greater than book and pamphlet literature, and relevant material can be hidden away in the most obscure places. Yet in many ways it is easier to locate, that is, if access to the following is available: *Architectural Periodicals Index*, *Avery Index to Architectural Periodicals*, *British Humanities Index* and *Current Technology Index* (formerly *British Technology Index*) (see Chapter 7).

The *Architectural Periodical Index* (*API*) is the first place to look for any article on architectural conservation. The *API* was first published in 1973 but for the period before that there is a microfilm index available for all periodical articles received by the RIBA Library from 1956 to 1970 (London: World Microfilms, 1971). More selective are the periodical lists in the *RIBA Library Bulletin* (1946–1972) which were cumulated annually between 1966 and 1972). As mentioned above, one needs to search very carefully here under the type of building for the sub-heading 'preservation, restoration' as well as under the section where that appears as a main heading. Conservation is not used as a term.

If the *API* fails to produce suitable references the *Avery Index to Architectural Periodicals* (Boston: G. K. Hall & Co., 1st edn, 1963, 12 vols plus 6 supplementary vols, 1965–1972: 2nd edn, 1973, 15 vols, plus continuing supplements) should be consulted. This is the periodicals index of the Avery Library of Columbia University, New York, one of the great architectural libraries of the world, is the next place to look. If often supplements the information found via the *API*. Indexing began selectively in 1934 and over the last few years retrospective indexing has been taking place to fill the gaps. It is therefore worth consulting the supplements even in the search for earlier works.

Often articles relevant to architectural conservation are to be found in non-architectural or town planning periodicals, and consequently do not find their way into the indexes of periodicals held by even the best architectural libraries. There are two ways of filling these gaps: via the *British Humanities Index* and the *Current Technology Index*. As a second line of approach they are most useful, and turn up a considerable number of conservation articles which could otherwise be missed. The *Current Technology Index* is particularly valuable in giving reference to conservation papers with an engineering bias, for example, technical articles concerned with the analysis of the structural defects of historic buildings and their repair, or articles on special types of structure, such as bridges. These papers often appear in engineering journals not normally taken by architectural libraries.

Current periodicals

While the above lists will yield almost all the English-language periodical literature that the architect, conservator or student is ever likely to need it is worthwhile noting some of the more important journals in the field. There is no one journal that satisfies, or could ever satisfy, all architectural conservation needs, but it is unfortunate, though perhaps inevitable in view of the number of disciplines it covers, that its literature is scattered through quite so many publications. Additionally, in a general architectural practice, conservation will be only one of a number of items competing to determine the choice of periodicals the practice will take. General architectural journals try to provide a complete service for their readers and so devote a significant proportion of their pages to conservation. They try to cover all aspects of the field, and articles can range from pieces on area conservation to those on specific aspects of single buildings, and from the very general to the extremely specific and technical. Many of the specialist studies are tucked away in the pages of a learned or professional society journal and, though these may be well known to the specialist, they often do not filter down to those who only tackle the occasional conservation work.

In listing the following journals it is inevitable that there will be some omissions for many periodicals carry only the odd conservation article. Such articles may be traced via the periodicals indexes. More deliberate is the omission of journals dealing purely with such related fields as architectural history, chemistry or museum studies, even though in a wider context they may be relevant to conservation.

Leading the field of the general architectural journals perhaps is the *Architects' Journal*. As well as carrying good single articles on individual subjects, it also includes continuing series of articles on single themes, which, when complete, make up the well-known *AJ Handbooks*. An individual handbook may run for a period of up to two years and they are often so popular and useful that the Architectural Press subsequently publishes them in book form. Examples of handbooks on conservation themes during recent years are *Stone* (later published as *Stone in Building: Its Uses and Potential Today*), the *Housing Rehabilitation Handbook* and the *Use of Redundant Buildings*. The usefulness of the *AJ* 'Annual Review' has been referred to above. Following closely on the heels of the *Architects' Journal* are a whole range of architectural periodicals which have a serious contribution to make in the field of conservation literature. The *Architectural Review* contains a significant proportion of conservation material, often describing individual projects, analysing historic towns or areas or assessing the harmonizing of infill buildings in historic settings. The *Architectural Review* is not so much concerned with the nuts and bolts of conservation, but attempts to stand back a little and make detached assessments of the areas or buildings it is featuring. The articles are generally longer than those in the *AJ* and often illustrated with high-quality colour photographs.

The magazine *Building*, which for a number of years has published worthwhile conservation articles, from November 1978 to April 1981 featured a monthly 'Building Rehab' section containing specialist articles, while the current interest in architectural conservation has led to a number of other new ventures in the conservation field. *Building Design*, a lively weekly newspaper, often contains short articles on conservation and in 1977 spawned an offshoot, *Building Refurbishment and Maintenance* (appearing every other month) which is 'free to people working in building refurbishment'. This has a certain trade element in it. In 1979 Northwood Publications Ltd began publishing the monthly magazine *Building Conservation*, the articles of which, though explaining principles, are not intended to act as manuals for conservation work. It is still too early to assess the permanent value of this publication. Among other general periodicals worth consulting for conservation literature are those such as the *RIBA Journal, The Architect, Period Home* and *Stone Industries. Country Life* also deserves a special mention, as among its very miscellaneous selection of articles are a significant number on conservation, frequently studies of individual towns and villages, plus a regular feature entitled 'Conservation in Action'. Urban conservation is also catered for in the planning journals such as *The Planner*, formerly the *Journal of the Royal Town Planning Institute*, and the *Town Planning Review. Town and Country Planning, Housing Review, Housing and Planning Review* also contain a number, as does the *Quarterly Bulletin of the Intelligence Unit of the Greater London Council.* Those carried by the last are very valuable, being carefully researched and presented in great detail.

For more specialist articles the journals, annual reports, transactions, newsletters, etc. of the various advisory bodies, lobby groups and the more specialist professional societies will provide the best source. It is in this range that journals devoted entirely to conservation will be found, but even here architectural conservation may not always form their major part. Some may be more concerned with fine-art conservation or the conservation of objects for display in a museum environment. Additionally, there are journals seemingly unrelated to conservation and often produced by professional societies in other disciplines, that contain a regular proportion of technical and specialist architectural conservation works.

The Association for Studies in the Conservation of Historic Buildings (ASCHB), a body composed largely of conservation architects, issues a regular series of newsletters outlining the work of the Association and providing good conservation book review sections. Their annual *Transactions* is a more formal publication containing longer articles with a high proportion of conservation case studies. The publications of the ASCHB are very practical and contain much that is of practical value to a conservation architect. They deserve to be more widely known. Churches are dealt with in the annual publication *Churchscape*, issued from 1981 onwards by the Council for the Care of Churches. This contains a miscellaneous selection of articles on all aspects of the care of churches and is issued mainly for the guidance of diocesan advisory committees on the care of churches. Up to half of the publication can consist of book reviews of works on the history and conservation of churches and their contents. These can be very useful in keeping up-to-date with current church and conservation literature. *Churchscape* is successor to the annual *Newsletter of the Council for Places of Worship*, the name by which the Council for the Care of Churches was known from 1972 to 1981, and, although not having a wide circulation, can be found in some architectural libraries. The Council for the Care of Churches also published a range of books and pamphlets on the care of churches. The *Annual Reports* of the Society for the Protection of Ancient Buildings (SPAB) go back to 1878 and contain reports on individual buildings running into thousands. These are now both historical and conservation records. There are cumulative indexes, but the value of the later reports is undermined by the lack of a recent index. The SPAB also produces a series of technical pamphlets which deal with such varied problems as outward-leaning walls and the cleaning of brick and stone. The *Transactions of the Ancient Monuments Society* also contain large numbers of case studies as well as a number of more general articles. The bi-monthly *Newsletter* of the Civic Trust concerns itself mainly with general urban and village conservation problems, with one of its main aims being to keep local amenity societies abreast of the latest developments in thinking, legislation, techniques and products. Of the internation journals, the most easily available is *Monumentum*, the office publication of the International Council of Monuments and Sites (ICOMOS). This is issued somewhat irregularly with sometimes two, but at least one issue per annum. It is international in scope, but sometimes devotes a whole issue to a single theme. Usually its articles are in English or French but it has a multi-language bibliography at the end of each issue. More irregular is the *ICOMOS Bulletin*, which tends to devote each volume to the host country comprising the editorial committee for the issue.

The engineering professions' contribution to conservation literature is made via the journals of its various professional bodies, such as the *Proceedings of the Institution of Civil Engineers, The Engineer, The Structural Engineer* and various others. Although they do not contain a high proportion of conservation material, what there is is usually of a very high quality. The articles are often set out in a standard form and provide a model which could be copied by others working in the conservation field. Usually the structure is described in detail, the defects are analysed and the programme of conservation is carefully set out to act as a guide to others with similar problems. A surprising journal sometimes carrying good background articles for the conservation practitioner is the *Transactions of the Newcomen Society*. It is a high-quality publication of very long standing.

Articles on legislation relating to conservation are difficult to find in the periodical literature: they are scattered through the complete range. Relevant articles tend to be found during periods leading up to, or following, the passing of a major piece of conservation legislation, or at times when some particular legal issue is dominating discussion. These articles can be found via the periodical indexes. There is one relevant periodical, the *Journal of Planning and Environmental Law,* but perhaps the best way to keep abreast with current legislation and legal matters is to use a basic guide such as *A Guide to Historic Building Law* (Cambridge: Cambridgeshire County Council, County Planning Department, 4th edn, 1979) and then keep up-to-date via something like the *AJ* 'Annual Review' and, most importantly, the *Circulars* issued by the Department of the Environment.

There are a number of journals that deal with the fittings and furnishings of historic buildings, as well as those that concern themselves with the science and technology of conservation processes. *Studies in Conservation*, the quarterly journal of the International Institute for the Conservation of Historic and Artistic Works (IIC), is very much concerned with the science of conservation, and very technical articles on subjects ranging from the conservation of wall-paintings, the consolidation of fragile stonework or the treatment of polychromed sculpture, to the study of the whole interior climate of a medieval building can be found within its pages. Many of its contributors work in conservation laboratories, often attached to large museums, so there is a tendency for museum-type conservation, that is, the conservation of objects that will face a future in a controlled environment, to predominate.

Similar in many ways to *Studies in Conservation*, but perhaps of more everyday use to conservators, is *The Conservator*, produced by the United Kingdom Institute for Conservation (UKIC), formerly the United Kingdom Group of the International Institute of Conservation (IIC/UKG). Again, there is much museum conservation work described here, but articles on structural conservation work in the field, for example, the conservation of church monuments, are also included. The *Newsletters* and *Bulletins* of the Association for Preservation Technology, a North American group, are very practical in their approach and can cover anything from locks to floors and ceilings or heating systems. The examples given are usually North American but the articles are still of value to readers on this side of the Atlantic.

There are a whole host of journals published by specialist societies concerned with the study and, as a corollary, the conservation of certain classes of items. It would be impossible to list them all here, but examples of the type are the *Transactions of the Monumental Brass Society*, the *Bulletin of the International Society for the Study of Church Monuments, Antiquarian Horology* and the *Journal of the British Society of Master Glass Painters*. The best way to identify a journal dealing with such a subject is via the relevant subject section of Smith's *Critical Bibliography of Building Conservation* (see Bibliographies above) or in the Craft Council's *Conservation Sourcebook* (see Organizations below).

Libraries

There is no doubt that the best library to consult on any building conservation topic is the British Architectural Library, housed in the headquarters of the Royal Institute of British Architects. It is a reference library, though having a separate loan section for members and students of the RIBA, with a large section on conservation, plus other relevant works scattered through the rest of the library. Between three and four hundred periodicals are taken by the Library and in addition there is a separate collection of early books relating to architecture, including a large number of pattern books and craftmen's handbooks. Associated with this is the RIBA Drawings Collection. The Early Works Collection and the RIBA Drawings Collection are also discussed in the following section. In the provinces the most useful libraries for the conservationist will most likely be those of the nearest university or polytechnic having a department of architecture or planning. Failing this, the student will have to use his public library and the inter-library loan system. Unfortunately, the inter-library loan service, particularly when borrowing via the British Lending

Library, is notoriously slow for some types of material, and there is a risk that the relevant book will arrive long after the problem has been solved or forgotten.

There are many more specialist libraries in existence which can be of great help. The Civic Trust specializes in town and village conservation and coordinates the work of the amenity society movement. Its library reflects this, housing the best collection of amenity society conservation reports anywhere. The most complete holding of local authority reports is at the Marsham Street Library of the Department of the Environment, while another extremely good collection is held by the Library of the University of Liverpool, Department of Civic Design. The Library of the Council for the Care of Churches holds a comprehensive selection of material on church buildings: church architecture, the history of their furnishings and fittings with a special emphasis on maintenance and conservation. In addition there are other institutions, which though having small libraries, may hold copies of specific works difficult to find elsewhere. The SPAB is such an institution. It is emphasized that the libraries mentioned here are not public libraries, but most will allow use by the serious student if prior arrangements are made.

Architectural history

Many conservation architects maintain that there can be no true architectural conservation without a sound basis of architectural history. Unfortunately, today there are a large number of architects currently in practice who have had little or no training in the subject. It is beyond the scope of this book to indicate the full range of sources in architectural history; Arntzen and Rainwater's *Guide to the Literature of Art History* (Art Book Co., 1981) may do that. There are some classes of information such as detailed descriptions of old buildings, drawings and photographs, or early pattern books and builders' guides, that can be of great help to the architect or conservator. There are a few general guides to sources for architectural history available, and one of the most useful is *Sources for Architectural History in England* by John Harris, to be found in the *Journal of the Society of (US) Architectural Historians* (**24**(1), March 1965, 297–300). This is particularly valuable to the architect or conservator not well versed in architectural history as it was written for Americans not familiar with the English scene. Complementary to this is *A Guide to the Sources of English*

Architectural History by H. M. Colvin (Shalfleet: Pinhorns, 1967, a revised version of an article appearing in *Archives*, Michaelmas, 1955). Specifically on houses is *Sources for the History of Houses* by John H. Harvey (Archives and the User, No. 3, London: British Records Association, 1974), which, though dealing mainly with documentary evidence, also includes sections on architectural evidence and the historical background.

Accurate descriptions, early photographs or other illustrations of buildings can be of immense practical value during conservation work, and with the completion of the *Buildings of England* series (Nikolaus Pevsner (ed.), Harmondsworth: Penguin Books, 1951 –1974), descriptions of almost every building of note in the country are now ready to hand. Parallel series for Wales, Scotland and Ireland have also been started. While 'Pevsner' is extremely useful, he can often provide only background information for conservation. More valuable, where they exist, are the architectural descriptions and scale plans appearing in the *Victoria County Histories* (VCH) and the inventories of the Royal Commissions on Historical Monuments (RCHM). There used to be considerable overlap between these two bodies, but in the more recent volumes the VCH has tended to leave detailed architectural coverage to the RCHM. In surveying an area the RCHM takes large numbers of high-quality photographs, which can be up to seventy years old in the earliest volumes. The Royal Commission photographs are deposited with its sister establishment, the National Monuments Record (NMR), which also holds large collections of other photographs and measured drawings. It may be worth supplementing the information provided in the RCHM inventories by an inspection of the original survey cards which are often in more detail. These are retained by the RCHM, and the London office, at the same address as the NMR, holds all pre-war records, plus the surveys of monuments destroyed or threatened. It also holds some microfilm copies of material held by the regional offices. These regional offices, in Cambridge, Salisbury and York, hold the original survey cards of the areas they have covered. Inspection of these cards may only be made by prior arrangement. The National Register of Archives has surveyed many regional and private collections publishing annual lists of additions with entries by subject, architect and place. There are other institutions which also hold drawings, plans, photographs or descriptions of individual buildings. The Council for the Care of Churches has a file on every Anglican Church in the country and the contents of these may range from a few odd photographs to complete surveys and detailed records of previous conservation work. Similarly, the

SPAB holds over 10 000 files on individual buildings, and it may be possible to arrange permission to consult these. The RIBA Drawings Collection holds many thousands of architectural drawings and the publication of its 21-volume catalogue is now almost complete. The nineteenth-century architectural and building periodicals are also a good source for measured drawings of historic buildings, and are often valuable in that they can show them in a pre-restoration state. The task of finding such drawings is made easier by the existence of an index produced at the turn of the century by the Victoria and Albert Museum, the *Topographical Index to Measured Drawings of Architecture which have appeared in the Principal Architectural Publications* (HMSO, 1908). Very useful also is the modern general guide by Maurice W. Barley, *A Guide to British Topographical Collections* (Council for British Archaeology, 1974). This is a county-by-county index of collections, many of which include illustrations of buildings, in public repositories and some private collections in England, Scotland and Wales. It is by no means exhaustive, but is still very useful. For early illustration of country houses, there is also John Harris's *A Country House Index* (Shalfleet: Pinhorns, 1971), which indexes 'over 2000 country houses illustrated in 107 books of country views published between 1715 and 1872'.

At the local level it is always well worth enquiring at the area record or archive office to see if any relevant plans or illustrations exist, and for churches, at the local diocesan record office, which in many cases is the same place. It is fortunate that for churches, plans and drawings deposited with earlier faculty applications often survive, as do many hanging on the walls of church vestries. Sometimes useful background material may be located through enquiries via the local historical, archaeological or amenity society.

Early pattern books, craftsmen's handbooks and builders' guides can also be of great value to the architect or conservator. No specific guide to them exists, but an acquaintance with them may be made via the catalogue of the Early Works Collection held by the British Architectural Library. This may be done in one of two ways: either by visiting the library and using its new and exhaustive catalogue and chronological index, or at a distance by consulting the short title list *Early Printed Works in the RIBA Library*, published in seven issues of the *RIBA Library Bulletin* between May 1949 and February 1951. Naturally, additions have been made to the collections over the last thirty years, but this short title list is still very useful if a visit to the library is not possible.

Organizations

The advisory organizations in the conservation field can be divided into three types: government and official bodies, organizations supported by and representing a particular trade or industry, and non-official groups such as the learned and professional societies and volunteer pressure groups. Each type has its strengths and weaknesses and it is essential to know these, not only to avoid the pitfalls but to take full advantage of the services provided. Unfortunately, it is not always immediately clear from all the guides and directories as to which categories any individual body belongs. Though the number of advisory bodies specializing in conservation is large, it is fortunate that, just as there is one single guide to the literature of conservation in Smith's *Critical Bibliography*, there is also one extremely useful general guide to the organizations. This is the *Conservation Sourcebook – for Conservators, Craftsmen and those who have Historic Objects in their Care*, published by the Crafts Advisory Committee, since renamed the Crafts Council (London: CAC, 1979: up-dating supplement issued 1981). This lists more than 250 organizations, and although its sub-title suggests that it is aimed at conservators and craftsmen, its general sections include much that is of use to the conservation architect. The work is divided into twenty-nine sections, the majority of which contain information relevant to the conservation of buildings, their fitting or their contents. Relevant sections are those on general buildings, ecclesiastical buildings, building materials (plus more specialized sections devoted to stone, wood, glass and metals), furniture, and other categories of objects, such as leather, textiles, paintings and clocks, that may be found in historic buildings. Each entry in the book lists the institution and the essential information of location, telephone number, chief officers, etc., and has a descriptive section stating aims, scope and services. Although the work is extremely useful, it does have one drawback: it is not a critical compilation and the information it contains seems to be based entirely on material supplied by the individual organizations. It also covers in sparse detail the work of the international bodies such as the International Centre for the Study of the Preservation and Restoration of Cultural Property (the Rome Centre or ICCROM), the Council for Europe's Committee on Monuments and Sites and Council for Cultural Cooperation, the Organization for Economic Cooperation and Development (OECD), the United Nations Educational, Scientific and Cultural Organization (UNESCO), all of which produce useful literature, if not specific services, for British conservators and architects.

A similar sort of publication to the *Conservation Sourcebook*, but carrying a slightly different emphasis, is the Civic Trust's *Environmental Directory*. This is up-dated at intervals and lists government departments and agencies, voluntary societies, professional institutions and trade associations. It is also a very useful work.

Perhaps one of the most important aspects of building conservation is the financial side, and a guide to sorces of financial help would be most useful. Unfortunately, the Ancient Monuments Society's *Sources of Financial Help for Buildings of Architectural and Historic Interest*, compiled by Ivor Bulmer Thomas (*Transactions AMS*, **16** (new series), 1969, 145–156) is very much out of date, though the parts on charities are still useful. These are covered in more detail in the *Directory of Grant Making Trusts* (Charities Aid Foundation, 6th edn, 1978). Up-dated at regular intervals), this work is an essential source of reference.

Summary

There are three main sources of information in building conservation: its literature, specialist advisory bodies and individual experts. Its literature may be identified by means of bibliographies of conservation, notably *A Critical Bibliography of Building Conservation* by J. F. Smith, and their inevitable obsolescence overcome by employing the techniques of up-dating given here; advisory bodies may be located via the *Conservation Sourcebook* produced by the Crafts Council, and individual experts may be traced by using a combination of the author and subject indexes and the special-subject sections of the bibliographies, or via the personnel of the specialist advisory bodies.

NOTES

Since this chapter went to press the Architectural Press has published *British and Irish Architectural History: a Bibiliography and Guide to Sources of Information* (1981) by Ruth Kamen. This is also a very valuable sourcebook for conservation. As well as the architectural history bibliography, it contains sections on how to find out about architects and buildings from published and unpublished sources and from indexes and catalogues. There are also useful sections listing organizations and indicating sources of architectural photographs (see also p. 378).

The appearance of new conservation periodicals continues: *Architectural Preservation* made its appearance early in 1982 and *Monumentum*, now subtitled *The Journal of Architectural Conservation*, was reshaped in March 1982 and is now appearing quarterly. First impressions are that this will becomes a first-class conservation journal and set a standard for other to follow. *Building Conservation* has now been incorporated into the *Building Trades Journal*.

16
Buildings, people, places: background information
Valerie J. Bradfield

How do you find out about a building, or place, or person? It is important to be able to locate information quickly on these topics in certain situations. Background work for rehabilitation and restoration work on older buildings must be done. A particular building may be cited as an example of the use of a certain type of construction or material. One must be able to follow up that reference just as one can follow up a bibliographic reference. Only the quickest ways of going about this search are covered in this chapter – knowledge of a few appropriate sources will provide the information more quickly than serendipity. Another guide would be necessary to cover architectural history in full. Information on famous buildings, people or places, Sydney Opera House, Marcel Breuer or Birmingham will present few problems, as texts will easily be located in library catalogues; whole books exist about them, and they are well covered in *API* and the encyclopedias, so this chapter will not discuss them. The problems occur when requiring information on Truman's brewery, Gimson or Dunton Bassett (Leicestershire). Guides such as Pevsner's *Buildings of England* covering (eventually) the whole of the British Isles, county by county, are sufficiently detailed usually to provide a start where a location is known – and, as most readers should be familiar with them, they will not be mentioned again – but where more detail is required, this chapter indicates alternative methods of approach.

Buildings, people, places: background information 363

To begin with, there are ways of approaching this sort of question which are similar for each aspect. Asking certain questions may ascertain the starting point of the enquiry:

Buildings: Do you know the architect's name?
When was it started? Completed? Rehabilitated?
What else is known about it? Construction? Material?
Who are the owners?
How would you describe its current use, type function?
Has this always been the same?
Has it any names? What is it usually called?
By what characteristics is it likely to be cited, known?

People: Are they living? or dead?
What qualifications do they have?
What trade were they in?
What are their countries of origin? Work? Influence?
What works by them are known?
How long have they been dead?
Why do you need to know about them? Does this give clues about the location of information?

Places: What is the exact location?
What is the name of the council responsible?
Have there been any relevant boundary changes?
What parish is it?
If older information is sought what hundred is it in?
What is there noteworthy about the place which might have been isolated for discussion elsewhere?
What is the local newspaper?
Where is the nearest local library, larger library?
Are there any persons of note associated with the place itself or in your work? Or known to be interested?

These are the sorts of question which give a starting point to the sources of information concerned. Each section below will take the discussion from here.

The strategy for such a search was recently outlined by Elizabeth Dixon, Librarian at the Architectural Association, in *Picture Librarianship* (H. Harrison (ed.), Library Association, 1981):

The sequence of search through the AA Library's resources for the design of a marble doorway by Grinling Gibbons for Blenheim Palace would be:
1. The information files of 40 000 classified periodical articles to look for Blenheim Palace in the large collection of articles on country houses arranged alphabetically by name.

2. The alphabetical place index of the catalogue to find the place number for Blenheim.
3. The topographical section of the classified catalogue to find the reference to David Green's book, *Blenheim Palace* . . .
4. The index and list of illustrations in this book.
5. The alphabetical Biography section of the catalogue to note the titles, class numbers and locations of books about Grinling Gibbons and Vanbrugh (the architect of Blenheim).
6. The indexes etc. of these books.
7. *Catalogue of the Drawings Collection* of the Royal Institute of British Architects.
8. The *Avery Index of Architectural Periodicals* to trace entries listed under GIBBONS, G. and Blenheim Palace.
9. Scan these articles. . .
10. The subject index of the catalogue . . . for country houses, doorways, and domestic architecture.
11. The classified catalogue to note . . . material on country houses and domestic architecture. . .
12. The place index and Topography section of the catalogue and shelves for material on the architecture and topography of Oxfordshire.
(The doorway is illustrated in . . . Green . . . and there is a more detailed illustration in an article on Grinling Gibbons at Blenheim . . . in *Country Life*, May 1949).

This illustrates clearly the detective work involved in a fairly easy search which was capable of being resolved within the confines of one library, albeit an architectural one. Other searches will be longer and need to involve a carefully selected range of the items discussed below.

Buildings

Introduction

Having looked at the questions on the previous page it is important to realize why they were asked. Everthing needs a point of access and the more obscure the building the more lateral thought which has to be applied in locating information. Sometimes the only information which can be found will be a discussion of the architect's work or a description of the locality, although it was a description of the building which you started looking for. Hence the interrelationship of the sections of this chapter.

A strategy is necessary. This will obviously vary according to what is known at the outset. It may be sensible to contact the architect's office, if he is alive and if his practice or name is known, to ask if they have any reference files on the building. The telephone directories, the various lists and guides in Chapter 6 may provide addresses. Local libraries, public and academic, often keep files on local buildings. The local architectural society (if there is one and it can be located), the contractors, if they are known, may be contacted asking for reference files – the last may have better files than the architect: practice varies.

Where to start

Some starting points should be considered and will be amplified:

Few buildings are indexed by name in journals but many articles written about them are usually indexed under building type of the place name.

Pevsner's volumes have been mentioned; they are not purely historical, twentieth-century buildings of note are included.

Studies of architecture generally, twentieth century or earlier, always cite particular buildings and usually discuss them in some detail, and the more recent ones tend not to rely on the few famous buildings of the era but to have a wider scope.

Studies of places usually mention buildings in more or less detail.

Studies of the architect may well give further information on his buildings.

Volumes like the *World Architecture* series, *Zodiac* (Zwemmer, Vol. 1–, 1957–) *Lotus*, (Milan, Lotus and London, Academy editions, varying frequency), discuss many contemporary buildings, as do the detail volumes (see p. 249).

Institutions like the RIBA have specialist reference files of buildings and architects, as well as a collection of drawings and manuscripts.

In desperation, look up information on the place as shown below.

If the building is modern, look in the trade literature, the bibliographies in the *AJ* 'Annual Review', and Mills for discussions.

Journals

All the main architecture journals cover specific buildings at some time, in more or less detail; journals which also do this but tend to be forgotten are those like *Chartered Surveyor*, *Building Trades Journal* and *Building Specification* because they take a different slant on the information. Local history and archaeological society journals often discuss local buildings and can be located either using *Ulrich's International Periodicals Directory* (19th edn, Bowker, 1980) and *Willing's Press Guide* (annual) or the indexing journals like *British Humanities Index* and *Art Index*. *Studies in Conservation* and *Vernacular Architecture* cover older buildings. The new *Period Home* (1980–) covers country houses, cottages and town houses. Local newspapers often report on notable old and new buildings, and their offices often have indexes to their issues, although sometimes it will be the local library or archive office which has to be consulted.

Abstracts and indexes

A word of warning is needed as very few indexes use proper names as index entries but many have separate author/person indexes which are useful if the architect/contractor of a building is known.

The main exceptions to the above are *British Humanities Index*, which uses place names and building names if sufficiently important, and the *Avery Index to Periodical Articles*. In this latter the name is usually qualified by the country because so many American place-names derive from British. *Art Index* does index places under county or country. *API* is essential but, when using issues prior to 1978, either the architect or type of building must be known: places and names of buildings are used as sub-divisions of type of building therefore the work at Magdalen College, Oxford (discussed in *AJ*, **160**(51), 1974, 1439–1440), can be found under the building type or by knowing that Ivor Smith and Cailey Hutton were responsible. However, they will also be found using the topographical index at the RIBA library itself which has been kept since 1974 and printed since 1978. *Applied Science and Technology Index* can help but *Construction References* and *Engineering Index* are little help unless a feature of construction is known and can be used as an index term.

Indexes and bulletins such as the *Bulletin of East Midlands Local History* (Deparment of Adult Education, University of Nottingham, annual) index specific buildings locally and many similar publications can be traced through local libraries. J. Harris compiled *A Country House Index: An Index to Houses Illustrated in 107 Books Published 1715–1872 with a List of English Country House Guides and Art Collection Catalogues 1726–1870* (Pinhorns, 1971). *Burke's and Savill's Guide to Country Houses* now covers Ireland in Volume 1, Herefordshire, Shropshire, Warwickshire and Worcestershire in Volume 2, and East Anglia in Volume 3

(Burke's Peerage Ltd, 1978–1982). Similar specialist lists may be found using the RIBA library, the *British Museum Catalogue* and the *British National Bibliography*.

Texts

Handbooks and encyclopedias are discussed separately, but for particular buildings where the architect is not known the period or country can be used as a means of entry to the books or texts which may have covered that building. Town guides, the motorist's AA and RAC volumes, the Shell Guides and the Blue Guides may help. Studies of style and design are useful but require time, browsing and an element of guided serendipity to locate the required building. In any architectural libraries use the subject index to get to the shelves under the architecture of the appropriate country or period and look for texts like *World Architecture* (J. Donat (ed.), Studio Vista, Vol. 1–, 1964–) or *A Visual History of Twentieth Century Architecture* by D. Sharp (Heinemann, 1972). Unfortunately twentieth-century architects work in many countries so their work may not be covered only in texts about the country of origin. Volumes like the *Building Dossier* (comp. A. Williams, Builder Publications, 1980) bring together studies published in *Building*, which may have been missed, although they should have been located if *API* was used. 'Architectural Record' books like *Office Buildings* and *Record Houses* are published regularly by Architectural Record and are purely catalogues of those building types. Where a type of building such as a hospital is concerned, volumes like Stone's *British Hospitals and Health Care Buildings* (Architectural Press, 1980) will mention notable examples and give bibliographies to pursue (see p. 212 for other titles).

Recent studies of vernacular architecture have tended to catalogue buildings, and range from the standard R. W. Brunskill, *Illustrated Handbook of Vernacular Architecture* (2nd edn, Faber, 1978) to P. Cunnington's *How Old is Your House?* (Alphabooks, 1980) and John Smith's bibliography (p. 344). The DoE *Ancient Monuments in England* (3 vols, HMSO, 1978) contains all 'listed' buildings, which are not necessarily so ancient as the title implies. The DoE also produces many guides to these. Buildings of note open to the public from castles and houses to windmills and the guides they issue may be the only source of written information on those buildings. The National Trust *Yearbooks* study many of their buildings. There are many lists and guides to parish churches, theatres, etc., all of which select different examples, but between them they cover almost all those in Britain.

Phillimore of Chichester publish many guides to local buildings. Some are very specific and their catalogue is a useful listing, giving items such as J. Roebuck's *Urban Development in Nineteenth Century London: Lambeth, Battersea and Wandsworth, 1838–1888* (1980) or S. Castle, *Timber-framed Buildings in Watford* (1979), or *Victorian Churches of Kent* by R. Homan (1982).

The new guide, *The Capitals of Europe: Guide to the Sources for the History of their Architecture and Construction*, edited by A. Sagvari for the International Council on Archives, provides basic information on origins and growth, site and building periods for the cities covered.

Handbooks

Larger tomes should perhaps be covered separately. They abound, and the most suitable might be selected from the library shelves or from those mentioned below. Continuing initially on the historical theme, the GLC *Survey of London* (University of London, Athlone Press) is slowly continuing to describe all buildings in distinct areas of London and extends already to forty or so volumes. The Royal Commission on Historical Monuments is doing the same for other places, and HMSO has issued a number of inventories which are listed either in the sectional lists, the pamphlet *Architecture and Building* (1981) or their large leaflet, *Surveying our Heritage*. From these studies have also emerged compilation volumes like *English Vernacular Houses* (HMSO, 1978). Areas already inventoried include London, Hertfordshire, Buckinghamshire, Huntingdonshire, Essex, Herefordshire, Westmorland, Middlesex, Oxford, Cambridge, York, Stamford, Cambridgeshire, Dorset, Gloucestershire Cotswolds, Newark-on-Trent, North-east Northamptonshire, Anglesey, Glamorgan, Caernarvonshire, Peebleshire, Lanarkshire, Argyll and Stirlingshire, with others in preparation. Not all are single volumes but all are copiously documented. The *History of the King's Works* (HMSO, various dates) supplements this for all public buildings. Other guides will be found in Fenton's 'Books of note on buildings' (*Vernacular Building*, **4**, 1978, 32–36) and Auld's 'Historical sources for vernacular building research' (*Vernacular Building*, **4**, 1978, 37–40). Foreign buildings are covered in B. Walker, 'Books on foreign vernacular buildings' (*Vernacular Building*, **5**, 1979, 44–51) (see also Chapter 14). J. Harvey's *Sources for the History of Houses* (British Records Association, 1974) is a clear guide for those researching a building locally and indicates how to use archives. S. Colman's 'Tracing the history of your house' (*Period Home*, **1**, Nos. 1, 2, 3) is useful, as are many of the Shire Publications' *Discovering* series.

Architectural Heritage Year Prompted many counties to look at their local buildings, old and new, and to publish volumes such as Leicestershire's *The Local Tradition* (Leicestershire County Council, 1975) and V. Doe, *Derbyshire's Architectural Heritage: A Bibliographical Guide* (Derbyshire County Council, 1975).

Indicative of other types of work are A. Whittick, *Encyclopedia of Urban Planning* (McGraw–Hill, 1974) and H. Stierlin, *Encyclopedia of World Architecture* (2 vols, Macmillan, 1977), with many plans and building studies. Hatje's *Encyclopedia of Modern Architecture* (Thames and Hudson, 1963) has many biographical articles as well as ones on style showing buildings, usually well-known ones. P. Guedes, *The Macmillan Encyclopedia of Architecture and Technological Change* (Macmillan, 1979) is useful. C. M. Harris' *Historic Architecture Sourcebook* and *Dictionary of Architecture and Construction* (McGraw–Hill, 1977 and 1975) cover many buildings internationally and the *Illustrated International Architecture Index* in a number of volumes (comp. D. Van der Kellen, The Hague, 1967+) illustrates buildings by type with location and architect indexes.

Most other useful volumes are more in the nature of studies of recent architecture like the Open University course units on *History of Architecture and Design 1890–1939*, R. Maxwell, *New British Architecture* (Thames and Hudson, 1972) covering the 1960s or Stern's *New Directions in American Architecture* (rev. edn, Brazillier, 1977). The range is very wide and only some indications of the useful types of title have been given here.

Institutions

It is often helpful to start by making requests to certain institutions like the RIBA who have special indexes and collections (see p. 373). Local ones can be found in the *Directory of British Associations* or the Library Association *Guide* to local libraries, who will have their own local address lists (see p. 33). Specialist institutions like the Sports Council, the Crafts Advisory Council or the Centre on Environment for the Handicapped will often have similar files which are not necessarily published.

Local detective work should include museums and art galleries – located in the *Libraries, Museums and Art Galleries Yearbook* – where there will often be pictures of local architecture, sometimes with specialists who know more or will direct you to the local archive office or other source of further information. Record offices include twentieth-century data as well as historical and are listed in *Record Depositories in Great Britain* (6th edn, HMSO, 1979). Plans of many types of building can be found here owing to their deposit as a result of certain Acts of Parliament or to the preservation of documents including them from the fire insurance societies, etc. Acts like the Local Health Act required the deposit of building plans. School plans were kept from the nineteenth century also. Specific place-name indexes to records in private and public custody can be consulted at the National Register of Archives. The photographic collections described briefly on p. 201 may also be useful.

The museum of building, architecture and the environment being planned for London should be a useful source of information and pictures once it is fully established. It was announced anonymously in *AJ* on 4 March 1981.

Many other examples can be found, and where historical buildings are concerned Ruth Kamen's recent handbook should be consulted (p. 373), and Watkins' *The Rise of Architectural History* (Architectural Press, 1980). Modern buildings present more problems but the above should have turned up some information, and given hints of new lines of enquiry such as persons who might be useful to contact.

People

Introduction

It is much easier to find out about a person if he or she is dead! Surprisingly, only a few of the most famous get written about in their lifetime to any extent, those like Breuer who died shortly previous to the writing of this section, or in Britain, Stirling or Spence. Lasdun's work as a practice has been published, *A Language and a Theme: The Architecture of Denys Lasdun and Partners* (RIBA Publications, 1976), and lists all their work. Architects and artists tend to be better documented than everyday people. Journals write up the work of notable or prize-winning practices and architects. However, the act of finding that information may be a different matter – more difficult because handbooks, bibliographies, etc. do not yet include them. Yet some series like the *Vance Bibliographies* include many biographical bibliographies and other sources exist as well. The starting point, if the person is alive, is likely to be a yearbook or handbook, quickly followed by a hunt for periodical articles by or about the subject/person.

However, for those long dead, brief biographies may exist, obituaries may be known and appraisals may have taken place at anniversaries of their passing, especially locally. Follow the same lines of search here as for buildings. Books and discussions of historic architecture may present the information needed in this case and there are handbooks to provide a starting point.

Indexes and abstracts

As all journals discuss people frequently but none is devoted solely to architectural biography it is best to start by looking at the indexes. Most have author indexes and these usually incorporate works – or rather articles – *about* people also. *API* and *British Humanities Index* have separate lists but *Art Index* and the *Avery Index* incorporates names into the main alphabetical order. It is therefore essential to remember to look separately for indexes and not to assume that a biography about a person will be treated as a subject. There are name-entries in the *Architectural Index* (E. J. Bell (ed.), Boulder, Colarado, ceased 1976) but its journal coverage is not very wide. The predecessors of *API* should also be consulted, but at the British Architectural Library there is a full name-index including all personal names, corporate names (organizations, firms, etc.) and some building names. This also notes any biographical information held in the library (not necessarily printed) and references to all obituaries in the *Builder*, now *Building*, since its beginning in 1843. Other indexes are also available (see p. 373).

Several biographical indexes exist, the most useful of which is *Biography Index* (Wilson, quarterly, 1946–). This indexes any biography appearing in book form, as an article in a book, proceeding or journal or handbook. Naturally this is the only index which will cover current biography easily. *Bibliographic Index* will list persons where a bibliography over fifty references long is published and *Current Biography* (Wilson, monthly, 1940–) has printed many short biographical articles of the living and dead in all spheres of interest.

Obituaries are often useful and the *New York Times* has issued a biographical edition weekly since 1970 with profiles of topical people and is especially valuable for searching as it has a cumulated index. There is also an *Index to Obituaries in the New York Times 1858–1968*. Not to be outdone, *Obituaries from 'The Times' 1961–1970* and *1971–1975* were published in 1975 and 1978 respectively by Newspaper Archive Developments of Reading.

Texts

Biographies should be found in any library catalogue by name since works 'by and about' are usually kept together. In the RIBA *Booklist 1980/1* major architectural ones were listed for the first time. Sharp's *Sources of Modern Architecture*, now in its second edition (Architectural Press, 1980), has brief biographies and longer lists of references, but tends to cover fairly well-known architects.

Printed catalogues may reveal less well-known biographies if there is time to obtain the references using the inter-library loans service. In particular the catalogue of the RIBA Library, The British Museum Library and the V & A will cover architects and the *British National Bibliography* will cover everyone. For non-British persons the appropriate countries' national bibliography will be useful provided that the language can be read.

Specialist biographies in the British Architectural Library at the RIBA range from G. Spain and N. Drampoole, *Theatre Architects in the British Isles* (Reprint from *Architectural History: Journal of the Society of Architectural Historians*, 13, 1970, 177–189) to D. Linstrum's *West-Yorkshire Architects and Architecture* (Lund Humphries, 1978).

Historical and twentieth-century figures may be covered in historical or other texts relating to types of buildings. But biographical information may not be given, just a catalogue of works, although this may be what is sought. Many of the encyclopedias cited above are heavily biographical in their entries, but tend to keep also to famous names.

If there is no success here then turn to the handbooks or journals.

Handbooks

Biography is a popular topic and there is no shortage of biographical dictionaries, provided the subject is dead. The encyclopedias have already been given (p. 368) – Hatje is heavily biographical.

Some of the more readily available lists are given here; S. Brookes, *Index to Information on Individual Architects in a Select List of Books* (Vance Bibliography A132, 1979); E. B. Chancellor, *Lives of British Architects* (Duckworth, 1908); H. Colvin, *A Biographical Dictionary of British Architects, 1600–1840* (Murray, 1978); M. Emanuel, *Contemporary Architects* (Macmillan, 1980) covers 600 international architects giving bibliographic information. It has a companion volume, *Contemporary Artists* (Macmillan, 1977) edited by Naylor and Orridge. J. Harvey, *English Medieval Architects: A Biographical Dictionary down to 1550* (Batsford, 1954), J. M. Richard, *Who's Who in Architecture: from 1400 to the Present Day* (Weidenfeld and Nicolson, 1976); H. V. M. Roberts, *Index of Architects of Several Countries and Many Periods (except English Medieval) in Nearly 60 Old and New Selected Indexes and Indexed Specialist Works* . . . (RIBA Library, 1956) are also useful. The Society of Architectural Historians of Great Britain's, *Research Registers* (various) begin with biographical studies. G. Vasari, *Lives of Painters, Sculptors and Architects* (4 vols, Everyman, 1963), H. F. and E. R. Withey, *Biographical Dictionary of American Architects (Deceased)* (Los Angeles, New Age Publications, 1956), L. Wodehouse, *British Architects 1840–1976* (Gale Research, 1979), L. Wodehouse, *American Architects from the Civil War to the First World War: A Guide to Information Sources* (Gale Research, 1976), L. Wodehouse, *American Architects from the First World War to the Present: A Guide to Information Sources* (Gale Research, 1976) are all useful. There is an American Association of Architectural Bibliographers who publish a regular series of papers which are entirely biographical.

It should not be forgotten that architecture is an art and, as such, many of the numerous art encylopedias and biographies include architects. Of these the most comprehensive is the German Thieme-Becker, *Allgemeines Lexikon der Bildenden Kunstler* (37 vols, and 6-vol. supplement). *Sculpture Index*, by Clapp (Scarecrow, 1970) is useful.

There are also a number of general biographical dictionaries which are too numerous to mention here. The greatest of the British ones is the *Dictionary of National Biography*, which has volumes for each decade of the twentieth century to bring the original multi-volume edition published at the turn of the century up-to-date. The rest will be found on library shelves, listed in Walford (p. 108) or in G. Higgens (ed.), *Printed Reference Material* (Library Association, 1980).

So much for the dead. The living must also have information published about them but with less formality. *Who's Who* is well known but not always reliable, since the articles are written by the biographers. Those who have died during any decade will be found in the volume of *Who was Who* for the decade – but this only reprints the last entry from *Who's Who*. It does not create a biography or obituary and so might best be read in conjunction with *The Times* obituary. There is a fairly current *Dictionary of International Biography* (7th edn, Melrose Press, 1970) and an annual *International Who's Who*. Unlike the *Building Societies Who's Who* (Franey, bi-annual) and the *Consulting Engineers' Who's Who and Yearbook* (Northwood, annual), the *Who's Who in Architecture* is historical (Richards, above). *Who's Whos* exist for many walks of life. But the more reliable sources of brief data and addresses are the yearbooks and directories of the associations to which the subject should belong if a practising professional. British Data Services of Frinton-on-sea, Essex, have been issuing *Selective Lists of Practising Architects* at intervals since 1975 among other professional lists. Academics can be found either in the *Academic Who's Who* (2nd edn, Black, 1978) or the *Commonwealth Universities Yearbook*, which has a list of names at the end and includes the staff of most institutions in the Commonwealth. However, because of time delays in publication they may well have left by the time the volume is in use. Other such aids for information on non-architects might include the *Civil Service Yearbook, Crockford's Clerical Dictionary*, the *Bar List* and the *Medical Directory*, all annuals.

Institutions

A number of associations have been mentioned in this section already but not all are readily contactable. The institutions to which persons may belong will be unlikely to divulge personal information, leaving only those like the RIBA to help in this instance. Kamen's *British and Irish Architectural History: A Bibliography and Guide to Sources of Information* (Architectural Press, 1981) will be helpful here. The British Architectural Library's indexes have been mentioned and include, as well as the periodical article index with its name index; also the Goodhart–Rendel index of Victorian church builders, in manuscript; the index of members, 1834–1886, with brief information; the Kendrick index of nineteenth-century British stained glass, by artist; the 'grey books index', listing work of RIBA members which has been illustrated in the press, 1900–1919 in one volume and 1920–1974 in 145 loose-leaf volumes. All these must be consulted at the library. In addition to these there are the printed catalogues to the Drawings Collection supplemented by the card index held there. This includes entry by name of architect and of building. Much other information is available from the staff with reference to other British collections of original work.

The Drawings Collection of the RIBA may also assist in identifying work of some architects. The catalogue is referred to on p. 201 and World Microfilms are embarking on a systematic programme to make the drawings available on microfiche. This work is following the published catalogue.

The Manuscripts Collection also includes information on the architects, including designers, builders, craftsmen and tradesmen, and architectural historians from the seventeenth century to today. Some of the manuscripts have been made available on microfilm by World Microfilm entitled *British Architectural Library, Unpublished Manuscripts* (16 reels, 35 mm, no date). A catalogue is being compiled for publication but the present listing for consultation is that of the National Register of Archives (NRA) for the Historical Manuscripts Commission. These have name and building indexes and may be consulted either at the Manuscripts Collection or the NRA. Volumes list all the major collections of manuscripts in Britain and the annual *Architectural History and the Fine and Applied Arts; Sources in the National Register of Archives* describes the lists added each year, briefly indexing them. The full lists are available at the NRA.

The British Library Reference Division, Department of Printed Books, has issued a number of Readers' Guides, No. 6, *English Places: Sources of Information* and No. 8, *Family and Personal Names: A Brief Guide to Sources of Information* may be useful here.

Places

The order of this section differs from the above since the type of information resource also differs – there is less overlap than between the last two sections, and journals, although useful for articles sometimes, take second place to other sources of information.

Reference

The first step is to establish exactly where a place actually is, obtain the map reference and locate its regional authorities for other types of information – the parish, district, county councils, the water, gas and electricity authorities, etc. Either the Ordnance Survey *Gazeteer of the British Isles* or *'The Times' Index Gazeteer of the World* (Times, 1965) will do this.

Reference handbooks then range from the local telephone directories (of which large public libraries have full sets) to some of the bibliographies and guides on pages 227, but a good starting-point for the background development of many places in

England is the *Victoria County History* for the county. This undertaking began in 1902 and is not yet complete. A list of the volumes available can be obtained from the Institute of Historical Research of London University. Every town, city and village is covered by parish and hundred, with general chapters on the county as a whole. All are thoroughly documented. The development of the place until Victorian times will be covered in the county history gathered together by the Victorian bibliographers. Almost every county has a large multi-volume history of varying reliability (some were pure hagiography), usually also covering every village and hamlet. They are listed in Humphreys, *Handbook to County Bibliography* (Dawsons, 1974 reprint of 1917 edn) and Anderson, *The Book of British Topography: A Classified Catalogue of the Topographical Works in the Library of the British Museum Relating to Great Britain and Ireland* (1970 reprint of 1881 edn).

Population, rating information, lists of councillors, officers and addresses are quickly located in the *Municipal Yearbook* and the architectural practices, estate agents, building societies, chartered surveyors, etc. in the appropriate yearbook or list of members. However, it is wise to be wary of some of these since not all professions require membership to practise as architecture does, and there are a number of different estate agent's directories, for example, which will all furnish different lists of the practices in any one place – only those of the RICS guarantee qualification but even then not necessarily for agency. Many larger places issue a commercial directory every year as a guide to commerce and industrial interests and these are circulated to most central libraries for reference.

Statistics on local problems can also be found at local level by using several of the statistical publications mentioned in Chapter 9. In particular, information on *Local Housing Statistics* is available for districts and major towns in each county and covers building, rehabilitation grants, etc. General figures are available in *Regional Statistics* and financial ones in *Rates and Rateable Values* and *Local Government Financial Statistics* as well as the CIPFA volumes. The *Guide to Official Statistics* will supply further titles.

Local publications abound, ranging from those of the council, not just the planning office, to the minutes of the full council and of committee meetings. These will usually be found in the local studies or local history section of the public library since this section usually works on the premise that history began yesterday, and if it is local information, that is where it belongs. The finer line is drawn as to when documents and books belong with the library or the record office, and here practice varies from place to place. A telephone call to these will be essential, but if it becomes necessary to look at older materials do use one of the guides mentioned on p. 367 or W. B. Stephens, *Sources for English Local History* (Manchester University Pres, 1973) or Tate's *Parish Chest* (Cambridge University Press, 1969) before starting. Their advice is valuable and eventually time-saving.

Texts

To cover all these would be impossible but there a number of guides and lists which can be used in addition to those on p. 367. The *BNB* and the *British Museum Catalogue* will list any works known about the place usually by name. There is also another printed catalogue, the *Research Catalogue of the American Geographical Society* (15 vols plus supplement, G. K. Hall, 1962) which covers all countries and is the largest geographical library in the world. Numerous smaller bibliographies can be traced; the most recent is perhaps A. Sutcliffe's *The History of Urban and Regional Planning: An Annotated Bibliography* (Mansell, 1981). Another annual volume is the *Urban History Yearbook* which, despite its title, is very much geared to the last two centuries and produced at the University of Leicester. It provides articles about the development of various places, a bibliography of items known to have appeared during the previous year and a list of current research in progress, all indexed by place-name.

Geographical texts are easier to locate but sometimes frustrating in their vague treatment of areas rather than specific places. The British Association for the Advancement of Science holds its meetings every four years in different locations and for each region produces a useful and detailed survey of the region, its growth, industries, etc. Hodder and Stoughton are currently producing county volumes in their *Making of the English Landscape* series to which Professor Hoskins wrote the title volume. Methuen and Nelson also produce regional series for Britain.

The history and development of individual towns will often be found shelved as planning, with local plans, or as history, thus unfortunately making the search through any library less simple. Following this logic through there will be architectural studies of the place with the appropriate period or general architecture books and conservation studies elsewhere, etc. Compound volumes also contain a lot of the information that can be sought in vain. Some examples are M. D. Lobel's *Historic Towns* (Lovell Johns, 1969), Ian Nairn's *Britain's Changing Towns* (BBC, 1967) and Alec Clifton-Taylor's *Six English Towns* (BBC, 1978) and *Six More English Towns* (BBC, 1981) which cover Chichester, Richmond (Yorks), Tewkesbury, Stamford, Totnes and Ludlow, then Warwick, Saffron Walden, Beverley, Berwick-upon-Tweed, Bradford-upon-Avon and Lewes.

Local and national contacts

It does not help to go straight to the Planning Officer for information about his locality – most of the basic documents will be available in the local public and academic libraries and much more freely accessible. It then makes sense to go to the Planning or Architect's Office for information not available elsewhere, having first refined the nature of what is required. Some academic institutions with planning departments will have a range of planning information better than many others in the locality and quite wide-ranging, e.g. Leeds Polytechnic.

Local history societies will usually be able and willing to help as will Adult Education Centres. The *Directory of British Associations* or the *Local Historian's Encyclopaedia* (Historical Publications, 1974) will help to trace these. Some diocesan archive offices will also be helpful to certain searches and the local record office may send enquirers there.

Some local collections of plans, maps and drawings exist. *Guide to Collections of Topographical Drawings* was published in 1973 (Council for British Archaeology). It was compiled by Maurice Barley, whose work on the use of inventories of historic buildings (mainly houses) also indicates what can be reconstructed from a variety of documents in local record offices.

Local and regional studies centres exist and not only do they have a number of study documents on locations in Britain, usually in the twentieth century, but they also have useful centres of expertise. Among others one might mention the Planning Department of Oxford Polytechnic, the Centre for Urban and Regional Studies at the University of Birmingham and the Local Government Operational Research Unit at the Unversity of Reading. Their strengths vary with their staff movements

Journals, abstracts and indexes

As with buildings, few indexes cover place-names adequately. In 1981 the GLC database from *Urban Abstracts, ACCOMPLINE*, became available and this may help with searching for information by name. *API* and *Avery* have already been discussed but most information retrieved via these will refer to the buildings in, rather than the background of, a place. *British Humanities Index* is useful here and the *RICS Abstracts and Reviews* indexes used to be good until shortage of manpower led to their cessation in 1977. The detail of these, with their five-yearly cumulations, makes any search for information very quick. The indexes to the *DoE Library Bulletin*, when they appear, include major place-names and counties. The bulletins themselves cover a lot of local information, especially that fed into the DoE for planning purposes.

Geoabstracts has a topographical index and the local bulletins have already been mentioned.

Local newspapers can be mines of information, and the current ones can be found in *Willings Press Guide* (annual) while there are a number of lists of older ones and their whereabouts. The most useful are P. E. Allen, *Catalogue of the Newspaper Collection in the British Library* (British Museum publications, 1975), D. Dixon, *Local Newspapers and Periodicals of the Nineteenth Century: A Checklist of Holdings in Provincial Libraries* (Leicester University, Department of Victorian Studies, 2 vols, 1973) and Crane and Kaye, *A Census of British Newspapers and Periodicals 1620–1800* (Holland Press, 1927, reprinted 1966). The Library Association's Reference Special and Information section is producing a county-by-county survey in *Bibliography of British Newspapers*, edited by C. Toase. Many of the local studies of all types were indexed in Mullins' two volumes, *Texts and Calendars: An Analytical Guide to Serial Publications* (Royal Historical Society, 1958) and *A Guide to the Historical and Archaeological Publications of Societies in England and Wales, 1901–1933* (1968).

This listing may seem daunting and cramped because an attempt has been made not just to cover a lot in a small space but also to select those sources likely to give a quick return and to be fairly readily available. This also reflects the needs likely to arise for users of this book rather than planners, geographers, etc., who can refer to more detailed studies among their own literature. Anyone requiring to delve deeper on the architectural side should follow Ruth Kamen's advice in her *British and Irish Architectural History: A Bibliography and Guide to Sources* (Architectural Press, 1981). This is the only British guide and has a very wide scope listing not only useful bibliographies, journals and handbooks but also associations and institutions giving addresses and contact names. It is, however, a series of lists rather than a discursive guide.

Appendix 1
Outline classifications

Dewey decimal classification

The outline below is not comprehensive; space is limited. It aims to show the major numbers which an architect is likely to require. This means that undue repetition has been avoided by omitting some minor numbers within a sequence and giving only an example to show how the breakdown works within that area.

A few references are given between numbers. The subject index to any system should always be used. Standard numbers for places may be added in many places but this has not been done – they are given under 940 History and are added as 0942 etc., e.g. 724.90942 20th Century architecture in Leicester.

19th edition

000	GENERALITIES	310	Statistics
010	Bibliographies & Catalogs	320	Political Science
		330	Economics
016	Bibliographies of specific subjects	340	Law
		343	Public Law
100	PHILOSOPHY AND RELATED DISCIPLINES	343.07869	Building regulations
		350	Public administration
150	Psychology	352	Local government
200	RELIGION	360	Social problems and services
300	SOCIAL SCIENCES		
301	Sociology	370	Education
307	Communities	380	Commerce

Appendix 1 Outline classifications

390	Customs and folklore
400	LANGUAGE
500	PURE SCIENCE
510	Mathematics
516	Geometry
520	Astronomy and allied sciences
526	Mathematical geography
526.1	Geodesy
526.9	Surveying
530	Physics
534	Sound & related vibrations
535	Visible light and paraphotic
536	Heat
537	Electricity
540	Chemistry
542	Laboratories, apparatus, equipment
550	Sciences of earth (Geology)
554	Geology of Europe
570	Life sciences
572	Human races
573	Physical anthropology
590	Zoological sciences
600	TECHNOLOGY
610	Medical sciences
614	Public health
614.7	Environmental problems
620	Engineering
624	Civil engineering
624.1	Structural engineering
624.15	Foundation engineering
624.151	Engineering geology
624.152	Excavation
624.154–8	Specific types of foundation
624.17	Structural theory
624.172	Loads
624.177	Structural design
624.1772	Beams, girders, cylinders, slabs
624.1773	Trusses & frames
624.1775	Arches, domes
624.1776	Shells & plates
624.18	Design in specific materials
624.182	Metals
624.183	Masonry
624.184	Concretes
624.2	Bridges
630	Agriculture & related
640	Domestic science
650	Management
658.1	Organization & finance
658.1141	Partnerships
659.2	Management of plant & buildings
660	Chemical & related technolgies
670	Manufactures
680	Miscellaneous manufactures
690	Building
690.1	Specific structural elements (This is built up as 721.1–8)
690.2	General activities
690.21	Structural analysis
690.22	Safety
690.23	Maintenance & repair (DIY = 643.7)
691	Building materials
691.1	Timber
691.2	Natural Stones
691.3	Concretes, artificial stone
691.4	Ceramic & clay
691.5	Masonry adhesives
691.6	Glass
691.7	Iron & Steel
691.9	Other
691.92	Plastics & laminates
692	Auxiliary construction practices
692.1	Plans & drawings
692.2	Detail drawings
692.3	Specifications
692.5	Estimates
692.8	Contract

693	Construction in material and for specific purposes	711.4	Local community (Conservation, rehabilitation)
693.1	Masonry	711.409	Specific towns – plans
693.2	Stabilized earth materials	711.41	Plans based on street patterns
693.22	Bricks		
693.5	Concrete	711.43	Plans based on size
693.8	Specific purposes	711.5	Plans for specific kinds of areas (renewal)
693.82	Fireproof		
693.83	Insulated	711.55	Functional
693.832	Thermal	711.552	Commercial, industrial
693.834	Acoustical		
693.84	Pest-resistant	711.5522	Commercial, shopping centres
693.89	Other		
693.892	Waterproof	711.554	Medical centre
694	Wood construction, carpentry	711.557	Hotel & restaurant
		711.57	Cultural & educational
695	Roofing		
696	Utilities	711.58	Residential
696.1	Plumbing	711.7	Transportation facilities
696.12	Water supply		
696.6	Hot water supply	712	Landscape design
697	Heating, ventilating & air conditioning	712.3	Professional practice, procedure
697.001	Theory	712.5	Public parks
697.02	Local heating	712.6	Private parks
697.03	Central heating	713	Landscape design of traffic ways
697.04	Sources of energy		
697.042	Coal		
697.043	Gas		
697.1	Heating with open fires	714	Water features
697.2	Heating with space heaters	715	Woody plants
697.3–7	Central heating, various methods	716	Herbaceous plants
		717	Structures
697.8	Chimneys	718	Cemeteries
697.9	Ventilation and air conditioning	719	Natural landscapes
		720	Architecture
698	Detail finishing	720.1	Philosophy & theory
698.1	Painting	720.2	Miscellany
698.12	Exteriors	720.22	Illustrations & models
698.14	Interiors	720.28	Techniques, procedures
698.142	Walls		
698.146	Floors	720.284	Architectural drawing
698.5	Glazing		
698.6	Paperhanging	720.288	Conservation, preservation
700	ARTS		
701	Decorative arts	720.4	Specific topics of general applicability
710	Civic & landscape arts		
711	Area planning	720.42	Architecture for the handicapped
711.1	Procedures		

Appendix 1   Outline classifications   383

720.43	Architecture for the aged, infirm	728.8	Recreation buildings
		725.82	For shows
720.47	Utilization of natural energy sources in architecture	725.822	Theatres
		725.827	Sports
		726	Buildings for religious purposes
720.9	History of architecture (But see 722)		
		726.1	Temples & Shrines
721	Architectural construction	726.2	Mosques & Minarets
		726.3	Synagogues
721.042	Specific shapes, e.g. skyscrapers	726.4	Accessory houses of worship; parish houses, chapels
721.044	Specific materials		
721.0441	Masonry	726.5	Christian buildings
721.0447	Metals	726.51	Structural elements
721.046	Other specific topics (as in 720.42–7)	726.58	Specific denominations
721.1	Structural elements, foundations	726.59	Parts
		726.6	Cathedrals
721.2	Walls	726.7	Monastic buildings
721.3	Columns	727	School and educational buildings
721.5	Roofs		
721.6	Floors	727.1	Elementary schools
721.7	Ceilings	727.2	Secondary schools
721.8	Other	727.3	Colleges & universities
721.82	Openings	727.38	Ancillary buildings
721.83	Vertical access	727.5	Research
721.832	Stairs	727.6	Museums
721.84	Extensions	727.8	Libraries
722	Ancient & Oriental architecture	728	Residential buildings
		728.1	Low cost housing
723	Medieval architecture 300–399	728.3	Conventional housing
		728.31	Multiple dwellings
724	Modern architecture 1400–	728.312	Town houses, terraces
724.1	Early modern 1400–1800	728.314	Flats
		728.37	Separate houses
724.2	Classical revival	728.4	Club houses
724.3	Gothic revival	728.5	Hotels, motels
724.9	20th century	728.6	Farmhouses, cottages, solar houses
725	Public buildings		
725.15	Courts	728.8	Large private dwellings
725.2	Commercial buildings	728.81	Castles
725.21	Retail, shops	728.82	Palaces
725.3	Transportation & storage buildings	729	Design & decoration & ancillaries
725.4	Industrial buildings	729.1	In vertical plane, facades
725.5	Health & Welfare buildings		
		729.2	In horizontal plane
725.6	Prison buildings	729.24	Interior arrangement
725.7	Refreshment facilities & park structures	729.28	Lighting
		729.29	Acoustics
725.71	Restaurants	729.3	On structural elements
725.74	Swimming pools	729.31	Walls

384 Appendix 1 Outline classifications

729.32	Columns	747.75	Living room
729.35	Roofs	747.8	Specific types of buildings (using the numbers following 72 in 725–8)
729.37	Floors		
729.38	Doors, windows		
729.39	Other, stairs, balustrades	747.9	Specific decorations
		747.92	Lighting
729.4	In paint	747.94	Colour
730	Sculpture	749	Furnishing
740	Drawing, decorative, minor arts	770	Photography
		800	LITERATURE
741	Drawing	900	GENERAL GEOGRAPHY & HISTORY
742	Perspective		
747	Interior decoration	910	Geography
747.1	Under specific limitations; e.g. on a budget	914	Europe
		940	History, Europe
747.2	History	942	British Isles
747.201	Up to 499 AD	942.1	Greater London
747.202	500–1399	942.191	Croydon
747.203	1400–1799	943	Germany
747.2037	18th century	944	France
747.204	1800–1999	945	Italy
747.2049	20th century	950	Asia, Orient, Far East
747.3	Ceilings, walls, doors, windows	960	Africa
		970	North America
747.4	Floors	973	USA
747.5	Draperies, carpets	980	South America
747.7	Specific rooms of residential buildings	990	Australasia & other parts

Universal decimal classification

Although similar to Dewey UDC is a refined version developing the principles of classification to allow more accurate coding of complex topics, especially when necessary for data, articles, etc. which have more precisely defined contents than books. The numerical allotment of the numbers 1–9 is the same as Dewey and the numbers for related topics are so similar that there is little point in repeating them here. The outline below is therefore restricted mainly to the scope of the 620, 69, 71 and 72 classes.

To any number of UDC there are a number of alternative sets which can be added to increase the meaning of the code. Most frequently used are;

: followed by any other number to express those two topics in relation to each other, e.g. 744:72 draughtsmanship for architects,

Appendix 1   Outline classifications   385

+   followed by any other number simply means the item covers both, e.g. 71 + 72 planning and architecture,
( )   with a number in the brackets relates to the country covered in that item, the numbers for countries, towns, etc. are those following 900 in Dewey, e.g. 72.036(42) English modern architecture,
(0)   as above but the numbers preceded by 0 mean form in which the work is written and are less frequently used, e.g. 72(061) directory of architects.

Few others are regularly used.

In this code also there may be any number of digits before the point, not just three, but two or one, although never more than three; and there may be second and third points introduced at three digit intervals.

624	Civil and structural engineering	643.5	Bed-, bath-, living rooms
624.01	Structures according to material used	65	Management
		651	Office management, practice
624.011	Timber and organic		
624.012	Masonry, ceramic, concrete	651.4	Office practice
		651.5	Record document files, archives
624.02	Parts of structures		
624.028	Doors, windows, fences etc.,	657	Accounting
		658	Business management
624.03	Form, permanence, location of structures	658.1	Forms of business, finance
624.04	Structural design	658.2	Establishments, works, plant, equipment
624.05	Site organization		
624.07	Structural elements and members	658.3	Personnel, human relations
624.1	Earthwork, foundations	658.5	Production management, control
628	Public health engineering		
628.1	Water supply	659	Publicity, advertising
628.2	Town drainage, sewerage	69	Building
		69.00	Practice and procedure
628.8	Indoor climate engineering	69.001.3	Specifications
		69.001.5	Research
628.9	Illuminating engineering	69.002	Execution of works
628.92	Illumination technique	69.003.1	Economic aspects
		69.02	Structural parts of buildings
628.97	Lighting according to purpose	69.021	Foundations
64	Domestic science	69.022	Walls and partitions
643	Home, household equipment	69.024	Roofs
		69.025	Floors, ceilings
643.2	Room size, layout	69.026	Stairs, ramps, lifts
643.3	Kitchens	69.028	Doors, windows, fences
643.4	Dining rooms etc.		

Appendix 1 Outline classifications

69.03	Building conditions, permanence	711.552	Commercial, shopping business areas
69.05	Site organization, methods	711.58	Residential areas
69.059	Maintenance, damage repair	711.582	Housing estates
		711.6	Site planning, grouping of buildings
691	Building materials		
691.1	Organic origin	712	Landscape
691.2	Natural stones	712.3	Garden planning
691.3	Artificial stone	712.4	Planting, vegetation
691.4	Earth, cob, ceramics	718	Cemeteries, crematoria
691.5	Binding materials, plasters	719	Preservation of rural and urban amenities
691.6	Glass	72	Architecture
691.7	Metals	72.00	Practice and procedure
691.8	Components		
693	Site construction	72.01	General aesthetics, design
693.1	Stone masonry		
693.2	Brickwork	72.011	Design, plan, layout
693.5	Concreting *in situ*		
693.6	Plastering and finishing	72.02	Technique, drawing
693.7	Paving	72.03	Periods, styles, influences (historical works by period then country)
693.9	Framed construction		
694	Carpentry		
696	Equipment, services, installations	721	Buildings generally
696.1	Plumbing, sanitary	721.011	Design considerations
696.2	Gas installation, fittings		
696.6	Electrical installation, fittings	725	Public, civil, commercial buildings
697	Heating, ventilating, air conditioning	725.1	Civic and public service buildings
698	Finishing, decorating	725.2	Commercial and office buildings
699.8	Protective, proofed construction	725.3	Transport, traffic, storage buildings
699.81	Fire-resisting		
699.815	Means of escape	725.4	Industrial buildings, factories
699.82	Water, dampproof		
699.84	Vibration, sound proof	725.5	Health and welfare buildings
699.86	Thermal insulation	725.6	Prisons
7	The arts	725.7	Public refreshment buildings, baths, spas
7.0	General		
71	Physical planning, landscape	725.8	Public entertainment and recreation buildings
711	Town and country planning		
		725.9	Other civil building
711.2	Regional planning	725.91	Exhibition buildings
711.3	Rural planning, development		
		726	Ecclesiastical architecture
711.4	Urban planning		
711.5	Units, areas, zones	727	Buildings for education, science, art etc.
711.55	Functional units, civic, transport	728	Residential buildings

Appendix 1   Outline classifications   387

28.1	Housing	729	Architectural details, decoration
28.2	Blocks, tenements, multi-family dwellings	73	Sculpture
728.3	Houses	74	Drawing
728.31	Terraced	744	Technical drawing, lettering
728.34	Semi-detached		
728.37	Detached	747	Interior decoration
728.5	Hotels, inns	75	Painting
728.6	Rural architecture	75.02	Technique, materials
728.8	Castles, country houses	77	Photography

Library of Congress classification

This classification scheme, unlike Dewey and UDC, was devised to fit the literature rather than to represent the intellectual breakdown of knowledge. Each category covers a distinct subject area and the outline below reflects only those areas likely to be of interest to the architect.

A	GENERAL	H	SOCIAL SCIENCES
B	RELIGION, PHILOSOPHY, PSYCHOLOGY	HA	Statistics
		HM	Sociology
		HT	Communities
BF	Psychology	HT 101–384	Urban renewal, sociology
BF 311–499	Cognition, perception, intelligence	390–395	Regional planning
C	HISTORY, auxiliary sciences	K	LAW
		KD	Law of England and Wales, UK
D	HISTORY, general and Old World	L	EDUCATION
DA	Great Britain	M	MUSIC
E–F	HISTORY: AMERICA	N	FINE ARTS
		N 400–4040	Museums, galleries, by country and town
G	GEOGRAPHY, ANTHROPOLOGY, RECREATION		
		NA	Architecture
		NA 190–700	History, general then by period
GA	Mathematical geography, cartography, including surveys	NA 701–1613	Architecture by country
		NA 2541	Climate
GN	Anthropology	NA 2543–	Special subjects and groups, e.g. handicapped
GV	Recreation		
GV 561–1198	Sports		

Appendix 1   Outline classifications

NA 2699–1790	Architectural design and drawing	TA 630–695 Structural engineering
NA 2880–	Details	TA 715–787 Foundations
NA 4100–	Types of building	TH Building construction
NA 9053–	Other aspects, city planning	TH 845–895 Architectural engineering
NA 9053.06	Conservation and restoration	TH 100–1725 Systems of construction, fireproof, wood, masonry, concrete and steel
NA 9053.G7	Greenbelts	
NA 9053.R45	Residential areas	TH 2031–3000 Details
		TH 4021–4970 Buildings, special constructions by types
NB	Sculpture	
NC	Drawing, design, illustration	TH 5011–5701 Construction by trades, masonry, carpentry...
ND	Painting	
NE	Printing	
NK	Decorative arts	TH 6014–7975 Environmental engineering, plumbing, heating, ventilation, lighting
NK 1700–1305	Interior decoration	
P	LANGUAGE AND LITERATURE	
Q	SCIENCE	TH 9025–9745 Protection – damp, fire...
QC 220–246	Acoustics	
QC 251–338	Heat	TJ Mechanical engineering
QC 350–467	Light	
QM	Human anatomy	TK Electrical engineering
R	MEDICINE	
S	AGRICULTURE	TK 4125–4399 Electric lighting
T	TECHNOLOGY	TR Photography
TA	Engineering, Civil engineering	U MILITARY SCIENCE
TA 401–492	Materials, properties, strengths	V NAVAL SCIENCE
		Z BIBLIOGRAPHY
TA 501–625	Surveying	Z 5051–7999 Subject bibliography

Appendix 1 Outline classifications 389

CI/SfB: Construction classification

TABLE 0. Physical environment
  Planning areas

0 Planning areas
01 Extra terrestrial areas
02 International national scale planning areas
03 Regional sub-regional scale planning areas
04
05 Rural, urban planning areas
06 Land-use planning areas
07
08 Other planning areas
09 Common areas relevant to planning

Facilities

1 Utilities, civil engineering facilities
11 Rail transport
12 Road transport
13 Water transport
14 Air transport, other transport
15 Communications
16 Power supply, mineral supply
17 Water supply, waste disposal
18 Other

2 Industrial facilities
21–25
26 Agricultural
27 Manufacturing
28 Other

3 Administrative, commercial, protective service facilities
31 Official administration, law courts
32 Offices
33 Commercial
34 Trading shops
35–36
37 Protective services
38 Other

4 Health, welfare facilities
41 Hospitals
42 Other medical
43
44 Welfare, homes
45
46 Animal welfare
47
48 Other

5 Recreational facilities
51 Refreshment
52 Entertainment
53 Social recreation, clubs
54 Aquatic sports
55
56 Sports
57
58 Other

6 Religious facilities
61 Religious centres
62 Cathedrals
63 Churches, chapels
64 Mission halls, meeting houses
65 Temples, mosques, synagogues
66 Convents
67 Funerary, shrines
68 Other

7 Educational, scientific, information facilities
71 Schools
72 Universities, colleges
73 Scientific
74
75 Exhibition, display
76 Information, libraries
77
78 Other

8 Residential facilities
81 Housing
82 One-off housing units, houses
83
84 Special housing
85 Communal residential
86 Historical residential
87 Temporary, mobile residential
88 Other

CI/SfB: Construction Classification TABLE 0. (cont.)

9 Common facilities, other facilities

91 Circulation
92 Rest, work
93 Culinary
94 Sanitary, hygiene
95 Cleaning, maintenance
96 Storage
97 Processing, plant, control
98 Other; buildings other than by function
99 Parts of facilities; other aspects of the physical environment; architecture, landscape

---

TABLE 1. Elements

(--) **Sites, projects, building systems**

Substructure

(1-) **Ground, substructure**
(10)
(11) Ground
(12)
(13) Floor beds
(14)-(15)
(16) Retaining walls, foundations
(17) Pile foundations
(18) Other substructure elements
(19) Parts of elements (11) to (18)
    Cost summary

Structure

(2-) **Primary elements, carcass**
(20)
(21) Walls, external walls
(22) Internal walls, partitions
(23) Floors, galleries
(24) Stairs, ramps
(25)-(26)
(27) Roofs
(28) Building frames, other primary elements
(29) Parts of elements (21) to (28)
    Cost summary

(3-) **Secondary elements, completion**
    if described separately from (2-)
(30)
(31) Secondary elements to external walls, external doors, windows
(32)*Secondary elements to internal walls, internal doors

Use for doors generally if required

(33) Secondary elements to floors
(34) Secondary elements to stairs
(35) Suspended ceilings
(36)
(37) Secondary elements to roofs, rooflights, etc.
(38) Other secondary elements (31) to (38)
    Cost summary

(4-) **Finishes**
    if described separately
(40)
(41) Wall finishes, external
(42) Wall finishes, internal
(43) Floor finishes
(44) Stair finishes
(45) Ceiling finishes
(46)
(47) Roof finishes
(48) Other finishes to structure
(49) Parts of elements (41) to (48)
    Cost summary

Services

(5-) **Services, mainly piped and ducted**
(50)-(51)
(52) Waste disposal, drainage
(53) Liquids supply
(54) Gases supply
(55) Space cooling
(56) Space heating
(57) Air conditioning, ventilation
(58) Other piped, ducted services
(59) Parts of elements (51) to (58)
    Cost summary

Appendix 1   Outline classifications   391

CI/SfB: Construction Classification   TABLE 1. (*cont.*)

(6–) **Services, mainly electrical**
(60)
(61) Electrical supply
(62) Power
(63) Lighting
(64) Communications
(65)
(66) Transport
(67)
(68) Security, control, other services
(69) Parts of elements (61) to (68)
   Cost summary

Fittings

(7–) **Fittings**
(70)
(71) Circulation fittings
(72) Rest, work fittings
(73) Culinary fittings
(74) Sanitary, hygiene fittings
(75) Cleaning, maintenance fittings
(76) Storage, screening fittings
(77) Special activity fittings
(78) Other fittings

(79) Parts of elements (71) to (78)
   Cost summary

(8–)***Loose furniture, equipment**
(80)
(81) Circulation loose equipment
(82) Rest, work loose equipment
(83) Culinary loose equipment
(84) Sanitary, hygiene loose equipment
(85) Cleaning, maintenance loose equipment
(86) Storage, screening loose equipment
(87) Special activity loose equipment
(88) Other loose equipment
(89) Parts of elements (81) to (88)
   Cost summary

External, other elements

(9–) **External, other elements**
(90) External works
(98) Other elements
(99) Parts of elements
   Cost summary

Use only (7–) if preferred

TABLE 2. Constructions

A* Constructions, forms
B*
C*
D*
E   Cast *in situ* work
F   Block work; blocks
G   Large block, panel work; large blocks, panels
H   Section work; sections
I   Pipe work; pipes
J   Wire work, mesh work; wires, meshes
K   Quilt work; quilts
L   Flexible sheet work (proofing); flexible sheets (proofing)

M   Malleable sheet work; malleable sheets
N   Rigid sheet overlap work; rigid sheets for overlapping
P   Thick coating work
Q
R   Rigid sheet work, rigid sheets
S   Rigid tile work, rigid tiles
T   Flexible sheet work; flexible sheets
U
V   Film coating and impregnation work
W   Planting work: plants, seeds
X   Work with components; components
Y   Formless work; Products
Z   Joints

*Used for special purposes e.g. specification

392 Appendix 1 Outline classifications

TABLE 3. Materials

a* Materials
b*
c*
d*

Formed materials e/o

e Natural stone
f Precast with binder
g Clay (dried, fired)
h Metal
i Wood
j Vegetable and animal materials
k
m Inorganic fibres
n Rubbers, plastics etc.
o Glass

Formless materials p/s

p Aggregates, loose fills
q Lime and cement binders, mortars, concretes
r Clay, gypsum, magnesia and plastic binders, mortars
s Bituminous materials

Functional materials t/w

t Fixing and jointing materials
u Protective and process/property modifying materials
v Paints
w Ancillary materials
x
y Composite materials
z Substances

Used for special purposes e.g. resource scheduling by computer

---

TABLE 4. Activities, requirements

Activities, aids

(A) Administration and management activities, aids
(Af) Administration, organization
(Ag) Communications
(Ah) Preparation of documentation
(Ai) Public relations, publicity
(Aj) Controls, procedures
(Ak) Organizations
(Am) Personnel, roles
(An) Education
(Ao) Research, development
(Ap) Standardization, rationalization
(Aq) Testing, evaluating

(A1) Organizing offices, projects
(A2) Financing, accounting
(A3) Designing, physical planning
(A4) Cost planning, cost control, tenders, contracts
(A5) Production planning, progress control
(A6) Buying, delivery

(A7) Inspection, quality control
(A8) Hand over, feedback appraisal
(A9) Other activities, arbitration, insurance

(B) Construction plant, tools
(B1) Protection plant
(B2) Temporary (non protective) works
(B3) Transport plant
(B4) Manufacture, screening, storage plant
(B5) Treatment plant
(B6) Placing, pavement, compaction plant
(B7) Hand tools
(B8) Ancillary plant
(B9) Other construction plant, tools

(C) *
(D) Construction operations
(D1) Protecting
(D2) Clearing, preparing
(D3) Transporting, lifting

* *Used for special purposes*

Appendix 1 Outline classifications 393

CI/SfB: Construction Classification   TABLE 4. (*cont.*)

(D4) Forming: cutting, shaping, fitting
(D5) Treatment: drilling, boring
(D6) Placing: laying, applying
(D7) Making good, repairing
(D8) Cleaning up
(D9) Other construction operations

Requirements, properties

(E/G) Description [2]
(E) Composition [2.01/2.03]
(F) Shape, size [2.04/2.06]
(G) Appearance [2.07]
(H) Context, environment [3]
(J/T) Performance factors [4/5]
(J) Mechanics [4.01]
(K) Fire, explosion [4.02]
(L) Matter [4.03/4.06]
(M) Heat, cold [4.07]
(N) Light, dark [4.08]
(P) Sound, quiet [4.09]
(Q) Electricity, magnetism, radiation [4.10]

(R) Energy [4.11]
    Side effects, compatibility [4.12/4.13] Durability [4.14]
(S)
(T) Application [5]
(U) Users, resources
(V) Working factors [6]
(W) Operation, maintenance factors [7]
(X) Change, movement, stability factors
(Y) Economic, commercial factors [8/10]
(Z) Peripheral subjects, forms of presentation; time; space [11]

Note: Codes in square brackets above are from *CIB Master Lists for structuring documents relating to buildings, building elements, components, materials and services* (CIB Report No. 18, 1972)

CISfB is a flexible system, e.g. free codes throughout the tables can be used for special purposes on information which is not for general publication; for Tables 0 and 1, headings and codes in colour will often provide sufficient breakdown

Appendix 2
Associations and abbreviations used

This list gives the name, address and telephone number of the major associations mentioned in the text as at 31 May 1982. It does not intend to be comprehensive. Lists of addresses are discussed in Chapter 2. Those in *Specification*, the *Barbour Design Library* index volume, the directory volume of the RIBA *Product Data*, the *AJ Annual Review* and *House's Guide to the Construction Industry* are fuller and most regularly up-dated.

Usual abbreviations are given first – but the order is alphabetical by name. Abbreviations of frequently used titles are given but the index should be used to locate page references.

ACCESS	see Greater London Council
ACCOMPLINE	see Greater London Council
API	*Architectural Periodicals Index*. RIBA
ASCE	American Society of Civil Engineers, 345 East 47th Street, New York, 10017
AJ	*Architects' Journal*, Architectural Press, 9–13 Queen Anne's Gate, London SW1H 9BY (01-222 4333)
ASLIB	Association of Special Libraries and Information Bureaux, 3 Belgrave Square, London SW1X 8PL (01-235 5050)
	Association of Danish Landscape Architects, Gammel Torv 22, 1457 København K (01 81 15 22)
BDL	*Barbour Design Library* from Barbour Index Ltd
	Barbour Index Ltd, New Lodge, Drift Road, Windsor, Berks, SL4 4RQ (034 47 4121)
BRS	Bibliographic Retrieval Services Inc., Corporation Park, Building 702, Scotia, New York 12302
BLAISE	BLAISE Marketing, 2 Sheraton Street, London W1V 4BH (01-636 1544, x 242)

394

… Appendix 1 Outline classifications 395

BDA	Brick Development Association, Woodside House, Winkfield, Windsor, Berks, SL4 2DX (034 47 5651)
BAL	British Architectural Library, see RIBA
	British Blind and Shutter Association, 251 Brompton Road, London SW3 (01-584 5552)
	British Carpet Manufacturers' Association, 26 St James's Square, London SW1Y 4JH (01-839 2145)
	Technical Centre, Ackroyd House, Hog Road, Kidderminster (0562 4053)
	British Colour Makers Association, 93 Albert Embankment, London SE1 7TU (01-735 3001)
	British Contract Furnishing Association Ltd, 73 Grosvenor Street, London W1X 9DU (01-499 2232)
BEAB	British Electrotechnical Approvals Board, Mark House, 9–11 Queens Road, Horsham, Surrey KT12 5LU (09322 44401)
BHI	*British Humanities Index*
	British Institute of Interior Design, 22–24 South Street, Ilkeston, Derbs DE7 5QE (0602 329781)
BIM	British Institute of Management, Parker Street, London WC2B 5PT (01-405 3456)
BL	British Library, Bibliographic Services Division, 2 Sheraton Street, London W1V 4BH (01-636 1544)
BLLD	Lending Division, Boston Spa, Wetherby, West Yorkshire LS 23 7BQ (0937 843434): Reference Division, Great Russell Street, London WC1B 3DG (01-636 1544)
BLSRL	Science Reference Library, 25 Southampton Buildings, Chancery Lane, London WC2A 1AW (01-405 9721)
	British Plastics Federation, 5 Belgrave Square, London SW1X 8PH (01-235 9896)
BSI	British Standards Institution, Library, 2 Park Street, London W1A 2BS (01-629 9000): Sales Dept, 101 Pentonville Road, London N1 9ND (01-837 8801)
	Building Centre, 26 Store Street, London WC1E 7BT (01-637 3151)
	Building Conservation Trust, Apartment 39, Hampton Court Palace, East Molesey, Surrey KT8 9BS (01-943 2277)
BCIS	Building Cost Information Service, 85–87 Clarence Street, Kingston-upon-Thames, Surrey KT1 1RB (01-546 7554)
BDUK	*Building Documentation UK*, see Building Centre (now ceased)
BMCIS	Building Maintenance Cost Information Service, 85–87 Clarence Street, Kingston-upon-Thames, Surrey KT1 1RB (01-546 7555)
BRE	Building Research Establishment, Garston, Watford, Herts WD2 7JR (092 73 74040)
	BRE Boreham Wood Laboratory, Herts WD6 2BL (01-953 6177)
	BRE Princes Risborough Laboratory, Aylesbury, Bucks HP17 9PX (084 44 3101)
BSRIA	Building Services Research and Information Association, Old Bracknell Lane, Bracknell, Berks RG12 4AH (0344 25071)
CISI	Campagnie Internationale de Services en Informatique, 35 Boulevad Brune, 75680 Paris Cedex 14 (1 539 2510)
C & CA	Cement and Concrete Association, Wexham Springs, Slough, Berks SL3 6PL (028 16 2737)
CATED	Centre d'Assistance Technique et de Documentation, 9 rue la Pérouse, 75784 Paris Cedex 16 (720 88 00)

396 Appendix 1 Outline classifications

CEH	Centre on Environment for the Handicapped, 126 Albert Street, London NW1 7NF (01-267 6111)
CIOB	Chartered Institute of Building, Englemere, King's Ride, Ascot, Berks SL5 8BJ (0990 23355)
CIBS	Chartered Institute of Building Services, 222 Balham High Street, London SW12 9BS (01-675 5211)
CIB	see International Council for Building Documentation
CIBDOC	Database from CIB
CITÈRE	64 rue de Ranelagh, 75016 Paris (1 5245222 x 304/303)
	City Business Library, Gillett House, 55 Basinghall Street, London EC2V 5BX (01-638 8215/6)
	Colour Group (GB), Bowater Technical Services Ltd, Callybank House, Gravesend, Kent DA11 9AG (0474 64444)
CAA	Commonwealth Association of Architects, 326 Grand Buildings, Trafalgar Square, London WC2N 5HB (01-930 0059)
CI/SfB	Construction Indexing Manual
CICA	Construction Industry Computing Association, Guildhall Place, Cambridge, CB2 3QQ (0223 311246)
CIIG	Construction Industry Information Group, 26 Store Street, London WC1E 7BT (01-637 1022)
CIRIA	Construction Industry Research and Information Association, 6 Storey's Gate, London SW1P 3AU (01-222 8891)
	Cotton Silk and Man-Made Fibres Research Association, Shirley Institute, Didsbury, Manchester M20 8RX (061 445 8141)
COFI	Council of Forest Industries of British Columbia, Tileman House, 131/3 Upper Richmond Road, London SW15 2TR (01-788 4446)
CP	Current paper from BRE *or* Code of practice from BSI
	Crafts Advisory Committee, 12 Waterloo Place, London SW1Y 4AU (01-839 1917)
CTI	*Current Technology Index*
DES	Department of Education and Science Library, Elizabeth House, York Road, London SE1 7PH (01-928 9222)
DHSS	Department of Health and Social Security, 14 Russell Square, London WC1B 5EP (01-636 6811)
DHSS	Department of Health and Social Security Library, Alexander Fleming House, Elephant and Castle, London SE1 6BY (01-407 5522)
DoE	Department of the Environment (see also BRE, PSA), 2 Marsham Street, London SW1P 3EB (01-212 3434)
	Design Council, 28 Haymarket, London SW1Y 4SU (01-839 8000)
DIALOG	Besselsleigh Road, Abingdon, Oxford OX13 6EF (0865 730969) *or* Lockheed Information Systems, 3460 Hillsview Drive, Palo Alto, California 94304 (800/227 1960)
DIALTECH	see Technology Reports Centre
DIMDI	Weisshausstrasse 27, Postfach 420580, D 5000 Köln 41, West Germany (02 221 47241)
DIANE	see *Euronet Diane*
	Disabled Living Foundation, 346 Kensington High Street, London W14 8NS (01-602 2491)
	Ergonomics Information Analysis Centre, Department of Engineering Production, University of Birmingham, PO Box 363, Birmingham B15 2TT (021 472 1301 x 2731)

Appendix 1 Outline classifications 397

EURONET	Euronet Diane, BP 777 Luxembourg, 40221 *or* Customer Contact, British Telecom International, 7th floor, St Alphage House, 2 Fore Street, London EC2Y 5DA (01-606 9716)
ESA	European Space Agency, see Technology Reports Centre
	Export Intelligence Service, British Overseas Trade Board, Export House, 50 Ludgate Hill, London EC4M 7HU (01-248 5757)
	Farm Building Information Centre, National Agricultural Centre, Stoneleigh, Kenilworth, Warks CV8 2LG (0203 22345)
	Federation of German Landscape Architects, 5300 Bonn, Colmanstrasse 32, West Germany (02221 65 54 88)
FT	Financial Times Business Information Ltd, Bracken House, 10 Cannon Street, London EC4P 4BY (01-236 3430)
FPA	Fire Protection Association, Aldermary House, Queen Street, London EC4N 1TJ (01-248 5222)
FIRA	Furniture Industry Research Association, Maxwell Road, Stevenage, Herts SG1 2EW (0438 3433)
GLC	Greater London Council, Research Library, County Hall, London SE1 7PB (01-633 6068)
	Guild of Master Craftsmen, Parklands House, Keymer Road, Burgess Hill, Sussex BN7 1YE (044 56 45267)
HMSO	Her Majesty's Stationery Office: to order by post, Government Bookshop, PO Box 569, London SE1 9NH. To order in person, 49 High Holborn, London WC1V 6HB (01-928 6977). Enquiries and Information, Atlantic House, Holborn Viaduct, London EC1P 1BN (01-583 9876)
	Historic Houses Association, 38 Ebury Street, London SW1W 0LU (01-730 9410/9419)
	Home Office Library, 50 Queen Anne's Gate, London SW1H 9AT (01-213 3646/4227)
	Home Office, Construction and Building Branch Library, Room 106, St Vincent House, 30 Orange Street, London WC2H 7HT (01-930 8499 x 144)
	Horticultural Trades Association, 18 Westcote Road, Reading, Berks RG3 2DE (0734 581 371)
	Housing Centre Trust, 33 Alfred Place, London WC1E 7JU (01-637 4202)
IES	Illuminating Engineering Society, now CIBS
INKA	Fachinformationszentrum Energie Physik Mathematik, 7514 Eggenstein, Leopoldshafen 2, West Germany (7247 824568)
INSPEC	Information Services for Physics and Engineering Communities, Institution of Electrical Engineers, Publishing Sector, Stations House, 70 Nightingale Road, Hitchin, Herts SG 5 1RJ (0462 53331)
	Institute of Housing, Victoria House, Southampton Row, London WC1B 4EB (01-242 3267)
ICE	Institution of Civil Engineers, Great George Street, Westminster, London SW1P 3AA (01-222 7722)
IHVE	Institution of Heating and Ventilating Engineers, now CIBS
ISE	Institution of Structural Engineers, 11 Upper Belgrave Street, London SW1X 8BH (01-235 4535)
	Interior Decorators and Designers Association Ltd, 24 Ormond Road, Richmond, Surrey TW10 6TH (01-948 4151)
ICB	International Council for Building Research Studies and Documentation, Weena 704, Postbus 20704, Rotterdam, Holland (010 116181) UK agent: BRE

… Appendix 2   Associations and abbreviations used

IFLA	International Federation of Library Associations, POB 95312, 2509 CH, The Hague, Holland
ISO	International Standards Organization, see BSI
IUA	International Union of Architects, 51 rue Raynouard 75016, Paris (288 47 82): UK agent: RIBA
	International Wool Secretariat, Wool House, 6–7 Carlton Gardens, London SW1Y 5AE (01-930 7300)
	Lambeg Industrial Research Association, The Research Institute, Lisburn, County Antrim, N. Ireland BT 27 4RJ (08464 2255)
	Landscape Institute, Nash House, 12 Carlton House Terrace, London SW1Y 5AH (01-839 4044)
	Lighting Industry Federation, 25 Bedford Square, London WC1B 3HH (01-636 0766)
MO	Meteorological Office, Enquiry Service, England and Wales: London Road, Bracknell RG12 2SZ (0344 20242 x 2278). Scotland: Corstophine Road, Edinburgh EH12 7BB (031 3349721 x 524). N. Ireland: Tyrone House, Ormeau Avenue, Belfast BT2 8HH (0232 28457)
MoPBW	Ministry of Public Building and Works, see DoE
NBA	National Building Agency (now ceased)
NFBTE	National Federation of Building Trades Employers, 82 New Cavendish Street, London W1M 8AD (01-580 5588)
	National Physical Laboratory, Queens Road, Teddington, Middlesex TW11 0LW (01-977 3222)
NPFA	National Playing Fields Association, 25 Ovington Square, London SW3 1LQ (01-584 6445)
NTIS	National Technical Information Service, 4 High Street, Alton, Hants GU34 1BA (0420 84300)
	Oil and Colour Chemists Association, 967 Harrow Road, Wembley, Middlesex HAO 2SF (01-908 1086)
	Paintmakers Association of Great Britain Ltd, 93 Albert Embankment, London SE1 7TY (01-582 1185)
	Paint Research Association, Waldegrave Road, Teddington, Middlesex TW11 8LD (01-977 4427)
	Photogrammetric Society, Department of Photogrammetry and Surveying, University College London, Gower Street, London WC1E 6BT (01-387 7050)
PTRC	Planning and Transportation Research and Computation Co. Ltd, 109 Bedford Chambers, King Street, London WC2 (01-836 2208)
	Plastic Coating Research Company Ltd, Swan Lane, Sandhurst, Camberley, Surrey GU17 8DB (0252 873470)
	Plastics and Rubber Institute, 11 Hobert Place, London SW1W 0HL (01-245 9555)
PSA	Property Services Agency, Whitgift Centre, Wellesley Road, Croydon CR9 3LY (01-686 8710)
PIRA	Research Association for the Paper and Board, Printing and Packaging Industries, Randalls Road, Leatherhead, Surrey KT22 7RU (037 23 76161)
RIBA	Royal Institution of British Architects, 66 Portland Place, London W1N 4AD (01-580 5533)
RIBAS	Royal Institution of British Architects' Services, 66 Portland Place, London W1N 4AD (01-637 8991)
RICS	Royal Institution of Chartered Surveyors, 12 Great George Street, Parliament Square, London SW1P 3AD (01-222 7000)

Appendix 2   Associations and abbreviations used   399

RTPI	Royal Town Planning Institute, 26 Portland Place, London W1N 4BE (01-636 9107)
	Rubber and Plastics Research Association, Shawbury, Shrewsbury, Shrops, SY4 4NR (0939 250383)
	Society of Industrial Artists and Designers, Nash House, 12 Carlton House Terrace, London SW1Y 5AH (01-930 1911)
	Society of Surveying Technicians, Aldwych House, Aldwych, London WC2B 4EL (01-242 4832)
	Sports Council, 70 Brompton Road, London SW3 1EX (01-589 3411)
SMM	Standard method of measurement
	Swiss Federation of Landscape Architects, Forchstrasse 287, 8008 Zurich, Switzerland (01 55 22 43)
SDC	Systems Development Corporation, Stuart House, 47 Crown Street, Reading, Berks RG1 2SG (0734 866811). SDC–ORBIT, 2500 Colorado Avenue, Santa Monica, California 90406, USA
THE	Technical Help for Exporters, BSI, Maylands Avenue, Hemel Hempstead, Herts HP2 4SQ (0442 3111)
TI	Technical Indexes Ltd, Willoughby Road, Bracknell, Berks RG12 4DW (0344 26311)
TRC	Technology Reports Centre, Department of Industry, Orpington, Kent BR5 3RF (0689 32111) *DIALOG* x255
	Textile Institute, 10 Blackfriars Street, Manchester M3 5DR (061 834 1457)
TRADA	Timber Research and Development Association, Hughenden Valley, High Wycombe, Bucks HP14 4ND (0240 24 3091)
TCPA	Town and Country Planning Association, 17 Carlton House Terrace, London SW1Y 5AS (01-930 8903)
	Zoological Society of London, Regent's Park, London NW1 4RY (01-722 3333)

Index

A & B Viewdata, 70
Abbreviations, 107, 394–399
Abstracting and indexing journals,
  127–134
  biography, 371–372
  conservation, 349–350
  energy, 270–271
  in searching, 42, 46
  interior design, 304–305
  landscape, 292–293
  photography, 200–201
  places, 378–379
  services, 270–271
  structures, 254–255
  surveying, 223–224
  (see also subject headings, titles)
Accidents,
  statistics, 185
ACCOMPLINE, 63,65, 131, 134, 378
Accuracy,
  in building, 220
ACE, 255
Acts see Statutes
Addresses, 100, 107–108, 235, 301
  (see also subjects)
Adhesives, 262
  directory, 140
Administrative buildings, 212, 213
Advertising agencies, 108
Advisory leaflets (DoE), 148, 248
Advisory services, 19–20

Aggregate Block Association, 259
Agrément Board, 145, 151, 158
AGRICOLA, 64
Agricultural buildings,
  databases, 64
AGRIS, 64
Air-conditioning, 268–278
  (see also Energy)
Air Infiltration Centre, 271, 278
Air photographs, 193, 221
Air turbulence,
  near high-rise buildings, 238
Airports, 22, 43
AJ handbooks, 39, 101, 351
Alternative technology, 267, 270, 273,
  277, 278
Aluminium,
  databases, 65, 261
ALUMINIUM, 65
Aluminium Federation, 26
Aluminium Window Association, 277
American Meteorological Society, 242
American Institute of Architects,
  213–214
American Society for Testing and
  Materials, 160, 302
American Society of Architectural
  Bibliographers, 373
American Society of Civil Engineers,
  254
  database, 65

Index

American Society of Landscape
    Architects, 292, 295
American Society of Surveying and
    Mapping, 225
American standards, 160
An Foras Forbartha, 288
Anatomy, 303
Anbar Abstracts, 327–328
Ancient Monuments, 357, 367
Ancient Monuments Society, 353, 360
Anthropometric data, 214–215,
    216–218, 303, 305
    databases, 65
Appeals,
    planning, 233
Aqua Group, 311
AQUALINE, 64
Arbitration, 326
Archaeology, 347, 348
Architects,
    biography, 370–375
    identification, 362–363
    information habits, 3
    information needs, 1–16, 18, 329–337
    lists, 374
    personal information systems, 3,
        37–57, 79–83, 136–138,
        142–143, 329–336
    practices, 106, 228, 338–342
    libraries, 109, 329–336
    registration, 322
    use of product information, 137–138,
        329–336
Architect's Data, 211, 213
*Architect's Guide to Sources of
    Information and Advice*, 28
Architect's Job Book, 330
Architect's Journal, 12, 13, 126, 148,
    250, 258, 260, 268, 292, 298, 318,
    324, 332, 351
    'Annual Review', 4, 23, 97, 100, 197,
        252, 267, 272, 292, 349, 365
    cost analyses, 283
    'Guide to Information Sources', 31,
        258
    interior planting schemes, 298
    planning, 236
    'Products in practice', 150
Architects Registration Council, 106,
    322
Architects Standard Catalogue, 146
Architectural Association, 363–364
    slide library, 204
Architectural design, 126, 189

Architectural history, 203, 356,
    362–370
    gardens, 292
Architectural illustration, 196–198
Architectural Index, 371
Architectural Periodicals Index, 129,
    134, 189, 201, 202,217, 236, 271,
    279, 283, 292, 316, 321, 327, 349,
    362, 363
    Keywords, 129
    proposed database, 64
Architectural photogrammetry,
    221–222
Architectural Review, 126, 303, 351
Architecture, *passim*
    schools, lists, 106
Archives, 300
ARGODATA, 64
ARIANE, 5, 66–67, 68, 218
ARKISYST, 66
*Art and Archaeology Technical
    Abstracts*, 347
Art galleries, 108, 369
Art Index, 366, 371
Arts and Humanities Citation Index, 47
Asbestos, 265
Aslib, 21, 320, 342
    on-line searching, 63
Aslib Directory, 32
Assessment of products, 158
    (*see also* Agrément Board, Quality
        assurance)
Association for Preservation
    Technology, 347, 355
Association for Studies in the
    Conservation of Historic
    Buildings, 352
Association of Construction
    Information Providers, 70
Associations,
    conservation, 359–360
    contract, 317
    fire, 267
    interior design, 299
    libraries, 25–26
    lists, 28–34, 140, 218, 302, 308,
        369–370, 394–399
    local, 377
    local history, 369–370
    maintenance, 290
    overseas work, 318–319
    specification, 285
    surveying, 221, 225–226
    (*see also* subject headings)

Atlases, 188, 192
Autoclaved Aerated Concrete Products
   Association, 259
*Avery Index to Architectural
   Periodicals*, 130, 349, 350, 364,
   366, 590
Avery Memorial Library,
   printed catalogue, 34

Banwell report, 312
Barbour Compendium, 21, 139, 141,
   143–144, 146, 252
Barbour Design Library, 25, 29, 43, 50,
   67, 147–148, 152, 155, 156, 214,
   246 *passim*, 258 *passim*
Barbour Index Ltd., 25, 143, 334
Barry, *Construction of Buildings*, 251,
   272
Bathrooms, 215, 309
BAUFO, 64
Beams, 259
Bedrooms, 215, 309
Bibliographia Cartographica, 189
Bibliographia Geodaetica, 223
Bibliographic Index, 104, 370
Bibliographical references,
   evaluation, 49–50
   format, 15, 49–51, 80, 88–89
   organization, 53, 80
   volume, 7
Bibliographies,
   climate, 241, 245
   conservation, 344–349
   content, 42, 241
   contract, 316
   cost, 279
   energy, 103, 104, 271
   energy conservation, 273–274
   insulation, 273
   landscape, 103, 293
   law, 316
   lighting, 275–276
   maintenance, 103, 287,288
   materials, 265
   places, 377
   planned preventive maintenance, 289
   planning, 345–346
   preparation, 53, 56–57, 88
   published, 97–104
   quality, 279
   quantity surveying, 279, 316
   research associations, 11
   solar energy, 103, 104
   structural design, 250–251

Bibliographies (*cont.*)
   structures, 253
   technical, 148, 250
   updating, 348–349
   working abroad, 321
Bills of quantity, 284–285, 311–317
Biographies, 370–375
Biography Index, 371
Biological Abstracts, 59, 293
BIOSIS, 72
BLAISE, 61, 62, 64
Blinds, 308
Blockwork, 263
Books, evaluating, 48–50
Books in Print, 102, 349
Bouwcentrum, 290
BRE News, 173, 248
Brick, 259, 262, 263, 265, 277, 346
Brick Development Association, 26,
   247, 259, 263, 266
British and Irish Architectural History,
   31, 204, 360, 373, 378
British Archaeological Abstracts, 348
British Architectural Library, 22, 26,
   319, 349, 355, 358, 372
   Drawings Collection, 23, 34, 201
   Manuscripts Collections, 375
British Association for the
   Advancement of Science, 377
British Blind and Shutter Association,
   308
British Books in Print, 102
British Carpet Manufacturers
   Association, 302, 307
British Colour Makers Association, 306
British Constructional Steelwork
   Association, 214, 249, 252
British Contract Furnishing
   Association, 306
British Council of Maintenance
   Associations, 290
British Education Index, 217
British Electrotechnical Approvals
   Board, 157
British Humanities Index, 132, 217, 349,
   350, 366, 371, 379
British Institute of Interior Design, 299
British Institute of Management, 322
British Library, 102
   computer search services, 63
   Lending Division, 135, 355–356
   maps, 194
   Official Publications Library,
      173–174, 185

British Library (cont.)
  periodicals holdings, 135
  Reference Division, 102, 367, 375
  Science Reference Library, 21, 27, 149, 277, 320
  standards, 166
  (see also BLAISE)
British Museum Library,
  catalogue, 34, 367, 377
  topography catalogue, 375
British National Bibliography, 34, 102, 349, 367, 372, 377
British Official Publications not Published by HMSO, 147, 174, 237
British Overseas Trade Board, 318, 319, 320
British Plastics Federation, 259
British Reports, Translations and Theses, 47
British standards, 20, 144, 154–158
  building regulations, 175–176
  lists, 139
British Standards Institution, 26, 153–166, 302
  information, online, 70
British Technology Index see Current Technology Index
BSI Yearbook, 33, 155, 247, 302
BRS, 62
Builders,
  weather reports, 242
Building, 126, 260, 268, 280, 283, 352, 371
  R & D report, 39, 270
Building Bulletins, (DES), 172
Building Centre, 21, 102, 145, 150, 257, 278, 290
Building Centre,
  energy products, 275
Building Centre and CIRIA Guide to Sources of Information, 30
Building Centre Group, 25
Building Centre Trust, 11
Building Control, 174–180
Building Cost Information Service, 282
Building Design, 126, 178, 256, 260, 268, 332, 352
Building Documentation UK, 145, 258, 268
Building Enclosure,
  AJ Handbook, 101, 250, 279
Building Environment,
  AJ Handbook, 269
Building failures, see Failures

Building Law Reports, 180
Building Maintenance Cost Information Service, 287, 290
Building Management Abstracts, 132, 279, 287, 289, 317
Building Materials Producers, 260
Building Product Index, 144
building Regulations, 155, 156, 175–177, 197–180, 319, 332
  guides, 177–178
  Scotland and Northern Ireland, 179–180
Building Research Centres and Similar Organisations through the World, 35
Building Research Establishment, 9–10, 12, 22, 27, 169–171, 246, 256, 278, 285, 306, 319, 346
  bibliographies, 103
  Current papers, 8, 148, 151, 169–170, 176, 248, 259, 266
  Defects Action Sheets, 151
  Defects News, 151
  Digests, 169, 220–221, 248, 255, 259, 268, 286
  failures research, 151
  Information Directory, 8, 102, 148, 173, 203, 252, 260, 266, 286, 348
  Information Papers, 8, 148, 248, 266
  Library, 19
  maintenance and design, 285
  materials, 267
  News of Timber Research, 264
  Princes Risborough Laboratory, 9, 22, 169
  proposed database, 64
Building Science Abstracts, 10, 64, 132, 254, 261
Building Services Research and Information Association, 10–11, 26, 132, 267, 270, 271, 278
  bibliographies, 103
  database, 65, 69
  lighting, 275
Building Services Viewdata Association, 70
Building Societies Association, 184
Building Specification, 140, 254, 260, 280
Building Structure,
  AJ Handbook, 101, 250, 262
Building surveying, 286
Building Trades Journal, 260
  on-line, 70

Index 405

Building types, 22, 40, 210–218
  interior design, 309
Buildings,
  descriptions, 357, 364–370
  identification, 362–363, 364–370
Business equipment, 140
Business information, 328
  databases, 67
Business International SA, 322
Bye-laws *see* London Building Acts
BYGGDOK, 64, 66
BYGGVARUREGISTRET, 64

CAB Abstracts, 64
Capital Planning Information, 63
CAPTAIN, 69
Card catalogues, 114
Card indexes, 51–52, 80–82, 114
Carpets, 262, 302, 307–308
Cars, 218
Cartography *see* Maps
Case law *see* Law reports
CASEARCH, 261
Catalogues, 110–120
  as bibliographies, 101–102
  bookshop, 260
  defined, 110
  drawings, printed, 201
  government publications, 172–174
  library, printed, 34
  maps, printed, 194
  official publications, 172–174
  trade, presentation of, 137
  using, 111
  (*see also* Product information)
CATED, 66
Catering buildings, 213, 309
CBC classification, 118
CEEFAX, 68
Ceilings, 309
Cembureau, 263
Cement, 260, 263–264
  high alumina, 5, 265
Cement and Concrete Association, 10, 26, 102, 148, 249, 259, 260, 263, 264
  bibliographies, 103
Center for Building Technology (USA), 274
Central Electricity Generating Board, 271
Centre de Création Industrielle, 299

Centre for Environmental Studies, 346
Centre on Environment for the Handicapped, 27, 102, 216, 368
Chairs, 308
Charities Digest, 107
Chartered Institute of Building, 12, 254, 285, 286, 290, 316
  bibliographies, 103
  Estimating service, 282
  maintenance, 287
Chartered Institute of Building Services, 267, 269, 270, 271, 275, 278, 305
  (*see also* CIBS)
Chartered Institute of Public Finance and Accountancy, 184
Chartered Surveyor, 222
Chemical Abstracts, 59, 201, 261
  database, 62, 65
Churches, 353, 356, 357, 374
  model specification clauses, 284
CIB *see* International Council for Building Documentation
CIBDOC, 66
CIBS Building Services Manual, 269
CIBS Energy Code, 274
CIBS Guide, 4, 244, 269
Cinemas, 212
Circulation, 215
CIRIA Guide . . . see Building Centre and CIRIA Guide . . .
CISI, 62
CI/SfB, 118–119, 339, 389–393
  coordination of information, 197
  for personal information collections, 51, 123, 143, 149
CIT Agency, 279
Citation indexes, 47, 224, 261, 271
CITERE, 62
Civic Trust, 353, 356, 360
Cladding, 249
CLASP classification, 118
Classification, 115–123, 338–339
Climate,
  indoor, 272
  outdoor *see* Meteorology
Coal, 268
Codes of Practice, 154–156
  surveying, 220
Colleges, 107, 172
  databases, 64
  environment, 180
Colour, 306
Colour Index, 306

Columbia University *see* Avery
    Memorial Library
Commercial buildings, 212, 213
Commonwealth Agricultural Bureau,
    293
Commonwealth Association of
    Architects, 35, 106, 322
Commonwealth Bureau of Horticulture
    and Plantation Crops, 293
Communications
    barriers, 12
    bibliographies, 56–57
    channels of, 330–331
    construction industry studies, 11–12
    construction information, 2
    in the office, 331
    making enquiries, 24–25
    need for, 329
    techniques, 77–78
*Communication in the Building
    Industry*, 11
Community Land Act, 233
Companies House, 142
Company information, 142, 182
COMPENDEX, 61, 62, 65, 73, 74, 132,
    224, 261
Competitions, 199–200
Components, 251
Compulsory purchase, 233
Computer-aided architectural design,
    43
*Computer Programs for the
    Construction Industry*, 58
Computer search services, 63
Computers,
    in construction, 218
    in practices, 328, 334–335
    information retrieval, 58–75, 116,
        355
    product information, 152–153
    programs, 257
    user needs, buildings, 210
Concrete, 249, 250, 252, 253, 259, 260,
    262, 263–264
    databases, 66
    directory, 140
Concrete in Print, 264
Condensation, 243, 275, 277
Conference of Commonwealth
    Surveyors, 225
Conference Papers Index, 64, 224
Conference proceedings, 47–48, 225,
    253, 266, 290
    CIB, 5, 9, 266, 275

Conference proceedings (*cont.*)
    energy, 275
    fire, 266
    maintenance, 290
Conference Proceedings Index, 64
Contracts, 311–317
Conservation, 203, 263, 288, 343–360
    bibliographies, 104
    energy, 273
    regulations, 178, 180
Conservation Sourcebook, 33, 355, 359,
    360
Constrado, 253
Construction (DoE), 171, 253, 254, 257,
    287
Construction industry,
    Europe, 321
    handbooks, 108
    information in, 6–7
    market information, 153
    overseas databases, 66
    Prestel, 68–70
    statistics, 182–185
Construction Industry Computing
    Association, 58
Construction Industry Europe, 35
Construction Industry Information
    Group, 32, 202, 342
Construction Industry Register, 142
Construction Industry Research and
    Information Association, 10–11,
    20, 152, 256, 265, 267
Construction Industry Thesaurus, 54,
    72, 115, 118, 121–123
Construction Industry UK, 30
Construction References, 42, 47, 120,
    130, 174, 217, 254, 256, 261, 271,
    279, 281, 288, 293, 348, 366
Construction Research International, 5,
    9, 266, 275
Construction sites, weather data, 242,
    243
Construction statistics, 183–185
    guides, 183
Construction surveys, 219–226
Consultants,
    engineering, 247
    international lists, 318
    planning, 228
    structures, 257
CONTEL, 69 (*see also Prestel*)
Contents lists, 256
Contractors, 247
    statistics, 184–185

Coordinate indexing, 53–56
Copper, 261
Copyright, 167
  maps, 191–192
Copyright deposit, 102
Corrosion,
  databases, 65
Cost information, 279–283, 285–290,
  databases, 69
  energy, 269
  housing, 184
  of using manufacturer's literature,
    136
Costs-in-use, 265, 285–290
Cotton Silk and Man-made Fibres
  Research Association, 307
Council for British Archaeology, 348
Council for the Care of Churches, 353,
  357
Council of Forest Industries of British
  Columbia, 259
Council for Planning Librarians, 103,
  273, 347, 369
Councils Committees and Boards, 31,
  301–302
Country houses, 358, 366, 368–369
Courts, law, 210
Craft Council, 355, 359, 360
Crafts Advisory Council, 359, 369
CSIRO, 271
Current Biography, 371
Current information, 43, 109, 125–127,
  223, 255–256, 260, 288, 293, 316,
  348
  databases, 74
  products, 150
  standards, 156
*Current Information in the Construction
  Industry*, 130, 174, 199, 256
Current Papers, *see* Building Research
  Establishment, Current Papers
Current Technology Index, 132, 217,
  224, 255, 261, 271, 349, 350

Danish Landscape Architects, 292
Damp proofing *see* Waterproofing
Data Express, 25, 145
Databases,
  availability, 21
  construction, 63–64
  costs, 59–60
  development, 59
  in literature searching, 40, 47, 134

Databases *(cont.)*
  international business information,
    318
  (*see also* subject headings)
Datastar, 62
Davis Belfield and Everest, 281, 283
Daylight, 243, 275
Defects, *see* Failures
Department of Education and Science,
  22, 172, 173, 180
  Building Bulletins, 172
Department of Energy, 275
Department of Health and Social
  Security, 22, 26, 148, 172
Department of Housing and Urban
  Development (USA),
  statistics libraries, 185
Department of the Environment, 26,
  169, 319, 320, 346
  Advisory leaflets, 148, 248
  Annual List of Publications, 192, 227,
    266, 285, 286
  bibliographies, 103, 273
  Central Register of Air
    Photography . . ., 221
  circulars, 232, 234
  classification, 118
  guidebooks, 367
  Information series, 33
  information studies, 2, 11, 75, 115,
    136, 197
  Library Bulletin, 42, 47, 131, 174,
    176, 236, 271, 348, 379
  library catalogue, 34
  Mechanical Data Book, 275
  press notices, 185
  Register of Research, 235
  Town and Country Planning, 227
  viewdata, 69
Department of Trade,
  overseas work, 318–323
Derelict land, 230–231
Design,
  bibliographies, 299
  computer-aided, 43
  databases, 65, 218
  interiors, 299–310
  journals, 126
  terotechnology, 288–290
Design Abstracts International, 201,
  216, 217, 305
Design Bulletins, (DoE), 148, 172, 217
Design Council, 218, 298, 299
  street furniture, 140

408 Index

Design data,
  interiors, 303
Design Office Consortium, 257
Design process,
  information in, 1–6
Detailing, 249–250
Development *see* Planning
Development and Materials Bulletin see
  Greater London Council
Development control, 234
Development Land Tax, 233
Development process, 229–234
Dewey Decimal Classification, 119,
  339, 349, 380–384
Diagrams,
  presentation in reports, 87
DIALTECH, 61, 62
DIANE see Euronet
Diary,
  use of, 79–80
Dictionaries, 98, 105–106, 250, 272
  bills of quantities, 284
  biography, 372–374
  construction, 105
  contract, 317
  definition, 98, 105–106
  fire, 265
  foundations and soil, 250
  heating, ventilating, 272
  materials, 262
  photogrammetry, 221
Dictionary of Architectural Science, 40
Dictionary of National Biography, 373
Digest of New Legislation, 226
Digests, see Building Research
  Establishment *Digests*
DIMDI, 62
Dimensional coordination, 212
DIN standards, 160
Directories,
  architects, 372–374
  concrete, 263
  definition, 98
  energy, 268–269
  furnishing, 306, 308
  interior design, 301–302
  lists, 109, 140, 262, 272, 301
  manufacturers, 140–142, 301–302
  materials, 262
  planning, 228
  products, 139–142
  services, 272
  surveying, 226
Directory of Building Associations, 31, 32

Directory of Building Research
  Information and Development
  Organisations, 35
Directory of European Associations, 31
Directory of International Practices,
  226, 247
Disabled, 175, 216–217, 309
Disabled Living Foundation, 309
Documentation,
  office, 330
Doors, 248, 249
Draughtsmanship, 195–198
Drawing, 195–201
Drawings,
  communication medium, 12, 84
  facsimile transmission, 22
Dry Lining and Partitioning
  Association, 257

Easibrief, 256
Ecological Abstracts, 293
Economics, 182, 280
  guides, 99
Edge-notch cards, 55
Education,
  buildings, 180, 212
  databases, 64
  (*see also*, Schools, Colleges,
    Universities)
EEC,
  construction in, 320
Elderly, *see* Disabled
Electrical Contractors Association, 272
Electrical Engineer's Reference Book,
  46
Electricity, 268–269
Electricity Council, 275
Electricity Council Research Centre,
  269
Elements, 247–257
Employment,
  statistics, 185
Encyclopaedias,
  architecture, 105, 369
  definition, 98, 105
  law, 180
  planning, 232, 233
Energy, 267–278
  bibliographies, 104
  conservation, 178, 180
  databases, 64
  periodicals, 125
Energy Abstracts, 64

Energy Cost Index, 287
Energy Index, 271
Engineering,
　databases, 65
Engineering contracts, 315–316
Engineering Index, 132, 224, 255, 261, 271, 365
Entertainment buildings, 212, 213
ENVIROLINE, 64
Environment, 108
　databases, 64
　in buildings, 214 (*see also* Services)
　planning, 227–237
Environmental Directory, 360
Environmental Impact Analysis, 231, 234
Environmental Powers,
　AJ Handbook, 101, 177
Equipment,
　surveyors, 225
Ergonomic data, 215–216, 303
Ergonomics Abstracts, 216, 217, 303
Ergonomics Information Analysis Centre, 216
ERIC, 64, 72, 217
ESA-IRS, 62
Estates Gazette,
　on *Prestel*, 225
Estimating, 171, 280, 281, 282
　for maintenance, 286
EUROLEX, 68
Euronet, 61, 62, 318
EURONEWS, 74
Europe,
　information sources, 35–36, 318, 323
European standards, 158–159
Eusidic Database Guide, 71
Evaluation,
　reading, 48–50
Events, 106
EXCERPTA MEDICA, 64
Exhibitions, 108, 309
　products, 150
Experimental Cartography Unit, 192
Export,
　architectural services, 318–323

Facsimile transmission, 22
Factories, 212, 213, 243, 250
Failures, 151–152, 248, 253
　bibliographies, 103
　feedback, 150–152, 171, 286
　liability, 5

Farm buildings, 173
Farm Buildings Information Centre, 27, 257
Feedback,
　in the office, 330–331
　(*see also* Failures)
Fibre Building Board Development Organisation, 277
Filing,
　practice records, 300
Films,
　availability, 203
　for conservation, 360
Financial information, 142, 182, 321, 325
　databases, 67
FIND, 25
Finishes, 251
Fire, 171, 265–267
　CIBS Guide, 269
　guides to regulations, 178
　libraries, 22
Fire Protection Association, 27, 266, 267
Fire Research Abstracts and Reviews, 266
Fire Research Laboratory, 9
Fire Science Abstracts, 266
Flat roofs, 22, 251, 255, 257
Floor coverings, 265, 307
Floors, 248, 249, 258
Floorspace statistics, 185
Forest Products Research Laboratory,
　see Building Research Establishment, Princes Risborough Laboratory
Forestry Abstracts, 293
Foundations, 248, 250, 252
　(*see also* Site investigations)
Furniture, 306–308
Furniture Industry Research Association, 308

Gardens, 292, 296, 297
Gas, 268
Gateway, 70
Gazeteers, 374
Genysys, 257
Geoabstracts, 223–224, 379
Geodex, 255
Geological Survey, 191–192, 221
Geology,
　databases, 65

Geomechanics Abstracts, 62
German Federation of Landscape
    Architects, 292
Glass, 264, 347, 374
    cooling, 239
    stained, 346
Glass reinforced concrete, 259, 265
Glossary of Construction Terms, 72
Goodey and Matthew, 12, 17, 137
Goodhart-Rendal Index, 374
Government,
    libraries, 26
    personnel, 106
    publications, 167–180
        increase, 7
        USA, catalogue, 64
Government Publications, 172–173
Government Reports Announcements, 47
Government Statistical Service, 181–182
Grants, 106
    for conservation, 360
GRC, 259, 265
Greater London Council,
    ACCESS, 25
    details, 250
    Development and Materials Bulletin, 147, 151, 254, 259, 286, 287
    Research library, 63, 131
    specification clauses, 284
Griffiths, 283
Guide to British Topographical Collections, 358, 378
Guide to Government Department and Other Libraries, 32, 185
Guide to Information Sources see Architect's Journal
Guide to Official Statistics, 182, 376
Guides to sources, 98–100
    art history, 356–357
    building regulations, 177–178
    climate, 244
    concrete, 263
    conservation, 344–347
    construction, 12–16
    cost, 279
    furniture, 308
    landscape, 293
    law, 176
    libraries, 28–34
    plastics, 308
    textiles, 307

handbook of Architectural Practice and Management, see Royal Institution
    of British Architects
Handbook of Sport and Recreation Buildings, 217
Handbook of Urban Landscape, 231
Handbooks, 251, 261, 271, 288
    definition, 98
    fire, 266
    maintenance, 288
    materials, 261–262
    services, 271–272
    structural design, 250–251
Hansard, 175, 183, 186
    proposed database, 67
Harvard system, for references, 88–89
Harvard University, Fine Arts Library,
    printed catalogue, 34
Health, 173, 177, 212
Heating, 268–278
Heating and Ventilating Trades
    Contractors Association, 272
Hierarchy, 117, 119–120, 122
High alumina cement, 5,265
High-rise buildings, 238
Historical Manuscripts Commission, 374
Historic buildings, 344–345, 352–355, 357, 364–365
History,
    architectural, guides, 99
    of landscape, 294
HMSO, 167 *passim*
    catalogues, on-line, 64
Home Office, 26
    Fire department, 266
Homeworld '81, 277
Honeywood, 324
Horticultural Abstracts, 293
Horticultural Trades Association, 296
Hospital Abstracts, 217
Hospitals, 22, 107, 172, 289, 296, 367
Hotels, 213, 275, 309
House-Builders' Reference Book, 108
House journals, 259, 307
House of Commons Information
    Service, 68
Houses,
    country, 358, 366
    wind pressure, 243
House's Guide to the Construction Industry, 10, 11, 13, 30, 69, 127, 134, 158, 177, 178, 211, 267

Housing, 35, 172, 215, 249, 251, 277, 281, 351, 357, 367–370, 374
Housing Rehabilitation Handbook, 101
Housing statistics, 181, 184–185
How to Find Out, 24, 29
How to Find Out in Architecture and Building, 99
Human dimensions, *see* Anthropometric data
Humanscale, 214
Hutchins, 283
Hutton and Rostron, 58, 123, 257

IBSEDEX, 65
ICE Abstracts, 255
ICOGRADA, 299
ICSID, 299
IEE Wiring Regulations, 46
IHVE Guide, see CIBS Guide
Illuminating Engineering Society, 305
Indexes, 110–123, 338–340
    card, 50–51, 80–82, 114
    coordinate, 53–54
    for bibliographies, 51
    format, 111
    in texts, 213
    peek-a-boo, 54
    to journals, 127–134
    uniterm, 52–56
Indexing journals, *see* Abstracting and indexing journals
Indoor climate, 272
Industrial buildings, 212,213, 297
Industrial Society, 215
INFOLEX, 68
INFOLINE, 61, 62, 70–71
Information,
    definition, 3
    evaluation of, 83
    generation, 4
    nature of, 37
    research, 9
    technical, sources of, 22
Information brokers, 63, 257, 334
Information explosion, 2, 6
Information need, 1–11, 18
Information retrieval,
    computer techniques, 58–75, 116
    search strategy, 39–48, 363–364
Information Sources in Science and Technology, 13, 99
Information Trades Directory, 63, 71
INKA, 62

INLOGOV, 235
INPADOC, 65
INSPEC, 65, 224,261, 269, 271
Institute for Aerial Survey and Earth Sciences, 224
Institute for the Conservation of Historic and Artistic Works, 354
Institute of Directors, 322
Institute of Environmental Science and Technology, Polytechnic of the South Bank, 244
Institute of Geological Sciences, 191–192
Institute of Landscape Architects, 296
Institute of Local Government Studies, University of Birmingham,235
Institute of Quantity Surveyors, 285, 315
Institution of Civil Engineers, 254,255, 256
Institution of Electrical Engineers, *see INSPEC*
Institution of Heating and Ventilating Engineers, *see* Chartered Institute of Building Services
Institution of Structural Engineers, 253, 256
Institutions *see* Associations
Insulation, 108, 258, 260, 263, 268, 270, 273–275, 276–278
    directory, 140
    regulations, 178
    thermal, 239, 263
Insurance, 326
Interior Decorators and Designers Association Ltd., 299
Interior Design Catalogue, 146
Interiors,
    design, 299–310
    planting, 292
Inter-library loan, 21, 355
International Building Services Abstracts, 132, 217, 271
International Council for Building Documentation, 9, 35, 66, 119, 152, 254
    Master List of Properties, 137, 145
International Council for Societies of Industrial Design, 299
International Council of Graphic Design Associations, 299
International Council of Monuments and Sites, 345, 353

International Ergonomics Association, 217
International Federation for Housing and Planning, 240
International Federation of Surveyors, 225, 226
International Institute for the Conservation of Historic and Artistic Works, 347
International Society of Photogrammetry, 225
International Solar Energy Society, 277
International Standards Organisation, 66, 154, 159, 166
International Union of Architects, 66
International Wool Secretariat, 307
Investigator's Handbook, 33
ISMEC, 65

JCT *see* Joint Contracts Tribunal
Job records, 330–331
Joint Contracts Tribunal, 313–314
Joint Council of Landscape Architects, 296
Journals,
  concrete, 264
  conservation, 249–355
  content, 46
  draughtsmanship and photography, 200–201
  energy, 125, 270
  foreign, lists of, 321
  houses, 365
  interior design, 303–304
  landscape, 292
  lists, 127, 135, 321, 365
  location, 127–135
  maintenance, 287
  materials, 260–261
  publishing pattern, 43
  science, 260–261
  services, 270
  structures, 253–254
  surveying, 222–223

Kamen, R., *see British and Irish Architectural History*
Keesing's Contemporary Archives, 43, 106
Kempe's Engineers Yearbook, 39, 46, 108, 214, 261
Kitchens, 215, 309
Kitemark, 157
Knowhow, 33

Land use, 227–237
  statistics, 183
Land Use and Built Form Study Group, 214
Land Use Classification, 295
Land use maps, 192
Landscape, 203, 291–298
  bibliographies, 103
  hard landscape, 259, 298
  planning, 230–231, 293–294
Landscape Institute, 291–292
Landscape reclamation, 231
Law,
  building, 316–317
  guides, 99
  information databases, 67
  on-line, 68
  planning, 231–234
Law Courts, 26
Law reports, 68, 180, 316–317
Laxton's, 283
Lead, 261, 264
Legal Handbook, AJ, 101, 177, 324
Legislation,
  building, sources of, 177, 320, 324–325, 354
  fire, 265–266
  guides, 5
  planning, 231–233
Legislative process, 175
Leisure buildings, 212, 213, 147
Lettering, 196
Liability, 4–5
Libraries, 213, 368–369
  academic, 27
  additions lists, 102
  company, 32
  conservation 356, 357–358
  databases, 64
  government, 10
  government publications, 185–186
  maps, 193–194
  map, equipment for, 195
  office, 20–21, 25, 96, 109, 148–149, 195, 300, 336–342
  personal, 96–97, 331–332
  photographs, 201,
  printed catalogues, 34
  products, 148–149
  public, 27

Libraries *(cont.)*
 research, 26–27
 slide, 203–207
 statistics, 185–186
 use of, 22–25
Libraries in the UK and the Republic of Ireland, 33
Library and Information Science Abstracts, 64, 217
Library Association, 33
Library buildings, 43
Library Bulletin see Department of the Environment
Library of Congress classification, 120, 387–388
Lighting, 203, 268, 275–276, 305–306
Lighting Industry Federation, 275
LISA, 64, 202, 217
Listed buildings, 366
Literature guides *see* Guides to sources
Literature,
 search, 2, 37–51
 structure, 37–38
Literature search, 2, 37–51
 making notes, 50–51, 78–82
 samples, 37–47, 363–364
Local authorities, 106, 228
Local history, 364–370
 records, 376
Lockheed *see* DIALOG
London Building Acts, 156, 178–179, 266
London,
 buildings, 368

Mackinder, 12, 17, 19
Magazines, *see* Journals
Maintenance, 171, 285–290, 346
 bibliographies, 103
 landscape, 295–296
Maltha, D, *Technical Literature Search and the Written Report*, 99
Management,
 costs, 285–290
 guides, 99, 108
 practices, 324–328
 principles, 327–328
 techniques, 325
Management and Marketing Abstracts, database, 62
Manuals,
 definition, 98
 maintenance, 288

Manufacturers,
 lists of, 140
 local, 140
Manufacturers' literature, 27, 136+, 248, 258+
 (*see also* Production information)
Maps, 187–195, 235, 377
Marketing, 326–327
 building products, 153
Masonry, 251
Materials, 40, 257–267
 databases, 65
 interior design samples, 300–301
 statistics, 184
Measured drawings, 358
Measurement, 280
 distance,
 in surveying, 219
Medical buildings,
 databases, 64
MEDLARS, 64, 72
MEDLINE, 61
METADEX, 65, 261
Metals, 261, 347
 databases, 65
Meteorological and Geoastrophysical Abstracts, 242
Meteorological Office, 221, 242, 244
Meteorology, 238–245
 databases, 65
 world, 244, 321–322
Method of Building, (PSA), 171, 248–249
Metropolitan Museum of Art,
 library catalogue, 34
Microfiche,
 'libraries', 147–148, 237
Microfilm, 195
Mills, E., *see Planning*
Minor works contract, 314
Mitchell's *Building Construction*, 251, 272
 errors, 48
Modelling, 198
Monumentum, 345, 353, 360
Museum of Modern Art, New York,
 library catalogue, 34
Museums,
 lists, 108, 369–370

National Building Agency, 10, 12, 13, 23, 69, 152, 178, 257
National Building Specification, 284
 classification, 118

National Bureau of Standards, (USA), 160, 274
National Council of Architectural Registration Boards of the United States of America, 322
National Federation of Building Trades Employers, 281, 287, 314
  JCT, 313–314
  System Builders Section, 251
National Housebuilders Council, 106
National Institute for Physical Planning and Construction Research, 288
National Monuments Record, 357
National Physical Laboratory, 22, 27
National Playing Fields Association, 27, 217
National Register of Archives, 357, 375
National Schedule of Rates, 281
National Trust, 367
Natural Energy Association, 277
NEDO cost indices,
  on-line, 69
  Price indices, 280–281
Negligence, 327
Neufert, *Architect's Data*, 211, 213
New Metric Handbook, 101, 104, 211, 212, 269, 340
New products, 138
  reviews, 139
New publications, 102
New York Public Library, Art and Architecture Division, printed catalogue, 334
Newspapers, 379
Noise, 175, 276
  Databases, 64
  levels at airports, 43
Nonferrous Metals Abstracts, databases, 261
Note-taking, 50–51, 78–83
NPM Information Services, 63
NTIS, 47, 63, 64, 224, 271, 322
Numeric system,
  for references, 89

Obituaries, 371
Office libraries, 21, 25, 96–97, 329–342
  product literature, 143, 148–149
Office Planning,
  AJ Handbook, 101
Office practice, 108, 324–328
Offices, 212, 213, 216, 292, 297–298, 305, 309, 367

Official publishing, 10, 167–18 (*see also* Government)
  databases, 67–68
  lists, 147–148, 368
Officials,
  lists, 376
Oil and Colour Chemists Association, 306
Online Information Centre, 63
Optical coincidence cards, 54–55
ORACLE, 68
Ordnance Survey, 167, 189–191, 221, 374
Organizations, *see* Associations
Otto, Frei, 252
Overseas Building Notes, 319
Overseas,
  practices, surveying, 226
  work, 35–36, 170, 299, 318–323
  databases, 66
  landscaping, 293

Paint, 258, 306, 346, 347
Paintings, 347
  conservation, 347
Paper, 347
Parker, C. *Information Sources in Science and Technology*, 99
Parliament, 107
Partnership, 325
Patent Office, 167
Patents,
  databases, 65, 71
  solar energy, 277
Patsearch, 62, 65, 71
Pattern books, 358
Peek-a-boo indexes, 54
Performance, 288
Performance appraisal, 330–331
Periodicals, *see* Journals
Personal contacts, 19
Personal information collections, 331
  organization, by CI/SfB, 51
  records, 78–83
Personnel, 108, 326
Perspective, 196, 198
Pevsner, N., 357, 362, 365
Photogrammetry, 221–222, 226
Photographic Abstracts, 201
Photography, 200, 307, 370
  aerial, 193, 221
Physics Abstracts, 201, 261
Piling, 257

PIRA Abstracts,
  databases, 62
Place names, 108
Places, 375–380
Planned preventive maintenance, 289
Planner, 235
Planning, 227–237, 345–346
  databases, 65
  maps, 192–193
  reports, 356
  site, 219–226, 295
  statistics, 183–184
Planning, 104, 211, 212, 236
Planning Appeals, 233
Planning applications, 184, 230
Plans, 378 (*see also* Maps)
Plant, 262
Planting,
  exterior, 295–296
  interior, 292
Plastics, 256, 259, 262, 265, 307–308, 346
Playgrounds, 297
POLIS, 68
Pollution,
  databases, 64
Pollution Abstracts, 64
Population, 182
Post-coordinate indexes, 52–56
Practices,
  foreign, 322, 323
  information in, 299–303, 329–336
  information needs, 336–337
  lists, 106, 247
    surveying, 226
  management, 324–328
  overseas, 318
  procedures, 312
  working abroad, 320–321 (*see also* Libraries)
precipitation, *see* Rain
Presentation,
  drawings, 84, 199–200
  reports, 86
  standards, 156
  technical information, 137
Preservation, 288
  timber, 263
  (*see also* Conservation, Maintenance)
Prestel, 67, 68–69, 152, 173, 224, 242, 271, 280, 282, 320
Price books, 282–283
  landscape, 293
  maintenance, 287

Price indices, 280–285
Princes Risborough Laboratory, *see* Building Research Establishment
Principles of Modern Building, 168, 171, 251
Proceedings, of conferences, *see* Conference proceedings
Product design, 299
Product information, 136–153, 258–268, 275, 301–302
  CI/SfB in, 249
  coverage of services, 146
  databases, 67
  foreign, 35
  needs, 5–6
  new products, 138, 150
  quality assurance, 157–158
  services, 270
  use in design process, 210–211
Products,
  new, 260
Property,
  statistics, 185
Property Services Agency, 12, 26, 130, 171, 173, 285, 287, 293, 346
  bibliographies, 103, 273
  feedback information, 151
Psychological Abstracts, 217
Public libraries, 27
Publishers,
  specialists, 49
Publishing, 199–200

Qualifications, 107
Quality assurance schemes, 157–158
Quantity surveying, 279, 321, 327

R & D Abstracts, 47, 64
Rain, 203, 243, 252
Ramsey and Sleeper, *see Architectural Graphic Standards*
Rayner report, 181
Reading, 50
Records,
  historical, 367
  of work done, 50–51
  repositories, 369–370
Recreation buildings, 212, 213, 297
Redland Guide to the Construction Industry, 30
Reference books,
  guides, 108–109

References, *see* Bibliographical
    references
Regional Surveys, 377
Registration,
    architects, 322–323
Rehabilitation, 281, 284 (*see also*
    Conservation, Preservation)
Reinforcement, 252
Religious buildings, 212, 285
Rendering, 197–198
Repairs, 286 (*see also* Maintenance)
Reports,
    energy, 269
    lists, 39, 47, 63, 100
    US lists, 224
    writing, 85–91
Research,
    application, 4
    commencing, 40 *passim*
    definitions, 4
    dissemination, 4, 248
    energy, 275
    grants, 106
    in information, 9
    lists, architectural history, 373
    lists, on-line, 64
    organization in Britain, 9–11
    overseas directories, 35–36
    planning, 235
    solar, 277
    structural elements, 255
    surveying, 225–226
Research reports, 100, 248
Research associations, 10–11, 22, 26
    directories, 11, 28–33
    information from, 10–11
    in construction, 10–11, 26
*Research in British Universities,
    Polytechnics and Colleges*, 64
Research Index, 43
Restaurants, 275, 309
Restoration, 288
Review articles,
    uses, 46
Reviews,
    of products, 139
RIBA Library, *see* British
    Architectural Library
RIBA Journal, 126, 260
RIBA Product Data, 21, 25, 101, 139,
    145–146, 148, 150, 151, 156, 177,
    247 *passim*, 258 *passim*, 265, 273,
    316, 324, 327

RICS Abstracts and Reviews, 109, 131,
    185, 223, 236, 265, 288, 327, 379
RILEM, 256, 263
Ronan Point, 42, 151
Roof gardens, 297
Roofs, 248, 249, 252, 257, 258, 346
Royal Architectural Institute of
    Canada, 274
Royal Commission on Historical
    Monuments, 357, 368
Royal Institution of British Architects,
    339, 365
    bibliographies, 103
    Drawings collection, 355, 358, 364,
        374
    Energy package, 274
    *Handbook of Architectural Practice
        and Management*, 312, 324–325,
        341
    information services on-line, 70
    JCT, 313–314
    Library Bulletin, 350
    National Building Specification, 284
    Office Library Service, 25, 144, 334
    Overseas Affairs Section, 318, 319,
        323
    photographic collection, 201
    Plan of Work, 312, 330, 332
    Product Selector, 145–146
    slide collection, 204
Royal Institution of Chartered
    Surveyors, 224–226, 232–233, 282,
    285, 287
Royal Photographic Society, 201
Royal Town Planning Institute, 228,
    234, 235, 236
Rubber and Plastics Research
    Association,
    database, 66, 261, 308
Rubicon File, 324

Safety, 173, 177
Samples, 149–150, 300
Schedule of Rates for Building Works,
    171
Schools, 22, 107, 172, 180, 210, 215, 370
    databases, 64
Science,
    building materials, 257–267
Science Citation Index, 47, 224
Science Reference Library, *see* British
    Library

Scientific buildings, 212
SCISEARCH, 261
Sculpture Index, 372
SDC Orbit, 621
Search, 27
Searching,
 literature, online, 71–72
Sectional Lists, 173, 348
Selective Dissemination of
 Information, 21, 255
Services, 267
 bibliographies, 104
 databases, 65
Shirley Institute, 307
Shops, 213, 305, 309
Shrubs, 295–296
Site investigations, 188, 219–226
Site planning, 229, 295
Site surveying, 219–226
SLASH, 286
Slate, 346
Slide programmes, 197, 202–203
 surveying, 220
Slides, 201–208
Smith, D. *How to Find Out in Architecture and Buildings*, 99
Social Science Citation Index, 47
Social services, 107
Social Services Abstracts, 217
Society for the Protection of Ancient Buildings, 353, 356, 358
Soiciety of Architectural Historians, 372, 373
Society of Chief Quantity Surveyors, 281
Society of Dyers and Colourists, 306
Society of Industrial Artists and Designers, 299
Society of Motor Manufacturers, 218
Soil, 219–226, 250
 landscape, 291
Solar data, 269
Solar energy, 42, 273, 274, 276–277
 bibliographies, 103
Solar gain, 239
Solar radiation, 272
Solid Fuel Heating Advisory Service, 268
Sourcebook of Planning Information, 100, 188, 202, 227, 345–346
Sources of Modern Architecture, 99
Space between buildings, 293, 294

Space requirements, *see*
 Anthropometric data, Ergonomic data)
Specification, 139, 141, 146–147, 148, 156, 247 *passim*, 258 *passim*, 284–285
 index, 111
Specifications, 284–285
Speeches, 91–95
Spon's, 283, 287, 293
Sports and Recreational Building Design,
 Handbook, 101
Sports buildings, 22, 212, 213, 215, 275
Sports Council, 22, 27, 217, 368
Stables, 28
Standard Form of Building Contract, 311–317
Standard Method of Measurement, 262, 281
Standardization, 153–154
Standards, 101, 153–166
 and building regulations,179
 anthropometrics, 216, 217
 colours, 306
 databases, 65
 design data, 213–218
 drawing, 197
 for trade literature, 137
 foreign, 159–166
 interior design, 302–303
 landscape, 293
 (*see also* British standards, British Standards Institution, BSI Yearbook)
Standing Committee Urban and Building Climatology, 240, 242
Statistics, 180–186, 321
 brief guides, 107
 collections, 321
 databases, 67
 local, 375
 sources, 180–188
Statistics and Market Intelligence Library, 185, 321
Statutes, 174–180
Statutory Instruments, 67, 175–176
 planning,232
Steel, 214, 249, 252, 260
Steel Window Association, 257
Stone, 171, 347, 351
Stonework,
 conservation, 354

Strategy,
  for research projects, 40
  search, 363
Street furniture, 140, 298
Stress, 253
Structural analysis, 252
  on-line databases, 67
Structural surveys, 286, 288
Structures, 203, 247–257
  databases, 65
  fire, 178
  overseas work, 319
Sunlight, 243, 275
Surface Coatings Abstracts,
  databases, 261
Survey of London, 367
Surveying, 219–228
Swedish Institute of Building
  Documentation,
  databases, 64
Swimming pools, 213
Swiss Federation of Landscape
  Architects, 292
Symbols, 196, 198
Systems Development Corporation, 59

Talks, 91–95
Tax, 326
Techalert, 47, 100, 255, 268, 269, 274
Technical Advisory Service, Crown
  Paints, 258
Technical handbooks, 108
Technical Help for Exporters, 31, 159, 319, 320
Technical Indexes Ltd., 144, 149, 166
Technical literature,
  energy, 268
  materials, 258–259
  presentation, 137
  structures, 248–249
*Technical Literature Search and the
  Written Report*, 99
Technical Services for Industry, 30, 218, 278, 326
Technology Reports Centre, 61
  computer search services, 63
Telecomunications, 58 *passim*
TELEDON, 69
Telefacsimile Information Network
  Data, 22
Telephone numbers, 23
Télèsystèmes Questel, 62, 70
TELETEL, 69

TELETEXT, 68–70
Television studios, 28
Temperatures, 243
Tenders, 311–317
Terminology, 25, 44–46, 120
Terotechnology, 288
Textile Institute, 307
Textiles, 307–308, 347
Theatres, 212, 213
  bibliographies, 104
  Thernal Abstracts, 132, 271
  Thesaurus, 121–123
  bill of quantity phraseology, 284
  in searching literature, 72
  (*see also* Construction Industry
    Thesaurus, CIT Agency,)
Theses, 47, 224
Tiles, 265
Timber, 171, 249, 252, 259, 262, 264, 347
  databases, 66
  libraries, 22
Timber Research and Development
  Association, 10, 26, 102, 249, 259, 262, 264
  bibliographies, 103
*Time-Saver Standards for Building
  Types*, 213
Topography, 358, 376, 378
Town and Country Planning, 227
Town and Country Planning
  Association, 236
Town planning, *see* Planning
Town plans, 40, 193
Towns, 352, 367, 375–379
Trade associations, 22, 26
  directories, 28–33
  in construction, 26
*Trade Associations and Professional
  Bodies of the UK*, 32
Trade literature, *see* Product literature,
  Manufacturers
Trade names, 141
  carpets, 302
  rubber and plastics, 308
Translation services, 48, 320
Translations, 21, 47, 320
Trees, 295–296

U-values, 277–278
United Kingdom Institute for
  Conservation, 354
United States Department of
  Commerce, 215–216

Universal Decimal Classification, 119–120, 339, 384–387
Universities, 107
  survey research, 226
University Grants Committee, 215
University of Cambridge, School of Architecture, 214
Urban Abstracts, 63, 131, 236
Urban History Yearbook, 376
Urban Landscape,
  AJ Handbook, 101
Urbandoc Microfile, 237
User requirements, 210–218, 303

Vance bibliographies, 103, 347 (*see also* Council of Planning Librarians)
Ventilation, 243, 268–278 (*see also* Energy)
Victoria and Albert Museum,
  architectural drawings, 358
  library catalogue, 34
  slide library, 204
Victoria County History, 357, 376
Videodiscs, 70–71
Viewdata, 68–70

Walls, 248
Warburg Institute,
  library catalogue, 34
Warehouses, 213
Warwick University, 185

Water, 258, 262
Water,
  databases, 64
Waterproofing, 244, 263, 346
Weather data, 242–245
Weathering, 171, 288, 346
  plastics, 265
WEEDASEARCH, 65, 261
Which?, 302
Who's Who, 373
  compilation, 49
Wind, 243
Wind loading, 203, 248
Windows, 203, 248–250, 257, 274, 276, 277
Wiring regulations, *see IEE Wiring Regulations*
Wood report, 312
Woodbine Parish, 17, 20
World Aluminium Abstracts, 66, 261
World Design Sources Directory, 299
World Surface Coating Abstracts, 306
World Textile Abstracts, 307
World Textiles, 62, 261
Worldwide List of Published Standards, 160, 302

Yearbooks,
  definition, 98

Zinc, 261